T3-BNL-485

THE
INSTITUTIONAL
INVESTOR
SERIES IN FINANCE

Japanese Capital Markets

The Institutional Investor Series in Finance

Implementing Capital Budgeting Techniques, *Revised Edition*
Harold Bierman, Jr.

The Institutional Investor Focus on Investment Management
Frank Fabozzi, editor

Solving the Global Debt Crisis: Strategies and Controversies by Key Stakeholders
Christine A. Bogdanowicz-Bindert, editor

The Financial Manager's Guide to Bond Refunding Opportunities
John D. Finnerty, Andrew J. Kalotay, and Francis X. Farrell, Jr.

The Debt/Equity Choice
Ronald W. Masulis

International Corporate Finance, *Second Edition*
Alan Shapiro

Managing Financial Risk
Clifford W. Smith, Jr., Charles W. Smithson, and D. Sykes Wilford

Corporate Restructuring and Executive Compensation
Joel M. Stern, G. Bennett Stewart III, and Donald H. Chew, Jr., editors

Marketing Financial Services
David B. Zenoff, editor

Customer-Focused Marketing of Financial Services
David B. Zenoff, editor

JAPANESE CAPITAL MARKETS

Analysis and Characteristics of Equity, Debt, and Financial Futures Markets

Edwin J. Elton
Martin J. Gruber

1817

Harper & Row, Publishers, New York
BALLINGER DIVISION

Grand Rapids, Philadelphia, St. Louis, San Francisco
London, Singapore, Sydney, Tokyo, Toronto

International Standard Book Number: 0-88730-339-0

Library of Congress Catalog Card Number: 89-36967

Printed in the United States of America

Library of Congress Cataloging-in-Publication Data

Japanese capital markets: analysis and characteristics of equity, debt, and financial futures markets / [edited by] Edwin J. Elton, Martin J. Gruber.

p. cm. – (The Institutional investor series in finance)

Includes bibliographical references.

ISBN 0-88730-339-0

1. Capital market–Japan. 2. Securities–Japan. I. Elton, Edwin J. II. Gruber, Martin Jay, 1937–. III. Series.

HG4523.J365 1990

332.63′2′0952–dc20 89-36967

CIP

90 91 92 92 93 HC 9 8 7 6 5 4 3 2 1

To Jonathan, Stacey, Joelle, and Ellie Gruber
and
To Annette, Ned, Kathryn, John Paul, and Diane Elton

CONTRIBUTING AUTHORS

Menachem Brenner
Stephen J. Brown
Edwin J. Elton
Cheol S. Eun
Robert Alan Feldman
Martin J. Gruber
Mustafa N. Gultekin
N. Bulent Gultekin
Yasushi Hamao
James E. Hodder
Kiyoshi Kato
Toshiyuki Otsuki
Alessandro Penati
Richard H. Pettway
Bruce G. Resnick
Eisuke Sakakibara
James S. Schallheim
Sandra L. Schwartz
Neil W. Sicherman
Marti G. Subrahmanyam
Adrian E. Tschoegl
Jun Uno
Takeshi Yamada
William T. Ziemba

Contents

Preface

Japanese security markets are among the largest in the world. Furthermore, the return on Japanese securities has been among the highest offered in any market. Despite these facts there has been a limited amount of research on these markets. This book presents a collection of papers studying the important characteristics of Japanese Capital Markets. Although some of the papers have been published previously, most were prepared specifically for this volume.

To put the size of the Japanese security markets in perspective, consider the market value of the stock in companies traded in the stock markets of different countries. Using this criterion Japan is about 80% of the size of the U.S. market and considerably larger than the sum of all stocks from all of the major stock markets in Europe. This is a dramatic increase in size: seven years ago the Japanese market was less than 20% the size of the U.S. market and less than half the size of the European markets. In addition, the rate of return on Japanese stocks has been among the highest of any major stock exchange (as has the risk) in recent years. In the 15 years ending in 1987, the annual rate of return was over 22% for Japanese stocks. The high return and large size of Japanese security markets provide a strong incentive to understand these markets.

The structure of Japanese security markets in many ways resembles the structure of security markets in the United States. Japanese markets are high-volume markets with large institutional participation. Many of the economic characteristics of the Japanese markets are similar to the U.S. market, but many are different. For example, commissions are fixed and high. Both the similarities and differences are intriguing. This brings us to the substance of this book. It seems appropriate to provide the reader with a brief description of what lies ahead.

This book is divided into five sections. Section I deals with descriptions of Japanese security markets and reviews their historical performance. Section II examines the risk structure of the equity markets. Section III also deals with equity markets, more specifically with the relationship between firm characteristics and share return and calendar time and return. Section IV examines the futures market in Japan. Finally, Section V examines mergers and acquisitions in Japan and their impact on stockholder wealth.

Section I. Characteristics of Japanese Financial Markets

The purpose of the opening section of this book is to provide some background on the historical performance and characteristics of security markets in Japan.

The first article, "Fifteen-Year Performance of Japanese Capital Markets" by Yasushi Hamao, is, as its title suggests, a review of the performance of the major security markets in Japan. Hamao presents a very succint yet informative description of each of the major stock exchanges and bond markets in Japan. He then presents year-by-year evidence of the performance of the Japanese markets (both denominated in yen and in dollars for the years 1973–1987). The facts over this 15-year period:

1. The average return in dollars from Japanese stocks was above 22%.
2. The average return in dollars from small stocks was higher than 32% per year.
3. The average return in dollars from bonds was higher than 17%.

This should be sufficient motivation for the reader to be interested in Japanese markets and to continue reading.

In the second article, "The Japanese Financial System in Comparative Perspective," Sakakibara and Feldman compare the Japanese and U.S. financial markets. Japanese markets are characterized by a high and accelerated growth rate, a high and rising savings ratio, and low government consumption measured as a proportion of GNP. The authors discuss the differences in the financial systems and speculate whether these differences could account for differences in macroeconomic characteristics of the two countries. For the two countries they highlight four major differences in the financial systems. First, Japanese nonfinancial corporations have continuously increased their liabilities, surpassing the U.S. level. Second, Japan has a high degree of intermediation reducing the risks of the high corporate debt level. Japanese save indirectly through the post office and banks rather than hold stocks and bonds directly. Third, the Japanese government acts more like an intermediary than a borrower. Postal savings, rather than government deficits, are used to finance investments and loans. Finally, consumer borrowing is low relative to the United States. The authors argue that Japanese Capital

Markets are highly competitive, and that while the risk is spread through intermediation, this has not affected competition.

In the third article, "Some Aspects of Japanese Corporate Finance," Hodder and Tschoegl examine Japanese financial markets from the perspective of the firm. Japanese firms are heavily debt-financed compared to U.S. firms. The public market for corporate debt is relatively small, with most of the financing being supplied by financial intermediaries. About 90% of the corporate lending is supplied by 25 to 30 institutions. For any individual firm the funding is likely to be supplied by a lead bank and its affiliates. Hodder and Tschoegl view Japanese capital markets as less competitive than do many of the other authors in this volume. Equity markets are large in size, but the authors state trading is not as active since much of the stock is held for business relationships. Capital gains have favorable tax advantages relative to dividends, and dividend payouts are small compared to U.S. standards. This article is rich in institutional detail about how corporations finance investment and how the capital markets behave in Japan.

In the final article of Section I, "Underwriting Japanese Long-Term National Bonds," Pettway examines the characteristics of Japanese government bonds. Compared to other major markets, the interest rates on Japanese bonds have been low, but their pattern of change over time has been very similar to other bond markets. Pettway continues his analysis with an examination of the size of the government bond market. He finds that government bonds currently represent about one-third of the market for all new issues of bonds. This percentage has varied from 8% to 42.4% in the last 20 years. Finally, Pettway examines issuance costs and the relationship between interest rates in the new issue market and the secondary market.

Section II. The Risk Structure of Japanese Equity Markets

This section deals with patterns of returns and risk in the Japanese stock markets. The process driving security prices in Japan seems to be more complex than the process that drives security prices in the United States. All of the papers in this section attempt to model the risk structure of Japanese stock prices.

The first article in this section, by Eun and Resnick, looks at simple models of estimating the correlation structure for Japanese stocks. Elton and Gruber have previously shown that, for U.S. stocks, simple models of the correlation structure of stock returns outperform more complex models.[1] In particular, single-index models often outperform multi–index models and simple averages of correlations outperform historical correlations as predictors of the future. Eun and Resnick repeat some of these tests for Japanese stocks. While they do not investigate index models per se, they do present strong evidence that the correlation pattern among Japanese stocks is much more complex than the correlation pattern among American stocks.

The article by Elton and Gruber presents a more complete modeling of the risk structure of Japanese stocks. They develop a robust four-index model of the Japanese stock market. The evidence of the need for a multi-index model in Japan is much stronger than the evidence in the United States. The single-index model explains much less of the return on Japanese stocks than it does in the United States. Furthermore, if risk is measured by the single-index model, small stocks are identified as having less risk and offering a higher return than large stocks. The use of the four-index model captures much more of the risk structure of Japanese stocks and captures much of the size effect in the Japanese market. This paper proceeds to examine the use of the four-index model in forecasting risk. In particular, it demonstrates that the four-index model, employing historical data, can be used to construct portfolios that mimic target sets of security holdings (index funds).

The third article in this section, by Hamao, attempts to identify sets of macroeconomic variables that are associated with returns in the Japanese stock market. Factors examined include industrial production, inflation, investor confidence, interest rates, foreign exchange, and oil prices. The importance of these factors as risk indexes is explored as well as their ability to explain differences in average return between securities.

The fourth paper in this section, by Brown and Otsuki, continues to explore the relationships between macroeconomic variables and Japanese stock prices. Using a new economic methodology and employing line of business data, the authors are able to present convincing evidence on the six or seven macroeconomic factors that are priced in the Japanese market.

The last paper in this section, by Gultekin, Gultekin, and Penati, employs the methodologies developed in Elton and Gruber and Hamao to test the extent of integration of the U.S. and Japanese stock markets. Both the methodologies are used to test whether the Japanese and American stock markets act as one market or as two segregated markets. The analysis in this study is divided into two periods; before and after December 1980. In December 1980 Japan enacted the Foreign Exchange and Foreign Trade Control Law, which significantly lessened capital controls. This paper presents strong evidence that the passage of this act increased the integration of the two stock markets.

In concluding our discussion of these five articles we should alert the reader to keep in mind that the papers do not all attempt to reach the same goals. The first two papers, by Eun and Resnick and Elton and Gruber, are concerned with measuring the risk of alternative securities in the Japanese market. These approaches are useful for such objectives as predicting the risk of any portfolio, forming index funds, or capitalizing on fundamental data to form active portfolios. The third and fourth articles are more concerned with explaining expected or average returns. The emphasis is on relating differences in return to the sensitivities to economic variables.

Section III. Patterns in Stock Prices and Effects of Expectational Data

The next section of this book deals with the impacts of calendar time and firm variables on Japanese stock prices. In particular, seasonal patterns in returns and the impacts of size and expectational data (sales and earnings predictions) on stock returns are investigated.

In the first paper, by Kato and Schallheim, the impact of both seasonal influences and size are investigated. The January size effect is well documented in the literature on American stock prices. For example, Keim has shown that not only do small stocks in the United States produce higher returns than large firms but that 50% of the excess returns occur in the month of January.[2] Kato and Schallheim present evidence of a size effect in Japanese stock prices, a January effect, and possibly a June effect. As the authors discuss, the presence of a January effect (often associated with taxes in the United States) is interesting in Japan because of the existence of a different tax regime.

The second paper in this section deals with daily rather than monthly anomalies. The day of the week effect and, in particular, large losses on Mondays have been well documented using U.S. data. The paper by Kato, Ziemba, and Schwartz analyzes the day of the week effect in Japan. Although a strong day of the week effect is present, its pattern is distinctly different from that found in U.S. markets. New insight into the process can be supplied by the fact that Japanese stock markets are open on some but not all Saturdays. The implications of this are investigated.

The third paper by Elton and Gruber examines the impact of sales and earnings expectations on returns in the Japanese Market. Elton, Gruber, and Gultekin have shown that expectational data on earnings drive stock prices in the United States.[3] Elton and Gruber show that in the Japanese Markets earnings have a stronger impact on stock prices than do sales. Furthermore, there is some lag in the market's incorporation of changes in forecast data. Strong evidence is presented that purchasing stocks where analysts revise upward their estimates of earnings per share leads to an excess return.

Section IV. Futures

The next section of this book deals with the pricing of stock index futures in Japan. The first stock index future was offered on June 9, 1987, and was based on a 50-stock portfolio traded on the Osaka Exchange. Brenner, Subrahmanyam, and Uno review the theoretical relationship that should determine futures prices and then examine the actual performance of futures in Japan. They find sizeable deviations from theoretical value in the Japanese market. They contrast these differences with those found in U.S. futures markets and the market for futures on the Nikkei Stock average traded on the Singapore International Monetary Exchange. As the authors point out, although deviations from the theoretical value for any futures contract can be expected in "new markets," trading practices may accentuate these deviations in the Japanese market. They describe restrictions on trading and added elements of execution risk that can cause actual futures prices to deviate from their theoretical value.

Section V. Mergers

The last section of this book consists of one article by Pettway, Sicherman, and Yamada that looks at the stockholder wealth impact of Japanese mergers. The impact of mergers on stockholder wealth has been a major topic in the academic and business literature in America. This article examines whether similar effects exist in Japan or whether institutional differences have a major impact on the results.

Notes

1. Elton, Edwin J., and Martin J. Gruber, "Estimating the Dependence Structure of Share Prices—Implications for Portfolio Selection," *Journal of Finance*, Vol. 28, p. 1203.
2. Keim, Donald B., "Size Related Anomalies and Stock Return Seasonality: Further Empirical Evidence," *Journal of Financial Economics*, Vol. 12, p. 13.
3. Elton, Edwin H., Martin J. Gruber, and Mustafa Gultekin, "Expectations and Share Prices," *Management Science*, Vol. 27 No. 9, September 1981, pp. 975–987.

PART I

Characteristics of Japanese Financial Markets

1

Fifteen-Year Performance of Japanese Capital Markets*

Yasushi Hamao
University of California, San Diego

I. Introduction

This paper presents carefully compiled Japanese financial data for the past 15 years and provides the investment community with the historical market performance of Japanese financial markets.[1] The emerging importance of Japan and the Japanese investors in the world of finance has raised much interest among researchers and investment professionals in Japanese markets. Although there has been some academic work in empirical research on Japanese markets, it has been very difficult to get access to a high-quality database.[2] In extending the Arbitrage Pricing Theory to the Japanese economy in Hamao (1987), we found it necessary to create a database of financial information hitherto unavailable to researchers and most investors. This paper is a description of the database on Japanese financial markets the author has established. Not only does it show the market results for the past 15 years, but it also serves as the basis for empirical studies of Japanese financial markets. For years, time series of historical returns for the American economy have been available from Ibbotson and Sinquefield (1976) and Ibbotson Associates (1988). This invaluable database is taken as a model for our presentation of Japanese data. This also makes it possible to compare the two systems.

The presentation in this paper is done in the form of summary statistics and graphs. The paper is divided into five sections. Section II describes basic series of various financial assets, Section III derives and describes

* I thank Rick Antle, Peter Bernstein, Philip Dybvig, William Goetzmann, Roger Ibbotson, Jonathan Ingersoll and Stephen Ross for helpful comments on earlier versions of this chapter.

component returns, Section IV gives highlights of the data, and Section V concludes the paper.

II. Basic Series

Notations and Definitions

Monthly and annual returns are denoted as R and R^*, respectively, where

$$R^* = \prod_{t=\text{Jan}}^{\text{Dec}} [1 + R(t)] - 1 \tag{1.1}$$

The wealth index $V(T)$ is the value of wealth at month T of initial investment (100 yen) at the beginning of the period. This index is initialized at December 1972, that is,

$$V(T) = 100 \prod_{t=1/73}^{T} [1 + R(t)]$$

Figures 1.1 and 1.2 show wealth indices for the series we describe as follows.

The geometric mean returns for the 15-year period are computed as

$$RG = \left(\prod_{t=1/73}^{12/87} [1 + R(t)] \right)^{\frac{1}{180}}$$

Notations for financial assets are as follows:

TSE-I: value-weighted Tokyo Stock Exchange Section I index (large, mature firms)

TSE-II: value-weighted Tokyo Stock Exchange Section II index (small, young, or troubled firms)

TSE-I small: value-weighted index for the smallest quintile of the Tokyo Stock Exchange Section I (smallest large firms)

LGB: long-term government bond index

CORP: long-term corporate bond index

SIR: short-term interest rate

INFL: inflation rate

Notations for derived series are given in Section III.

Figure 1.1. Index Values (in Yen-Term)

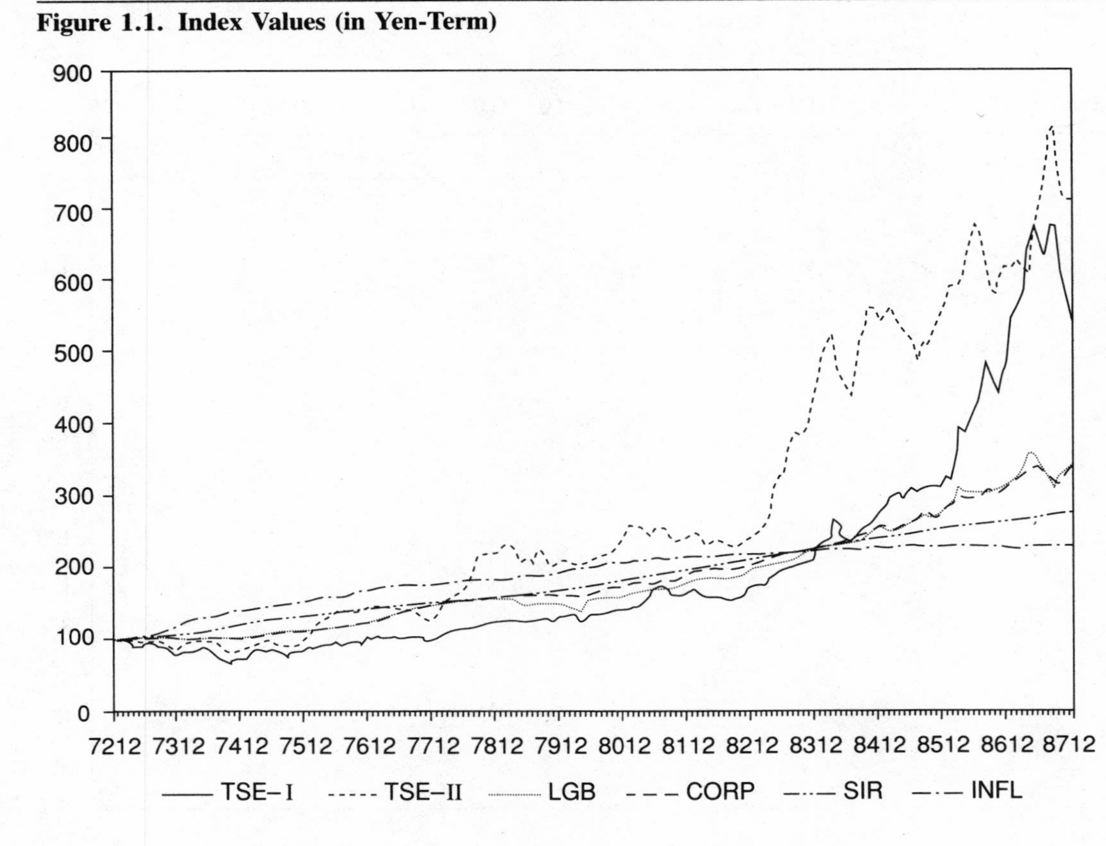

Figure 1.2. Stock Index Values (in Yen-Term)

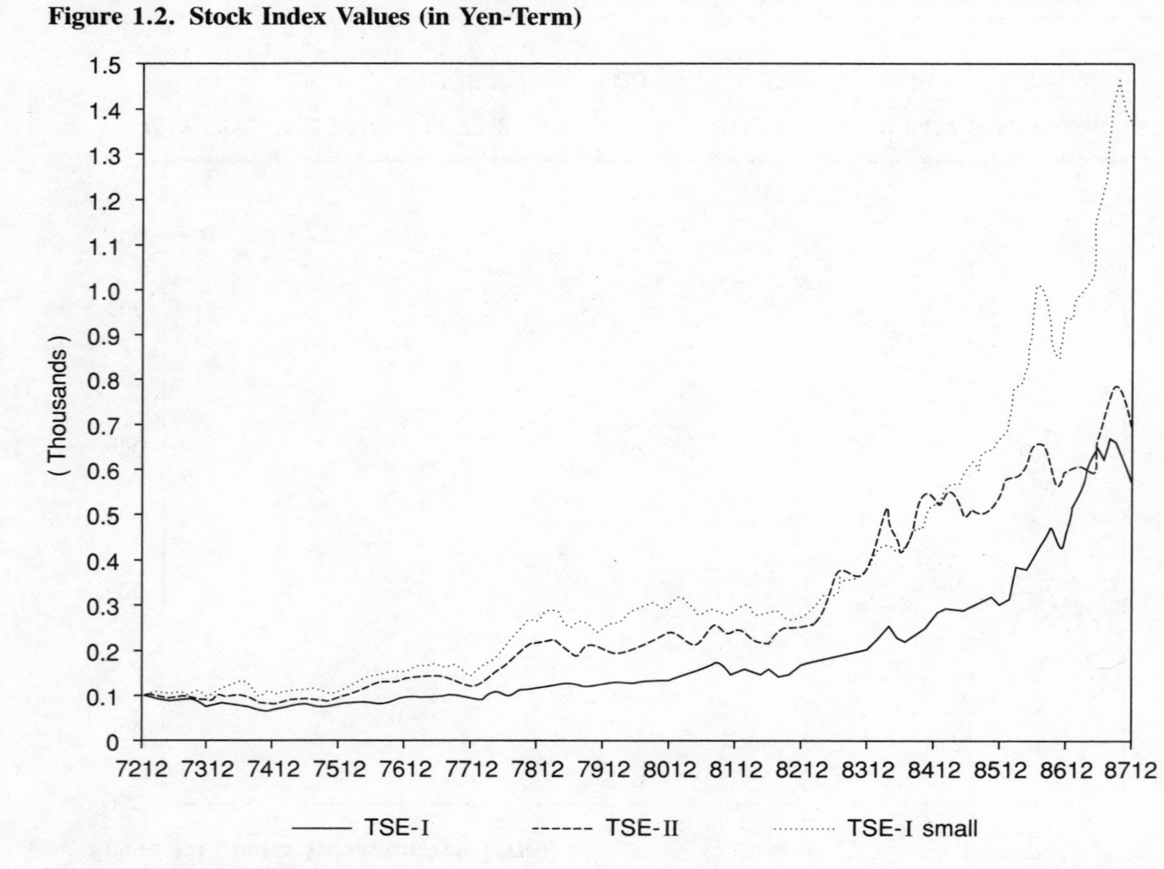

Common Stocks

Eight stock exchanges exist in Japan—Tokyo, Osaka, Nagoya, Kyoto, Hiroshima, Fukuoka, Niigata, and Sapporo. The Tokyo Stock Exchange has more than 95% of the whole market value and is divided into two sections according to a standard set by the exchange. The standard stipulates the required number of outstanding shares and trading volumes and the minimum dividend payment of the listed companies. Although it is customary for new companies to be listed in TSE-II first, before they satisfy the standard for TSE-I listing and get transferred to TSE-I, transition from the first section to the second section can also occur.

As of the end of 1987, the first section has 1101 companies and 351 trillion yen (2.9 trillion U.S. dollars) of market capitalization. It is larger than the NYSE, which has 1.8 trillion dollars. The second section has 432 companies and 11.3 trillion yen (92 million U.S. dollars) of market value. The largest company is Nippon Telegraph and Telephone Company (NTT), which went public in February 1987, with 33.7 trillion yen (276 billion U.S. dollars) as of December 1987. This is a clear outlier (second largest is Sumitomo Bank with 7.5 trillion yen (62 billion U.S. dollars) and is almost twice the size of the West German market. The distributions of capitalizations of all the listed companies in each section are shown in Figures 1.3 and 1.4. For practical reasons, NTT and the other 18 largest companies are not included in Figure 1.3. We notice that the distribution is skewed to the right, that is, there are relatively few but quite large companies that are dominating in market value in TSE-I. Indeed, the number of companies with a capitalization exceeding 500 billion yen (4.1 billion U.S. dollars) is 137, which is 12% of the 1101 companies, yet they account for 68% of the total market value of the TSE-I.

Market Indices. The market indices we present first are value-weighted indices of Tokyo Stock Exchange Section One (TSE-I) and Section Two (TSE-II). Dividends paid are considered to be reinvested in these indices for the purposes of calculating returns. These indices are different from the Tokyo Stock Price Index (TOPIX) published by the Tokyo Stock Exchange, and the Nikkei 225 Index by the Nikkei Newspaper Company. TOPIX is a value-weighted index of the first section, but it does not include dividends, and Nikkei 225 is similar to the Dow index and is an equal-weighted index of only 225 companies. Dividends

Figure 1.3. Distribution of Capitalizations (TSE-I, December 1987)

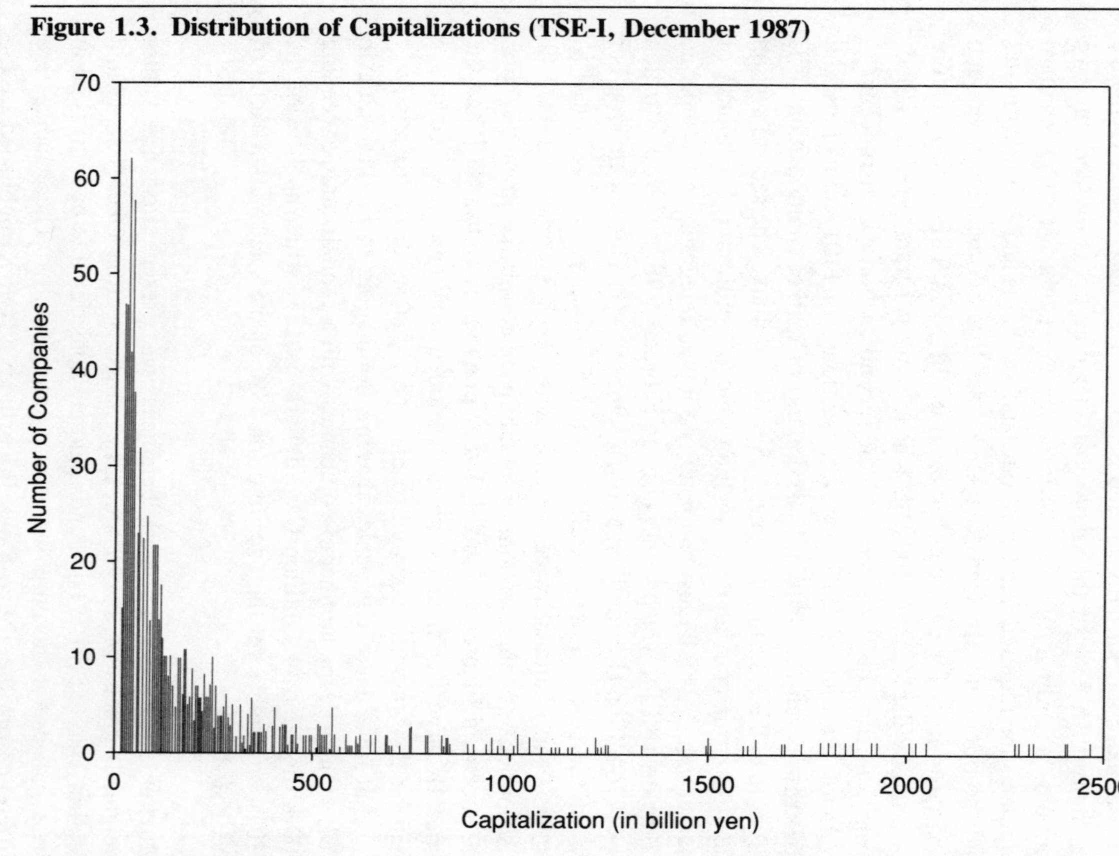

Figure 1.4. Distributon of Capitalizations (TSE-II, December 1987)

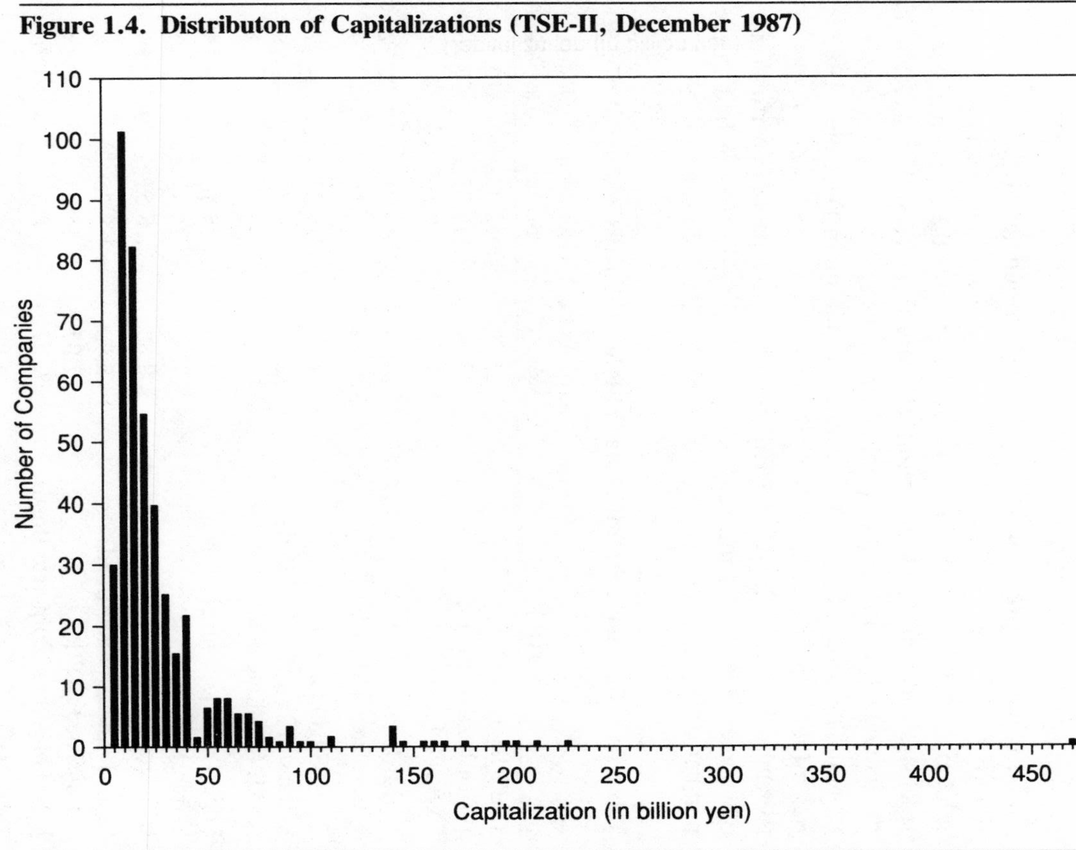

are less significant in Japan than in the United States. Out of the average annual total return of 13.29% of the TSE-I index (Table 1.1), income accounts for 1.70%, whereas S&P income return is 4.59% out of an 11.42% total return.

Small Capitalization Stocks. The smallest quintile of the capitalization of TSE-1 is extracted and the value-weighted index of these stocks is computed. The portfolios have approximately the same number of stocks (about 200), and are reformed every five years. The weights of the individual stocks are their capitalizations as of the end of the previous month. The capitalization of the smallest quintile in December 1987 is 6.3 trillion yen (51.6 billion U.S. dollars) which accounts for 1.79% of the entire TSE-1. Although the TSE-II index also represents performance of smaller companies, the small quintile of TSE-I is about half in the number of stocks and is smaller in market value compared to TSE-II.

Table 1.1. Summary Statistics, Basic Series (1973–1987). Annual. (In %)

Variable	Arithmetic Mean	Geometric Mean	Standard Deviation
TSE-I Index	13.29	12.07	16.31
$-Translated TSE-I Indes	22.09	19.05	27.66
S&P 500 Index	11.42	9.86	17.94
TSE-II Index	16.74	14.07	26.72
$-Translated TSE-II Index	25.88	21.18	35.79
TSE-I Small Quintile	21.67	19.27	24.92
$-Trans. TSE-I Small Quintile	32.71	26.70	40.99
NYSE Small Quintile	19.24	16.18	25.68
Long-Term Government Bonds	8.88	8.70	6.15
$-Translated LGB	17.16	15.48	19.49
U.S. Long-Term Government Bonds	8.88	8.53	13.30
Long-Term Corporate Bonds	8.90	8.76	5.56
$-Translated CORP	17.07	15.53	18.88
U.S. Long-Term Corporate Bonds	9.37	8.57	13.76
Short-Term Interest Rate	7.26	7.24	2.47
$-Translated SIR	14.97	13.92	15.39
U.S. Treasury Bills	8.20	8.17	2.64
Inflation	6.08	5.92	5.94
U.S. Inflation	6.96	6.90	3.57

Average Returns by Month. The above returns are then grouped by month and the averages are computed. Size-related seasonality in stock return patterns has often been discussed for the U.S. market [see Keim (1983)]. Monthly averages allow us to address the same effect in the Japanese market. Figure 1.5 displays TSE-I, TSE-I small quintile, and TSE-II indices.

Bonds

Japan did not develop active bond markets until the late 1970s. The first issue of long-term government bonds occurred in 1966 on the amendment of the fiscal law that had prohibited the government from issuing debt, and massive offerings started in 1975. Corporations depended mostly on bank loans. Government policy to maintain artificially low interest rates kept investors away from the bond markets. Therefore, the availability of the data is limited from the 1970s. The bond data before this database is almost meaningless because of the lack of a liquid market.

Long-Term Government Bonds. Returns on long-term government bond portfolios are computed using prices, including accrued interest. The LGBs have a 10-year maturity and pay semiannual coupons. The portfolios are for bonds with 9 to 10 years to maturity and are weighted by the outstanding volume. Notice that this is not "yield," which is most commonly found in bond literature in Japan.[3]

Long-Term Electricity Company Bonds. It is difficult to obtain corporate bond returns for the entire 15 years, but the long-term bonds issued by nine electricity companies offer the most consistently available data. These bonds have a 10-year maturity (12 years after March 1981) and the coupons are paid semiannually. Portfolios containing electricity company bonds and other small numbers of corporate bonds with 9 to 10 years to maturity are formed and the returns are computed. The electricity bonds represent about 85% of the portfolio contents.

Short-Term Interest Rates

Call money rate has often been used as the short-term interest rate in empirical studies of the Japanese economy. Since only the financial institutions participate in the call money market, it is often argued that

Figure 1.5. Average Returns, By Month (1973–1987)

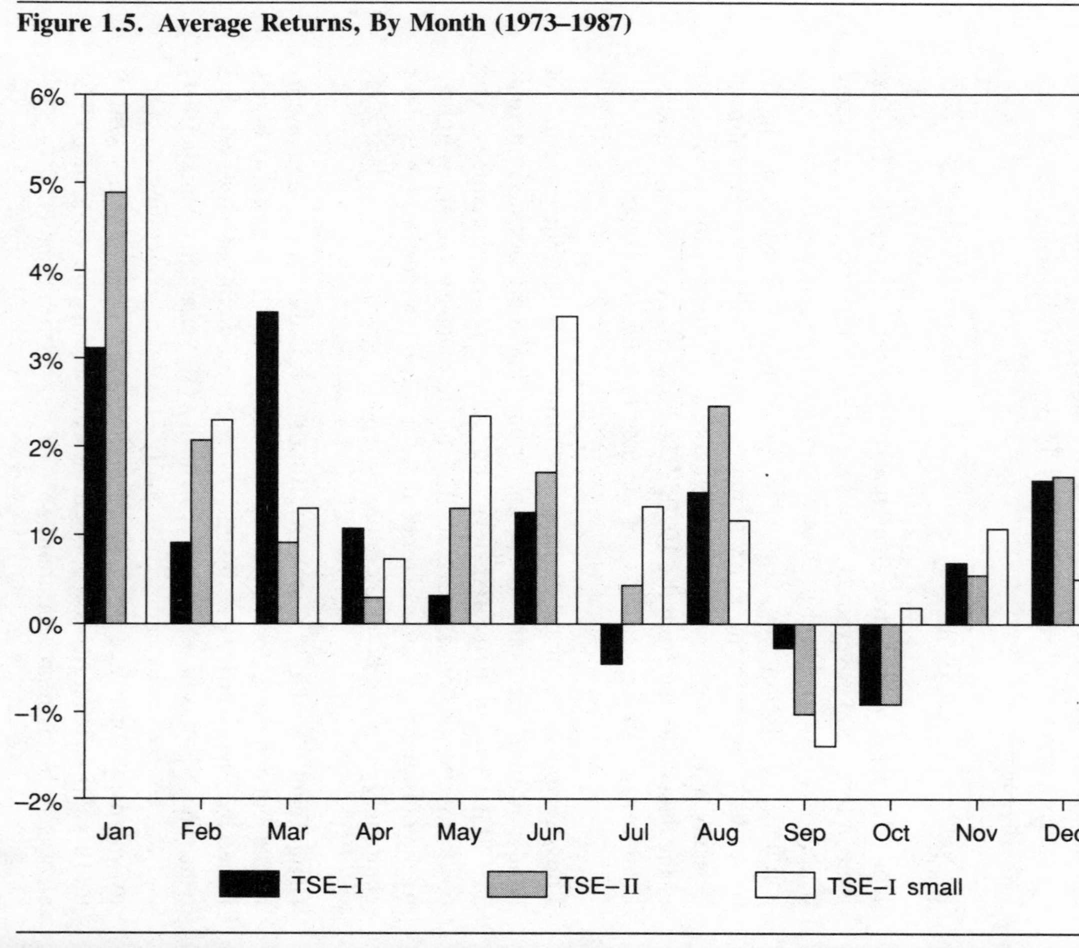

the call money rate is poor proxy for the riskless rate seen by investors. We will therefore present another short-term interest rate, the *Gensaki* rate.

Although the Gensaki market has existed since the early 1960s, it grew substantially in volume in the late 1970s. Gensaki rate is the interest rate applied to bond repurchase agreements which, as in the United States, are essentially collateralized loans.[4] The agreement period varies from one month to three months and, unlike the call money rate, participants are not limited to financial institutions, but also include corporations, government pension funds, and nonresidents.

In this study, the overnight call money rate was used through November 1977 and was replaced by the one-month Gensaki rate prevailing around the 25th of each month after December 1977.

Inflation

To measure inflation, we use the consumer price index (general, not seasonally adjusted) taken from the *Bank of Japan Monthly Statistics*. The inflation rate is the first log relative to the monthly CPI. We must note that this data is not contemporaneous with other asset returns since the prices for the index are taken during the month, whereas other asset returns are measured at the end of the month.

Dollar-Translated Returns

In order to facilitate international comparison with U.S. data, we transform the above asset returns into dollar terms. The month-end spot exchange rates are used to compute the dollar-translated returns, $\$R(t)$, as follows:

$$\$R(t) = \frac{S_{t-1}}{S_t}[1 + R(t)] - 1$$

where S_t = spot exchange rate (yen/dollar, interbank rate) at the end of month t. Because of the depreciation of the dollar over the 15-year period, especially after 1984, the dollar-translated Japanese returns are uniformly higher than their yen-term returns. Figures 1.6 and 1.7 show cumulative index values using the dollar-translated returns and the U.S. security returns.

Figure 1.6. Stock Index Values ($-Translated)

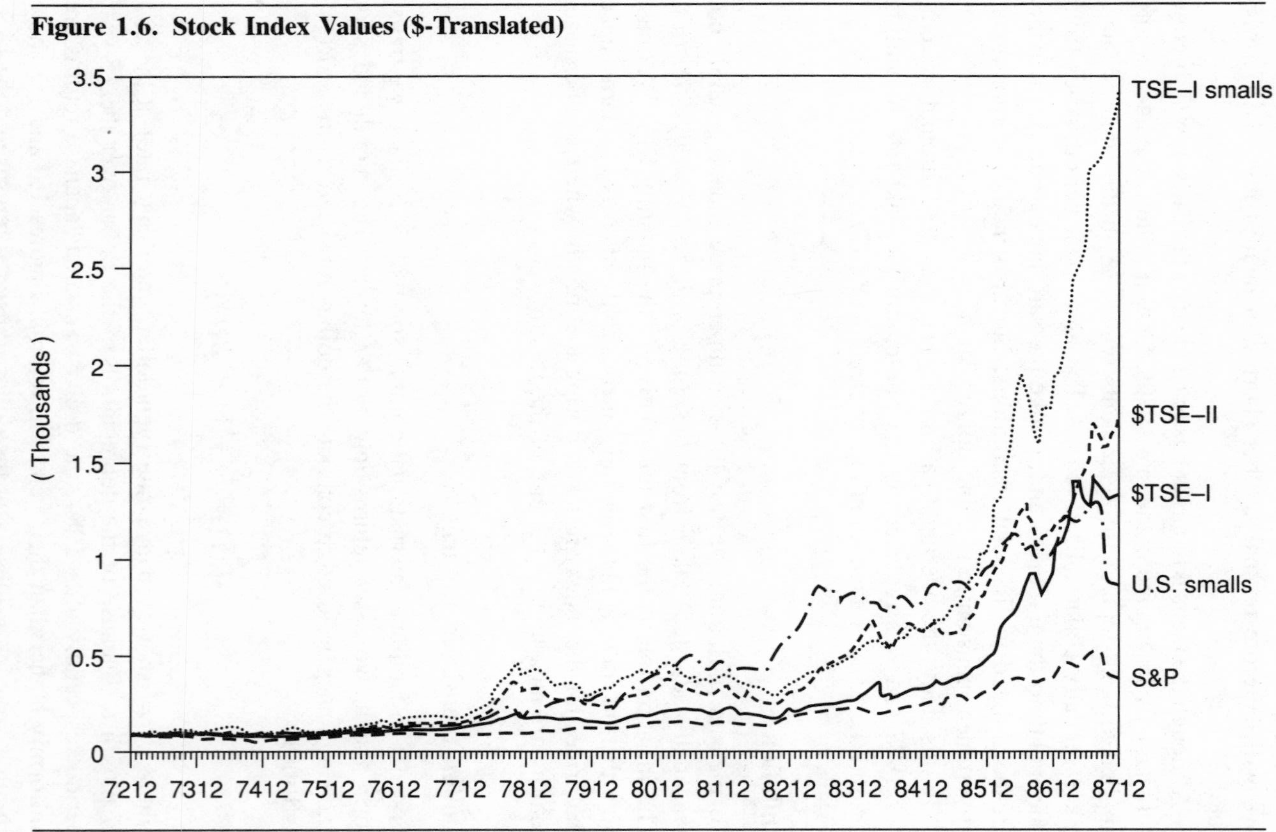

Figure 1.7. Fixed Income Index Values ($-Translated)

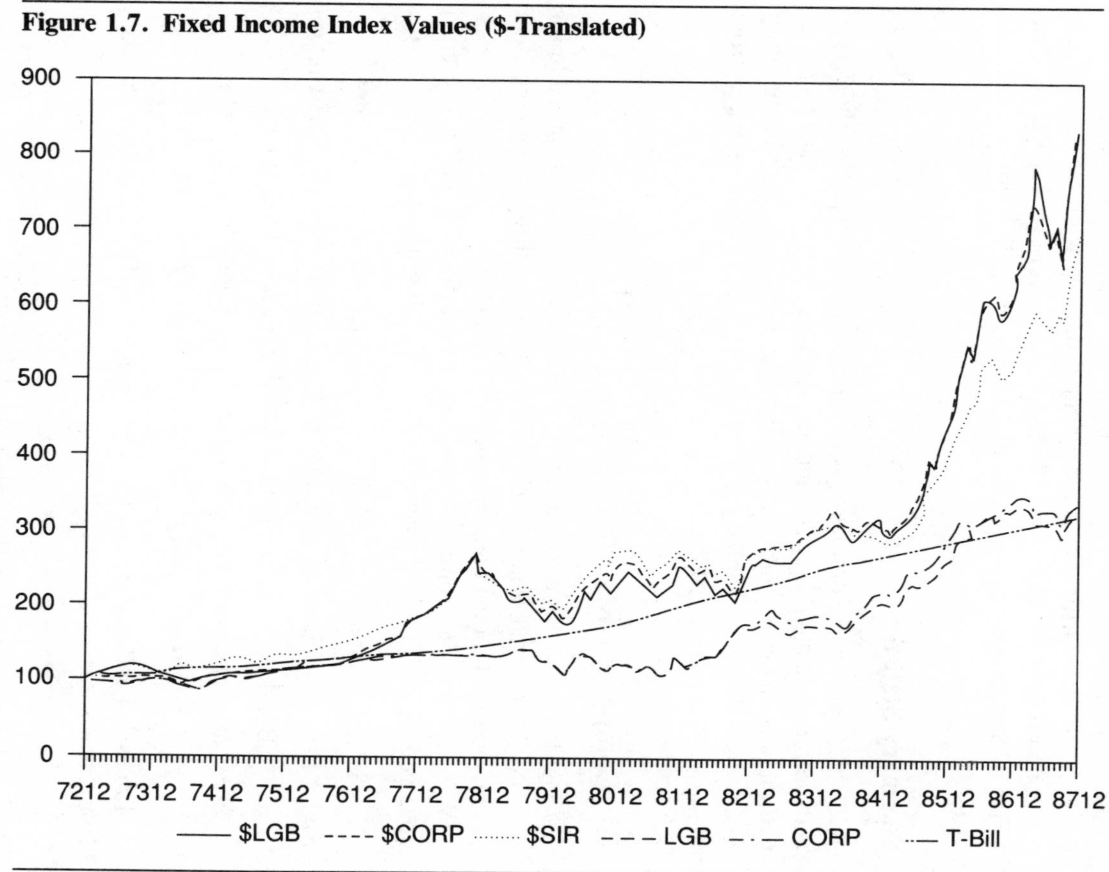

Annual Returns

Since the returns data are only available from 1973, our presentation of data is done using monthly returns. However, for a comparison with the U.S., it is informative to have annual data as well. Annual returns are computed using Equation 1.1. Figures 1.8 through 1.10 show time series of annual returns of stocks and bonds, including dollar-translated data.

Summary Statistics

Table 1.1 presents summary statistics for annual returns (both yen and dollar-translated figures) and the U.S. data for the same period. Correlation matrices and autocorrelations with one lag for monthly returns are shown in Tables 1.2 and 1.3. The U.S. data are taken from Ibbotson Associates (1988).

III. Component Returns

Having described basic return series of financial assets, it is possible for us to derive separate components of the returns, following the procedure established by Ibbotson and Sinquefield for the U.S. data.

We compute the nominal returns (net of inflation) and risk premia observed in the financial market in the following manner:

Equity premium = TSE-I return − Short-term interest rates

Small-firm capitalization premium = TSE-I small return − TSE-I return

Bond default premium = CORP return − LGB return

Bond maturity premium = LGB return − Short-term interest rates

Inflation-adjusted returns = Returns − INFL

Tables 1.4 and 1.5 present summary statistics. The U.S. data are taken from Ibbotson Associates (1988).

IV. A Close Look at the Historical Returns

Common Stocks

In the period of 1973–1987, all of the common stock indices outperformed other assets (Figures 1.1 and 1.2). TSE-I achieved the record

Figure 1.8. Annual Returns (Compounded Monthly)

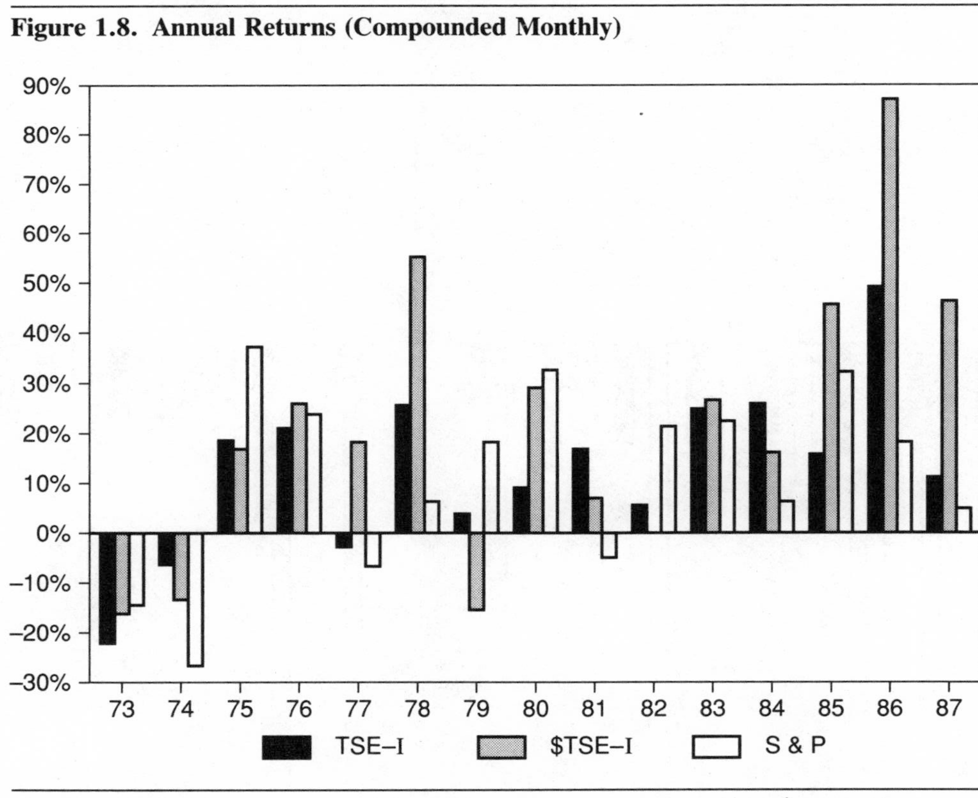

Figure 1.9. Annual Returns (Compounded Monthly)

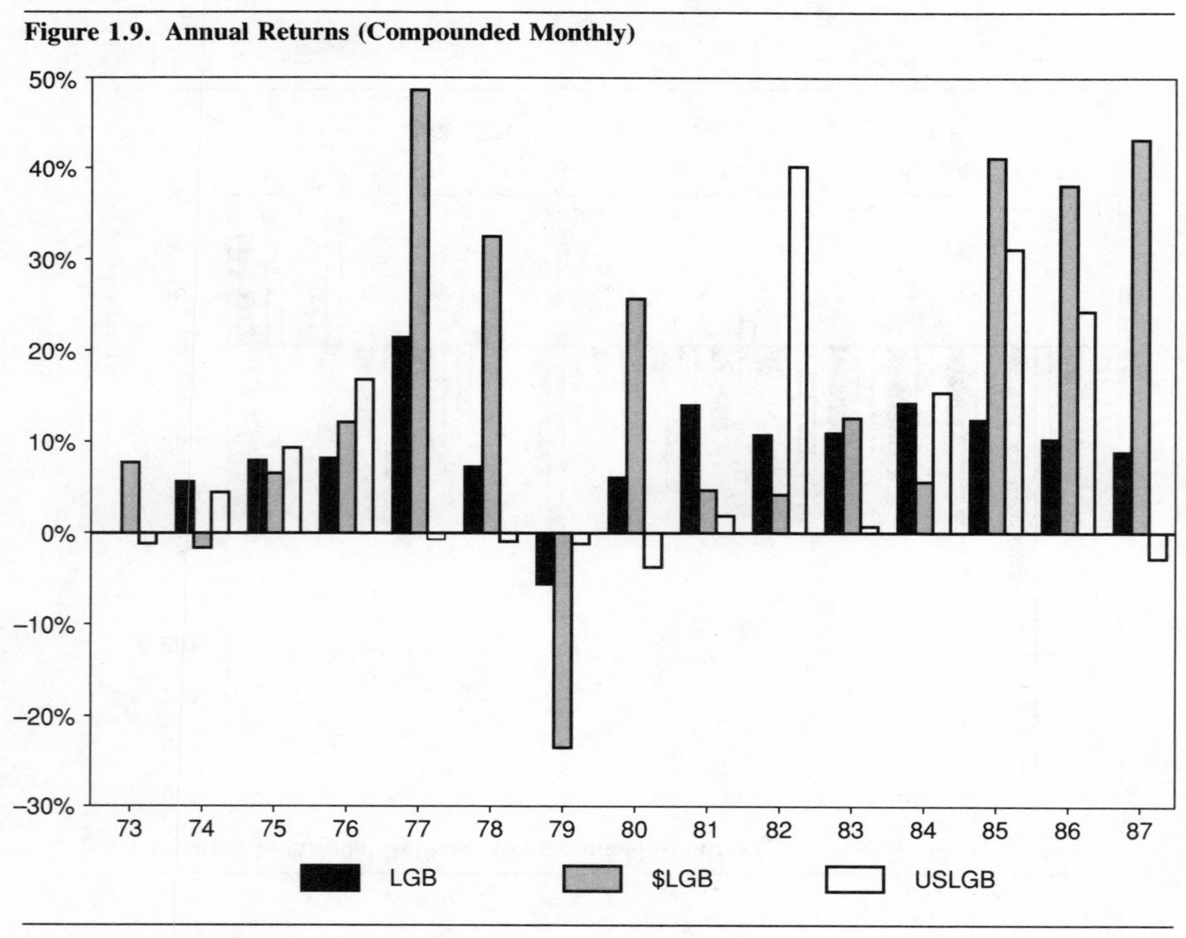

Figure 1.10. Annual Returns (Compounded Monthly)

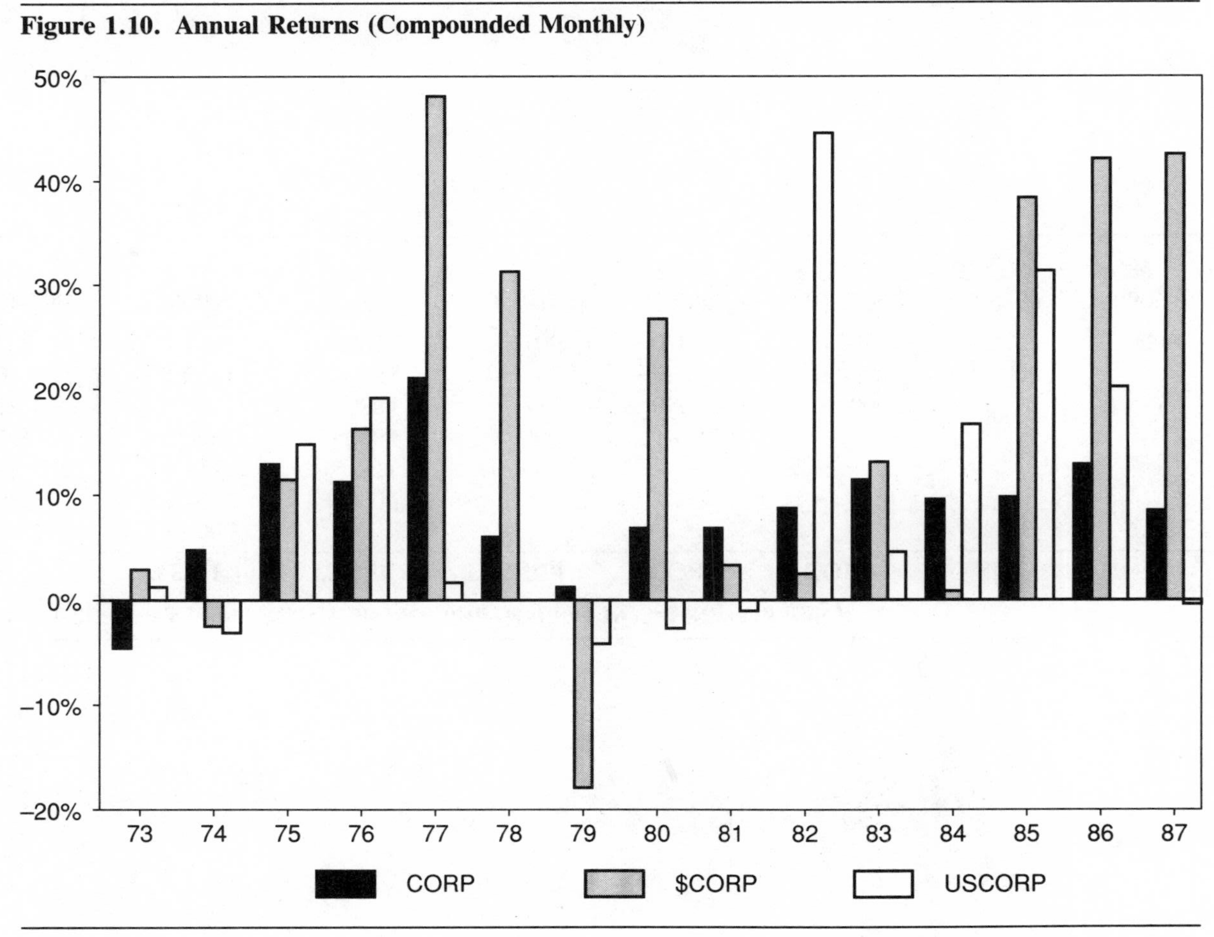

Table 1.2. Correlation Matrix and Autocorrelations 1973–1987 (Monthly)

	TSE-I	TSE-II	TSE-Ism	LGB	CORP	SIR	INFL
TSE-I	1.0000						
TSE-II	0.5032	1.0000					
TSE-Ism	0.5184	0.7871	1.0000				
LGB	0.2288	0.0083	0.0900	1.0000			
CORP	0.2194	0.0884	0.1188	0.8103	1.0000		
SIR	−0.0941	−0.0553	−0.1362	−0.0249	−0.0280	1.0000	
INFL	−0.1343	−0.0951	−0.1106	−0.1346	−0.2082	0.3637	1.0000
Autocorr	0.0631	0.3125	0.1638	0.0980	0.2299	0.9730	0.3090
t-stat	0.83	4.38	2.22	1.31	3.12	53.50	4.32

high cumulative index value of 688 in August 1987. 100 yen invested in December 1972 would have grown to 552 yen in December 1987. As in the U.S. market, small capitalization stocks recorded even higher index values, 721 yen for the TSE-II index and 1406 yen for the smallest quintile of TSE-I.

The TSE-I averaged 12.07% compounded annual return, which is 2.21 percentage points higher than the U.S. S&P 500 index in the same period (Table 1.1). The volatility of the TSE-I index is slightly lower than the U.S. figure for this period. The dollar-translated TSE-I index returns are more volatile than the yen returns but are higher in means as well. The same observation holds for the dollar-translated TSE-II returns.

The autocorrelation of TSE-I returns are quite low (Table 1.2). Given the *t*-statistics, we cannot reject the hypothesis that the true autocorrelations are zero with 95% of confidence level. This suggests that the TSE-I index returns can be characterized as a random walk.

1978 was an extremely "good" year for small stocks: both the TSE-I small quintile and the TSE-II index had compounded returns of more than 70% in one year.[5] We also notice that TSE-I small quintile performed very well after 1985 (Figure 1.6). In addition to higher returns, the small stock returns displayed higher volatility as well (Table 1.1). They are moderately correlated with each other, but the autocorrelations of both the TSE-I small quintile and TSE-II index are quite high (Table 1.2). It is not surprising given the inactive trading for smaller companies. All the stock indices have negative correlations with inflation.

The NYSE small quintile displays lower means and similar volatility to the yen-term TSE-I small quintile (Table 1.1). The yen-term TSE-I small quintile returns are lower in means and standard deviation than their dollar-translated figures. For a U.S. investor, $100 invested in Japanese small stocks would have become $3,480 over the 15-year period (Figure 1.6). Dollar-translated stock returns show low correlation coefficients with corresponding U.S. returns, suggesting that investment in Japanese equities provides good diversification to the U.S. investors (Table 1.3).

Equity risk premium, which is often used in the context of the Capital Asset Pricing Model, has annual figures of 4.51% geometric mean and 5.8% arithmetic mean (Table 1.4). Small stock premium is 5.55% in geometric mean and 6.94% in arithmetic mean, which is similar to the U.S. small stock premium (5.76% geometric mean and 6.92% arithmetic mean).

Table 1.3. Correlation Matrix and Autocorrelations 1973–1987 (Monthly)

	$TSE-I	$TSE-II	$TSE-I	$LGB	$CORP	$SIR
$TSE-I	1.0000					
$TSE-II	0.7231	1.0000				
$TSE-Ism	0.7433	0.8806	1.0000			
$LGB	0.6966	0.6008	0.6519	1.0000		
$CORP	0.7025	0.6411	0.6764	0.9743	1.0000	
$SIR	0.6899	0.6570	0.6881	0.9306	0.9552	1.0000
USS&P	0.2728	0.2314	0.1763	−0.0022	0.0299	0.0020
USSMALL	0.4753	0.6912	0.8266	0.1657	0.1805	0.1625
USCORP	0.1243	0.0979	0.1207	0.2382	0.2207	0.1682
USGOVT	0.1518	0.0930	0.1221	0.2534	0.2242	0.1596
USTBILL	−0.1327	−0.1597	−0.1931	−0.1469	−0.1739	−0.1633
USINFL	−0.2195	−0.1627	−0.1595	−0.1997	−0.2055	−0.1188
−0.1844	−0.1153	−0.1983	−0.2091	0.3095	1.0000	
Autocorr	0.1275	0.2807	0.2008	0.0994	0.1157	0.0559
t-stat	1.71	3.87	2.73	1.31	1.52	0.73

Table 1.4. Summary Statistics, Risk Premia (1973–1987). Annual. (In %) Numbers in parentheses are U.S. data for 1973–1987

Variable	Arithmetic Mean	Geometric Mean	Standard Deviation
Equity Risk Premium	5.80	4.51	16.26
	(3.04	1.56	17.42)
Small Stock Premium	6.94	5.55	17.42
	(6.92	5.76	16.10
Bond Default Premium	−0.06	−0.11	3.11
	(0.46	0.41	3.25)
Bond Maturity Premium	1.58	1.37	6.54
	(−0.69	−0.03	12.92)

Glossary:

Equity Risk Premium = (Tokyo Stock Exchange Section I Index Return) − (Short-Term Interest Rate)

Small Stock Premium = (TSE-I Smallest Quintile Return) − (TSE-I Index Return)

Bond Default Premium = (Long-Term Corporate Bonds Return) − (Long-Term Government Bonds Return)

Bond Maturity Premium = (Long-Term Government Bonds Return) − (Short-Term Interest Rate)

Table 1.3 (Continued)

	USS&P	USSMALL	USCORP	USOVT	USTBILL	USINFL
	1.0000					
	0.2374	1.0000				
	0.3487	0.0329	1.0000			
	0.3138	0.0402	0.9372	1.0000		
	−0.0871	−0.1347	0.0587	0.0859	1.0000	
	0.0217	0.1075	0.1416	0.0595	0.9044	0.6449
	0.29	1.44	1.90	0.80	28.01	11.20

Table 1.5. Summary Statistics, Inflation-Adjusted Series (1973–1987). Annual. (In %)

Variable	Arithmetic Mean	Geometric Mean	Standard Deviation
Tokyo Stock Exchange-I Index	6.80	4.54	20.74
S&P 500 Index	4.47	2.78	18.53
Tokyo Stock Exchange-II Index	10.67	7.58	27.66
TSE-I Small Quintile	19.89	16.58	27.42
NYSE Small Quintile	11.62	8.70	24.97
Long-Term Government Bonds	2.98	2.53	9.47
Long-Term U.S. Government Bonds	2.18	1.16	15.53
Long-Term Corporate Bonds	3.01	1.17	4.23
Long-Term U.S. Corporate Bonds	2.28	1.58	16.06
Short-Term Interest Rate	1.26	1.17	4.23
U.S. Treasury Bills	1.25	1.20	3.51
Inflation	6.08	5.92	5.94
U.S. Inflation	6.96	6.90	3.57

Inflation-adjusted series are defined as (Total Return) − (Inflation) for each series.

Although TSE-I as a whole does not show a specific pattern of seasonality, the small quintile of TSE-I does; its January (and June) returns are considerably high (Figure 1.5) for TSE-II, the August return is its second highest next to January. The small firm/January effect seems to be present in the data, but less obvious than in the U.S. data, if only because of the smaller sample size.[6]

Bonds

100 yen invested at the end of 1972 would have become 350 yen for the long-term government bond and 352 yen for the long-term corporate bond (Figure 1.1). Both bonds had less volatile returns compared to common stocks, but the long-term government bond returns have slightly higher volatility than the long-term corporate bonds (Table 1.1).

Both return series display higher serial correlation that the TSE-I index (Table 1.2). The *t*-statistics for the serial correlation of the CORP is 3.12, that is, we can reject the hypothesis that the true autocorrelation is zero. If the inflation is largely unanticipated, negative correlation coefficients of LGB and CORP with inflation seem plausible since bonds are fixed income securities. We also notice that the default premium is much smaller than the U.S. data, and indeed it is negative (Table 1.4). One of the reasons is that the electricity bond, which comprises the majority of the corporate bond, is a very low-risk bond.

Compared with the U.S. data in the same period, both bonds had similar returns and much lower standard deviations (Table 1.1). Translating bond returns into dollar terms increases the mean return as well as volatility. Although dollar-translated LGB and dollar-translated CORP, U.S. Government Bonds and U.S. Corporate Bonds show high correlation pairwise, dollar-translated bond returns and U.S. bond returns have low correlations (Table 1.3).

Short-Term Interest Rates and Inflation

The index values for the short-term interest rates and cumulative inflation grew to 285 and 237, respectively (Figure 1.1). The short-term interest rates and U.S. T-bill returns have similar summary statistics, except that the autocorrelation of Japanese rates is close to one, suggesting stepwise movements (Tables 1.1 and 1.2). The inflation rate is lower than in the U.S., but it has more variability. Japan had high inflation in 1973 and 1974, but it has come down to a lower level and, in August 1983, the cumulative index for short-term interest rates exceeded the inflation (Figure 1.1).

V. Conclusion

We presented and characterized Japanese financial data for the past 15 years in summary statistics and graphs. We also transformed Japanese data into dollar terms and provided a comparison with the U.S. data over the same period from a perspective of U.S. investors.

Common stocks follow a random walk and have higher returns than other assets. Small stocks, above all, have even higher returns but higher volatility as well. The January anomaly of small firms exists, but to a less obvious extent than in the U.S. data. Bond returns show moderate autocorrelations and less volatility than stocks. Compared with the U.S. series, Japanese common stocks are higher in means and similar in standard deviation. Bonds and the short-term interest rates are comparable to the U.S. in both mean returns and standard deviation. Translation to dollar-terms adds more returns as well as risk. For the U.S. investors, the data show that investment in Japanese securities provides good diversification.

Notes

1. Throughout this paper, the original raw data were provided by the Daiwa Securities. The data were recalculated and recompiled according to the author's specifications. The author wishes to thank Daiwa Securities for their cooperation.
2. Some examples of empirical research in Japanese markets are Gultekin, Gultekin, and Penati (1987), Hamao (1987), Hoshi(1987), Kato and Schallheim (1985).
3. The "yield" for Japanese bonds often represents current coupon yield and is computed as follows (assuming annual coupon payments):

$$\text{price} = \frac{(\text{number of remaining years})\times(\text{coupon}) + \text{face value}}{1 + (\text{number of remaining years})\times(\text{yield})}$$

4. See Stigum (1978) for a description of the U.S. repurchase agreement (*repo* for short). The name *Gensaki* stands for "spot-and-forward."
5. Graphs showing annual returns for small stocks are omitted. They are available from the author upon request.
6. For other documentation of the size effect in the Japanese market, see Kato and Schallheim (1985) and Nakamura and Terada (1984).

References

Gultekin, Bulent, Mustafa Gultekin, and Alessandro Penati, (1987). "Capital Controls and International Capital Markets Segmentation: the Evidence from the Japanese and American Stock Markets," Working Paper, the Wharton School, University of Pennsylvania.

Hamao, Yasushi, (1987). "An Empirical Examination of the Arbitrage Pricing Theory: Using Japanese Data," Ph.D. Dissertation (Chapter 2), Yale School of Management, forthcoming in *Japan and the World Economy: International Journal of Theory and Policy*.

Hoshi, Takeo, (1987). "Stock market Rationality and Price Volatility: Tests Using Japanese Data," *Journal of the Japanese and International Economies*, Vol. 1, pp. 441–462.

Ibbotson, Roger, and Rex Sinquefield, (1976). "Stocks, Bonds, Bills, and Inflation: Year-by-Year Historical Returns (1926–1974), *Journal of Business*, Vol. 49, pp. 11–47.

Ibbotson Associates, (1988). *Stocks, Bonds, Bills, and Inflation: 1988 Yearbook*, Chicago, Capital Market Research Center.

Kato, Kiyoshi, and James Schallheim, (1985). "Seasonal and Size Anomalies and the Japanese Stock Market," *Journal of Financial and Quantitative Analysis*, Vol. 20, pp. 243–260.

Keim, Donald, (1983). "Size-Related Anomalies and Stock Return Seasonality: Further Empirical Evidence," *Journal of Financial Economics*, Vol. 12, pp. 13–32.

Nakamura, Takeo, and Noboru Terada, (1984). "The Size Effect and Seasonality in Japanese Stock Returns," paper presented at the Institute for Quantitative Research in Finance (The Q Group).

Stigum, Marcia, (1978). *The Money Market*, Homewood, IL, Dow Jones-Irwin.

2

The Japanese Financial System in Comparative Perspective[1]

Eisuke Sakakibara
Ministry of Finance, Tokyo, Japan

Robert Alan Feldman
Department of Economics, Massachusetts Institute of Technology, Cambridge, Massachusetts 02139

I. Introduction

The conventional view of postwar[2] Japanese financial markets is that they were highly regulated. Authorities were alleged to control both absolute level and allocation of funds among firms and individuals.[3] Moreover, financial controls were seen to form the basis of industrial policy favoring growth industries, which in turn made high growth of GNP possible. Thus, direct control by authorities over asset choice by intermediaries is alleged to have generated high growth.

Ironically, however, most accounts of the Japanese financial structure are critical of the controls, which are considered, a priori, to be inefficient or irrational. But this puts proponents of the conventional view in a difficult position. They must choose among several unattractive ways of reconciling control with high growth: (1) that controls in Japan were ineffective; (2) that growth would have been even faster without controls; or (3) that controls are more efficient than markets. The common resolution of the dilemma was a variant of the last point. Japan's controls, it is alleged, were effective because of "peculiarities" of Japanese financial markets, such as predominance of indirect finance, "excessive" indebtedness of commercial banks to the Bank of Japan, high dependence of

Journal of Economic Literature Classification Number 053, 310.

nonfinancial corporations on bank loans, and heavy borrowing of city banks from local banks.

The theories constructed within this framework are logical and internally consistent, but they also contradict the widespread belief that Japanese society is highly competitive in nature. Why would the Japanese financial industry submit to controls when other (but not all) industries were competitive? The question itself suggests an answer: perhaps the financial subsectors, on the contrary, actively sought and encouraged controls, in a version of rent seeking, and then competed among themselves for the spoils. The appropriate model is then that of monopolistic competition.

How, then, are we to evaluate Japanese financial performance? If the appropriate model is that of monopolistic competition, then was the system more monopolistic or more competitive? Did the monopolistic elements cause suboptimalities, or did the competitive aspects dominate and bring overall efficiency? Finding statistical indicators of monopoly levels and degrees of competition is difficult, but we do try to present some. More importantly, we judge the success of the financial system by the degree of intermediation it brought. We make this concept precise below. In particular, we compare the Japanese pattern of financial markets to that of the United States, and examine how differences in structure affected performance. The role of government is also considered.

II. The Interrelationships among Macroeconomic Performance, Structure of Financial Markets and Conduct of Financial Policies in Japan

The most striking fact about postwar Japan is that the real rate of growth of GNP was not only high but also accelerated.[4] Surges are common to late starters in industrial revolutions, but Table 2.1 shows that the surge in Japan persisted and accelerated. Growth in the 1950s might be linked to recovery from the war. But why did the acceleration continue?

Since acceleration started in the 1930s, we suspect that structural changes in the economy then, with modifications during the occupation, may have been conducive to acceleration. For example, the basic foundation of current Japanese financial markets was laid during the 1930s. The reforms of the occupation did not have much impact on the organization of financial markets. Indeed, *zaibatsu* (conglomerate) dissolution and the de facto confiscation of equity actually accelerated the trend

Table 2.1. Real GNP Growth (%/yr)

	Japan	U.S.	Germany	U.K.
1931–1937	5.7	3.1	8.5	3.1
1938–1956	1.8	4.8	—	1.9
1957–1962	9.4	3.2	5.5	3.1
1963–1969	10.3	4.4	4.9	2.9
1970–1974	6.0	3.0	2.9	2.7
1975–1979	5.8	4.4	4.0	2.3

Sources: 1931–1938: Nakamura (1978, p. 12); 1936–1956: for U.K.: Mitchell (1975); for the U.S.: U.S. Dept. of Commerce, *Historical Statistics of the United States*, p. F-31; and for Japan: Ohkawa and Shinohara (1980, Tables A2, A50, and A57); 1957–1979: IMF, *Internat. Fin. Stat.*, May 1977 and December 1980.

from direct to indirect financing.[5] It is only conjecture at this stage, but such structural changes may have stimulated trend acceleration.

The second critical fact of the postwar Japanese economy concerns the savings ratio. Table 2.2 shows the ratio of gross savings of all sectors to GNP for some major nations. The pattern is quite similar to that of Table 2.1; a major upward shift occurred in the 1930s, and the rise continued until the early 1970s. The issue is not merely the high level of the savings ratio, but its continued rise.

Table 2.2. Ratio of Gross Saving to GNP

	Japan	United States	Germany[a]
1932–1937	17.9	6.4	7.3
1938–1957	27.0	12.8	—
1958–1962	33.6	15.2	25.9
1963–1969	36.5	16.2	26.4
1970–1974	37.3	15.8	26.2
1975–1979	30.5	15.7	22.3

Sources: Japan: 1932–1969: Ohkawa and Shinohara (1980, Tables A1 and A6); 1970–1979: Bank of Japan, *Internat. Compar. Stat.* (in Japanese), 1980. U.S.: 1932–1937: Dept. of Commerce, *Long-Term Economic Growth;* 1938–1979: *Economic Report of the President* (1980, Tables B-23 (p. 260) and B-1 (p. 233). Germany: 1932–1937: Mitchell (1975, p. 785); 1938–1979; IMF, *Internat. Fin. Stat.*, May 1977 and December 1980. Data listed are gross fixed capital formation plus increase in stocks as a percent of GNP.

a. Capital formation as % of GNP.

Conventional macro models of Japan normally ignore the structure of financial intermediation as a determinant of the savings rate. This may be justified if financial markets are perfectly competitive, and if individuals and corporations can borrow and lend unlimited amounts with perfect certainty at the market interest rate. This textbook framework is what has guided research that attributed Japan's high saving to the higher rate of growth of income, the low asset/income ratio, and institutional characteristics such as the bonus system.

But market structure, imperfect information, and uncertainty play crucial roles, particularly in retail markets for bank deposits and bank loans. Given imperfections and uncertainty, the structure of financial intermediation will affect the overall level and sectoral distribution of savings. It is intriguing to note that the shift toward more indirect financing in Japan coincided with the rise in the savings ratio.

The third critical characteristic of the postwar Japanese economy is the share of government in overall economic activity. Many analysts believe there was a substantial government role in many sectors, but in fact both the level of aggregate government spending and tax revenue as a proportion of GNP have been considerably lower than in other developed countries. Although the government share (consumption, investment, plus transfer payments of all kinds as a percentage of GNP) has increased somewhat in recent years, it was only 30.5% in 1978, compared to 34% in the United States and 43.9% in the United Kingdom in 1977.[6]

The reason is lower government consumption; government consumption was only about 10% of GNP in Japan in 1978, versus about 20% in the United States, Germany, and the U.K. The low figure for Japan is due to low defense expenditures and a much smaller number of government employees. Japanese defense expenditures in 1979 were 0.95% of GNP, compared to 5.05% for the United States. The total numbers of government employees (central, local, and public corporations) per 1,000 population in 1976 were 92 and 169 in Japan and the United States respectively, excluding military personnel. (The numbers were 93 and 205, respectively, when military personnel were included.) On the other hand, Japan shows a much higher ratio of government investment to GNP than any other advanced country. In 1978, the ratio of government gross capital formation to GNP was 6.3%, compared to 1.6% in the United States in 1977.[7]

But there is another critical role government can play, that of financial intermediary. Government can socialize risks, coordinate private interests, and improve flows of information. Both the U.S. and Japanese governments have acted as intermediaries. United States financial intermediation policy attempted to channel a certain proportion of a given amount of savings into housing and agricultural sectors; Japanese financial intermediation policy attempted not only to channel savings into both productive social infrastructure and manufacturing, but also to raise savings in the aggregate.

To summarize, the three major aspects of the postwar Japanese economy that we emphasize in the context of their interactions with financial markets and policies are (1) high and accelerating rate of growth of real GNP, (2) the high and rising savings ratio, and (3) a frugal, investment-prone, intermediation-oriented government sector.

III. The Characteristics of the Japanese Financial System

Following a framework similar to that used by Friedman (1981), we directly examine changes in the liability-issuing and asset-holding behavior of the economy's various financial and nonfinancial sectors, and compare Japan's experience with that of the United States. Four important characteristics of Japanese financial markets emerge.

Continuous Deepening of Debts

One distinctive development of the Japanese financial markets since World War II has been the rapid, continuing rise in the ratio of financial liabilities of nonfinancial sectors to total GNP. Unlike the U.S. case, in which Friedman found long-run stability of this ratio,[8] the postwar Japanese figure showed an upward trend, and now stands above the U.S. level.

Table 2.3 shows this liability ratio, both in the aggregate and by major sectors or categories of borrowers (central government, local government, incorporated business, and individuals).

The rapid rise in the liability/GNP ratio in early postwar years can be explained, at least partially, as a restoration of earlier liability/GNP levels. But the ratio continued rising well into the 1970s. Thus, the Japanese nonfinancial sector today is more deeply in debt than its U.S. counterpart.

A natural counterpart of the liability deepening by the nonfinancial sector is the accumulation of financial assets. In Table 2.4, one aspect

Table 2.3. Financial Liabilities as a Share of Total GNP[a]

	Total		Central Government		Local Authorities		Corporations		Individuals[b]	
	Japan	U.S.	Japan	U.S.	Japan	U.S.	Japan	U.S.	Japan	U.S.
1953–1955	0.779	1.374	0.085	0.605	0.076	0.108	0.547	0.288	0.091	0.372
1956–1960	0.995	1.411	0.072	0.500	0.101	0.130	0.682	0.325	0.138	0.454
1961–1965	1.211	1.480	0.043	0.422	0.128	0.149	0.851	0.360	0.189	0.548
1966–1970	1.387	1.422	0.084	0.323	0.175	0.148	0.890	0.396	0.238	0.574
1971–1975	1.598	1.476	0.108	0.279	0.214	0.151	0.965	0.444	0.307	0.601
1976–1978	1.761	1.503	0.222	0.300	0.273	0.137	0.897	0.452	0.364	0.614

Sources: Data are from the Flow of Funds Accounts of the Federal Reserve System and of the Bank of Japan. Flow-of-funds data for Japan used in the SNA accounts were not used because they do not go back far enough in history and because of the incompleteness of that set of data.

a. Figures in the table represent the geometric averages of ratios for the years listed.

b. The sector "Individuals" includes unincorporated business in both countries.

Table 2.4. Marshallian *K* for Currency, M_1, and M_2

	Currency/GNP		M_1/GNP		M_2/GNP	
	Japan	U.S.	Japan	U.S.	Japan	U.S.
1953–1955	0.084	0.074	0.298	0.373	0.609	0.638
1956–1960	0.082	0.062	0.319	0.323	0.783	0.637
1961–1965	0.085	0.055	0.364	0.284	0.936	0.697
1966–1970	0.083	0.050	0.382	0.246	1.040	0.699
1971–1975	0.093	0.048	0.434	0.220	1.198	0.747
1976–1978	0.085	0.047	0.407	0.189	1.250	0.765

Sources: Flow-of-funds data from the Bank of Japan and the Federal Reserve System; Bank of Japan *Economic Statistics Annual* for GNP of Japan; *Economic Report of the President* for U.S. GNP and currency outstanding.

of accumulation of financial assets is shown, the ratios of M_1 and M_2 to GNP. (M_2 here includes postal savings deposits, which are only part of M_3 in the Bank of Japan's classification system.) The ratio of money to GNP is often called the Marshallian *K* (or reciprocal of velocity), and is usually assumed in monetary theory to be stable. The Marshallian *K* for M_2 was indeed rather stable in the United States, but rose chronically in Japan. Since M_2 constituted about 65% of all financial assets (excluding trade credit) of the nonfinancial sector in Japan throughout the postwar period, it is only natural that M_2/GNP follow a path similar to that of the liability ratio in Table 2.3. Although the upward trend in M_1/GNP is weaker, the trend is still discernible. On the other hand, the currency/GNP ratio is quite stable.

These trends in the components of money reflect standard Japanese practice; most Japanese households do not open checkable bank accounts. The bulk of M_1 is interest-bearing, noncheckable demand deposits. Thus, both demand and time deposits in Japan should be treated not as money but as nonnegotiable assets.

The High Degree of Financial Intermediation

Many analysts have discussed the predominance of indirect financing in Japan. But Kuroda and Oritani (1979) have pointed out that consistent classification of privately placed bonds and bonds purchased by financial intermediaries changes the conventional picture of sharp contrast between U.S. and Japanese patterns of direct versus indirect financing: if one includes privately placed bonds and bonds purchased by financial intermediaries as a part of indirect financing, and also adjusts properly for differences in accounting methods between the two countries, the proportions of indirect financing in the two countries are not that much different.

Moreover, the distinction between direct and indirect financing is somewhat misleading. Suzuki (1980, pp. 67–68) has said that "To express this in the most extreme terms, the reason why direct financing is preferable to indirect financing is that funds are then allocated through the interest-rate mechanism by competition, whereas the policy of artificially low interest in Japan prevented the development of competitive . . . markets." But the assertion that direct financing is better completely ignores the question of risk. Even if bank-bought bonds are considered "direct" financing, they are not nearly as direct as individual-bought bonds. In short, because of the structure of purchase of bonds and stocks, the distinction between direct and indirect financing may be a red herring. Better insight is gained by measuring the degree of financial intermediation relative to economic activity.

Financial intermediaries' basic activity is to hold a single liability, usually deposits, and transform this liability into assets. This activity is important to an economy because it not only reduces costs of financial activity to depositors but also transforms the nature of risks. For example, one result is maturity transformation; that is, financial intermediaries collect deposits of short maturity and make investments or loans of long maturity. The extent of the mismatch of asset-side and liability-side maturities cannot be too large since financial intermediaries must have sufficient liquidity for unforeseen withdrawals of deposits. But the risk of a liquidity crisis is reduced by interbank markets, money-market instruments, and central-bank financing.

Table 2.5 shows one measure of the importance of financial intermediation, the ratio of total liabilities of financial intermediaries to GNP. Because of intercountry, intertemporal, and compositional differences of intermediaries' liabilities, the ratios of Japan and the United States in Table 2.5 are not directly comparable. But we do see several facts. The degrees of financial intermediation rose in both countries, but much less in the United States than in Japan. In the United States, "the continuation and even acceleration of the trend toward intermediate markets" has been accompanied by the "simultaneous rise in the economy's reliance on privately issued debt."[9] That is, despite the small rise in the overall

Table 2.5. Financial-System Liabilities as a Proportion of GNP

	Japan	U.S.
1953–1955	0.919	1.106
1956–1960	1.238	1.166
1961–1965	1.566	1.313
1966–1970	1.729	1.371
1971–1975	1.961	1.427
1976–1978	2.044	1.486

Source: Calculated from Flow of Funds Accounts of the Federal Reserve System and the Bank of Japan.

ratio in the United States, the amount of risk increased. This is because, as seen in Table 2.4, the composition of liabilities shifted substantially from public to private. Since private debt is more risky than public debt, overall risk rose. This increase in aggregate liability-side risk in America encouraged advances in financial intermediation, to blunt the effect on individuals' asset-side risk.

In Japan, the rise in financial intermediation was extremely rapid and closely associated with overall deepening of debts. Moreover, the share of public debt in total financial debt rose after 1960, implying less risk; but the rapid surge in the overall ratio of liabilities to GNP more than offset this change in composition. In Japan the increase in intermediation was encouraged not by the shift in debt composition, but by overall deepening of debts.

Table 2.6 shows the composition of financial assets of nonfinancial sectors in both countries. Holdings of equities and bonds are much larger in the United States, while M_2 is much more important in Japan. The figures clearly indicate that intermediation in Japan is dominated by banks and the post office. Moreover, the proportion of financing through trade credit is much larger in Japan than in the United States, reflecting the fact that Japanese nonfinancial corporations, particularly trading companies, engage in substantial financial intermediation to their customers and subsidiaries. Hence, the degree of overall intermediation is even larger than implied by the ratio of liabilities of financial intermediaries to GNP. All in all, postwar Japan saw a tremendous rise in financial intermediation, to a level greater than that in the United States.

Table 2.6. Wealth Composition of Nonfinancial Sector (Assets) (% of Total)

	M_1		M_2		Long-term savings[a]		Equities	
	Japan	U.S.	Japan	U.S.	Japan	U.S.	Japan	U.S.
1953–1955	0.249	0.153	0.526	0.298	0.047	0.136	0.124	0.272
1956–1960	0.189	0.122	0.491	0.272	0.065	0.140	0.147	0.320
1961–1965	0.159	0.096	0.438	0.273	0.072	0.145	0.137	0.344
1966–1970	0.154	0.085	0.446	0.279	0.087	0.149	0.110	0.333
1971–1975	0.161	0.084	0.467	0.336	0.091	0.160	0.102	0.245
1976–1978	0.149	0.078	0.487	0.367	0.104	0.167	0.088	0.204

	Financial investments[b]		Loans		Trade Credit	
	Japan	U.S.	Japan	U.S.	Japan	U.S.
1953–1955	0.025	0.201	0.010	0.023	0.263	0.065
1956–1960	0.028	0.180	0.006	0.019	0.260	0.068
1961–1965	0.047	0.151	0.002	0.019	0.303	0.067
1966–1970	0.038	0.139	0.001	0.021	0.318	0.078
1971–1975	0.045	0.142	0.000	0.021	0.293	0.087
1976–1978	0.060	0.154	0.000	0.023	0.261	0.084

Source: Calculated from Flow of Funds Accounts of the Federal Reserve System and the Bank of Japan.

a. Includes trusts and insurance.

b. Includes securities other than equities.

Low Public Debt and High Public Financial Intermediation

Another striking contrast between the United States and Japan is the evolution of public debt. In the United States the ratio of outstanding public debt to total nonfinancial sector liabilities was 71% in 1946. For Japan the ratio was only 10% in 1953. Gradual and steady decline in the United States and rapid increase in Japan after 1971 brought the ratios to 19% in the United States and 14% in Japan at the end of 1978. The low initial value for Japan was the result of the rampant inflation of the late 1940s. This low initial value, together with balanced budgets of the central government, made possible extremely low stocks of public debt. The central government deficit started to bulge after 1971, and has grown very rapidly throughout the 1970s. But despite this bulge, it is legitimate to characterize the years 1953–1973 in Japan as a period when the share of public debt remained low.

A natural counterpart of the low liability share of the government was the high share of the private sector. In particular, the share of financial liabilities of corporations remained extremely high through the period for Japan. By 1978, their share had fallen to "only" 47%, compared to 30% in the United States. But before the first oil shock, the share had never gone below 60%, and stayed near 70% most of the time. This high liability share for corporations was no doubt a major underpinning for high investment and high growth of GNP. The low public debt share contributed to growth by avoiding significant crowding out and by encouraging financial intermediaries to take more risk on private debts. Although the direction of causality is ambiguous, we could argue that the paucity of riskless government securities induced the economy to devise more ways to bear more risk. The chief method was more intermediation.

The Japanese government itself played a significant role in raising the degree of financial intermediation. Table 2.7 gives two indicators of this, the share of government financial institutions in loans granted, and the share of government intermediaries in total liabilities of all intermediaries. The shares for Japan are significantly higher than those of the United States throughout the period. Moreover, as discussed below, the significance of this intermediation is much greater than the numbers suggest. On the liability side, the postal savings system, administered through post offices, created an atmosphere of intense competition in the collection of deposits. On the asset side, lending by official banks

Table 2.7. Government Financial Intermediation (Shares of Government Financial Institutions in Loans and Total Liabilities of the Financial Sector)

	Loans (Assets)			Total liabilities	
	Japan				
	Gross	Net[a]	U.S.	Japan	U.S.
1953–1955	0.221	0.191	0.043	0.191	0.010
1956–1960	0.228	0.179	0.045	0.192	0.015
1961–1965	0.206	0.156	0.065	0.171	0.020
1966–1970	0.215	0.156	0.066	0.184	0.027
1971–1975	0.220	0.156	0.073	0.202	0.046
1976–1978	0.283	0.210	0.086	0.232	0.063

Source: Calculation from Flow of Funds Accounts of the Federal Reserve System and the Bank of Japan.

a. The net column excludes loans among government institutions.

(e.g., the Japan Development Bank) not only injected extra funds into the system but also gave de facto government guarantee to projects in which they participated.

Low Levels of Consumer Credit

Another distinctive feature of Japanese financial markets is the low level of liabilities of individuals. The category "individuals" includes unincorporated business in the Japanese flow of funds statistics, and American statistics are adjusted by us accordingly. Hence, numbers in Table 2.3 include, among other things, bank loans to unincorporated business. Although consumer and mortgage credit in Japan have expanded quite rapidly in the 1970s, they were still only 17.5% of GNP in 1978, versus 70.1% in the United States. It is fair to characterize the postwar Japanese financial markets as closed to consumers. When liquidity constraints are binding, the life-cycle pattern of income affects the life-cycle pattern of consumption. In Japan, the pattern of income is skewed toward old age, because of the seniority wage system. And due to postwar borrowing constraints, the young had to save to build houses instead of borrowing to do so, while the old saved whatever remained after consumption. Thus the combination of the seniority wage structure and poor consumer financing generated higher overall savings.

Summary

Comparison of flow-of-funds data of the United States and Japan during the postwar period yields the four distinct features of Japanese financial evolution just analyzed. These seem to provide some suggestions about why the savings rate, and perhaps the real growth rate, accelerated. The ability to deepen debts made it possible for corporations to borrow heavily, raise investment, and reduce the real cost of financing. The small amount of government debt, along with the de facto closure of markets to consumers until the 1970s, meant that most funds could go only to corporations and investment. These developments were encouraged by the rapid advancement of financial intermediaries, which raised savings by lowering average risk per yen of assets.

IV. Deepening of Liabilities; Growth of Financial Intermediation

What factors made possible the deepening of liabilities and the advance of intermediation? The answer, we feel, lies in the intensity of competition among the individual institutions within sectors of the financial market, even though some had monopoly power as sectors. Government regulation indeed granted certain market powers to sectors of the financial market, and restrained price competition; but policy also encouraged nonprice competition among the privileged.

We hope to show that Japanese financial intermediaries competed fiercely, despite regulations. Qualitative judgment on the relative tightness of regulations is not easy, but evidence indicates that many statutory regulations in Japan were less extensive, both in scope and stringency, than those in the United States. "Administrative guidance" in Japan, although pervasive in some areas, did not prevent effective competition among intermediaries of a given class. Moreover, there has always been intense competition from intermediaries not subject to guidance, that is, those not under jurisdiction of either the Ministry of Finance or the Bank of Japan. On the liability side, fierce competition forced strenuous efforts at deposit collection. On the asset side, each commercial bank has competed quite vigorously to become the "main bank" (primary lender) to good customers.

Some academic analysts have questioned whether the loan market was actually competitive. Main banks were often described as focal points of *keiretsu* (corporate groups) and keiretsu were often alleged to be nothing but reformulations of old zaibatsu. Mitsubishi Bank, for example, is main bank to a large number of companies of the old Mitsubishi group, and Sumitomo is main bank to a group of old Sumitomo corporations. However, the importance of grouping has been exaggerated. Main banks were usually followed closely by second and third banks that had no group connections. Practitioners were virtually unanimous in saying that pervasive competition existed among banks to secure as many good loans as possible.

However, the evidence against competitiveness of the financial market cannot be ignored. Deposit rates and government bond rates were controlled, and direct credit controls by authorities were also a standard macroeconomic policy tool. These controls and others gave rise to monopoly rents and taxes.

Which, then, were more important, the monopolistic aspects or the competitive ones? One method of determining this would be to attach dollar values to the costs of various distortions and the benefits of competitive aspects. Then a social welfare function could be used to weight the costs and benefits. Unfortunately, the assignment of values to costs and benefits is difficult, and the definition of a social welfare function even more difficult. Instead, we adopt a less rigorous but easier procedure. We compare stringency of regulations and other aspects of the Japanese financial markets to those in the United States. If there is a low number of areas where distortions in Japan appear worse than in the United States, and if these distortions appear small in relation to total funds for allocation, then, we say that the effects of competition in Japan outweighed those of monopoly.

Historical Background

Before turning to details on monopoly and competition, a brief discussion of the history of the Japanese financial system is in order.

As in the United States, many Japanese financial regulations date back to the late 1920s and early 1930s. The Banking Act was enacted in 1927, in the midst of a string of financial panics, and remained in effect until 1982. The Japanese Banking Act mandated strong national leadership in bank regulation, and the result of the act was merger and consolidation. The total number of commercial and savings banks fell from 1541 in 1926 to 498 in 1936, and finally to 65 in 1945. By one measure, deposit concentration in the five major banks rose during this period; the Big Five share of deposits of all regular banks (Big Five and the locals) went from 20.5 to 31% between 1920 and 1930. But much more significant was the increase in the share of the post office and thrift institutions in total deposits of all financial intermediaries. Their combined share rose from 10.4 to 25.4%.[10]

These thrift institutions throve throughout the postwar period. In 1979, they alone still held 25% of total deposits. The development of thrifts seems extremely important in explaining the very competitive and pervasive nature of retail banking in the postwar period. Commercial banks, despite their relatively strong position in the market, were forced into so-called massive deposit collection drives as early as the 1950s, to counter competition in deposit collection from the thrift institutions and post offices. Prewar development of these institutions laid the foundation for intense postwar competition in retail banking.[11]

The occupation period (1945–1952) was also a crucial phase in the evolution of the financial system. Though occupation policies took little direct action on the financial sector, the reforms still affected financial markets in fundamental, though indirect, ways.

First, the dissolution of the zaibatsu—which, when coupled with inflation, resulted in de facto confiscation of equities—completely changed the ownership structure of assets. Dissolution put an end to private placement of equities with wealthy individuals, zaibatsu corporations, and zaibatsu holding companies. As a result, demand for loans from intermediaries rose drastically.

Second, specialized banks were reorganized into long-term-credit banks, and new public financial institutions, such as the Housing Finance Corporation (*Jutaku Kinyu Koko*) and the Japan Development Bank (*Nihon Kaihatsu Ginko*), were established between 1949 and 1952. This laid the groundwork for effective syndication of loans and coordination of underwriting.

Third, the Dodge Line and later legislation established a policy regime that banned flotation of national bonds to cover current deficits. The Japanese government could not borrow significant amounts from financial markets; however, it could lend since it had enormous funds from postal savings deposits, which had previously funded national debt.

Thus, the Japanese financial structure received a substantial bequest from history, namely, (1) an active, competitive set of thrift institutions, (2) an emphasis on multitiered intermediation, (3) a set of core institutions to organize syndications, and (4) a government budget in chronic surplus.

Commercial Banking Regulations

Virtually every nation regulates its banking industry. Bitter experience has taught that faith in the financial system is a public good, and economic theory teaches that public goods are most efficiently provided by government. Thus, the main rationale for banking regulation is to maintain the public good of depositor confidence by assuring bank solvency.

Banking is highly regulated in both the United States and Japan, and Japan's banking literature normally assumes that Japanese regulations are more stringent than those of the United States. But detailed documentation reveals this to be an exaggeration. The evidence is as follows.

(i) Branching. Limitations on geographic expansion are much stricter in the United States than in Japan. U.S. banks are not allowed "full service" offices in more than a single state. This restriction may not be circumvented by holding companies, because the same regulation applies to banking offices owned by bank holding companies. Moreover, even within a state, branching by banks and acquisitions by bank holding companies are subject to restrictions imposed by each state. As of July 1979, 11 U.S. states prohibited bank branching; of these 11, 5 prohibited more than one banking office for a bank holding company. Among the 38 states that allow branching, only 22 permit statewide branching.

There are no major geographic restrictions on bank branching in Japan. Even nonbank commercial depository institutions enjoy freedom in geographic expansion. There are no geographic restrictions on mutual-bank branching. Only credit associations are limited to branching within prefectures, but prefectures are usually large enough for this constraint not to bind.

There is voluminous literature about effects of U.S. branching restrictions on the competitiveness in banking.[12] The general conclusion is that restriction prevents competition and lowers efficiency. One report of the president to Congress notes that "Existing restraints on geographic expansion create artificial, arbitrary barriers to entry, and therefore are anticompetitive."[13]

Some analysts have called Japan's Ministry of Finance branch-expansion policies conservative and anticompetitive, despite the absence of geographic restrictions. For example, city banks were treated relatively unfavorably in branching policy. However, the post offices, local banks, and thrift institutions quickly filled the gap left by exclusion of major banks from the branch-expansion race. Commercial banks, mutual banks, credit associations, agriculture and fishery cooperatives, and post offices all competed fiercely for deposits, and all but the latter competed for commercial loans to creditworthy borrowers. Indeed, competition among these institutions is often called "excessive" by both the Ministry of Finance and the press. The role of Japan's Ministry of Finance in branching regulations seems to have been to prevent large banks from monopolizing the deposit market.

Table 2.8 shows the number of financial institutions and branches in the United States and Japan. A hasty observer may see only 86 commercial banks in Japan compared to 14,705 in the United States. But because of the similarity in deposit-gathering functions between commercial banks and thrifts, at least mutual loan and savings banks, credit associations, and credit cooperatives in Japan should be included. This adds 1016 institutions and 11,566 branches. Moreover, considering the powerful competitive pressure applied by agricultural cooperatives (4564 institutions and 16,949 offices) and post offices (22,074 deposit-taking offices), and then considering that all of Japan is only the size of Montana, the numbers shown in Table 2.8 clearly suggest more severe competition in Japan.

Price competition in deposit collection was highly regulated in both nations. Monetary authorities in both set maximum interest rates on deposits depending on length of deposit, and allowed higher rates to thrift institutions than to commercial banks. In Japan, the post office was also allowed higher interest rates for deposits, often after acrimonious negotiations between the Ministry of Posts and Telecommunications and the Ministry of Finance. Moreover, intermediaries in both nations sought to circumvent the interest-rate controls with gifts for new accounts and special collection and payments services. There appears to have been at least as much price competition in Japan as in the United States, though neither nation had much before the late 1970s.

Though most analysts have deplored deposit-rate controls, it is not clear how distortionary they were. It is hard to imagine that savings could have been higher with deposit rates free from control. Japanese savers clearly showed sensitivity to interest rates in how they allocated their savings; large flows of deposit transfers from one institution to another occurred when the gap between postal savings rates and commercial

Table 2.8. Number of Financial Institutions and Their Offices: United States and Japan

United States (December 31, 1977)			Japan (December 31, 1979)		
	No. of institutions	No. of offices		No. of institutions	No. of offices
Commercial banks	14,705	32,880	Commercial banks	86[a]	8,510
Mutual savings banks	467	2,314	Mutual loan & savings banks	71	3,712
Savings & loan associations	4,761	17,848	Credit associations	462	5,350
Credit unions	22,380	NA	Credit cooperatives	483	2,504
			Agricultural cooperatives	4,564	16,949
			Post offices	NA	22,074

Sources: U.S.: Board of Governors of the Federal Reserve System; U.S. League of Savings Association; National Credit Administration. Japan: Bank of Japan.

a. Includes long-term credit banks.

bank rates expanded. But the total quantity of savings did not seem to be affected by the level of interest rates. Thus, the distortion of the savings-investment balance caused by deposit-rate controls was probably minor. Moreover, by preventing rapid transfers of deposits in deposit-rate wars, the deposit-rate controls enabled banks to keep lower reserves and thus allocate more of their own portfolios to earning assets.

It is difficult to assess objectively the relative competitiveness of United States and Japanese banking markets. But data on three– and five-firm concentration ratios of bank deposits show clearly that Japan is more competitive. These ratios were 29.1 and 41.2%, respectively, for Tokyo, and 37.2 and 55.1% for New York (see U.S. Department of Treasury, 1981, and Bank of Japan, 1967).

(ii) Segmentation. Another important comparison is market segmentation, particularly between nonbank depository institutions and commercial banks. Until the Monetary Control Act of 1980 in the United States, there were distinct differences in what U.S. regulatory authorities regarded as the business activities of commercial banks and those of thrifts. For example, the former offered checking accounts, and the latter did not. The U.S. asset- and liability-side regulations, which naturally lead to segmentations of markets, were far less strict in Japan. For example, the proportions of housing loans in commercial bank, mutual bank, and credit association assets in Japan were 5.2, 8.5, and 10%, respectively, of residential mortgages in similar institutions in the United States at the same time. Note, however, that the term "less segmentation" means only that Japanese intermediaries were less restricted in choice among existing assets. It does not mean that all assets existed. The problem of nonexistence of a consumer loan market in Japan was not a problem of segmentation, but rather one of exclusion.

(iii) Other Regulations. It is difficult to make an unambiguous judgment on the relative stringency of other regulations, but the widespread perception of tighter regulations in Japan is not obvious.

For example, equity investments are prohibited in the United States but permitted in Japan, as long as a single bank's holdings do not exceed 5% of the total equity of a company. Moral suasion and jawboning in the United States are the counterparts of Japan's administrative guidance. It is widely believed that moral suasion is ineffective in the United States, but some analysts feel administrative guidance is important. The present authors believe its importance is exaggerated.

Administrative guidance on deposit collections in Japan is typically conducted against such practices as (a) deposit drives to commemorate openings of new branches, decentennials of foundings of banks or changes in management, or (b) imposition of de facto quotas or too ambitious deposit targets for branches. Neither practice even exists in the United States. But they persist in Japan, despite years of guidance against them; and even if the Ministry of Finance succeeded in repressing these practices, only the mode of competition would change, not the amount.

Of course, not all administrative guidance in Japan was toothless. But when effective, the effectiveness was due to the needs of the banks, securities firms, and other regulatees for cooperation from the Ministry of Finance in regulatory decisions on financial structure. In short, administrative guidance was effective only when the Ministry of Finance could make a credible threat to alter the balance of regulatory privilege. However, the Ministry itself gained many advantages (e.g., low-interest bond flotations after 1965) from the de facto taxes on the returns to regulation-generated monopoly power. In this sense, the Ministry of Finance was a prisoner of its own regulatory system, and had difficulty using administrative guidance in areas of critical importance to the profits of regulatees. Since the effectiveness of administrative guidance was restricted to areas of lesser importance, it cannot have lowered the competitiveness of the financial system greatly.

Regulatory authorities in the United States and Japan must also assure the soundness of bank portfolios. Japanese restrictions are weaker. For example, Japanese banks can lend up to 20% of their own capital to a single borrower, versus 10% in the United States. Use of real estate as collateral is subject to substantial legal restriction in the United States, but to none in Japan.

(iv) Long-Term Lending. The perfectly competitive Walrasian auctioneer model lies behind most criticism of Japanese long-term lending markets. It is normally alleged that dominance of indirect financing in Japan has made the system less efficient than that of the United States.

In fact, the United States is not as competitive as analysts of Japan often imagine. First, some 30% of corporate bonds are privately placed in the United States. In substance, this process is very close to bilateral monopoly, though both parties operate under threat of exit by the other. Second, even public placements are underwritten by investment bankers in a process far from the ideal of Walrasian auctions. Practitioners agree that close relations of issuer and manager are essential for successful issues of corporate bonds. Usually the same investment bank serves as lead manager for a company over many years, and for every type of issue. These managers have full knowledge of the strengths and weaknesses of the issuing company, and participating investment banks rely most on lead managers' assessments of companies in deciding whether to join a syndicate. Moreover, the issuing company itself relies on the judgment of its lead manager about current and future market conditions. These judgments help determine the amount and terms of issue. The managers take responsibility for maintenance of market strength for the issue afterward, and assume risks if their judgment turns out to be wrong.

The above procedures are very similar to making ordinary syndicated loans in Japan. Banks negotiate with borrowing companies about the amount and terms of loans, based on knowledge of creditworthiness and capital-market conditions. The main bank acts as wholesale financial intermediary, collecting funds from syndicate participants and lending them to the issuer.

Thus, long-term lending through bonds in the United States and through commercial bank-loan syndication in Japan do not differ much in competitiveness; they do differ in the ultimate source of funds attracted. In the United States long-term funds come most often from insurance companies and pension funds, whose liabilities are long in maturity and low in volatility. But in Japan, 65% of financial assets (excluding trade credit) held by the nonfinancial sector take the form of deposits, versus only 40% in the United States. It is only natural that the main instrument of long-term lending reflect the asset preferences of the intermediaries with the most money to lend.

At first sight, it may seem ironic that extensive loan syndication was compatible with competition. But in fact, syndication is only necessary when financial power is dispersed. When no one institution's participation in a project is crucial, no threat aimed at securing a larger return can be successful. Extensive syndication is evidence in favor of high competition, not against it.

But syndication and diversification of long-term loans were not sufficient to reduce the asset-side risk of Japanese commercial banks to levels suitable to the liability-side risk; a sufficient quantity of long-term funds was simply not forthcoming from commercial banks. The shortfall was filled by long-term credit banks. There is a significant differentiation between these long-term credit banks and regular commercial banks. On the asset side, the credit banks are largely restricted to long-term instruments, both loans and bonds. On the liability side, they are permitted to issue debentures (about half of which are purchased by other financial intermediaries, and half by individuals) and are allowed deposits only from government and from borrowers. In practice, most funds come from debentures. With much less volatility on the liability side, credit banks could easily devote almost all their resources to long-term assets.

Long-term credit banks also perform a critical role in the Japanese bond market. The market has a unique feature called commissioned underwriting, in which banks act as "commissioned" companies advising on amount, timing, and terms of flotation, coordinating negotiations, preparing contracts, receiving proceeds, and delivering certificates. Securities companies only underwrite in the strict sense, that is, ensure that the issuer obtains the funds it requires in the event of undersubscription. Thus, the functions performed by investment banks in the United States are undertaken jointly in Japan by banks and securities companies.

Some analysts have argued that bank dominance in long-term lending is due to controls on the bond market. But given the similar functions of regular and long-term banks in Japan in making long-term loans, and those of investment banks in the United States in corporate-bond issues, Japanese banks seem very natural candidates for the central locus of long-term lending.

Moreover, a stable market in corporate bonds would have required the existence of a deep market in risk-free government securities to act as a scale against which to determine appropriate corporate-bond yields. The low quantities of government bonds outstanding in Japan before 1975 would have prevented the existence of a deep government-bond market, even if resale controls imposed on members of the government-bond syndicate had been nonexistent. Hence, with no stable frame of reference within which to set corporate-bond rates, development of a major market in long-term corporate bonds would have been difficult.

Commercial and long-term credit banks were dominant suppliers in the long-term credit markets in Japan because of their abundance of resources and their experience in appraising creditworthiness, not because of controls.

Thus, we see private financial intermediation in Japan to have been highly competitive. The overwhelming source of funds was deposits, so banks and thrifts were the primary type of intermediary. Relatively weak regulation (compared with the United States) on bank-deposit collection and asset composition of banks and thrifts encouraged competition. But substantial innovation was necessary to reduce risk enough to allow banks to make long-term loans. Loan syndication and long-term credit banks were the answer. Hence, the absence of an active bond market reflected not an absence of competition but rather an absence of need. Firms did not need a bond market because maintenance of competition in the loan market did not require the threat of exit. The government did not need one since regulations favoring banks could generate monopoly profits sufficiently large to allow the Ministry of Finance to take de facto taxes in the form of low rates on nonmarketable government securities. The role of regulation was not to restrict competition but rather to ensure the government access to cheap borrowings.

V. Government Role in Financial Markets

Government has various functions in financial markets, the most significant of which are (1) issuance of national debt, (2) regulation of financial markets, and (3) financial intermediation through public institutions. We propose to show that the role of the Japanese government during the postwar period has the following characteristics: the government acted more as financial intermediary than as borrower or regulator; and the government was quite active as direct collector of deposits, and allocated these deposits largely to public bodies, often for further intermediation.

The existence of government intermediaries allowed the Japanese financial system to pool, socialize, and diversify risk in a highly effective manner. In addition to providing standard benefits of intermediation, that is, reduced transactions costs, lower risk for depositors, and maturity transformation, the government intermediaries facilitated risk pooling and diversification through participation in syndicates. Private long-term-credit banks were usually managers or comanagers for loan syndicates, but government financial intermediaries, such as the Japan Development Bank or the Japan Export Import Bank, often had to join in order for syndicates to succeed.

Public financial intermediaries normally participate in loan syndications only for larger and riskier projects. Though public banks' shares in syndications are not usually large, their participation gives the project an effective government guarantee. The role of public financial intermediaries is not to undertake projects with lower expected return, but rather to reduce the exposure of private institutions in risky projects with *higher* expected return. Thus, the country as a whole undertakes the risky, high-return projects, and cultivates the potential for a higher rate of GNP growth.

Government intermediaries in Japan are separated into those whose primary job is collecting deposits and those whose primary job is using them. The primary collector is the postal-savings system, whose 22,000 offices hold about 20% of total deposits in the nation. The main contribution of the postal-savings system was to help raise the financial-savings rate. The ubiquity of branches made deposit easier, particularly in rural and poorer urban areas. It also forced other institutions to try harder to gather deposits. Less well publicized is the postal system's role as the basis of an illegal subsidy to "small" savers. It is quite legal for savings up to a certain limit (currently ¥3 million—about $13,500) to earn interest tax free; but the postal system has allowed multiple accounts and the inevitable tax evasion under the name of "privacy." This opportunity to evade taxes was (and is) cherished by the Japanese, so the laxity of the postal-savings administration in this regard may have encouraged people to spend less and save more.

However, the postal-savings system does little allocation of funds to investors. Rather, most post-office funds are entrusted to the Portfolio Management Department (*Shikin Unyo Bu*) of the Ministry of Finance. The PMD also receives funds from national pension funds,[14] from surplus funds of special accounts of the government, and from public corporations. Post-office funds have comprised a bit more than half of total PMD liabilities throughout the postwar period.

The PMD is primary allocator of funds deposited and entrusted to the government. Until the early 1950s, the PMD mostly supported central and local governments. Indeed, at the end of World War II postal savings were merely small-denomination government savings bonds. But after the balanced-budget rule of 1949, funds were increasingly allocated to loans to public corporations, including those to other public financial intermediaries.

PMD funds allocated to loans and investment are the overwhelming source of funds to the main direct government investor, the Fiscal Investment and Loan Program (FILP). But even half of FILP funds are earmarked for further financial intermediation, to such institutions as the Japan Development Bank and the Housing Finance Corporation. In the 1950s and early 1960s, FILP stressed large-scale industrial projects, foreign-trade finance, and some financing of small and medium enterprises. In the 1970s, the focus shifted to mortgage financing and social development.

But "off-budget" financing is by no means uniquely Japanese, as exemplified by U.S. agencies such as the Federal Housing Authority and the Small Business Administration. Indeed, rapid growth of "off-budget" public credit agencies is one of the major characteristics of the postwar U.S. financial market. As a ratio to GNP, assets of U.S.-sponsored credit agencies and mortgage pools have increased from 1% during 1946–1950 to 8% in 1976–1978.[15] However, there is a difference in kind. U.S. agency support is largely restricted to agriculture and housing, while Japanese agencies also supply funds for industrial plants and equipment.

However, looking only at the level of public intermediation seriously underestimates its significance. Even if only 10% of funds for a project come from public sector intermediaries, private intermediaries feel much more secure in extending their own loans. In Japan, the principle of implicit guarantee was applied over a broad range of activities, both in favor of large-scale industry and in favor of small business and housing. In the United States, however, the use of government guarantee to encourage private lending to business has met with stiff political resistance (e.g., the Lockheed and Chrysler cases), though the same power used in favor of private housing (eg., through FHA) or agriculture (e.g., tobacco warehousing) is considered politically sacred.

Implicit guarantee did not mean that the Japanese government could do as it pleased with industry. Funds could not be channeled to sectors where expected returns were low, since private institutions simply would not lend to such sectors. However, in cases where both expected returns and risk were high, the involvement of public entities was quite significant.

Thus, we see that the Japanese government has played a much more active role as intermediary, both in collecting and in allocating funds, than has the U.S. government. Moreover, the objects of public intermediation have been on a much broader scale in Japan. Detailed explanation of why this was possible is beyond the scope of this paper, but we would like to make a tentative guess.

The perception widely held by the Japanese people, that the government, as distinct from political parties, is free from direct corruption, gives public financial institutions the reputation of acting on policy consensus. The Japanese people have the choice of letting bureaucrats or politicians choose projects. The widely held view that many Japanese politicians participate—when given the chance—in wholesale influence selling makes the bureaucrats practice of *amakudari* (retirement of bureaucrats to plush industry jobs) seem relatively mild. Thus, the government financial institutions in Japan always support policy objectives, but seldom purely political ones. The United States has not been so fortunate; a typical example in the United States is the Synthetic Fuel Corporation, which was widely believed—whether justly or not— to be a political creation of the Carter administration. The existence of honest public institutions seems to be a prerequisite for successful financial intermediation by the government.

VI. Conclusions

This essay has focused on three major aspects of the relationship between real and financial sectors of the postwar Japanese economy: (1) high and accelerating rate of growth of GNP, (2) a high and rising savings ratio, and (3) low government consumption but high government savings as a ratio to GNP. In particular, we hypothesized a causal relationship between the structure of financial intermediation and the accelerating growth of the real economy.

Four major characteristics of Japanese financial markets have been identified by comparison of the Japanese with the U.S. system.

First, financial liabilities of Japan's nonfinancial sector have deepened continuously, surpassing the U.S. level. Liabilities of the corporate sector were particularly deep while those of the government and individuals remained less than their U.S. counterparts.

Second, the high degree of financial intermediation helped make this liability deepening possible, since intermediation reduced both costs and risks of the average portfolio. Financial assets of Japanese savers have accumulated mostly in post office and bank deposits, while a substantial part of American assets is held in equities and bonds. The proportion of assets in trade financing is much larger in Japan than in the United States also, confirming the proposition that Japanese nonfinancial firms engage in extensive intermediation.

Third, the Japanese government was more a financial intermediary than a borrower or regulator. The share of public debt in total liabilities of nonfinancial sectors remained relatively small, though a conspicuous bulge occurred in the late 1970s. In particular, the balanced-budget principle contributed to the low level of public debt and postal savings were used for investments and loans.

Fourth, consumers were largely excluded from borrowing in financial markets until the 1970s; the proportion of mortgage and consumer loans has remained extremely small compared to that of the United States.

What were the major institutions underlying these facts? A crucial one was intense competition in deposit collection due to less restrictive regulations on commercial banking and pervasive diversification of financial intermediaries. Thrift institutions and post offices, in particular, competed fiercely with commercial banks.

Long-term credit banks were another important institution. These banks provided a core for loan syndications and coordination of corporate financing. The system of loan consortia allowed the scope of investment to become both larger and more long-term.

Socialization of risk must be distinguished clearly from government planning or control. Even when the government socialized risk, primary responsibility for the projects remained with the private sector. But government was active in collecting deposits through the postal-savings system. And while government consumption was quite low, government investment, funded through FILP and the PMD by postal savings, was high.

Japan's financial markets were quite different from those in the U.S. Retail competition, long-term credit banks, and government intermediaries gave Japan some notable strengths that the United States lacked. Japan's financial structure provided the advantages of competition to both Japanese corporations and consumers, though most competition took the form of service and quantity competition rather than price competition.

In short, we feel there is substantial evidence in favor of the following conclusion about the postwar Japanese economy: intense financial intermediation by both private and public sectors was a key factor in liability deepening, and this in turn raised savings, investment, and GNP growth.

Notes

1. A longer version of this paper was presented as part of the Program on U.S.-Japan Relations of the Center for International Affairs at Harvard University. E. Sakakibara was Visiting Associate Professor of Economics at Harvard when the project was undertaken: The authors are indebted to Mr. Yuzo Harada who assisted in the project, and who is co-author of an

earlier version of the paper. The authors also thank members of the Japan Economic Seminar and two anonymous referees for comments on an earlier draft. The views expressed in this paper are solely those of the authors, and do not reflect those of any institution with which they are affiliated.

2. By the term "postwar" we mean, in general, the years 1953–1973, after recovery from the devastation of World War II, but before the great changes of the 1970s.
3. As an example of this line of argument, see Wallich and Wallich (1976). The conventional view is well elaborated in Suzuki (1980).
4. See Ohkawa and Rosovsky (1973).
5. Hadley (1970) notes that "the [Edwards] mission proposals in finance were curiously weak; somehow it never came to grips with a key element of the issue, the integral union of commercial banking with industrial and commercial undertakings."
6. See Japan, Ministry of Finance (1980).
7. Classification of what is consumption and what is investment differs among countries. A referee pointed out that the United States includes major portions of road building expenditures in consumption. To the extent that this is true, the meaning of this set of data is weakened.
8. Friedman (1981) excludes equity from consideration and includes the unincorporated business sector in the corporate sector. Due to data and conceptual differences, we have included equity and classed unincorporated business as part of the individuals' sector. The stability that Friedman found in the U.S. data is robust to these changes.
9. See Friedman (1981, p. 36).
10. See Sakakibara et al. (1981).
11. See Patrick (1981).
12. See Heggestad (1979) and Rhoades (1977).
13. The *Report of the President* (1981, p. 12).
14. As of 1980, the four major categories of pensions were the Welfare Program for employees of private corporations, the National Pension for any citizen, the Corporate Pension for employees of government and public corporations, and Private Pensions. Accumulated funds for the Welfare and National Pensions are deposited with the PMD.
15. See Friedman (1981).

References

Bank of Japan (*Nohon Ginko*), (1967).

Friedman, Benjamin, (1981). "Postwar Changes in the American Financial Market," in Martin S. Feldstein, ed., *The American Economy in Transition*, Chicago, University of Chicago Press.

Hadley, Eleanor M., (1970). *Antitrust in Japan*, Princeton, N.J., Princeton University Press.

Heggestad, Arnold A., (1979). "Market Structure, Competition, and Performance in Financial Industries: A Survey of Banking Studies," in Franklin R. Edward, ed., *Issues in Financial Regulation*, New York, McGraw-Hill.

Japan, Ministry of Finance, (1980). *Saishutsu Hyakka* (Fact Book on Public Finance).

Kuroda, Iwao, and Yoshiharu, Oritani, (1979). "A Re-examination of the 'Peculiarities of Financial Structure' in Japan: Through Comparison of Balance Sheets of Japanese and American Corporations" (in Japanese), in *Kinyu Kenkyu Shiryo*, Bank of Japan, April.

Mitchell, Bridger R., (1975). *European Historical Statistics*, New York, Columbia University Press.

Nakamura, Takafusa, (1978). *The Japanese Economy, Growth and Structure*, Tokyo, Tokyo University Press.

Ohkawa, Kazushi, and Henry Rosovsky, (1973). *Japanese Economic Growth: Trend Acceleration in the Twentieth Century*, Palo Alto, CA, Stanford University Press.

Patrick, Hugh T., (1981). "Evolution of the Japanese Financial System in the Interwar Period," in T. Nakamura, ed., *Analysis of the Japanese Economy in the Interwar Period* (in Japanese), Tokyo, Yamakawa Press.

Report of the President—Geographic Restrictions on Commercial Banking in the United States, (1981). Washington, D.C., U.S. Dept. of the Treasury.

Rhoades, Stephen A., (1977). "Structure-Performance Studies in Banking: A Summary and Evaluation," Staff Economic Studies, No. 92, Board of Governors, Federal Reserve System.

Sakakibara, Eisuke, Robert Feldman, and Yuzo Harada, (1981). "The Japanese Financial System in Comparative Perspective," Mimeo, Program on U.S.–Japan Relations, Harvard University.

Suzuki, Yoshio, (1980). *Money and Banking in Contemporary Japan*, New Haven, CT, Yale University Press.

Wallich, Henry, and Mable I. Wallich, (1976). "Banking and Finance," in Hugh, Patrick and H. Rosovsky, eds., *Asia's New Giant*, Washington, Brookings.

3

Some Aspects of Japanese Corporate Finance*

James E. Hodder
Stanford University,
Stanford, CA 93405

Adrian E. Tschoegl
SBCI Securities (Asia) Ltd.,
Tokyo, Japan

I. Introduction

In this paper, we attempt to blend economic theory with an understanding of the historical context and regulation of Japanese financial markets, particularly during the 1950s and 1960s. The historical and regulatory context is critical since it represents the framework within which the economic forces operated. That is, we are interested in examining how a particular structure, characterized by controlled interest rates, segmentation of markets and functions, and limited entry, gave rise in understandable ways to distinctive corporate financial practices.

There have been a number of recent publications that attempt to describe and explain the Japanese corporate financial system.[1] Perhaps the most discussed topics are the relatively high degree of financial leverage for the "typical" Japanese firm and the predominance of bank financing for the external funding of large corporations. There also has been discussion of such apparent peculiarities in the equity markets as the issue of shares at a par value of 50 yen when their market value is 1,000 yen or more, as well as the extensive cross holdings of shares between corporations. The role of a firm's "main bank" as not only lender and financial advisor, but, in some cases, exercising management control, also has received attention.

* The authors would like to thank John G. McDonald, Tom Roehl, and Toshiharu Takahashi for their helpful comments on drafts of the original paper. This paper originally appeared in the *Journal of Financial and Quantitative Analysis*.

Before we address these issues, we wish to make two points. First, the structure of the Japanese financial system changed radically after World War II as a consequence of legislation introduced by the Occupation Authorities and the need to rebuild. For example, with respect to high debt to equity ratios and heavy dependence on bank loans, Nakamura (1981) cites evidence that equity comprised 67% of gross capital (total assets) for manufacturing industries in 1935. In a related vein, Kurosawa (1981) provides figures that external funding by Japanese corporations during the 1931–1936 period was only 4% from bank loans, with 96% through stocks and industrial bonds.

Second, the Japanese financial system has been evolving continuously since the war. Thus, to speak of "traditional" practices, even if one restricts the term to the postwar era, is to freeze a stylization of a much more complex reality.

In Section II, we begin by describing the debt markets, both bond and bank, and endeavor to explain firms' apparent preference for the latter. Section III discusses some characteristics of the equity market, dividend practice, and par value issues. Section IV addresses the economic rationale for a highly levered capital structure in light of current financial theory, as well as the historic and regulatory context in Japan. Section V focuses on the main bank phenomenon. Section VI examines our findings in light of the substantial deregulation of Japanese financial markets since 1970 and the slower economic growth since the "oil shock" of 1973 and provides some concluding comments.

II. Debt Markets

The vast majority of borrowing by major Japanese corporations is from private financial institutions (banks and insurance companies) rather than through bonds or commercial paper (see Table 3.1).

The Japanese bond market is dominated by government issues (including local and government guaranteed), which comprise roughly 75% of the outstanding amount. Corporate bonds (including convertibles) account for only around 6.5% of the total outstanding bonds of nonfinancial corporations. During 1980–1983, nonconvertible corporate bonds were less than 5% of total public bond offerings. Of that small fraction, three-quarters were issued by electric power companies. If we set aside the electric power companies as something of a special case and exclude convertibles on the grounds that they are primarily an equity-

Table 3.1. Net Supply of Industrial Funds by Source (%)

Year	Sale of Stocks & Shares	Industrial Bonds	Borrowing from Private Financial Institutions	Borrowing from Gov't. Institutions
1950	6.2	8.5	72.6	12.7
1955	14.1	3.9	68.9	13.0
1960	16.1	5.2	71.2	7.5
1965	5.3	4.4	81.4	8.9
1970	7.9	2.8	81.2	8.0
1972	5.7	1.8	86.8	5.7
1973	5.4	3.6	82.8	8.1
1974	5.8	3.3	79.6	11.3
1975	6.6	6.7	74.9	11.8
1976	4.8	3.6	80.2	11.4
1977	7.1	4.5	75.2	13.2
1978	8.0	5.2	73.0	13.8
1979	8.5	5.7	69.3	16.5
1980	7.4	2.9	77.0	12.7
1981	9.1	4.5	72.8	13.6
1982	8.9	2.8	78.1	10.2

Source: The Bank of Japan, *Economic Statistics Annual*.

raising mechanism, then bonds all but disappear from the balance sheets of large Japanese industrial corporations.

A key reason for the post-World War II preponderance of bank over bond debt was the government's policy of keeping bond interest rates low. As a result, there was little public demand for bonds. In fact, after the oil shock of 1973–1974, the city banks were required to buy government bonds at par. The government essentially preempted the bond market for itself, plus public corporations, the railways, and utilities. Furthermore, corporate bond issues have been strictly controlled by a group composed of underwriters and those banks that act as agents for bond issues. Because bonds are discountable at the Bank of Japan, there was a further reason to insure that issued bonds were of high quality. In fact, the Bank of Japan and the Ministry of Finance monitored and occasionally exercised control over the selection of corporations qualified to issue bonds, the issuing terms, and even the total monthly amount of new issues (Goto, 1980).

Of the corporate bonds that were issued, a proportion ended up in the portfolios of the major banks. These could afford to hold the bonds of their loan customers because they would use compensating balances to raise the effective rate (Suzuki, 1980).

There were several other legal and institutional restrictions on the ability of corporations to issue domestic debt, which also inhibited development of the corporate bond market. The Commercial Code prohibited corporations from issuing bonds in excess of stated capital and reserve funds (Goto, 1980). Until 1979, Japanese corporate bonds were all issued on a secured basis, typically with the main bank acting as a trustee. The issuing criteria for unsecured bonds are rather stringent, but are less so for convertibles than for straight debt. These rules are being relaxed somewhat, but the requirements as of December 1983 still make issuing unsecured bonds difficult for all but the largest and most credit-worthy companies (Japan Securities Research Institute, 1984). Apparently the restrictions under the Commercial Code were eased recently at a time when corporations were reducing their debt (and hence were less dependent on the goodwill of their banks) and when monetary conditions were easier (Goto, 1980). Nevertheless, the rationing of corporate access to the bond market remains an important explanatory factor in the development of Japanese corporate financial policy (Royama, 1983–1984).

A second reason for the preponderance of bank over bond debt has to do with the relative newness of Japanese companies after World War II. The Occupation Authorities broke up the pre-war *zaibatsu* (holding companies), dismissed all the senior management, largely dispossessed the original owners, and redistributed the shares fairly widely. These measures, together with the physical destruction of the war, insured that the companies that emerged, while carrying old names, were, to a significant degree, new organizations.

Diamond (1984*a*, 1984*b*) argues that new companies that do not yet have a reputation will prefer to issue their debt via intermediaries rather than in arms-length markets. They find it cheaper to purchase the delegated monitoring services of intermediaries than to pay a premium in bond markets for the fact that lenders cannot adequately observe and control the borrowers' decisions. Thus, not only were firms rationed out of the bond markets, but, at least in the early years, they might have encountered reputational difficulties when seeking bond financing.

The debt markets in Japan are highly segmented, both from international markets and internally. This isolation of the Japanese markets from the international ones was an important factor in sustaining the repression of the domestic ones. Within each segment domestically, the number of actors is limited and there has been little or no entry since the early 1950s. As we discuss in Section V, this structure has had important consequences for the control of lending risks.

Until recently, the ability of Japanese firms to borrow from foreign lenders was heavily regulated. Prior to the amended Foreign Exchange and Foreign Trade Control Law of 1980, overseas borrowing by Japanese residents required prior approval by the Ministry of Finance (MOF). Although a few large corporations received approval for foreign bond issues in the 1960s, such issues were a negligible aggregate funding source until the mid-1970s.

Similarly, the access of foreign banks to the Japanese markets was strictly controlled. A few foreign banks reestablished branches after the war, but further entry was essentially precluded until approximately 1969.[2] Even now, the relative position of foreign banks is very small. At the end of 1983, they accounted for only about 3% of total bank lending in Japan. For all practical purposes, foreign sources provided negligible debt or equity capital during the rapid growth phase (1950–1973) of Japanese industry.

Domestically, the number of major lenders to large business is also limited. Excluding the government agencies, there are the 13 City Banks, 3 Long-Term Credit Banks, and 7 Trust Banks as well as the large life insurance companies. Among the 21 domestic life insurance companies at the end of 1980, the top 3 (Nippon, Dai-Ichi, and Sumitomo) controlled 50% of total assets while the top 8 controlled 82%. The nonlife insurance companies also lend to large business but are not a significant fraction of the total. The 63 Regional Banks generally focus on loans to smaller firms and individuals. Regional Banks represented 28% of bank loans outstanding at the end of 1983; however, given the focus of their lending, they should be a much smaller fraction of total lending to large corporations—perhaps 10% of the total. In summary, perhaps 90% or more of private lending to large industrial firms is controlled by 25 to 30 institutions.

In practice, the number of key lending institutions has been even smaller than the 25 to 30 indicated above. Realistically, the top six to eight City Banks plus the Industrial Bank of Japan (a long-term credit bank) and, to some extent, the Long-Term Credit Bank of Japan have largely controlled lending to major corporations in Japan.[3]

This group of major banks and insurance companies is informally interconnected. Their senior executives know each other, many went to school together, and a number are former MOF officials. They have offices within blocks of each other in central Tokyo and socialize at, for example, the Banker's Club. In some cases, several institutions belong to the same *keiretsu* (a group of firms with extensive business relations and cross-shareholdings)—for example, Sumitomo Bank, Sumitomo Trust and Banking, and Sumitomo Mutual Life are all members of the Sumitomo keiretsu. The high degree of contact facilitates coordination of lending policies, especially in financial distress situations.

This coordination does not imply a noncompetitive environment. The relationship between the banks is relatively complex and involves intense competition (Sakakibara & Feldman, 1983), but this occurs within accepted bounds. In examining the behavior of Canadian banks, Breton and Wintrobe (1978) point out that "moral suasion" (i.e., window guidance) can also be viewed as a mutually advantageous exchange between the central bank and the commercial banks. That is, the latter cooperate with the regulator not just out of fear of administrative or legislative sanctions, but also because the central bank offers a quid pro quo of information and other services that facilitate collusion among the banks. Thus, the banks cooperate to maintain a system that places bounds on competition.

As a final point under this section, a substantial fraction of firm borrowing is short term and tends to be concentrated within a few large banks. Indeed, short-term borrowing actually exceeds long-term borrowing, both of which are substantially larger than borrowing via bonds. This is largely explained by the traditional practice among Japanese banks of making short-term loans and then continuously renewing ("rolling over") those loans effectively to provide longer term financing. Although the maturity structure has been lengthening, as of March 1983, only 34% of the outstanding loans from the City, Regional, and Trust Banks had maturities greater than one year. The exceptions to this practice are the three Long-Term Credit Banks with 79% of their loans having maturities of over one year.

This pattern is a consequence of regulatory requirements. The City, Trust, and Regional Banks are not permitted to issue medium- and long-term liabilities. The regulatory authorities therefore require them to limit the nominal maturities of their loans. By contrast, the Long-Term Credit Banks may issue debentures, and correspondingly make longer term loans. This loan maturity structure has important implications for the main bank relationship (see Section V).

III. Equity Market

The Tokyo Stock Exchange is both large and active—second only to New York in terms of both total market value and value of shares traded annually. In 1983, the value of shares traded on the Tokyo exchange represented 48.8% of the total market value. However, one should treat share values and price appreciation figures with caution since trading has, in effect, been restricted to a relatively small fraction of the potentially available shares.

Table 3.2 gives a breakdown of ownership in 1983 for all companies listed on any of the eight Japanese stock exchanges. Of particular interest are the heavy institutional holdings (72% of total shares and 73.7% of market value). There also have been pronounced trends in the composition of share ownership, with the holdings of private domestic institutions increasing more or less continuously from 28.1% of total shares in 1950 to the current 66.7%. Over the same period, individual holdings declined from 69.1 to 28%. Among domestic institutions, holdings by financial institutions increased from 9.9 to 37.7% of total shares, while nonfinancial corporations increased their shares from 5.6 to 26.0%. In contrast, holdings by security companies fell from 12.6 in 1950 to the current, relatively insignificant, 1.8%. Investment trusts

Table 3.2. 1983 Share Ownership by Type of Investor, All Listed Companies

	Percentage of Listed Shares	Percentage of Market Value
Gov't. and Local Gov't.	0.2	0.3
Financial Institutions	37.7	37.0
Investment Trusts	1.2	1.6
Securities Companies	1.8	1.7
Business Corporations	26.0	25.4
Individuals & Others	28.0	26.3
Foreigners	5.1	7.6

Source: *Tokyo Stock Exchange Fact Book 1984.*

(similar to U.S. mutual funds) are not currently a major factor in the market and were negligible in 1950; however, they were much more significant in the early 1960s. Foreigners (almost entirely institutions) have been investors in Japanese securities for years. Their holdings have recently surged, more than doubling since 1980.

The major security holders in Japan basically hold shares to maintain or enhance business relationships and do very little trading. Among financial institutions, the major shareholders are banks and insurance companies, with each holding 17.6% of total listed shares. Although these institutions collectively hold over 35% of listed shares, they were involved in only 3.7% of the stock transactions (Tokyo, Osaka, and Nagoya exchanges) during 1983. Business corporations were somewhat more active, but still engaged in only 7% of stock transactions. Thus, the major institutional holders (banks, insurance companies, and nonfinancial business corporations) collectively held 61.2% of listed shares, but engaged in only 10.7% of trades. By contrast, member security firms, individuals, and foreigners accounted for 81.5% of trading, despite holding less than 35% of the listed shares. If we exclude trades by member security firms acting as dealers (23.9% of the total), individuals and foreigners accounted for 75.7% of remaining trades. Thus, we get a rather clear picture of an economy where over 60% of listed shares are held by institutions that do very little trading.

Most of the institutional shareholding is intra– rather than intergroup in nature (Okumura, 1982). The resultant cross-holding acts as a barrier to hostile takeovers and mergers by ensuring that a blocking percentage is in friendly hands. The two great waves of stock interchanges occurred in the early 1950s and early 1970s. In the first period, the keiretsu emerged from the remains of the pre-war zaibatsu. The second wave followed the 1971 liberalization of capital flows into Japan when managements feared acquisition by foreign firms.

Traditionally, large Japanese firms have paid dividends based on the par value of their stock (usually 50 yen per share). Indeed, there is a widely held view that annual dividends should be at least 10% of par value (5 yen per share for most companies). This view is strongly reinforced by listing criteria for the Tokyo Stock Exchange that virtually mandate a minimum annual cash dividend of 5 yen per share. Firms can be demoted from the First to Second Section of the exchange or even delisted entirely for failure to pay cash dividends; however, the delisting criteria are relatively lenient and happen only after five consecutive years of no cash dividends.[4]

As a consequence of this, dividends of at least 10% of par are paid, except under dire circumstances. Indeed, failure to pay such a dividend is taken as a strong signal of serious financial difficulties. On the other hand, firms have not generally increased dividends as a fraction of par value despite increases in earned income and market prices for their shares. Thus, average dividends per share for First Section stocks that paid dividends fluctuated between 6.88 and 5.92 yen per share from 1960 through 1983. During the same period, the TSE Stock Price Index increased approximately sevenfold, with the result that average dividend yields have declined to approximately 1% of the average share price.

Individual shareholders prefer capital gains to dividends because of an asymmetric tax treatment.[5] Firms, too, prefer to minimize dividends because of investment needs (see Section IV) and because of the relatively more favorable corporate tax treatment of interest payments.

The purchase of stocks with low dividend yields, however, creates a problem for most Japanese institutional shareholders. Banks have cash flow requirements for payment of interest to depositors. Insurance companies face restrictions on declaring policy dividends (currently around 7.5%) without adequate reported income and they are generally not allowed to treat capital gains (even when realized) as income. Most nonfinancial corporations are, at least partially, financing their shareholding by loans with associated interest payments. Thus, we have a set of institutional shareholders who need substantial dividend yields, but traditionally follow policies of buying and holding shares to enhance business relations with the firms issuing those shares. Consequently, the purchase of low yielding market issues squeezes these institutions' ability to meet other commitments.[6]

Prior to 1969–1970, virtually all new issues were rights offerings to existing shareholders at par, with unsubscribed shares offered to the public at market prices. From 1956–1968, the amount raised at market prices was less than 5% of total funds raised domestically on new equity issued by listed companies. The first completely public issue at a market price apparently took place in January 1969.[7] Since then, market price issues have become very important, accounting for approximately three-quarters of new equity funds raised from 1980–1983. Rights offerings still account for approximately 20% of new equity funds, with the remainder coming through private placements that are frequently priced at substantial discounts from market.

One possible interpretation of par value issues is that this practice was basically a mechanism for increasing total dividend payments to shareholders. With a 5 yen per share dividend commitment, a rights issue at less than market effectively increases dividend yield on total shareholdings. However, stock splits (which were legal and not uncommon) or simply announcing a higher dividend per share have the same effects, without the expense of registration statements, etc. Thus, it seems that these par value issues were at least partially for the purpose of raising additional equity funds.

Although market issues now dominate in terms of funds raised, they are a much smaller fraction of new shares issued, as seen in Table 3.3. Rights offerings and private placements account for almost twice as many new shares as market issues. Conversions of convertible bonds as well as gratis issues were both considerably greater than market issues. Thus, in terms of voting power, market issues have not been much of a factor. Even if we add conversions to market issues, the total for 1979–1981 represents only 5.2% of listed shares for TSE firms in 1981. Furthermore, existing shareholders are buying most of the market issues and convertibles.

It's clear that conversions of convertible bonds are becoming a substantial source of additional equity. Since the late 1970s, the annual market value of new convertible bond issues has generally exceeded that for public offerings of new equity. From 1978–1983, convertible issues totaled 6.4 trillion yen of which 63% was issued in overseas markets

Table 3.3. New Share Issues by TSE Listed Companies 1979–1981

	Million Shares	% of Total
Market Issue	4902	17
Rights Offering	8655	29
Private Placement	505	2
Conversions	6568	22
Gratis Issue	8390	28
Stock Dividends	101	0
Mergers	539	2
TOTAL	29,660	100

Source: Tokyo Stock Exchange, *Annual Statistics Report*.

(primarily Europe). During the same period, public offerings amounted to 5.1 trillion yen, including a 548 billion yen equivalent in foreign markets.

When issuing these bonds, the conversion price is set quite close to the market price for the firm's shares—the current guideline is a 5% premium. As a consequence, the vast majority of these bonds are converted. In some cases, this occurs very rapidly—e.g., 85% conversion within six months of issue. Thus, the issue of convertibles by Japanese firms can be largely viewed as an equity-raising mechanism (at least in the long run).

IV. Leverage

In this section, we focus on the generally higher debt to equity ratios in Japan. The data in Table 3.4 represent the aggregate balance sheet

Table 3.4 Balance Sheets of All Nonfinancial Corporations Listed on the Tokyo Stock Exchange in 1983

	Trillion Yen	Percentage of Total
Assets		
Current Assets	110.3	67.0
Fixed Assets	54.3	33.0
Deferred Assets	0.1	0
Total Assets	164.7	100.0
Liabilities		
Notes and Accounts Payable (Trade Payables)	38.2	23.2
Short-Term Borrowing	30.5	18.5
Bonds	5.6	3.4
Long-Term Borrowing	21.3	12.9
Other Liabilities	32.7	19.9
Total Liabilities	128.3	77.9
Shareholders Equity	36.3	22.0
Total Liabilities and Shareholder's Equity	164.7	100.0

Source: *Tokyo Stock Exchange Fact Book 1984.*

for all nonfinancial companies listed on the Tokyo Stock Exchange in 1983. Although the fraction of shareholders equity (22%) has increased in recent years, it is still quite low by U.S. standards.

The aggregate figures on leverage in Table 3.4 conceal extremes in both directions. There are companies, such as Matsushita or Toyota, that have relatively little debt and massive financial resources, including billions of dollars in cash and marketable securities. At the other extreme are companies, such as Maruzen Oil, that had large losses in 1981 and 1982, resulting in a negative book value.

Accounting differences as well as the enormous appreciation in market values of book assets (particularly land and securities) have raised questions about reported debt/equity ratios for Japanese firms. Some authors have even suggested that the apparent disparity between Japanese and U.S. practice may be largely a reporting artifact (Kuroda & Oritani, 1980) and, at the very least, is great exaggerated (Choi, et al., 1983). For example, Aoki (1984) attempts to adjust for a variety of possible distortions using aggregate numbers for all nonfinancial corporations listed on the Tokyo Stock Exchange. His results indicate that adjusted equity values for 1981 represent about 40% of total assets for a typical firm, roughly twice the reported figure.[8] Thus, the financial leverage of an average large Japanese firm may be substantially less than popularly supposed. Nevertheless, 60% debt is still a lot of borrowing on average, particularly since reported equity to asset ratios have been increasing since the mid-1970s. There are also numerous firms that are much more highly levered than average and would have equity to total asset percentages of perhaps 10 to 20% even after a variety of adjustments.

Clearly, it has been possible to operate a major firm in Japan on a much more highly levered basis than would be generally acceptable to lenders in the United States. Given that the bond market was not a meaningful financial option for most Japanese firms during the postwar period, the question of the preference for bank borrowing over equity still remains. We advance two complementary explanations for the apparent preference for debt funding.[9] The first is a static argument based on regulated and apparently below-market interest rates (Suzuki, 1980) plus an internal capital market role by corporate groups. The second, and more novel, explanation is a dynamic theory that relates corporate financing preferences to investment opportunities.

Our first explanation rests on the fact that Japan has been characterized until recently by an elaborate system of interest rate controls and credit allocations (Bank of Japan, 1978, p. 13.) The government imposed its own system of ceilings on loan and deposit rates, which was later replaced by voluntary ceilings based on negotiations among the Federation of Bankers' Association, the Ministry of Finance, and the Bank of Japan. The government's apparent intention was to keep down the cost of capital to Japanese business firms in order to promote economic development and improve their competitive position in world markets.[10] The ceilings were, therefore, generally below equilibrium rates. To keep loan rates low, deposit rates were also restrained. When interest rates are not free to balance loan supply and demand, credit rationing (i.e., quantitative allocation) is inevitable.

One can exaggerate the rigidity of the loan rate ceilings. Some loans (small or long-term ones) were not regulated. The Japanese banks often required heavy compensating balances and fees that raised the effective interest rate. Had the compensating balances not usually earned interest, the amounts held presumably would have been lower. Finally, the rate controls were not always observed. Nevertheless, the ceilings were sufficiently binding to provide an impetus for the formation of ties between banks and firms. The effect was even more pronounced during the recurring periods of tight money (Teranishi, 1982). Under these circumstances, banks rationed their loans on the basis of stable borrower-lender relations as well as on the size and financial health of the firm. This provided a strong incentive for firms to develop and maintain close bank relations.

Banks also had incentives to develop and maintain good customers. First, the Bank of Japan allowed the city banks to have high ratios of loans to deposits, which has come to be known as the "over-loan" phenomenon. The city banks augmented their deposits by borrowing from the provincial banks and from the Bank of Japan through a rediscount window at concessionary rates. The latter has provided between 1 and 12% of the city banks' total capital, and has averaged about 7% for the 1968–1975 period (Bronte, 1982, p. 143). The allocation of "over-loan" credit depended on the amount of loans the banks had made in previous periods. Second, Caves and Uekusa (1976, p. 82) provide evidence that group firms made higher average payments for borrowed capital than did independent companies.

In addition to its interest rate policies, in the 1950s and early 1960s, the government attempted to channel funds. One of the Bank of Japan's (BOJ) most important tools was what has come to be known as window guidance. This involved direct, frequent contact between the BOJ and the commercial banks, with the former setting bank-by-bank quotas on loans to customers. In addition to limiting total bank credit, the BOJ directed the banks' sectoral allocations in general and, sometimes, in considerable detail. These policies also encouraged the formation of interfirm relationships in which the credit allocation could be modified through intragroup reallocation.

Both interest rate suppression and credit allocation would have encouraged higher leverage among major firms. First, those large, stable, and favored firms that had access to below-free-market rates had an incentive to borrow. They would have done so until, at the margin, the interest savings equalled the additional cost shareholders faced because of the increased risk. Furthermore, the recurring periods of tight money gave firms an incentive to borrow up to their credit limits, even if they had no current need for the full amount.

Second, credit allocation by the government through the banks pushed the capital market into the large firms. That is, one can think of large firms as part industrial or trading firm and part bank. It is clear that Japanese firms engage in extensive intermediation. Trade credit is a much larger proportion of the assets of the nonfinancial sector in Japan than it is in the United States (Sakakibara & Feldman, 1983). Thus, we get the following stylized picture of financial intermediation. The government channeled low-cost funds to the major banks, directly and indirectly. These, in turn, lent the funds to large companies with whom they were affiliated, who proceeded to borrow heavily. The large companies, including the trading companies, then lent the funds to their subsidiaries, affiliates, and suppliers. Thus, as Aoki (1984) and Bronte (1982, p. 9) point out, netting out trade payables and receivables to remove the effect of the companies' banking role causes the apparent leverage to decline.

Our second, dynamic, explanation of leverage relates directly to what Myers (1984) has called the "Pecking Order Theory" of capital structure. This theory suggests that managers have asymmetric information regarding the firm's investment opportunities that is difficult to convey in a believable manner to potential investors. New investors believe that management may be trying to exploit them for the benefit of "old" shareholders and consequently tend to undervalue new shares issued to finance favorable investment opportunities. In the model of Myers and Majluf (1984), this leads to a pecking order in which internal financing is preferred, with low risk debt as a second choice. Only as debt becomes relatively risky does it become potentially desirable to issue equity. It may instead be desirable to forego the investment project, unless its NPV is sufficiently high to offset the undervaluation of new equity.[11]

From the early 1950s until the mid-1970s, major Japanese firms were growing at generally rapid rates. Kurosawa (1981) provides estimates that total assets for such firms grew at an average annual rate of 15.6% from 1955–1974. During that same period, these firms had annual operating profits before interest or taxes that averaged 9.4% of assets. If these firms had been all equity financed and paid no dividends, their after-tax earnings would have financed roughly a 4.7% growth rate, less than one-third of the rate that actually occurred. Furthermore, they were both highly levered and paying substantial dividends.

Although dividend yield is low relative to market price (slightly over 1% on average with 88% of listed securities in 1983 having yields below 2.5%), it represents a substantial payout rate relative to earnings (38% on average, in 1983). Consequently, firms had enormous external funding requirements in order to finance their rapid growth.

Even at par value, rights issues during the 1950s were capable of raising total sums comparable in real terms to more recent market issues. For example, from 1959–1960, listed firms raised 224.8 billion yen annually through equity issues (94% via rights offerings). In the 1976–1980 period, listed firms raised 842 billion yen annually or 3.75 times the earlier figure (26% was via rights offerings). However, the Consumer Price Index increased an average of 3.85 times between these periods. Thus, listed firms actually raised less in real terms during the later period, although there were over twice as many listed companies.

The per share dividend commitment means that dividend cash flow requirements for a par value issue exceed (perhaps substantially) those on a market price issue. Thus, they do not appear, at first glance, to be an efficient way to raise capital. In the context of the Myers and Majluf model, however, rights issues make a great deal of sense because they avoid the problem of potential exploitation of new shareholders.

V. The Main Bank Lending System

While firms had a clear incentive to borrow, lending to highly levered firms would seem extremely risky from the banks' perspective. What evolved in Japan was a set of clever mechanisms for reducing lending risks, allowing continued borrowing up to seemingly extraordinary debt to equity ratios.

A point worth mentioning is the consequence of the banks' legal right to own shares. The limit currently is 10% of a firm's outstanding shares, falling to 5% after 1987. A firm's bank is far more likely to own shares in the firm than are its nonmain bank lenders. In many cases, the legal ceiling is nonbinding. However, the fact that they can and do hold shares reduces the lending risks the Japanese banks face. By being both creditor and stockholder, the banks make themselves indifferent to any attempt to make the firm more risky than anticipated by creditors and, in this way, to transfer wealth from them to shareholders. However, this is not enough to explain the Japanese banks' ability to support debt. The key factor is the main bank relationship.

Typically, each major industrial borrower had one of the top eight to ten banks acting as its main bank. The relationship between a firm and its main bank tends to be both long term and very close, with the bank being privy to extensive and confidential information on the firm's operations as well as its medium and long-range plans. Consequently, the main bank's loan evaluation was typically accepted with little question by other lenders.

The intensity of the main bank relationship appears to be largely a function of the indebtedness and consequent need for bank support by the client firm.[12] At one extreme, the main banks of cash-rich companies such as Matsushita or Toyota primarily benefit from corporate deposits as well as foreign exchange and fee-generating transactions. There is apparently relatively little flow of confidential information.

For heavy borrowers, there are extensive formal and informal contacts between the firm and its main bank at a variety of levels. In addition to providing a substantial fraction of the firm's borrowed funds, the main bank acts as a financial advisor as well as an agent on other loans and such bond issues as do occur. The bank has considerable influence and, in some cases, veto power over capital spending plans. In the extreme, a firm in financial difficulties may suddenly find several of its top executives replaced by bank personnel.

The main bank has enormous power. It can refuse to rollover short-term loans. Assuming other short-term lenders follow suit, the firm is more-or-less instantly insolvent. Also, Japanese banks have "rights to take assets, seize collateral or offset holdings to counter possible losses in the event of a threatened insolvency even though there is no literal default."[13] These rights are part of a set of General Business Conditions based on the General Banking Agreement (1948), which are the same for all Japanese banks and must be accepted by client firms in order to establish a borrowing relationship. These General Business Conditions effectively replace the variety of loan covenants prevalent in the United States while giving Japanese banks more flexibility and power.

The other side of the main bank's role is an implicit guarantee to other lenders. The main bank is providing a monitoring function for itself and those other lenders. It has much better information and the other lenders rely on its evaluation. They also typically expect the main bank to absorb a disproportionate share of loan losses in the event of a client bankruptcy.[14] Consequently, it has both a responsibility and a strong incentive to act on behalf of not only itself, but also other lenders.

There are several striking examples that illustrate these aspects of the main banking relationship. When Ataka (a large trading company) went bankrupt in 1977, its two main banks took almost all the losses. Sumitomo Bank wrote off 106 billion yen, while Kyowa Bank lost 46 billion yen. According to Prindl (1981), foreign creditors of Ataka lost nothing, although their loans were basically unsecured.[15]

In the case of Toyo Kogyo (Mazda), Sumitomo Bank orchestrated a rescue effort. In late 1974, the bank sent several of its own executives to top positions at Toyo Kogyo, called a meeting of the firm's lenders, and announced that it would stand behind the automaker, in effect, guaranteeing the other lenders' loans. It also announced that Sumitomo Trust (Toyo Kogyo's second largest lender and a member of the Sumitomo Group) would provide any necessary new loans. According to Pascale and Rohlen (1983), not one of the other 71 lenders called a loan or refused to rollover existing credits.

In order for the main bank system to work well, there needs to be a small number of major lenders with considerable confidence in each other. Minor lenders can be repaid, if necessary, to eliminate disagreements, so they are not a major factor in the viability of the system. However, as the number of major lenders enlarges, the system becomes unwieldy and starts to break down. We have only to look at the LDC debt reschedulings to see the difficulties in coordinating the views of a large number of lenders. Thus, the restriction of foreign borrowing and the concentration of Japanese lenders were crucial in the development of a main bank lending system.

Another significant factor was the relatively minor use of corporate bonds. Bondholders would potentially have to agree to the main bank's actions (or be repaid). If large amounts of a firm's debt were held by individual bondholders, this could prove problematic. However, the banks were generally in a position to discourage or veto bond issues, particularly by major borrowers, which includes the vast majority of Japanese firms. Furthermore, and in part as a consequence, the amounts of outstanding bonds are relatively small and mostly held by financial institutions.

The other critical feature of this system is confidence that the main bank will carry out its responsibilities and not abuse its position with respect to both the other lenders and the client firm. As in a variety of other markets, it appears the enforcement mechanism here is reputation. Any failure reduces a bank's ability to get other independent firms as customers and will cause customers already in a main bank relationship to reduce or transfer their dependence. Regulatory limits on lending to each customer have resulted in a situation in which even the main bank seldom provides more than 30% of a firm's loans. This makes it easier for nongroup companies to switch their allegiance in a market where all the banks are constrained to offer otherwise virtually identical services.

In summary, the main bank lending system allowed sufficient monitoring and control by the main bank to overcome most of the agency problems associated with lending.[16] There were efficiencies in that one bank did the monitoring, which minimized associated costs. The level of monitoring also seems to have been an increasing function of the firm's debt level—a monitoring cost versus risk reduction tradeoff. This system appears to be capable of dramatically reducing deadweight losses in financial distress situations. The main bank can make a liquidation or rescue decision and take control rather smoothly without resorting to time-consuming bankruptcy procedures and litigation of asset claims. In addition to saving possible legal costs, it is clear that the ability to reorganize with minimum disruption to customer, supplier, and employee relations is quite valuable.

IV. Concluding Remarks

Since roughly 1970, there has been a dramatic and continuing relaxation of both formal and informal government controls over Japanese financial markets. Obviously, this can have substantial implications for Japanese corporate finance.

The phased deregulation of interest rates will permit the introduction of new instruments, such as commercial paper and bankers acceptances, and the growth of demand for bonds. At the same time, there are now many firms that are sufficiently well established that they could and would wish to dispense with intermediaries and instead borrow directly. Because of the importance of legal and regulatory strictures, the rate at which the shift takes place will depend on a complex political process involving the Ministry of Finance, the Bank of Japan, banks, securities firms, and borrowers and investors.

To the degree that the existence of new, free market rate instruments undermines the traditional low-interest rate policy, they remove a major cause of high corporate leverage. First, as rates throughout the economy become market-determined, firms have a reduced incentive to substitute cheap debt for equity. Second, as rates come to equilibrate supply and demand, credit rationing will be reduced, removing the need or opportunity for nonfinancial firms to assume as great a role in financial intermediation.

In addition, several studies document a substantial increase in earnings volatility as well as a somewhat lower return on assets for Japanese firms since 1974.[17] This shift in the business environment increased the probability of financial distress for Japanese firms generally and resulted in considerable pressure for reduced leverage. The main bank system is good at dealing with financial distress occurring relatively independently across numerous firms. However, what happened was a systematic risk increase across most of the economy. Consequently, the position of main banks was weakened and the motivation for borrowers to reduce their leverage was substantial. In fact, the degree of leverage has been decreasing in recent years perhaps, in part, for this reason and, in part, due to a decreased rate of growth of assets.

In contrast with earlier rapid growth rates, the rate of growth in total assets of major manufacturing firms dropped to an average of 6.4% annually during 1974–1982. This allowed relatively greater internal funding and less reliance on debt. When coupled with new equity issues and conversions, the result was roughly a 40% increase in equity relative to total assets during 1977–1983.

Since 1974–1975, interest rate deregulation and slower economic growth have acted in the same direction in reducing corporate leverage. Intuition would suggest that the latter has had the greatest effect, partially because the former process is still in its early stages.

As indicated earlier, a critical feature of the main banking system is a small number of lenders who can be counted on to fulfill their obligations. Opening the Japanese markets to foreign lenders as well as allowing firms to borrow abroad seriously undermines the system. Not only is the number of potential lenders large, but their actions are difficult for a main bank to control. Aside from coordination problems and generally differing perspectives, reputational threats regarding the Japanese market are apt to be much less effective with foreign lenders. Indeed, recent major bankruptcies such as Riccar and J. Osawa seem to have occurred because of a breakdown in the main bank lending system.[18] In both cases, borrowing from foreign lenders appears to have precluded effective main bank control.

The crucial question for the continuance of the existing system is whether a main bank can induce client firms to limit their borrowing from nontraditional sources. A little bit of nontraditional borrowing is not a major problem since it can be repaid, if necessary. But significant borrowings from a highly diversified group of lenders essentially inhibit the main bank's ability to intervene effectively. Main banks can probably enforce borrowing restrictions on small or financially weak firms. Large and financially strong firms do not really need the main bank system to support their borrowing and may turn more to bond markets. However, if these firms get into financial difficulties in the future with large diversified borrowings, rescue operations may be much more difficult than in the past.

Two important observations emerge from an examination of the characteristics of Japanese corporate finance in the post-World War II era. The first is that the suppression of external markets does not necessarily mean the disappearance of their functions. Instead, the location of the allocation function may shift, as it appears to have done in the Japanese case, to internal capital markets within economic groups of firms and to the firms themselves. In fact, it is possible that these internal markets contributed to economic development by mitigating bureaucratic credit allocation errors.

The second observation has to do with the responsiveness and congruence of institutions. That is, incentives for high leverage were accompanied in Japan by the development of institutions, such as the main bank relationship, that could accommodate them. This again suggests the sociologists' paradigm of "unexpected consequences." That is, one cannot change one part of a system without it having far-reaching consequences.

Thus, deregulation will have many consequences, only some of which are visible now.

Notes

1. See, for example, Elston (1981); Bronte (1982); Wright & Suzuki (1979); Kurosawa (1981); and International Business Information, Inc. (1983).
2. See Prindl (1981) for a discussion of this situation.
3. This is, of course, subject to the view of the MOF and the Bank of Japan, which exerted considerable and sometimes detailed influence over major lenders.
4. See Japan Securities Research Institute (1984) or Tokyo Stock Exchange (1984) for other listing criteria.
5. Capital gains are free of income tax, depending on the size and number of transactions. Dividends are taxed at both the corporate and individual levels, but the corporate tax rate on earnings paid out as dividends is lower than the rate on retained earnings (Baldwin, 1985).
6. Many of the institutions described apparently objected to the issuance of shares at market when it started taking place in the late 1960s and early 1970s. The result was a compromise in which issuing firms agreed to return a portion of the premium (between the issue price and par) to their shareholders in the form of subsequent gratis stock issues. Coupled with the traditional dividend practice, this had the effect of raising dividend yields over time, relative to the issue price.

   Accounts vary regarding how much of this premium was to be returned. Kurosawa (1981) states that it was all to be returned within a 10-year period with 20% before the next stock issue. Currently published guidelines confirm the 20% return before issuing stock again, but suggest that the firm is not obliged to return the other 80%. This requirement is also applied to stock issued in connection with conversions of convertible bonds. In practice, most firms seem to be observing the 20% guideline, but some are not (particularly with overseas convertible issues). There also seems to be heavy and increasing pressure to eliminate the requirement. Probably the initial concept was 100% return of premium, but has deteriorated over time.
7. The company was Nihon Gakki, a musical instruments maker. By market price issues we mean underwritten public offerings or the granting of subscription rights to a selected person or persons. Unlike par-value issues, the price of the new shares is based on the current market price of the outstanding equity (Japan Securities Research Institute, 1984), though the new shares may be sold at a slight discount.
8. Aoki adjusted for the undervaluation of real estate and securities that were carried at historic cost and par, respectively, for certain pension reserves

and for trade credit. These results are also consistent with those from confidential studies by the Japanese Government and various securities firms, as summarized in Bronte (1982).

9. Our explanations concern firms' demands for equity capital. Toshiharu Takahashi has suggested an explanation based on the supply of equity capital. His argument is that the supply of funds was limited because: (a) foreigners could not buy Japanese shares; (b) the ultimate institutional holders, banks and insurance companies, had a limited demand; and (c) individuals tended to prefer to hold their savings in the form of bank deposits because the securities companies did not seek out investors and because of a fear of insider trading and stock price manipulation.
10. This does not mean that rates of return in Japan were below world levels. They may have been above world rates and thus capital controls were necessary to keep foreign funds from flowing into Japan (Suzuki, 1980). In the late 1970s, the evidence is that differences between interest rates in Japan and the unregulated Euro-yen rates on similar securities is slight (Otani & Tiwari, 1981). Furthermore, Baldwin (1985) presents evidence indicating that in the period 1960–1980, the effective cost of capital in Japan was probably very close to that in the United States.
11. Recent empirical evidence for the United States suggests that the announcement of a new equity issue reduces the value of previously outstanding shares by 30% of the value of the issue (Asquith & Mullins, 1986).
12. This statement is based on the first author's interviews with bankers, financial managers, and consultants in Japan in 1983 and 1984.
13. Prindl (1981), p. 60.
14. Wallich and Wallich (1976, p. 273) describe the situation as follows: "It is taken for granted that the main bank assumes a special responsibility with respect to the borrower. In an emergency other creditors therefore can expect their claims to effectively though not legally outrank those of the main bank."
15. Prindl was General Manager of Morgan Guaranty's Tokyo office at the time.
16. See Barnea, Haugen, and Senbet (1981) for a review of the literature on such problems.
17. For example, see Kurosawa (1981) or Kurosawa & Wakasugi (1984).
18. For an interesting account of the Osawa failure, see International Business Information, Inc. (1984).

References

Aoki, M., ed., (1984). *The Economic Analysis of the Japanese Firm*, New York, North-Holland, Chapter 1.

Asquith, P., and D. W. Mullins, (1986). "Equity Issues and Stock Price Dilution," *Journal of Financial Economics* Vol. 15, Jan/Feb, pp. 61–89.

Baldwin, Carliss Y., (1985). "The Capital Factor: Competing for Capital in a Global Environment," in *Competition in Global Industries*, Michael A. Porter, ed., Boston, Harvard Business School.

Bank of Japan, Economic Research Department, (1978). *The Japanese Financial System.*

Bank of Japan, *Economic Statistics Annual* (various years).

Barnea, A., R. A. Haugen, and L. W. Senbet, (1981). "Market Imperfections, Agency Problems and Capital Structure: A Review," *Financial Management*, Vol. 10, Summer, pp. 7–22.

Breton, Albert, and Ronald Wintrobe, (1978). "A Theory of 'Moral Suasion'," *Canadian Journal of Economics*, Vol. 11, pp. 210–219.

Bronte, S., (1982). *Japanese Finance: Markets and Institutions*, London, Euromoney Publications.

Caves, Richard E., and Masu Uekusa, (1976). *Industrial Organization in Japan*, Washington, D.C., The Brookings Institution.

Choi, F. D. S., S. K. Min, S. O. Nam, H. Hino, J. Ujie, and A. Stonehill, (1983). "Analyzing Foreign Financial Statements: Use and Misuse of Ratio Analysis," *Journal of International Business Studies*, Vol. 14, pp. 113–131.

Diamond, D. W., (1984). "Financial Intermediation and Delegated Monitoring," *Review of Economic Studies*.

Diamond, D. W., (1984). "Reputation Acquisition in Debt Markets," Unpublished Paper, University of Chicago.

Elston, C. D., (1981). "The Financing of Japanese Industry," *Bank of England Quarterly Bulletin*, pp. 510– 518.

Goto, Takeshi, (1980). "Bond Market: Current Situation and Legal Aspects," in *Lectures on Japanese Securities Regulation*, Tokyo, Japan Securities Research Institute.

International Business Information, Inc., (1984). "J. Osawa & Co., Ltd.: An Assessment of What Went Wrong." Report prepared by International Business Information, Inc., Tokyo, March.

International Business Information, Inc., (1983). "Recent Trends in Japanese Corporate Finance," Report prepared by International Business Information, Inc., Tokyo.

Japan Securities Research Institute, (1984). *Securities Markets in Japan 1984.*

Kuroda, Iwao, and Yoshiharu Oritani, (1980). "A Reexamination of the Unique Features of Japan's Corporate Financial Structure," *Japanese Economic Studies*, Vol. 8, Summer, pp. 82–117.

Kurosawa, Yoshitaka, (1981). "Corporate Financing in Capital Markets," Mimeo, Research Institute of Capital Formation, The Japan Development Bank.

Kurosawa, Y., and T. Wakasugi, (1984). "Business Risk, Dividend Policy and Policy for Capital Structure," Staff Paper, Research Institute of Capital Formation, The Japan Development Bank, August.

Myers, S. C., (1984). "The Capital Structure Puzzle," *Journal of Finance*, Vol. 39, July, pp. 575–592.

Myers, S. C., and N. Majluf, (1984). "Corporate Financing and Investment Decisions When Firms Have Information Investors Do Not Have," *Journal of Financial Economics*, pp. 187–221.

Nakamura, T., (1981). *The Postwar Japanese Economy: Its Development and Structure*, Tokyo, University of Tokyo Press.

Okumura, Hiroshi, (1982). "Interfirm Relations in an Enterprise Group: The Case of Mitsubishi," *Japanese Economic Studies*, pp. 53–82.

Otani, Ichiro, and Siddarth Tiwari, (1981). "Capital Controls and Interest Rate Parity: The Japanese Experience, 1978–81," *IMF Staff Papers*, Vol. 28, December, pp. 793–815.

Pascale, R. T., and T. P. Rohlen, (1983). "The Mazda Turnaround," *Journal of Japanese Studies*, Vol. 9, pp. 219–263.

Prindl, A. R., (1981). *Japanese Finance: A Guide to Banking in Japan*, New York, John Wiley & Sons.

Royama, Shoichi, (1983–1984). "The Japanese Financial System: Past, Present and Future," *Japanese Economic Studies*, Winter, pp. 3–31.

Sakakibara, Eisuke, and Robert A. Feldman, (1983). "The Japanese Financial System in Comparative Perspective," *Journal of Comparative Economics*, Vol. 7, March, pp. 1–24.

Suzuki, Yoshio, (1980). *Money and Banking in Contemporary Japan*, New Haven, CT, Yale University Press.

Teranishi, Juro, (1982). "A Model of the Relationship Between Regulated and Unregulated Financial Markets: Credit Rationing in the Japanese Context," *Hitotsubashi Journal of Economics*, February, pp. 25–43.

Tokyo Stock Exchange. *Annual Statistics Report,* (various years).

Tokyo Stock Exchange, (1984). *Tokyo Stock Exchange Fact Book 1984*.

Wallich, H. C., and M. I. Wallich, (1976). "Banking and Finance," in *Asia's New Giant*, Hugh Patrick and Henry Rosovsky, eds., Washington, D.C., Brookings Institute.

Wright, R. W., and S. Suzuki, (1979). "Capital Structure and Financial Risk in Japanese Companies," *Proceedings of the Academy of International Business Conference: Asia-Pacific Dimensions of International Business*, pp. 367–375.

4

Underwriting Japanese Long-Term National Bonds*

Richard H. Pettway
University of Missouri-Columbia

After the dramatic appreciation of the Japanese yen and after the financial liberalization of the Japanese national bond market and financial deregulation in Japan, many investors have become increasingly interested in Japanese national bond issues. The purposes of this article are to describe the levels of interest rates on government bonds of comparable countries, focus on the size and characteristics of new issues of Japanese national bonds, and describe the mechanics of underwriting these national bonds.

Interest Rates Are Low on Japanese National Bonds

Japan has followed a long-standing policy of low interest rates, particularly during the 1960s and early 1970s, to encourage economic growth and to keep interest costs on the national debt as low as possible. The interest rates on long-term national bonds of six comparable countries are listed in Table 4.1. Over the period from 1984 through 1988, all the yields of the six countries' national bonds move in generally similar patterns, but the yields on Japanese national bonds were lower than those

* This article is an extension of an earlier paper (Pettway 1982) that was completed when he was a Fulbright Research Scholar to Japan and China in 1982 and a Visiting Professor to Keio University in Tokyo. Special thanks are due to the New York Office of Daiwa Securities Research Institute, which supplied the issues of their *Investor's Guide*. Professor Takeshi Yamada, Hosei University, Tokyo, and Professor Takashi Kaneko, Keio University, Tokyo, were very helpful and provided comments and suggestions.

Table 4.1. International Long-Term Interest Rates for National Bonds of Major Countries

Date		Japan 10 Year Mat. (%)	U.S.A. 10 Year or More (%)	U.K. 20 Year Mat. (%)	F.R.G. 10 Year Mat. (%)	France Long-Term (%)	Canada 10 Year or More (%)
Month	Year						
6	1984	7.51	13.43	11.15	8.24	13.12	13.81
9	1984	7.21	12.34	10.88	7.90	12.01	12.63
12	1984	6.65	11.51	10.61	7.18	11.79	11.66
3	1985	6.91	11.91	11.01	7.64	11.31	11.93
6	1985	6.52	10.47	10.86	7.06	10.90	10.88
9	1985	5.78	10.77	10.57	6.54	10.90	10.96
12	1985	5.89	9.68	10.69	6.67	10.47	10.06
3	1986	4.55	8.15	9.94	6.21	8.43	9.54
6	1986	4.78	9.13	9.77	6.30	7.95	9.42
9	1986	5.72	8.88	10.36	6.15	7.80	9.45
12	1986	5.42	8.49	10.94	6.32	9.07	9.23
3	1987	4.37	8.36	9.70	6.20	8.51	8.98
6	1987	4.61	9.37	9.55	6.16	9.40	9.78
9	1987	6.73	10.18	10.43	6.77	10.49	11.14
12	1987	5.07	10.10	10.08	6.54	9.93	10.34
3	1988	4.73	9.38	9.78	6.26	9.36	10.13

Source: *Investors' Guide*, Tokyo, Daiwa Securities Research Institute, Various Months.

of the other countries. In fact, these yield differences remain within a reasonably narrow band that has been consistent over the 1980s. The rates for Japan are the lowest, followed by Germany, with the other four countries being much higher. For example, a comparison of interest rates shows that the rates on long-term U.S. government bonds were between 300 and 600 basis points higher than the Japanese bonds from 1984 through 1988. Pettway (1982) found that during 1981 and 1982 the yields on long-term U.S. government bonds were between 365 and 606 base points higher than comparable Japanese national bonds.

The Size of the Japanese National Bond Market Is Growing

The Japanese national bond sales were less than 1.77 trillion yen per year until 1974. From 1975 through 1979 the amounts issued per year grew steadily and reached a high point of 10.97 trillion yen in 1979. During the 1980s the new issue volume rose even more and reached 21.7 trillion yen in 1987.[1] The size of the new issues of national bonds for each month is provided from June 1984 through March 1988 in Table 4.2. During this period the new issues of government bonds averaged 1.7 trillion yen per month. Using a 132 yen/dollar exchange rate, this average new bond sale per month would be equivalent to 13.2 billion dollars per month.

Notice that the three major categories of national bonds are also presented in Table 4.2, long-term (10-year maturity), medium-term (5-year maturity), and discount bonds (5 years or less). The majority of each monthly new issue is long term (i.e., an average of 76% of all government bonds issued during this period were long term). The vast majority of the monthly issues was interest paying, not discount bonds. Of the long-term bonds issued, most were sold through public offerings. In fact, 49% of each monthly sale of national bonds was through public offering.

The issuance of government bonds has constituted a major part of the entire new issue market in Japan. Government bonds were less than 8% of the total new bond issues sold in 1970. They rose to 19.6% in 1974. The most dramatic rise occurred in 1975, when national bonds were 32.2% of all new bond issues. The percentage of all new bond sales of government securities reached a peak of 42.4% in 1979. During the 1980s, this percentage remained below the 1979 record and was 32.7% in 1986.

Table 4.2. Amount of Japanese National Bonds Issued Per Month (6/1984–3/1988; Billion Yen)

Date		Total Government Bonds	Long-Term Bonds	%	Long-Term Public Offering	%	Medium-Term Bonds	%	Discount Bonds	%
Month	Year									
6	1984	918	600	65	600	65	318	35	0	0
7		408	0	0	0	0	408	100	0	0
8		2,458	2,223	90	1,400	57	235	10	0	0
9		2,053	1,600	78	600	29	313	15	140	7
10		1,750	1,480	85	700	40	270	15	0	0
11		1,659	1,131	68	750	45	368	22	160	10
12		1,049	700	67	700	67	349	33	0	0
1	1985	1,065	678	64	678	64	251	24	137	13
2		1,236	1,084	88	600	49	152	12	0	0
3		709	388	55	200	28	183	26	137	19
4		2,227	1,900	85	1,000	45	327	15	0	0
5		3,196	2,397	75	940	29	661	21	138	4
6		1,874	1,558	83	702	37	316	17	0	0
7		3,410	2,780	82	600	18	494	14	136	4
8		1,026	920	90	700	68	107	10	0	0
9		2,208	1,700	77	1700	77	373	17	135	6
10		1,119	900	80	900	80	219	20	0	0
11		1,493	1,493	100	700	47	0	0	0	0
12		1,575	900	57	900	57	675	43	0	0
1	1986	1141	712	62	712	62	294	26	134	12
2		2,137	1,707	80	500	23	298	14	133	6
3		563	563	100	563	100	0	0	0	0
4		1,649	1,200	73	1,200	73	449	27	0	0

5		1,837	1,345	73	608	33	365	20	127	7
6		1,406	900	64	900	64	506	36	0	0
7		2,187	1,871	86	450	21	188	9	127	6
8		3,137	2,873	92	600	19	264	8	0	0
9		1,357	1,000	74	1,000	74	228	17	128	9
10		1,103	900	82	900	82	203	18	0	0
11		2,754	2,348	85	700	25	276	10	130	5
12		1,061	800	75	800	75	261	25	0	0
1	1987	2,870	2,487	87	900	31	257	9	126	4
2		1,964	1,509	77	1,108	56	455	23	0	0
3		476	476	100	476	100	0	0	0	0
4		1,770	1,400	79	1,400	79	290	16	80	5
5		2,668	2,289	86	1,109	42	259	10	120	4
6		1,253	800	64	800	64	453	36	0	0
7		876	450	51	450	51	302	34	124	14
8		2,122	1,866	88	400	19	256	12	0	0
9		2,440	2,057	84	1,356	56	257	11	126	5
10		204	0	0	0	0	204	100	0	0
11		1,808	1,682	93	700	39	0	0	126	7
12		3,267	2,970	91	1,233	38	297	9	0	0
1	1988	2,866	2,455	86	730	25	286	10	0	4
2		1,526	1,339	88	600	39	187	12	0	0
3		1,829	1,829	100	1,188	65	0	0	0	0
Averages		1,733	1,397	76	777	49	279	20	56	3

Source: *Investors' Guide*, Tokyo, Daiwa Securities Research Institute, Various Months.

Finally, as the primary market of Japanese national bonds (or in Japanese, *Kokusai*) rose in size, the secondary market also grew substantially. In fact, 8.8 trillion yen of government bonds were traded on the Tokyo Stock Exchange's bond market in 1983. The size of these secondary market trades in government bonds was 22.6 trillion yen in 1984, 39.4 trillion yen in 1985, 49.9 trillion yen in 1986, and 56.9 trillion yen in 1987.[2]

Mechanics of the Underwriting and Sale of Long-Term National Bonds

The issuance and trading of Japanese national bonds are governed under the Japanese Securities and Exchange Law that went into effect on May 7, 1948. Americans will understand the Japanese law because it was patterned after the U.S. 1933 Securities Act and the 1934 Securities Exchange Act. The Japanese law has been revised several times with the most important revisions occurring in 1965 and 1971.

National bonds sold in Japan may be legally classified into construction bonds and deficit-financing bonds. Construction bonds are issued under the Public Finance Law within the government budget for public works, fiscal investments, and loans. Deficit-financing bonds are special legislative authorized bonds to finance general account expenditures.

Government bonds in Japan, at present, consist of four types of securities: (1) long-term interest-bearing bonds, initially issued with 10-year maturities; (2) intermediate-term interest-bearing bonds, initially issued with 5-year maturities; (3) intermediate-term discount bonds, initially issued with 5-year maturities; and (4) short-term bonds, initially issued with 2- to 4-year maturities.

In the monthly sale of new government bonds, there are some specific steps in the process. First, the government is represented by the Ministry of Finance (MOF) and MOF acts through the Bank of Japan (BOJ, the central bank of Japan), which is responsible for the contract on the underwriting of bonds and handling of public offering.[3] This is generally similar to the relationship between the Treasury and the Federal Reserve System in the United States.

Japan has followed a low interest policy, under which interest rates of all kinds remained unresponsive to the changing conditions of the market. Historically, the bond market of Japan has had two distinct and not organically connected markets: the issuing market and the distribution market. This resulted in terms of issue that failed to reflect adequately the market value of the issue involved, since original coupon rates were pegged below secondary market yields. Lately the issuing terms of bonds have become more flexible and issuing prices and yield reflect current yields on traded government bonds in the secondary market.

Generally, short-term bonds are not underwritten since they are distributed by means of competitive bids. The short-term government bonds are issued under a "Public Tender" method, the first of which was held in June 1978. Since 1982, the Ministry of Finance has used a fixed-rate public offering method on these short-term bonds. The issuer fixes the nominal interest rates, the prices of a proposed bond issue, and invites bids from tender participants.

Underwriting of national bonds other than short-term bonds is performed using an underwriting syndicate generally composed of 13 city banks, 3 long-term credit banks, 64 local banks, 7 trust banks, 68 mutual loan and savings banks, 6 credit associations, the Central Cooperative Bank for Commerce and Industry, the Central Cooperative Bank for Agriculture and Forestry, 25 foreign banks, 21 securities companies, 2 foreign securities companies, 22 life insurance companies, and 22 nonlife insurance companies.[4] This syndicate will typically distribute the bonds directly to individuals and other investors or sell them to a bond-selling group. Prior to 1983, commercial banks in Japan were not allowed to sell long-term or intermediate-term national bonds directly to individuals. Now commercial banks can participate in over-the-counter sales of outstanding government bonds.

Typically, the procedures for a government bond issue are as follows. First, there is a resolution of the Japanese Diet on the amount of bonds issuable. Second, there is a meeting of underwriters where notification on the terms of issue and instructions to prepare for the underwriting contract are provided. The underwriting group has two contracts: a contract for handling the public offering and a contract among syndicate and selling group members. There is a specific beginning of the subscript and a specific time limit for subscription. After the subscription ends, there is a specific payment date when the members of the syndicate make payment for and receive delivery of the government bonds from the Bank of Japan.

The pricing procedures on these long-term national bonds generally work in the following manner. During the last week of a month prior to the sale, representatives of the MOF, BOJ, and the underwriting syndicate establish the size of the issue and its maturity (normally 10 years), and begin to discuss the pricing of the issue. During the first week of the sales month, both the MOF and the underwriting syndicate make a proposal on pricing. Usually each issue is priced slightly below par (99.75% to 98.25%), so the main concern is establishing the coupon and thereby the yield on each issue. After negotiations and agreement as to price, yield, and coupon rate, a contract is signed between the underwriting syndicate and the BOJ (acting as fiscal agent for MOF). During the offering period, underwriters, securities companies, and members of the selling group obtain orders and commitments on the issue at the agreed-on price. The date of issuance and settlement is usually the 20th day of the selling month. Subsequently, after the issue has been sold, members of the underwriting group, securities companies, and selling group members will receive commission payments from the BOJ. Generally these commissions are approximately 1% of the value of the bonds sold. Thus, the government, through the BOJ, receives the total gross receipts from the sales of national bonds and disburses a commission for the sale rather than the netting process at the underwriter level employed in Europe and America.

Since Japanese commercial banks play a large role in the underwriting of national bonds, the separation of banking and securities business should be discussed. Traditionally, the countries that believe the strongest in the separation of banking and securities businesses are the United States, the U.K., Canada, and Japan. In Japan the legal separation of banking and securities business was established by Article 65 of the Securities and Exchange Law (enacted during an occupation period in 1948 and based on the U.S. Glass-Steagall Act). There are some very important differences between the Glass-Steagall Act and Article 65. The Glass-Steagall Act imposes strict controls, even on the acquisitions of securities for investment purposes. U.S. financial institutions were permitted to buy only negotiable securities and not allowed to purchase equities. However, in Japan under Article 65 there are no controls on the acquisitions of securities and equities for investment purposes. The Anti-Monopoly Law of Japan does restrict the size of equities held for investment by financial institutions. More importantly, banks and trust banks are allowed to underwrite national government bonds, local government bonds, and government-guaranteed bonds. Thus, even though Japan is a stronger supporter of the separation of banking and securities businesses, Japanese commercial banks may hold limited equity shares as investments and may underwrite government bonds.[5]

Comparisons between Subscriber's Yield and the TSE Yield on Long-Term Bonds

In the past, primary market yields on national bonds were not tied directly to yields in the secondary markets of comparable securities. As of September 30, 1981, the Japan Securities Research Institute (JSRI) found a differential of 135 to 143 basis points between the current market yield of 10-year national bonds selling in the secondary market on the Tokyo Stock Exchange, TSE, and the subscriber's yield on newly issued national bonds.[6] The JSRI stated,

> It has long been pointed out that the differential between the current yields of outstanding bonds with the longest maturity and subscriber's yields of new issue tended to undermine the development of the bond market. Because the terms of issue of some of the new issues have tended to be fixed artificially at a low level, such differential grew larger, particularly during periods of monetary stringency, making outstanding bonds with a longer maturity much more attractive than new issues, with the result that issuers of new bonds, except private placeable bonds, have often encountered difficulty in selling their securities.

Using an "event method" of measurement, however, Pettway (1982) found that on 16 new issues of national bonds during 1981 and 1982 that new issues of national bonds were competitively priced with very small differences between the subscriber's yield and current market yields of reasonably comparable bonds.

To retest this issue with current data, the coupon yields on all new national bonds issued for each month from June 1984 through June 1988 were gathered and displayed in column 3 of Table 4.3. The subscriber's yields are also displayed for each new issue. Notice that the subscriber's yield is always equal to or higher than the new issue coupon rate, which indicates that all new issues are sold to underwriters at a small discount, usually 99.75% to 98.25% of par. This difference between yields is presented in column 6 and ranges from 47 basis points to zero, with an average of 17 basis points that is, statistically, significantly different from zero. Thus, it could be inferred that, on average, the underwriting

Table 4.3. Interest Rates on 10-Year Japanese National Government Bonds (6/1984–6/1988)

(1)	(2)	(3)	(4)	(5)	(6)	(7)	(8)
Date		Coupon	Subscriber	TSE	(4)−(3)	(5)−(3)	(5)−(4)
Month	Year	Yield (%)	Yield (%)	Yield (%)	Diff. (%)	Diff. (%)	Diff. (%)
6	1984	7.00	7.346	7.51	0.35	0.51	0.16
7		7.00	7.346	7.77	0.35	0.77	0.42
8		7.30	7.698	7.41	0.40	0.11	−0.29
9		7.10	7.538	7.21	0.44	0.11	−0.33
10		7.10	7.448	6.96	0.35	−0.14	−0.49
11		6.80	7.055	6.64	0.25	−0.16	−0.42
12		6.80	6.969	6.65	0.17	−0.15	−0.32
1	1985	6.50	6.666	6.46	0.17	−0.04	−0.21
2		6.50	6.666	7.14	0.17	0.64	0.47
3		6.80	7.099	6.91	0.30	0.11	−0.19
4		6.80	6.926	6.88	0.13	0.08	−0.05
5		6.80	6.842	6.62	0.04	−0.18	−0.22
6		6.50	6.708	6.52	0.21	0.02	−0.19
7		6.50	6.624	6.42	0.12	−0.08	−0.20
8		6.20	6.405	6.37	0.20	0.17	−0.03
9		6.20	6.405	5.78	0.20	−0.42	−0.62
10		6.00	6.120	6.59	0.12	0.59	0.47
11		6.50	6.708	6.35	0.21	−0.15	−0.36
12		6.50	6.582	5.89	0.08	−0.61	−0.69
1	1986	6.10	6.262	5.89	0.16	−0.21	−0.37
2		6.00	6.000	5.37	0.00	−0.63	−0.63
3		5.70	5.778	4.55	0.08	−1.15	−1.23
4		5.10	5.100	4.60	0.00	−0.50	−0.50
5		5.10	5.100	5.02	0.00	−0.08	−0.08

6		5.10	5.100	4.78	0.00	−0.32	−0.32
7		5.10	5.329	5.23	0.23	0.13	−0.10
8		5.10	5.329	5.15	0.23	0.05	−0.18
9		5.10	5.252	5.72	0.15	0.62	0.47
10		5.10	5.567	5.72	0.47	0.62	0.15
11		5.40	5.555	5.44	0.16	0.04	−0.12
12		5.30	5.454	5.42	0.15	0.12	−0.03
1	1987	5.30	5.376	5.70	0.08	0.40	0.32
2		5.00	5.151	4.85	0.15	−0.15	−0.30
3		5.00	5.075	4.37	0.08	−0.63	−0.71
4		4.70	4.736	4.00	0.04	−0.70	−0.74
5		4.00	4.141	3.88	0.14	−0.12	−0.26
6		3.90	3.969	4.61	0.07	0.71	0.64
7		4.30	4.667	5.45	0.37	1.15	0.78
8		4.60	5.051	5.71	0.45	1.11	0.66
9		4.90	5.126	6.73	0.23	1.83	1.60
10		4.90	5.126	5.40	0.23	0.50	0.27
11		5.00	5.075	5.26	0.08	0.26	0.18
12		5.00	5.000	5.07	0.00	0.07	0.07
1	1988	4.90	5.050	4.15	0.15	−0.75	−0.90
2		4.80	4.874	4.53	0.07	−0.27	−0.34
3		4.80	4.800	4.73	0.00	−0.07	−0.07
4		4.70	4.740	4.79	0.04	0.09	0.05
5		4.60	4.600	5.12	0.00	0.52	0.52
6		4.80	5.102	5.54	0.30	0.74	0.44
Averages					0.17*	0.09	−0.08

*Significant at 0.01 level

Source: *Investors' Guide*, Tokyo, Daiwa Securities Research Institute, Various Months.

spread on the Japanese national bonds averaged 17 basis points over the past four years.

In column 7 are found the differences between the coupon rate set by MOF and BOJ (i.e., the Ministry of Finance and the Bank of Japan) on each issue and the current yield on the longest national bond traded on the Tokyo Stock Exchange (TSE) designated as the TSE yield in column 5. The data show that the original coupons on average are set 9 basis points above the current yield on comparable traded national bonds. Even though there were some significant differences such as +183 basis points in September of 1987 and −115 basis points in February of 1986, the average across the 47 observations of 9 basis points was not significantly different from zero. Thus, it appears that, generally, the coupon on a new issue of Japanese national bonds is placed close to the current yield of traded long-term national bonds on the TSE. Additionally, the differences between the subscriber's yield and the TSE yield found in column (8) varied from −123 basis points to +160 basis points, but on average there were only 8 basis points of difference which is, statistically, insignificantly different from zero. These values are reasonably similar to those of Pettway (1982). This study reconfirms that the subscriber's yield is not always less than the yields on comparable traded bonds that were found in earlier studies by the Japanese Security Research Institute and finds that, on average, there is no significant difference between these two yields. Thus, the conditions in the primary market for national bonds have improved to the point that previous impediments to its efficiency and growth no longer exist.

Summary and Conclusions

As the budget deficits of the Japanese government increased in the late 1970s and in the 1980s, the sizes of new issues of Japanese national bonds began to grow. Even with the historic low-interest policy of the government and its historical desire to separate the yields on new long-term national bonds sold in the primary market from the current yields of comparable bonds in the secondary market, the government was forced to liberalize and make its issuing policies more flexible. With increased financial deregulation in Japan, this study that details the current mechanics of underwriting of new issues of national bonds in the primary market in Japan finds that there is evidence that the yields set on new issues (i.e., subscriber's yields) are not statistically different from the yields on comparable issues traded on the secondary market. Thus, the current Japanese national bond primary market reflects reasonable required returns and, therefore, there are no artificial barriers to their efficiency and growth.

Notes

1. See *Securities Market in Japan, 1988,* (1987), p. 72.
2. These values exclude the over-the-counter sales of government bonds. See *Tokyo Stock Exchange Fact Book, 1988,* (1988), p. 25.
3. A good source for these types of details is *Securities Market in Japan, 1988,* (1987), Chapter 5.
4. See *Securities Market in Japan, 1988,* (1988), p. 70. The number of foreign banks and foreign security companies has changed recently.
5. A good discussion of this issue is found in Suzuki (1987), pp. 38 and 134–135.
6. See *Securities Market in Japan, 1982,* (1982), p. 81.

References

Handbook of the Japanese Bond Market, 1982, Tokyo, The Industrial Bank of Japan, Limited.

Investor's Guide, Tokyo, Daiwa Securities Research Institute.

Pettway, Richard H., (1982). "Interest Rates of Japanese Long-term National Bonds: Have Interest Rates Been Liberalized?" *Keio Economic Studies*, Vol. 19, No. 1, Tokyo, The Keio Economic Society, Keio University, pp. 91–100.

Securities Market in Japan, 1982, (1982). Tokyo, Japan Securities Research Institute, February.

Securities Market in Japan, 1988, (1987). Tokyo, Japan Securities Research Institute, December.

Suzuki, Yoshio, (1987). *The Japanese Financial System*, Oxford, Clarendon Press.

Tokyo Stock Exchange Fact Book, 1988, (1988). Tokyo, International Department, Tokyo Stock Exchange.

PART II

The Risk Structure of Japanese Equity Markets

5

Estimating the Dependence Structure of Japanese Share Prices

Cheol S. Eun
College of Business and Management, University of Maryland

Bruce G. Resnick
School of Business, Indiana University

I. Introduction

The purpose of this study is to provide empirical documentation concerning the best possible method for estimating the correlation structure of Japanese share prices and, consequently, to make modern portfolio theory (MPT) amenable to implementation in the Japanese stock market, which is now the largest stock market, in terms of the capitalization value, in the world.

Since the pioneering works of Markowitz (1959) and Tobin (1958) appeared, MPT has exerted a profound influence on the development of the theory of finance. For example, the implications of MPT for equilibrium asset prices were independently explored by Sharpe (1964), Lintner (1965), and Mossin (1966), leading to the development of the Capital Asset Pricing Model (CAPM). In contrast to such a rapid theoretical development, the implementation of MPT has been, at best, slow. This is due to two main obstacles: input requirements and computational procedure.

In order to apply MPT, the investor must obtain accurate estimates of the expected return, the variance of return for each security, and the correlation coefficients of returns between each pair of securities. As has been recognized in the literature, the task of obtaining accurate estimates of these parameters is particularly difficult with respect to the matrix of correlation coefficients. The reason for this is partly because there are a large number of correlations to be estimated, and partly because the organizational structure of the securities industry does not easily lend itself to extensive interfirm analysis. Hence, it is not likely that security analysts can generate accurate estimates of correlations between all pairs of securities, even if they could do so for small subsets of securities. The second obstacle to the implementation of MPT is the necessity to solve a quadratic programming problem to determine an optimal portfolio.

To overcome these obstacles, a number of simplifying models were developed and tested in the context of the U.S. stock market.[1] As was shown by Elton and Gruber (1973) and Elton, Gruber, and Urich (1978), such simplifying models as the Mean Model and the Single-Index Model with adjusted betas provided reasonably accurate estimates of future correlations. Furthermore, these models made it possible to develop simple algorithms for computing the composition of the optimal portfolio. Owing to these studies, MPT is now amenable to implementation in the context of the U.S. stock market. However, no parallel effort has yet been made to make MPT applicable to non-U.S. stock markets, including the Japanese stock market.

In this paper, we first present a variety of forecasting models that can be employed to estimate the dependence structure of Japanese share prices. In addition to the "traditional" models previously tested by Elton and Gruber and by Elton, Gruber, and Urich, we propose a class of "composite" models which can potentially outperform the traditional models. The composite models involve an adjustment of the sample estimates of the correlation coefficients toward the best prior estimate. We evaluate the performance results of each of the forecasting models from the viewpoint of an investor who uses the Japanese yen in measuring asset returns.

In this paper, we use monthly return data for a sample of 72 Japanese firms, representing 10 major industries, from the period of January 1973 through December 1982. The data were obtained from *Capital International Perspective*, Geneva, Switzerland. The first six years of data (estimation period) are used to produce forecasts of the last four years (forecast period).[2] In evaluating the performance of the alternative forecasting models, we use two major criteria: the mean squared forecast error and the stochastic dominance based on the frequency distribution of the squared forecast errors. Finally, to ensure the robustness of our findings, the empirical tests are replicated for two nonoverlapping subsamples of 36 firms.

The plan of the paper is as follows. Section II describes the alternative forecasting models. In Section III, the performance evaluation criteria are discussed. In Section IV, the empirical results are presented. Section V summarizes and concludes.

II. The Alternative Forecasting Models

In this section, we describe the nine forecasting models we employ for estimating the correlation structure of Japanese share prices: a full historical model, three index models, two mean models, and three composite models. The first three types of forecasting models have been previously used to estimate the correlation structure of U.S. share prices. In addition to these "traditional" models, we develop a class of "composite" forecasting models.

Full Historical Model

The Full Historical Model calculates each pairwise correlation coefficient over a historical period and assumes that the historical values of these coefficients are the best estimates of their future values. Since each pairwise correlation has to be directly estimated, the Full Historical Model is the most disaggregate of all models under consideration. For the entire sample of 72 firms we calculate the 2556 historical correlation coefficients over the estimation period. Furthermore, for each of the two nonoverlapping samples of 36 firms we calculate the 630 historical correlation coefficients. Throughout the paper, the test results for the Full Historical Model serve as the benchmark against which the performance results of the more aggregate mean models and sophisticated behavioral and composite models are evaluated.

Index Models

An alternative to direct estimation of the correlation coefficients via the Full Historical Model is to assume that assets co-vary only because of their common response to a single index or multiple indices. Given a specific behavioral assumption, one can derive the implicit correlation matrix.

Single-Index Model. The Single-Index Model assumes that assets are correlated with one another only through their common response to the market index. Formally, the Single-Index Model is described by the following basic equation:

$$R_i = \alpha_i + \beta_i R_M + e_i \qquad i = 1, \ldots, n \tag{5.1}$$

with the assumption that

1. $E(e_i) = 0, \qquad i = 1, \ldots, n$
2. $\text{Cov}(e_i, R_M) = 0, \qquad i = 1, \ldots, n$
3. $\text{Cov}(e_i, e_j) = 0, \qquad i,j = 1, \ldots, n \quad i \neq j$

where R_i and R_M are, respectively, the rates of return on asset i and the market index; α_i and β_i are stable parameters specific to asset i.

Once β's are estimated via Equation 5.1, the implicit correlation coefficient can be calculated as follows:

$$\rho_{ij} = \frac{\beta_i \beta_j \sigma_M^2}{\sigma_i \sigma_j}, \qquad i,j = 1, \ldots, n \qquad i \neq j \tag{5.2}$$

As a proxy for the market, we used the value-weighted Japanese market index constructed by *Capital International Perspective*. In this study, two different estimates of β are used for calculating the correlation coefficients: an unadjusted historical β and a Bayesian β derived by Vasicek (1973). The Bayesian estimation of β involves an adjustment of the sample estimate of β toward the best prior estimate, which is taken to be the average value of the sample cross-sectional betas.[3]

Industry Multi-Index Model. In contrast to the Single-Index Model, the Industry Multi-Index Model purports to capture the industry influence beyond the market influence. The Industry Multi-Index Model assumes that assets co-vary because of their common response to the industry index as well as to the market index. The Industry Multi-Index Model tested is of the following specification:

$$R_i = \alpha_i + \beta_i R_M + \gamma_i R_J + \epsilon_i \qquad i = 1, \ldots, n \tag{5.3}$$

with the assumption that

1. $E(\epsilon_i) = 0 \qquad i = 1, \ldots, n$
2. $\text{Cov}(\epsilon_i, R_M) = 0 \qquad i = 1, \ldots, n$

3. $\text{Cov}(\epsilon_i, R_J) = 0 \qquad i = 1, \ldots, n \quad J = 1, \ldots, N$
4. $\text{Cov}(R_J, R_M) = 0 \qquad J = 1, \ldots, N$
5. $\text{Cov}(R_J, R_K) = 0 \qquad J, K = 1, \ldots, N \quad J \neq K$
6. $\text{Cov}(\epsilon_i, \epsilon_j) = 0 \qquad i, j = 1, \ldots, n \quad i \neq j$

where α_i, β_i, and γ_i are stable parameters specific to asset i (of industry J); R_J is the residual return to industry J's index, constructed to be orthogonal to the market index. Equation 5.3 assumes that the returns to an asset are affected only by the market influence and the influence of the particular industry to which the asset belongs.[4]

Given the Industry Multi-Index Model of Equation 5.3, the implicit correlation coefficients can be calculated as follows:

$$\rho_{ij} = \frac{\beta_i \beta_j \sigma_M^2}{\sigma_i \sigma_j} \tag{5.4}$$

$$\rho_{ij} = \frac{(\beta_i \beta_j \sigma_M^2 + \gamma_i \gamma_j \sigma_J^2)}{\sigma_i \sigma_j} \tag{5.5}$$

between firms from different industries, and between firms from the same industry respectively. It is clear from examining Equations 5.2, 5.4, and 5.5 that the Single-Index Model and the Industry Multi-Index Model will produce identical estimates of interindustry pairwise correlations, but different estimates of intra-industry correlations. This implies that any difference in performance between these two types of models should be attributed to their differential estimates of intra-industry correlations. Table 5.1 shows the distribution of the sample firms by industry membership.

Mean Models

Another alternative to the Full Historical Model is to assume that the historical correlation matrix contains information about the future mean correlations, but not information about pairwise differences from the mean correlation. The mean models hypothesize that since the pairwise differences are very unstable through time, it is better to estimate them as being zero, rather than their historical level. The idea of averaging the historical correlations to estimate their future values was first tested by Elton and Gruber (1973), resulting in a surprisingly robust performance with U.S. data.[5]

Table 5.1. Sample Firms Classified by Industry Membership[a]

Industry	Entire Sample	Subsample 1	Subsample 2
1. Automobiles	5	3	2
2. Capital Goods	8	4	4
3. Chemicals	8	4	4
4. Consumer Goods	14	7	7
5. Electrical & Electronics	8	4	4
6. Energy	4	2	2
7. Finance	8	4	4
8. Materials	5	2	3
9. Merchandising & Trade	7	3	4
10. Leisure & Airlines	5	3	2
Total	72	36	36

a. For the list of sample firms, see Appendix.

In this study, two such models are tested: the Overall Mean Model and the Industry Mean Model. The Overall Mean Model, which is the most aggregate of all models under consideration, estimates every pairwise correlation coefficient as being the average of all historical pairwise correlation coefficients sample-wide. Recognizing, however, that there could be a common mean correlation only within and between industry groups, we choose to test the Industry Mean Model. The Industry Meal Model estimates every "intra-industry" pairwise correlation coefficient as being the average of all pairwise correlation coefficients among the sample firms within the industry. Further, every "interindustry" pairwise correlation coefficient between assets from two different industries is estimated as being the average of all interindustry pairwise correlations between the sample assets from the two industries.

Composite Models

In addition to the traditional models described above, we propose a class of "composite" forecasting models that can potentially outperform the traditional models: the Naïve Composite Model, the (historical) Optimal Composite Model, and the Bayesian Composite Model.

Naïve Composite Model. Estimation of future correlation coefficients by a composite model involves an adjustment of the sample historical values of correlation coefficients toward the average value of the sample cross-sectional correlation coefficients. In general, the forecast value for the *i*th entry of the correlation matrix ρ_i provided by a composite model can be written as follows:

$$\rho_i = wH_i + (1 - w)\overline{H} \tag{5.6}$$

where H_i is the *i*th entry in the correlation matrix of sample correlations estimated from the historical period, $\overline{H}$ is the average of the sample cross-sectional correlations, and w is the weight assigned to the sample correlation. It is evident from Equation 5.6 that the composite model generates forecasts by combining the forecasts of the Full Historical Model and the Overall Mean Model. To the extent that the historical correlation matrix contains information together with noise, it may be possible to filter the noise and more fully utilize the information by means of composite forecasting.

Clearly, the performance of a composite model will depend on the particular weighting scheme adopted. In the special case where w is unity, Equation 5.6 reduces to the Full Historical Model. Alternatively, when w is zero, Equation 5.6 reduces to the Overall Mean Model. Both the Full Historical Model ($w = 1$) and the Overall Mean Model ($w = 0$) implicitly assume that the minimum MSE occurs, respectively, at opposite "corners." However, if the minimum MSE occurs at an interior point, that is, $0 < w* < 1$, the composite forecast will be superior to either constituent model. This implies that neither constituent model is utilizing all of the information contained in the historical data in an optimal fashion. Our Naïve Composite Model simply assumes that an equally weighted composite forecasting, $w* = 0.5$, will produce the most accurate forecast.

Optimal Composite Model. Recognizing that the equal weighting of the Naïve Composite Model is, as its name implies, a naïve estimate of $w*$, the Optimal Composite Model tries to determine the "optimal" weighting scheme based on the historical data which will minimize the MSE loss function:

$$\text{MSE} = \frac{1}{n}\sum_{i=1}^{n}(\rho_i - A_i)^2 \tag{5.7}$$

where ρ_i and A_i are, respectively, the forecast and the actual value of the ith entry of the correlation matrix. Substituting Equation 5.6 into Equation 5.7, we obtain

$$\text{MSE} = \frac{1}{n}\sum_{i=1}^{n}[(wH_i + (1-w)\bar{H}) - A_i]^2 \tag{5.8}$$

It is evident from Equation 5.8 that the MSE is dependent on the numerical value assumed by w.

Differentiating Equation 5.8 with respect to w, the following first-order condition obtains

$$\sum_{i=1}^{n}[w(H_i - \bar{H})^2 + (H_i - \bar{H})(\bar{H} - A_i)] = 0 \tag{5.9}$$

Solving Equation 5.9 for the optimal w^* yields

$$w^* = \frac{\sum_{i=1}^{n}(H_i - \bar{H})(A_i - \bar{H})}{\sum_{i=1}^{n}(H_i - \bar{H})^2} \tag{5.10}$$

Defining $d\bar{H} = \bar{H} - \bar{A}$, Equation 5.10 can be rewritten as

$$w^* = \frac{\sum_i(H_i - \bar{H})(A_i - \bar{A}) - d\bar{H}\sum_i(H_i - \bar{H})}{\sum_i(H_i - \bar{H})^2} \tag{5.11}$$

Noting that the second term in the numerator of the right-hand side of Equation 5.11 is zero, a simplified expression for the optimal weighting scheme results:

$$w^* = \frac{\text{Cov}(H, A)}{\text{Var}(H)} \tag{5.12a}$$

$$= \left(\frac{\sigma_A}{\sigma_H}\right)\gamma_{AH} \tag{5.12b}$$

where γ_{AH} refers to the correlation coefficient between the A_i and H_i. Given σ_A and σ_H, a higher γ_{AH} leads to a higher w^*, that is, a higher weight for H_i in Equation 5.6. If $\gamma_{AH} = 0$, then $w^* = 0$, and the Overall Mean Model results. If $\sigma_H = \sigma_A\gamma_{AH}$ on the other hand, then $w^* = 1$, and we obtain the Full Historical Model. Finally, it is pointed out that to estimate w^*, two nonoverlapping time series are needed. In this study, we divide the six-year estimation period into two equal parts to make the estimates. Obviously, the performance of the Optimal Composite Model would critically depend on the intertemporal stability of γ_{AH}.

Bayesian Composite Model. As was mentioned previously, the Composite Model involves an adjustment of the sample estimate H_i toward the mean of the sample estimates $\bar{H}$. In making the adjustment toward the mean, both the Naïve and the Optimal Composite Models make the same degree of adjustment, w, for all n entries in the correlation matrix. This implicitly assumes that the variance of the sample correlation coefficient is the same between all pairs of assets. The consequence of this approach is to underadjust the less accurate estimates and to overadjust the more accurate ones.

The Bayesian Composite Model makes an adjustment of the sample estimate of H_i toward the mean $\bar{H}$, with the degree of adjustment determined by the precision of both the sample estimate and the mean of the sample estimates. The correlation estimator can be written as follows:

$$\rho_i = w_i H_i + (1 - w_i)\bar{H} \qquad i = 1, \ldots, n \tag{5.13}$$

where

$$w_i = \frac{\mathrm{Var}(\bar{H})}{\mathrm{Var}(H) + \mathrm{Var}(H_i)} \quad \text{and}$$

$$1 - w_i = \frac{\mathrm{Var}(H_i)}{\mathrm{Var}(H) + \mathrm{Var}(H_i)}$$

$\mathrm{Var}(\bar{H})$ denotes the variance of the distribution of the historical estimates of the correlation coefficients over the sample of assets, and $\mathrm{Var}(H_i)$ denotes the square of the standard error of the sample estimate of the ith entry in the correlation matrix. The Bayesian Composite Model calls for more (less) adjustment toward the mean of the sample estimates with large (small) standard errors.[6]

The weighting scheme of Equation 5.13 makes it necessary to estimate $\mathrm{Var}(\bar{H})$ and $\mathrm{Var}(H_i)$. While estimation of the former poses no problem, estimation of the latter is more difficult. The difficulty stems from the fact that the distribution of the sample correlation coefficient tends to be skewed, and also that the sample correlation coefficient does not provide interval estimates for the true value of the future correlation coefficient. As shown by R.A. Fisher, however, we can derive the confidence intervals by using a particular function of the sample correlation coefficient H_i, rather than the sample correlation coefficient itself. This function is known as the Fisher "H to z" transformation function.[7]

The Fisher transformation function is given by the following rule:

$$z = \frac{1}{2} \ln \left[\frac{1 + H_i}{1 - H_i} \right] \tag{5.14}$$

Since for each possible value of H_i there exists an unique value of z, and vice-versa, it is possible to convert an H_i value to a z value, make inferences in terms of z, and finally translate these into inferences about H_i. From Equation 5.14 we can derive the following relationship:

$$H_i = \frac{e^{2z} - 1}{1 + e^{2z}} \tag{5.15}$$

For samples of moderate size, the sampling distribution of z is approximately normal, with the sampling variance of z given by

$$\text{Var}(z) = \frac{1}{(T - 3)} \tag{5.16}$$

where T is the number of observations. Using Equation 5.16, we can construct an approximate 95% confidence interval in terms of z, $[z^-$ to $z^+]$, as follows:

$$\left[z - 1.96\sqrt{\frac{1}{T - 3}} \text{ to } z + 1.96\sqrt{\frac{1}{T - 3}} \right]$$

Now, translating the above confidence interval for z to that for H_i, we obtain the following approximate 95% confidence interval in terms of H_i, $[H_i^-$ to $H_i^+]$:

$$\left[\frac{e^{2z-} - 1}{1 + e^{2z-}} \text{ to } \frac{e^{2z+} - 1}{1 + e^{2z+}} \right]$$

Noting that

$$H_i^+ - H_i^- = z(1.96\sigma_{Hi}) \tag{5.17}$$

we obtain the following estimation of $\text{Var}(H_i)$:

$$\text{Var}(H_i) = \left[\frac{H_i^+ - H_i^-}{2(1.96)}\right]^2 \tag{5.18}$$

In estimating the dependence structure of Japanese share prices, we test the following nine forecasting models in this study:

1. Full Historical Model
2. Single-Index Model with the Historical Beta (SIM-H)
3. Single-Index Model with the Adjusted Beta (SIM-V)
4. Industry Multi-Index Model (MIM-I)
5. Overall Mean Model
6. Industry Mean Model
7. Naïve Composite Model
8. Optimal Composite Model
9. Bayesian Composite Model

III. Evaluation Criteria

Two different, but complimentary criteria are employed in evaluating the performance of each of the forecasting models: the mean squared forecast error (MSE) and stochastic dominance in terms of the frequency distribution of the forecast errors (SDF). Given n pairs of corresponding forecasts and actual values (ρ_i, A_i), the MSE criterion measures the seriousness of forecast errors via the calculation:

$$\text{MSE} = \frac{\sum_{i=1}^{n}(\rho_i - A_i)^2}{n} \tag{5.19}$$

To establish the dominance of one model over a second model under the MSE criterion, we first compute the difference, D_i, in the squared forecast errors between each pair of forecasting models for each entry of the correlation matrix:

$$D_i = (\rho_{i1} - A_i)^2 - (\rho_{i2} - A_i)^2 \tag{5.20}$$

where ρ_{i1} and ρ_{i2}, respectively, refer to the forecast values of model 1 and model 2 for the ith entry of the correlation matrix, and A_i refers to the actual value of the entry. Model 1 is judged to dominate Model 2 if the mean of these differences is negative and significantly different from zero at the 5% level. Since each pair of forecasting models produces a "paired" forecast for each entry of the correlation matrix, an ordinary two-tailed T-test can be applied to a "single" mean calculated from the n values of D_i.

To evaluate the forecasting models relative to the benchmark of the Full Historical Model, we compute the Theil Inequality Coefficient (TIC) for each of the forecasting models:

$$\text{TIC} = \left[\frac{\sum_{i=1}^{n} (\rho_i - A_i)^2}{(H_i - A_i)^2} \right] \tag{5.21}$$

where H_i is the value for the ith entry of the full historical correlation matrix. It is clear from Equation 5.21 that TIC > 1, if the forecasts are less accurate than those provided by the historical extrapolation, and TIC < 1 if the opposite is true.[8]

Under the SDF criterion, we examine the distribution of the differences in the squared forecast errors for the purpose of determining if a model is less likely to make any size error than a second model. Taking a pair of models, one model is said to "dominate" the other if its cumulative frequency function of squared forecast errors, $(\rho_i - A_i)^2$, is larger than or equal to that of the other at all intervals and strictly larger at one or more intervals. In this study, we examine the frequency distribution at 15 different intervals.[9] In the absence of a strict stochastic dominance relationship, one model is said to be "superior" to the other if its cumulative frequency function is larger than that of the other at 8 or more intervals out of the 15.

IV. Empirical Results

The most significant finding of the empirical tests is that as a class, the composite models tend to outperform the more traditional models with the Japanese stock market data. Empirical results for the entire sample show that the three composite models are, in fact, the three best performing models, with or without the mean adjustment. This is true under both the MSE and SDF criteria. In particular, the Naïve Composite Model exhibits the best overall performance.

As shown in Panels A and B, respectively, of Table 5.2, the Naïve Composite Model has a lower MSE at a statistically significant level than all other models for both the entire sample and subsample 1. The Optimal Composite and the Bayesian Composite Models rank second and third, respectively; but they are not significantly different from one another in terms of forecasting accuracy. The Industry Mean Model, which was the best performing model tested by Elton and Gruber (1973), ranks fourth. Its MSE is not significantly different from the Bayesian Composite Model, however. The MSE comparison is not quite as clear-cut for subsample 2. As can be seen from Panel C of Table 5.2, the Industry Mean Model ranks first, with the Naïve, Optimal, and Bayesian Composite models ranking second, fourth, and sixth, respectively. Nevertheless, the MSE of the Industry Mean Model is only statistically significantly different from that of the Optimal Composite Model and not the Naïve or the Bayesian Composite Models.

Table 5.3 presents the test results from applying the SDF criterion to the entire sample (Panel A) and the two subsamples (Panels B and C). It can be seen from the table that no single model strictly dominates all of the others. However, as a class, and in general, the composite models tend to produce lower errors of any size than the traditional models. Specifically, the Naïve Composite Model dominates, or is at least superior to, all the other models for both the entire sample and subsample 1. For subsample 2, the Naïve Composite Model places first in overall performance, but it is not superior to either the Bayesian Composite or the Full Historical Model. The Bayesian and Optimal Composite Models have an overall placement of second and third, respectively, for the entire sample and each subsample. Moreover, both of these two models are at least superior to all models with a lower overall placement, except in subsample 2 where neither model is superior to the Full Historical Model.

Our results from testing the more traditional models when using Japanese data are clearly at odds with the earlier work of Elton and Gruber (1973) and Elton, Gruber, and Urich (1978), who used U.S. data. As can be seen from Table 5.2 (with the exception of Panel B) and Table 5.3, the Full Historical Model is superior to the Overall Mean Model for forecasting future correlation coefficients under both the MSE and SDF criteria. This is opposite to the results obtained by Elton and Gruber and Elton, Gruber, and Urich. In addition, the Elton-Gruber-Urich results indicated a distinct superiority of the Overall Mean Model

Table 5.2. Performance, Decomposition of the MSE, and Forecast Characteristics of the Alternative Models (Unadjusted)

Forecasting Model	Performance Measures		Decomposition of MSE			Forecast Characteristics		
	MSE[a]	TIC	U_m	U_v	U_c	ρ	σ_ρ	τ
Panel A: Results from Entire Sample								
1. Naïve Composite	0.0500	0.9074	0.2502	0.3486	0.4011	0.2832	0.0817	0.4258
2. Optimal Composite	0.0509	0.9238	0.2455	0.4714	0.2831	0.2832	0.0587	0.4258
3. Bayesian Composite	0.0516	0.9365	0.2744	0.1649	0.5606	0.2903	0.1214	0.4424
4. Industry Mean	0.0526	0.9546	0.2378	0.3872	0.3749	0.2832	0.0710	0.3528
5. Full Historical	0.0551	1.0000	0.2268	0.0459	0.7273	0.2382	0.1634	0.4258
6. SIM-H	0.0556	1.0091	0.1726	0.2530	0.5744	0.2693	0.0951	0.2139
7. SIM-V	0.0565	1.0254	0.1714	0.3197	0.5089	0.2698	0.0793	0.1510
8. Overall Mean	0.0582	1.0563	0.2150	0.7850	0.0000	0.2832	0.0000	0.0000
9. MIM-I	0.0661	1.1996	0.2522	0.0717	0.6761	0.3005	0.1448	0.2781
Panel B: Results from Subsample 1								
1. Naïve Composite	0.0405	0.8766	0.2329	0.3335	0.4336	0.2650	0.0761	0.4005
2. Optimal Composite	0.0414	0.8961	0.2277	0.5120	0.2603	0.2650	0.0467	0.4005
3. Bayesian Composite	0.0418	0.9048	0.2569	0.1636	0.5795	0.2715	0.1098	0.4269
4. Industry Mean	0.0443	0.9589	0.2129	0.2832	0.5039	0.2560	0.0804	0.2777

5. Full Historical	0.0462	1.0000	0.2043	0.0348	0.7608	0.2650	0.1523	0.4005
6. Overall Mean	0.0465	1.0065	0.2031	0.7968	0.0000	0.2650	0.0000	0.0000
7. SIM-V	0.0488	1.0563	0.1384	0.3307	0.5309	0.2501	0.0653	−0.0313
8. SIM-H	0.0489	1.0584	0.1548	0.2964	0.5488	0.2549	0.0720	0.0319
9. MIM-I	0.0545	1.1797	0.2297	0.0845	0.6857	0.2798	0.1245	0.2199
Panel C: Results from Subsample 2								
1. Industry Mean	0.0599	0.9131	0.3278	0.3028	0.3693	0.3041	0.0970	0.5083
2. Naïve Composite	0.0620	0.9451	0.3164	0.3415	0.3422	0.3041	0.0861	0.4682
3. SIM-H	0.0626	0.9543	0.2288	0.2236	0.5476	0.2836	0.1134	0.3476
4. Optimal Composite	0.0631	0.9619	0.3109	0.4207	0.2683	0.3041	0.0687	0.4682
5. SIM-V	0.0633	0.9649	0.2339	0.2738	0.4922	0.2856	0.1000	0.3282
6. Bayesian Composite	0.0637	0.9710	0.3434	0.1593	0.4973	0.3119	0.1309	0.4772
7. Full Historical	0.0656	1.0000	0.2991	0.0538	0.6471	0.3041	0.1723	0.4682
8. MIM-I	0.0708	1.0793	0.0282	0.1221	0.5957	0.3054	0.1387	0.3437
9. Overall Mean	0.0733	1.1174	0.2677	0.7323	0.0000	0.3041	0.0000	0.0000

a. All differences in MSE are statistically significant at the 5% level, except among the following groups of models (2, 3), (3, 4), and (5, 6, 7) in Panel A; (2, 3), (3, 4), (4, 5, 6), (5, 6, 7, 8), (6, 8), and (7, 8) in Panel B; and (1, 2, 3, 5, 6), (3, 4, 6, 7), (4, 5, 6, 7), (7, 8), and (8, 9) in Panel C.

Table 5.3. Dominance by Cumulative Frequency Distribution of the Squared Forecast Errors[a] (Unadjusted)

Forecasting Model	Naïve Comp.	Opt'l Comp.	Bayes. Comp.	Indu. Mean	Full Hist.	SIM −H	SIM −V	Over. Mean	MIM − I	Total
				PANEL A: Results from Entire Sample						
1. Naïve Composite		13	10	15	14	15	15	15	15	112
2. Optimal Composite	2		5	15	11	15	15	15	15	93
3. Bayesian Composite	5	10		13	14	15	14	15	15	101
4. Industry Mean	0	0	2		6	13	15	15	15	66
5. Full Historical	1	4	1	9		13	13	13	15	69
6. SIM-H	0	0	0	2	2		13	13	15	45
7. SIM-V	0	0	1	0	2	2		11	11.5	27.5
8. Overall Mean	0	0	0	0	2	2	4		8	16
9. MIM-I	0	0	0	0	0	0	3.5	7		10.5
				PANEL B: Results from Subsample 1						
1. Naïve Composite		$9(0.5)^2$	10.5	11	14	14.5	15	15	15	$103(0.5)^4$
2. Optimal Composite	$4(0.5)^2$		5	12	13	15	15	15	15	$94(0.5)^2$
3. Bayesian Composite	4.5	10		12	15	14.5	14	15	15	$99(0.5)^2$
4. Industry Mean	4	3	3		8.5	15	14.5	12	15	$74(0.5)^2$

5. Full Historical	1	2	0	6.5		14	14	10	15	62.5
6. SIM-H	0.5	0	0.5	0	1		$5(0.5)^5$	3	14.5	$23(0.5)^8$
7. SIM-V	0	0	1	0.5	1	$5(0.5)^5$		3	11.5	$21(0.5)^7$
8. Overall Mean	0	0	0	3	5	12	12		13	45
9. MIM-I	0	0	0	0	0	0.5	3.5	2		$5(0.5)^2$
PANEL C: Results from Subsample 2										
1. Naïve Composite		12.5	7.5	9	6.5	12.5	14	15	14	$89(0.5)^4$
2. Optimal Composite	2.5		6.5	9	6.5	11	12	15	14	$75(0.5)^3$
3. Bayesian Composite	7.5	8.5		9	$7(0.5)^4$	$10(0.5)^2$	13	15	15	$84(0.5)^8$
4. Industry Mean	6	6	6		6	6	9	15	8.5	62.5
5. Full Historical	8.5	8.5	$4(0.5)^4$	9		9.5	10	12	13	$73(0.5)^7$
6. SIM-H	2.5	4	$3(0.5)^2$	9	5.5		11.5	15	15	$64(0.5)^5$
7. SIM-V	1	3	2	6	5	3.5		15	12	47.5
8. Overall Mean	0	0	0	0	3	0	0		3.5	6.5
9. MIM-I	1	0	0	6.5	3	0	3	11.5		$24(0.5)^2$

a. A number in the table represents the number of times, out of 15 intervals examined, that the left-hand side model has a larger cumulative frequency function, that is, smaller errors, than the model on the top. In cases where two models have the same cumulative frequency function once or *n* times, that is indicated by (0.5) or $(0.5)^n$, respectively. To facilitate multilateral comparison, the sum of these numbers is provided for each model in the last column.

in comparison to the SIM-H and SIM-V Models. This is not the case with the Japanese data. From Table 5.2, it can be seen that each of the two single index models has a significantly lower MSE in comparison to the MSE of the Overall Mean Model for the entire sample and for subsample 2. For subsample 1, the MSE of the Overall Mean Model is lower, but not significantly different, than the two Single Index Models. From Table 5.3, it can be seen from Panel A for the entire sample (Panel C for subsample 2) that the two Single Index Models are superior to (dominate) the Overall Mean. In Panel B for subsample 1, however, the Overall Mean Model is superior to the SIM-H and SIM-V.

In summary, with Japanese data, as with U.S. data, there appears to be a fairly strong industry factor in the pairwise correlation coefficients which is captured by aggregation at the industry level. This industry factor apparently does not allow itself to be captured by the more behaviorally sophisticated MIM-I model, as is indicated by its generally poor performance under either evaluation criterion. Of the traditional models, the Industry Mean, the Full Historical, and the Overall Mean all predict the same mean correlation coefficient. The Industry Mean Model produces a smaller MSE than the Full Historical, which in turn has a smaller MSE than the Overall Mean. However, in general, the Full Historical Model is superior to either of these two models in terms of the SDF criterion, with the Industry Mean also being at least superior to the Overall Mean. This may suggest that valuable information pertaining to the industry factor is lost in the extreme aggregation of the pairwise correlation coefficients by the Overall Mean Model. It also suggests that there is some random noise in the historical data that prevents the Full Historical Model from capturing the industry factor in the pairwise correlation coefficients as well as does the Industry Mean Model.

In turn, the relative superiority of the composite models could be attributed to their ability to retain the influence of the important industry factor captured by the Full Historical Model, yet eliminate some of its inherent random noise by combining it with the Overall Mean Model by some weighting scheme. The fact that the Naïve Composite Model outperforms the other two composite models suggests that attempting to "fine-tune" the weighting scheme only adds more random noise. Evidence of this is provided by a comparison of the estimated w^* used for the Optimal Composite Model with what the actual w^* turns out to be. For the entire sample and subsamples 1 and 2, w^* was estimated as 0.3596, 0.3069, and 0.3990, respectively. The actual values of w^* turn out to be 0.5569, 0.5060, and 0.6296, respectively. Hence, using a fixed weight of 0.5000, as we did for the Naïve Composite Model, allowed the estimated value to be closer to the actual value than was the case from using a more sophisticated estimation technique.

As was shown by Theil, the MSE can be decomposed into three terms, each of which represents a particular kind of forecast error.[10]

$$\text{MSE} = \frac{\sum_{i=1}^{n}(\rho_i - A_i)^2}{n} = (\bar{\rho} - \bar{A})^2 + (\sigma_\rho - \sigma_A)^2 + 2(1-\tau)\sigma_\rho\sigma_A \tag{5.22}$$

where $(\bar{\rho}, \bar{A})$ and (σ_ρ, σ_A) are, respectively, the means and the standard deviations of the forecast and the actual correlations, and τ is the correlation coefficient between the forecast and the actual correlations. The first term of Equation 5.22 measures the error due to a biased forecast; the second term measures the error due to unequal variation; and the third term measures the error due to an imperfect correlation. Dividing through the right-hand side of Equation 5.22 by the MSE results in three "inequality proportions," which measure the relative importance of the components. These three terms are, respectively, labeled:

Bias proportion $$U_m = \frac{(\bar{\rho} - \bar{A})^2}{\text{MSE}} \tag{5.23a}$$

Variance proportion $$U_v = \frac{(\sigma_\rho - \sigma_A)^2}{\text{MSE}} \tag{5.23b}$$

Covariance proportion $$U_c = \frac{2(1-\tau)\sigma_\rho\sigma_A}{\text{MSE}} \tag{5.23c}$$

Obviously, the three proportions add to unity. An immediate implication of the preceding analysis is that once the MSE criterion is accepted, the character of a forecasting model is fully specified by three parameters: $\bar{\rho}$, σ_ρ, and τ. The values of these parameters were computed for each of the forecasting models, and they are presented in the third panel of Table 5.2. It should be noted that the standard deviation of the forecast correlations, σ_ρ, reflects each model's propensity to differentiate individual pairwise correlations from the forecast mean correlation, $\bar{\rho}$. The lower σ_ρ is, the more aggregate is the forecast that the model provides. Examination of the table clearly indicates that the Overall

Mean Model results in complete aggregation.[11] In addition, it can be seen that the Optimal Composite Model provides the second most aggregate forecast; this is a result of the underestimation of the optimal weight values, w^*, having placed a major emphasis on the overall mean pairwise correlation coefficient.

The middle section of each panel in Table 5.2 provides the inequality proportions for each of the forecasting models. With the exceptions of the Overall Mean Model and the Optimal Composite Model, imperfect correlation, as measured by U_c, is in general the largest source of forecast error. For the seven other models, U_c ranges from 0.3749 for the Industry Mean Model to 0.7273 for the Full Historical Model for the entire sample. For subsample 1 (subsample 2), U_c ranges from 0.4336 (0.3422) for the Naïve Composite Model to 0.7608 (0.6471) for the Full Historical Model. The average U_c for these seven models is 0.5462, 0.5776, and 0.4988 for the entire sample and subsamples 1 and 2, respectively. In like order, the average values of U_m are 0.2265, 0.2043, and 0.2902 and for U_v they are 0.2273, 0.2181, and 0.2110. Noting the results from the entire sample, as presented in Panel A, and the calculation of U_c in Equation 5.23*c*, it is not surprising that the composite models, which as a class perform best, all have a high τ and only a moderate σ_ρ. This suggests that in forecasting correlation coefficients, some aggregation is necessary to eliminate random noise, but no so much as to completely eliminate the unique elements in the historical data, which are possibly due to an industry factor.

As an additional method of testing, we examine the performance when each model is adjusted to have the same forecast of the mean correlation as the average of the historical correlations. Elton and Gruber (1973) and Elton, Gruber, and Urich (1978) noted that this method of performance evaluation is useful in determining to what extent the forecasting accuracy of a model is dependent on its forecast of the mean correlation. As can be seen from Table 5.1, the mean forecast correlation ranges from 0.2693 for SIM-H to 0.3005 for MIM-I for the entire sample. For subsample 1 (subsample 2) the range is from 0.2501 (0.2836) for SIM-V (SIM-H) to 0.2798 (0.3119) for MIM-I (the Bayesian Composite). It can also be seen from the table that the Full Historical, Overall Mean, Industry Mean, and the Naïve and Optimal Composite Models all forecast the mean correlation as the average of the historical correlations. Relative to that value, the Single-Index Models underestimate the mean correlation and the MIM-I and

Table 5.4. Performance and Decomposition of the MSE of the Alternative Forecasting Models (Adjusted)

Forecasting Model	Performance Measures		Decomposition of MSE		
	MSE[a]	TIC	U_m	U_v	U_c
PANEL A: Results from Entire Sample					
1. Bayesian Composite	0.0499	0.9056	0.2503	0.1704	0.5793
2. Naïve Composite	0.0500	0.9074	0.2502	0.3486	0.4011
3. Optimal Composite	0.0509	0.9238	0.2456	0.4714	0.2830
4. Industry Mean	0.0526	0.9546	0.2378	0.3873	0.3749
5. Full Historical	0.0551	1.0000	0.2268	0.0459	0.7273
6. Overall Mean	0.0582	1.0563	0.2150	0.7850	0.0000
7. SIM-H	0.0585	1.0617	0.2137	0.2405	0.5458
8. SIM-V	0.0593	1.0762	0.2108	0.3045	0.4847
9. MIM-I	0.0619	1.1234	0.2019	0.0765	0.7216
PANEL B: Results from Subsample 1					
1. Bayesian Composite	0.0404	0.8745	0.2332	0.1688	0.5980
2. Naïve Composite	0.0405	0.8766	0.2329	0.3335	0.4336
3. Optimal Composite	0.0415	0.8983	0.2278	0.5120	0.2602
4. Industry Mean	0.0443	0.9589	0.2129	0.2832	0.5039
5. Full Historical	0.0462	1.0000	0.2044	0.0348	0.7608
6. Overall Mean	0.0465	1.0065	0.2031	0.7969	0.0000
7. SIM-H	0.0508	1.0996	0.1859	0.2855	0.5286
8. MIM-I	0.0514	1.1126	0.1835	0.0896	0.7269
9. SIM-V	0.0515	1.1147	0.1832	0.3135	0.5033
PANEL C: Results from Subsample 2					
1. Industry Mean	0.0599	0.9131	0.3278	0.3029	0.3693
2. Bayesian Composite	0.0615	0.9375	0.3192	0.1652	0.5157
3. Naïve Composite	0.0620	0.9451	0.3164	0.3415	0.3422
4. Optimal Composite	0.0631	0.9619	0.3109	0.4207	0.2683
5. Full Historical	0.0656	1.0000	0.2991	0.0538	0.6471
6. SIM-H	0.0679	1.0351	0.2890	0.2062	0.5048
7. SIM-V	0.0681	1.0381	0.2882	0.2544	0.4574
8. MIM-I	0.0704	1.0732	0.2786	0.1227	0.5988
9. Overall Mean	0.0733	1.1174	0.2677	0.7323	0.0000

a. All differences in the MSE are statistically significant at the 5% level, except among the following groups of models: (1, 2), (1, 3), (6, 7, 8), and (8, 9) in Panel A; (1, 2), (1, 3), (4, 5, 6, 8), and (7, 8, 9) in Panel B; and (1, 2, 3), (2, 4), (4, 5, 6, 7, 8), and (8, 9) in Panel C.

Table 5.5. Dominance by Cumulative Frequency Distribution of the Squared Forecast Errors[a] (Adjusted)

Forecasting Model	Bayes. Comp.	Naïve Comp.	Opt'l. Comp.	Indu. Mean	Full Hist.	Over. Mean	SIM −H	SIM −V	MIM −I	Total
PANEL A: Results from Entire Sample										
1. Bayesian Composite		10	11	13	14	15	15	15	15	108
2. Naïve Composite	5		13	14	14	15	15	15	15	106
3. Optimal Composite	4	2		14	11	15	15	15	15	91
4. Industry Mean	2	1	1		6	15	15	15	9	64
5. Full Historical	1	1	4	9		13	13	13	15	69
6. Overall Mean	0	0	0	0	2		11	11	5	29
7. SIM-H	0	0	0	0	2	4		11.5	3.5	$20(0.5)^2$
8. SIM-V	0	0	0	0	2	4	3.5		2	11.5
9. MIM-I	0	0	0	6	0	10	11.5	13		40.5
PANEL B: Results from Subsample 1										
1. Bayesian Composite		$9(0.5)^2$	11	$12(0.5)^2$	15	15	15	15	15	$107(0.5)^4$
2. Naïve Composite	$4(0.5)^2$		$9(0.5)^2$	11	14	15	14.5	15	15	$97(0.5)^5$
3. Optimal Composite	4	$4(0.5)^2$		12	13	15	15	15	15	$93(0.5)^2$
4. Industry Mean	$1(0.5)^2$	4	3		8.5	12	15	15	14	$72(0.5)^3$
5. Full Historical	0	1	2	6.5		10	14	14	11.5	$58(0.5)^2$

6. Overall Mean	0	0	0	3	5		14	14.5	8.5	$44(0.5)^2$
7. SIM-H	0	0.5	0	0	1	1		$11(0.5)^2$	2	$15(0.5)^3$
8. SIM-V	0	0	0	0	1	0.5	$2(0.5)^2$		2	$5(0.5)^3$
9. MIM-I	0	0	0	1	3.5	6.5	13	13		$36(0.5)^2$
PANEL C: Results from Subsample 2										
1. Bayesian Composite		10	10	10	12	15	14	14	15	100
2. Naïve Composite	5		12.5	9	6.5	15	15	15	14	$91(0.5)^2$
3. Optimal Composite	5	2.5		9	6.5	15	15	14.5	14	$80(0.5)^3$
4. Industry Mean	5	6	6		6	15	13	13	8.5	72.5
5. Full Historical	3	8.5	8.5	9		12	12.5	13	12	$77(0.5)^3$
6. Overall Mean	0	0	0	0	3		2	3	$2(0.5)^2$	$10(0.5)^2$
7. SIM-H	1	0	0	2	2.5	13		11.5	4.5	$33(0.5)^3$
8. SIM-V	1	0	0.5	2	2	12	3.5		2	$22(0.5)^2$
9. MIM-I	0	1	1	6.5	3	$11(0.5)^2$	10.5	13		$45(0.5)^4$

a. A number in the table represents the number of times, out of 15 intervals examined, that the left-hand side model has a larger cumulative frequency function, that is, smaller errors, than the model on the top. In cases where two models have the same cumulative frequency function once or *n* times, out of 15 intervals, that is indicated by 0.5 or $(0.5)^n$, respectively. To facilitate multilateral comparison, the sum of these numbers is provided for each model in the last column.

Bayesian Composite Models overestimate the mean correlation. Considering that the mean of the actual correlations is 0.1713 for the entire sample, 0.1679 for subsample 1, and 0.1640 for subsample 2, all of the forecasting models overestimate the actual mean correlations. But some models do so more than others. Hence, the bias of a model is altered by making a mean adjustment. In our samples, the models that overestimate the mean correlation relative to the average of the historical correlations will have a reduction in bias, and vice-versa.

Table 5.4 presents the MSE performance results and Table 5.5 the SDF results of the forecasting models when the forecasts of each model are mean adjusted. Tables 5.4 and 5.5 are the direct counterparts to the unadjusted results presented in Tables 5.2 and 5.3, respectively. The most notable change caused by the mean adjustment, as can be seen from Table 5.4, is the improvement in ranking of the Bayesian Composite Model due to the bias reduction. The Bayesian Composite Model now ranks first for both the entire sample and subsample 1 instead of third, and it ranks second in subsample 2 instead of sixth. Moreover, by the SDF criterion, as evidenced by Table 5.5, the Bayesian Composite Model now dominates, or is superior to, all other models. In general, the Naïve Composite Model performs second best by either criterion; however, its MSE is not significantly larger than the Bayesian Composite Model's MSE for the entire sample or either subsample. In addition, the Naïve Composite Model is never strictly dominated by the Bayesian Composite. This suggests that the extra computational effort required to "fine-tune" a composite model to achieve a slightly superior performance than the Naïve Composite Model may not be justifiable. The simple Naïve Composite Model performs very well overall with Japanese data.

V. Concluding Remarks

The purpose of this paper was to assist in making modern portfolio theory amenable to the Japanese securities markets and to expand the knowledge of modern portfolio theory in general. To this end, we have evaluated the performance of nine alternative forecasting models that can be used to estimate the correlation structure of Japanese share prices, or any country's share prices. Three of the models we tested are new, and they can be classified as composite models. As is conventional with the literature, the results from the Full Historical Model were used as the benchmark against which the other eight models were evaluated.

The most important result emerging from our empirical tests is that as a class, the composite models tended to be superior to the more traditional models employed in the previous studies. Specifically, the Naïve Composite Model produced the best overall results in terms of forecast accuracy when the individual forecast correlations were unadjusted. When each pairwise forecast correlation was adjusted by the mean of the historical correlations, the Bayesian Composite Model produced slightly, but not significantly, superior results than did the Naïve Composite Model. This suggests that efforts to "fine-tune" the composite forecasting models are not justifiable. Because of the relative ease of forecasting correlation coefficients by the Naïve Composite Model, the results of this study should be beneficial to making modern portfolio theory applicable to the Japanese stock market.

It was also noted that the results of our unadjusted tests of the traditional models were clearly at odds with the results obtained by Elton and Gruber and Elton, Gruber, and Urich when using U.S. data. Our mean adjusted tests of these models were consistent with their results, except for the fact that the Full Historical Model performed very well when using Japanese data while it did not with U.S. data. We interpret this result as implying that there is a strong industry factor in Japanese data that is captured by the Full Historical Model.

Appendix

Industry and Subsample Membership of Sample Firms

Name	Industry	Subsample
1. Ajinomoto	Consumer Goods	2
2. Asahi Brewery	Consumer Goods	1
3. Asahi Chemical	Chemicals	2
4. Banyo Chemical	Chemicals	2
5. Bridgestone Tire	Capital Equipment & Components	2
6. Calpis Food	Consumer Goods	1
7. Canon	Leisure, Tourism, & Airlines	2
8. Chiyoda Chemical Engineering	Capital Equipment & Components	2
9. Daiei	Merchandising, Wholesale, & Int'l Trade	2
10. Daiichi Kangyo Bank	Finance	2

Industry and Subsample Membership of Sample Firms (continued)

Name	Industry	Subsample
11. Daimaru	Merchandising, Wholesale, & Int'l Trade	2
12. Daishowa Paper	Materials	2
13. Daiwa Bank	Finance	1
14. Fuji Bank	Finance	2
15. Fuji Photo Film	Leisure, Tourism, & Airlines	2
16. Fugisawa Pharmaceutical	Consumer Goods	1
17. Fujitsu	Electrical & Electronics	1
18. Hattori	Leisure, Tourism, & Airlines	1
19. Hitachi	Electrical & Electronics	2
20. Honda Motor	Automobiles	2
21. Ishikawajima-Harima	Capital Equipment & Components	1
22. Isuzu Motors	Automobiles	1
23. Itoh (C.) & Co.	Merchandising, Wholesale, & Int'l Trade	1
24. Japan Airlines	Leisure, Tourism, & Airlines	1
25. Kajima	Capital Equipment & Components	1
26. Kanegafuchi Chemical	Chemicals	1
27. Kansai Electric Power	Energy	2
28. Kao (Soap)	Consumer Goods	1
29. Kawasaki Heavy	Capital Equipment & Components	1
30. Kirin Brewery	Consumer Goods	2
31. Kamatsu	Capital Equipment & Components	2
32. Kubota	Capital Equipment & Components	2
33. Kyoto Ceramic (Kyocera)	Materials	2
34. Makita Electric	Electrical & Electronics	2
35. Marubeni	Merchandising, Wholesale, & Int'l Trade	2
36. Matsushita Electrical Industrial	Electrical & Electronics	2
37. Mitsubishi Chemical	Chemicals	1
38. Mitsubishi Corp.	Merchandising, Wholesale, & Int'l Trade	1
39. Mitsubishi Heavy	Capital Equipment & Components	1
40. Mitsukoshi	Merchandising, Wholesale, & Int'l Trade	1

Industry and Subsample Membership of Sample Firms (continued)

Name	Industry	Subsample
41. Mitsui & Co.	Merchandising, Wholesale, & Int'l Trade	2
42. Nippon Electric (NEC)	Electrical & Electronics	2
43. Nippon Kokan	Materials	1
44. Nippon Oil	Energy	2
45. Nippon Sheet Glass	Materials	1
46. Nippon Steel	Materials	2
47. Nissan Motors	Automobiles	2
48. Nomura Securities	Finance	2
49. Oki Electric	Electrical & Electronics	1
50. Osaka Gas	Energy	1
51. Pioneer Electronics	Consumer Goods	2
52. Ricoh	Electrical & Electronics	1
53. Sankyo Co.	Consumer Goods	1
54. Sanwa Bank	Finance	1
55. Sanyo Electric	Consumer Goods	2
56. Sharp	Consumer Goods	1
57. Shiseido	Consumer Goods	2
58. Showa Denko	Chemicals	1
59. Sony	Consumer Goods	2
60. Sumitomo Bank	Finance	1
61. Takeda Chemical	Chemicals	1
62. TDK Electronics	Electrical & Electronics	1
63. Teijin	Chemicals	2
64. Tokio Marine & Fire Insurance	Finance	2
65. Tokyo Electric Power	Energy	1
66. Toray	Chemicals	2
67. Toyo Kogyo	Automobiles	1
68. Toyota Motor	Automobiles	1
69. Victor Co. of Japan	Consumer Goods	1
70. Wacoal	Consumer Goods	2
71. Yamaha Motor	Leisure, Tourism, & Airlines	1
72. Yasuda Fire & Marine	Finance	1

Notes

1. For a detailed discussion of these models, refer to Cohen and Pogue (1967), Elton and Gruber (1973), Elton, Gruber, and Urich (1978), Jobson, Korkie, and Ratti (1979), Markowitz (1959), and Sharpe (1963).
2. The division of data into a six-year estimation period and a four-year forecast period is similar to the proportional split employed by Elton and Gruber (1973) and Elton, Gruber, and Urich (1978) in their studies of U.S. correlation structure.
3. For a detailed discussion of this type of adjustment, see Vasicek (1973).
4. Underlying the Industry Multi-Index Model of Equation 5.3 is the assumption that the inclusion of additional industry indices is likely to add random noise rather than additional information.
5. Elton and Gruber (1973) found that the Industry Mean and the Overall Mean Models outperformed the Full Historical and the Single– and Multi-Index Models in forecasting the dependence structure of U.S. share prices.
6. It is pointed out that the adjustment technique of the Bayesian Composite Model is essentially in the same spirit as that used by Vasicek (1973) in adjusting the sample estimate of beta.
7. Refer to Winkler and Hays (1975, pp. 652–655) for a detailed discussion of the Fisher transformation function.
8. See Theil (1971, p. 28) for a detailed discussion of the Inequality Coefficient.
9. Fifteen intervals are taken over the error size range of 0.000 to 0.220, at which the cumulative frequency distribution reaches at least 0.9286 for all of the models. Due to the heavy skewness of the relative frequency distribution toward zero, intervals are taken over increasing distances, that is, the first four intervals are of 0.005, the second four intervals are of 0.010, the next five intervals are of 0.020, and the last two intervals are of 0.030.
10. Refer to Theil (1971, p. 29) for a detailed discussion of the decomposition of the MSE.
11. For the Overall Mean Model, U_c is zero because it offers a uniform forecast for each and every pairwise correlation; consequently, it will have a very high value for U_v. The opposite is true for the Full Historical, the most disaggregate model; it has a very high U_c value, whereas U_v is close to zero.

References

Cohen, Kalman, and Gerald Pogue, (1967). "An Empirical Evaluation of Alternative Portfolio Selection Models." *Journal of Business*, Vol. 45, April, pp. 166–193.

Elton, Edwin, and Martin Gruber, (1973). "Estimating the Dependence Structure of Share Prices—Implications for Portfolio Selection," *Journal of Finance*, Vol. 28, December, pp. 1203–1232.

Elton, Edwin, Martin Gruber, and Thomas Urich, (1978). "Are Betas Best?" *Journal of Finance*, Vol. 33, December, pp. 1375–1384.

Jobson, J., B. Korkie, and V. Ratti, (1979). "Improved Estimation for Markowitz Portfolios Using James-Stein Type Estimators." *Proceedings of the American Statistical Association, Business and Economic Statistics Section*, pp. 279–284.

Lintner, John, (1965). "The Valuation of Risk Assets and the Selection of Risky Investments in Stock Portfolios and Capital Budgets." *The Review of Economics and Statistics*, Vol. 47, February, pp. 13–37.

Markowitz, Harry, (1959). *Portfolio Selection*, New York, John Wiley and Sons.

Mossin, Jan, (1966). "Equilibrium in a Capital Asset Market," *Econometrica*, Vol. 34, October, pp. 768–783.

Sharpe, William F., (1963). "A Simplified Model of Portfolio Analysis," *Management Science*, Vol. 10, January.

Sharpe, William F., (1964). "Capital Asset Prices: A Theory of Market Equilibrium Under Conditions of Risk," *Journal of Finance*, Vol. 19, September, pp. 425–442.

Theil, Henri, (1971). *Applied Economic Forecasting*, Amsterdam, North-Holland.

Tobin, J., (1958). "Liquidity Preferences as Behavior Towards Risk," *The Review of Economic Studies*, Vol. 26, February, pp. 65–86.

Vasicek, Oldrich, (1973). "A Note on Using Cross-sectional Information in Bayesian Estimation of Security Betas," *Journal of Finance*, Vol. 28, December, pp. 1233–1239.

Winkler, Robert L., and William L. Hays, (1975). *Statistics: Probability, Inference, and Decision*, 2nd ed., New York, Holt, Rinehart and Winston.

6

A Multi-Index Risk Model of the Japanese Stock Market*

Edwin J. Elton
Nomura Professor of Finance, The Graduate School of Business Administration, New York University

Martin J. Gruber
Nomura Professor of Finance, The Graduate School of Business Administration, New York University

The two largest stock exchanges in the world are in Tokyo and New York. The Tokyo Stock Exchange is now larger than the New York Stock Exchange in the aggregate market value of listed companies. Despite the size and importance of the Japanese market there is a paucity of research on Japanese security markets compared to the enormous amount of research on U.S. securities markets.

One of the major current areas of research in U.S. markets is estimating the influences or factors that affect returns.[1] Identifying these influences and estimating the return-generating process is important for a multitude of applications, such as estimating the variance-covariance structure of returns, for equilibrium pricing, and for event studies. This study is of interest both because it examines a different (and important) market than that examined in previous studies and because it uses methodology that has not previously been employed. To the best of our knowledge, this is the first examination of the number of factors affecting Japanese security prices.

Our methodology differs from past methodology in two ways. First, we employ a new set of statistical techniques to examine the hypothe-

* This paper owes much to our collaboration with the quantitative analysis team of the Nomura Securities group (MERRIT 21). In particular, our research would have been almost impossible without the efforts by two individuals, Mr. Y. Akeda and Mr. Y. Kato of the Nomura Research Institute.

sized return-generating structure across samples at a point in time. This allows us to determine whether the structure is a common structure or unique to a particular sample. Second, we examine the reasonableness of our estimated return-generating process by examining how useful it is for decision making in a forecast mode. There are a number of alternative ways that a return-generating process can be estimated; there are arguments for and against each. One test that any estimated model ought to meet is that its use leads to better decisions.

The paper is divided into five sections. In the first section, we examine how many factors are in the return-generating process for Japanese securities and discuss the estimation of these factors. In the second section, we compare the performance of our multifactor return-generating process to the single-index model as a model for describing security returns. In the third section, we examine how well our return-generating model performs, compared to a single-index model, for decision making purposes. In the fourth section, we examine how well the return-generating process, which was determined on statistical grounds, can be explained in terms of economic variables.

Though the analysis in the first three sections develops and tests a risk structure for Japanese stock prices, the fourth section begins the exploration of a new topic. For many modeling purposes, for example, the creation of index funds, all that is needed is a model that describes the pattern of returns and that is reasonably robust over time. However, it is useful if the statistically derived indexes are associated with economic influences. This is true for it raises our confidence that the indexes we have found are not due to chance, and it may lead eventually to the development of a forecasting model based on macrovariables. In the fourth section of this paper we present some evidence that the indexes we have developed in the earlier sections are in fact associated with economic variables. Although the analysis is preliminary at this stage, it suggests that further research in this area might be fruitful. In the fifth section we return to the indexes developed in earlier sections and perform standard A.P.T. tests to examine how many factors are priced in the sense that greater sensitivity to these factors leads to differential average return.

I. Identifying the Factors

The first step we use to estimate the return-generating process involves factor analyzing the historical time series of returns. The advantages and disadvantages of using factor analysis to identify the influences present in the return generating process are well documented in the literature of financial economics.[2] One key aspect of the controversy over the use of factor analysis is the problem of identifying the number of factors that are significant in explaining the covariance structure of security returns.[3] A large part of the problem stems from our inability to factor analyze large numbers of securities. Two methods have been introduced to deal with this problem. The first involves performing factor analysis on subsets or groups of securities. This multisample approach was introduced by Roll and Ross (1980). The second is the portfolio approach introduced by Chen (1983).

In the group or multisample approach, securities are divided into samples and maximum likelihood factor analysis is used to extract factors from each sample.[4] The difficulty with this approach is that the factors extracted in each sample need not be extracted in the same order or even with the same sign. How then can one determine whether one has extracted the same factors or different factors (unique to each group) as one goes from group to group? Although this is a problem, its solution represents an opportunity to improve our identification of the return-generating process when we use the grouping technique. By analyzing the factors produced from different groups and identifying those influences that are common across two or more groups, we can differentiate between unique and general factors.

Chen's portfolio approach rests on examining the return behavior of portfolios of securities rather than individual issues. There are two disadvantages to this approach. First, no matter how large the sample used to form portfolios, one cannot tell whether one has measured factors unique to that sample or general factors common to all securities. Second, the results obtained by this methodology are very sensitive to the portfolio formation technique employed.

There are two previous papers, Cho (1984) and Brown and Weinstein (1983), which sought, as we will, to identify the common factors across groups. Cho (1984) used interbattery factor analysis, a technique that looks directly at the intergroup correlation matrix to produce estimates of the number of factors. This technique allows the estimation of the number of common factors present for any particular significance level. The results reported by Cho (1984) show that the number of factors found

1. Is very sensitive to the significance level selected.

2. Depends on the members of the sample. The number of factors found across 21 samples varied from three to nine.

A related approach was used by Brown and Weinstein. They divided a group into two subgroups and performed factor analysis on each subgroup and on the overall group. They examined differences in the unexplained sum of squares between the overall group and the total of the two subgroups. Since the unexplained sum of squares is unaffected by an orthogonal transformation of any factor structure, Brown and Weinstein could compare the residual sum of squares from the subgroups with the residual sum of squares from the overall group with the same number of factors extracted. If the factors from one group are merely an orthogonal transformation of the factors from a second group, the residual sum of squares should not be statistically different.

Our major tests are very much in the spirit of the Cho and Brown and Weinstein papers. We initially divide our 393 stock sample into four samples, each containing either 98 or 99 stocks.[5] We then perform maximum likelihood factor analysis within each of the four samples. While we examine some standard estimating techniques to determine the number of factors within a sample, our primary tool to determine the number of factors is to test whether the factors extracted from any sample are linear transformations of the factors extracted from other samples. We use canonical correlation to perform these tests.

The remainder of this section is divided into three parts: In the first, we briefly describe our overall sample. In the second we discuss the method used and the empirical results in determining the number of factors. In the third, we discuss the determination of which factor solution we use as the return-generating process.

Sample Selection

Our sample was the 400 stocks comprising the NRI 400 stock index. We were interested in the NRI 400 stock index because it is one of the most widely used indexes in Japan. In addition, the 400 stocks in the index constitute 70.9% of the total capitalization of the first section of the Tokyo Stock Exchange and 62.9% of the total Tokyo Stock Exchange. The value of the NRI 400 was 266,092 billion yen and 1905 billion dollars as of April 1987.

We had 180 months of price and dividend data on the stocks making up the NRI Index: from April 1971 through March 1986. Because of missing data we had to delete 7 of the 400 stocks. The remaining 393 stocks were broken into four samples, with the first three samples containing 98 stocks and the fourth, 99 stocks. The four subsamples were formed both because of the limitations of the maximum likelihood factor analysis program employed and because of the advantages of testing factor structures across different samples. It is to this topic that we now turn.

How Many Factors?

Tests of the appropriate number of factors to include in the return-generating process can be separated into those that look at one group at a time and those that take advantage of the fact that solutions for more than one group have been obtained. Although we will emphasize the latter because, as explained in what follows, it considers the commonality of the factors selected, we will briefly examine the standard single group tests.

Single Group Tests. To obtain an initial idea of how many factors might be present in the return-generating process, 10 factor solutions (using maximum likelihood factor analysis) were performed on each of our four samples. That is, for each sample, a maximum likelihood solution involving first one factor, then two factors, then three factors, and continuing through 10 factors was found. There are three commonly used techniques, in the literature on factor analysis, which are employed to decide on the correct number of factors needed to explain the covariance matrix. These are Chi Square (Lawley & Maxwell, 1971), Akaike's Information Criteria (Akaike, 1974), and Schwartz's Baysian Criteria (Schwartz, 1978). Of these three criteria, Schwartz's is the most conservative in estimating the number of significant factors. The Chi Square Test and Akaike's Information Criteria tend to include factors that, while statistically significant, have little economic importance. When we use either of the latter two tests the results show that there are at least 10 factors present, for each sample, in the return-generating process. We did not test for the optimum number since we had not performed factor solutions involving the extraction of more than 10 factors and since our alternative tests and previous attempts by others to identify the return generation processes on other samples of securities indicate the presence of fewer than 10 factors.[6]

When we employ Schwartz's Baysian Criteria we get a much more parsimonious description of the return-generating process. Schwartz's criteria produces a statistic that reaches its minimum at the "correct" number of factors extracted. The value of Schwartz's statistic for each group for alternative numbers of factors 1 through 10 is shown in Figure 6.1. Schwartz's criteria identified three factors as significant in the return-generating process for sample 1, and four factors for samples 2, 3, and 4.

The conclusion from examining the number of factors present in the return-generating process of each sample separately is somewhat ambiguous. It rests on the choice of the test employed to determine significance. The answer would seem to be either 4 or 10, or more. The next step is to use information from more than one group to decide on the number of factors.

Multiple-Group Tests. The intent of our analysis is to estimate a return-generating process that describes the return on all stocks that are like the stocks in the NRI 400 Index. When we examine any one of our four samples as we add more factors to the solution, we increase the probability that the added factors are idiosyncratic to the stocks in that sample or subset of those stocks rather than factors that explain the covariance structure of returns among large groups of securities. If, in fact, our factor solution from a sample has measured general influences, then the solution from a second group should capture the same general influences. However, we cannot simply compare the first factor from a sample with the first factor from another sample and the second with the second, et cetera. Factor solutions are not unique up to a linear transformation. Therefore the first factor from one sample may be the second factor from a second sample or even a linear combination of the first, second, third, and fourth factors from the second sample. Although there are some attributes of maximum likelihood factor analysis that will tend to extract factors in a parallel manner, and to some extent lessen this problem, they do not eliminate it.[7] There is a method for correcting this problem.

What we would like to do for an *n*-factor solution is to find that linear combination of the *n* factors from one sample that is most highly correlated with the best linear combination of the *n* factors from a second sample. After removing this correlation we would like to find the second linear combination of the *n* factors from the first sample that is

Figure 6.1. Schwartz's Baysian Criterion

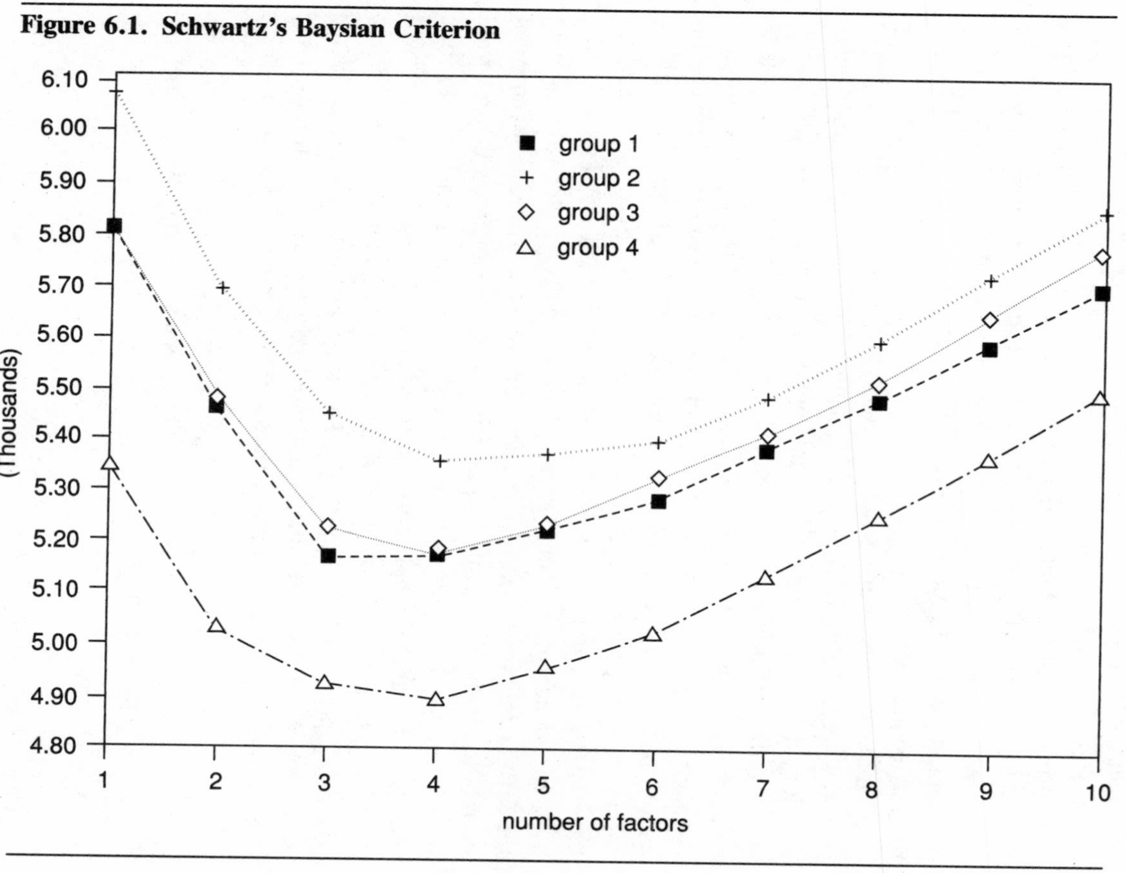

most highly correlated with the linear combination of the n factors from the second sample. We would like to do this n times. This is exactly what canonical correlation does. By finding best-fit linear combinations it removes the problem of the factors from one sample being linear transformations of the factors from a second sample. If, in fact, one has estimated too many factors—for example, n instead of $n - k$—then the $n - k + 1$ canonical variates (linear combination of the n factors) from one sample should be uncorrelated with the $n - k + 1$ canonical variate from a second sample.

In Table 6.1 we present the average (across four samples) squared canonical correlation for the first canonical variate out of the one-factor solution, the second canonical variate out of the two-factor solution, proceeding through the seventh canonical variate out of the seven-factor solution. Examining these results it appears likely that the correct solution is either four or five factors. The association of the fourth linear combination from a four-factor solution is almost 60%, while for the fifth linear combination from a five-factor solution it is just above 20%, and for the sixth linear combination of the six-factor solution it is less than 5%.

The evidence so far would seem to support a four-factor solution with the fifth factor worth considering. Though we have argued that canonical correlation is the correct way to determine whether factor structures from one group are the same as those from a second group, it is worthwhile taking a look at the simple correlation pattern between factors. This will allow us to see the type of orthogonal transformation that can take place. Table 6.2 presents the simple correlation between the factors extracted from samples 1 and 2 for the four-factor and five-factor solutions. Note that in the four-factor solution, the only correlations above 0.10 occur

Table 6.1. Canonical R, ith Canonical R^2 from the i Factor Solution

i	R^2
1	0.929
2	0.799
3	0.664
4	0.589
5	0.211
6	0.043
7	0.028

Table 6.2. An Example of a Factor Pattern: Correlation of Factor between Samples 1 and 2

sample 1:	F1	F2	F3	F4	F5
		1. Four Factors			
F1	0.974	—	—	—	
F2	—	0.895	—	—	
F3	—	—	0.904	—	
F4	—	—	—	0.690	
		2. Five Factors			
F1	0.973	—	—	—	—
F2	—	0.863	—	0.220	—
F3	—	—	0.901	—	—
F4	—	—	—	—	0.721
F5	—	0.174	−0.185	—	—

Note: dash = less than 0.1

for the first factor from sample 1 with the first factor from sample 2, the second with the second, et cetera. When we go to the five-factor solution the clear pattern fractures. In addition to the correlation pattern being much less clear, some factors from one group do not seem to be associated at all with factors from the other group. For example, factor 5 from sample 1 and factor 4 from sample 2 have only minimal correlation with any of the factors arrived at from the other group. Once again we see support for the four-factor solution.

Correlation Test. As a final check on the decision to use a four-factor model, we examined the association between solutions involving alternative numbers of factors and returns over time. We could have examined this for individual stocks or for the market as a whole but instead decided to employ a portfolio approach. The portfolio approach is not only useful for estimating time series association, it will allow us to obtain better estimates of sensitivities and will be useful later in this paper in examining cross-sectional relationships. Because we wished to form portfolios for cross-sectional testing as well as time series analysis, we wished to have portfolios that would have differences in average return. An instrumental variable was needed for return. Because of the documentation of the size effect in the Japanese market (as well as the

U.S. market), size was chosen as the instrumental variable.[8] The 393 stocks in our sample were divided into 20 portfolios based on size.

These portfolios were formed every month and the returns computed over the next month. For each portfolio the returns were regressed against the two–, three–, four–, five–, and six-factor solutions from each of our samples. The average R^2 for each of the four solutions (one from each sample) over the 20 groups is shown in Table 6.3 and plotted in Figure 6.2. The additional explanatory power from increasing the number of factors beyond four is very small in absolute terms and relative to the contribution of the first four factors. This reinforces the earlier evidence that four factors are adequate to define the return-generating process for large stocks in the Tokyo Stock Exchange.

Which Four-Factor Solution?

Having decided to employ a four-factor model we still have a problem to solve. We have four different four-factor models, one derived from each of our four samples. One must be selected as the basis for the remainder of our tests. This is not as important a decision as it may at first seem. We know from the results of our canonical correlation tests that each of the sets of four factors (actually linear transformations of the four factors) are very highly correlated with each other. We have previously presented evidence that the four factors are capturing the same fundamental influences in the return-generating process and hence it should not make much difference which of the four factor solutions we use.

Nevertheless, we have to make a choice of one solution (or sample) to use for the remainder of this study. To make this choice we performed two types of tests. The first looked at the R^2 of each of our sample four-factor solutions with two different return series. The second examined the residual correlation of returns after the correlation with the four indexes had been removed.

Table 6.3. Average R^2 Across 20 Size Portfolios with Alternative Factor Solutions

	2 Factors	3 Factors	4 Factors	5 Factors	6 Factors
Sample 1	0.686	0.713	0.771	0.772	0.772
Sample 2	0.663	0.700	0.763	0.777	0.779
Sample 3	0.673	0.681	0.764	0.768	0.769
Sample 4	0.678	0.731	0.763	0.770	0.775

Figure 6.2. R^2 **of Factors with 20 Portfolios**

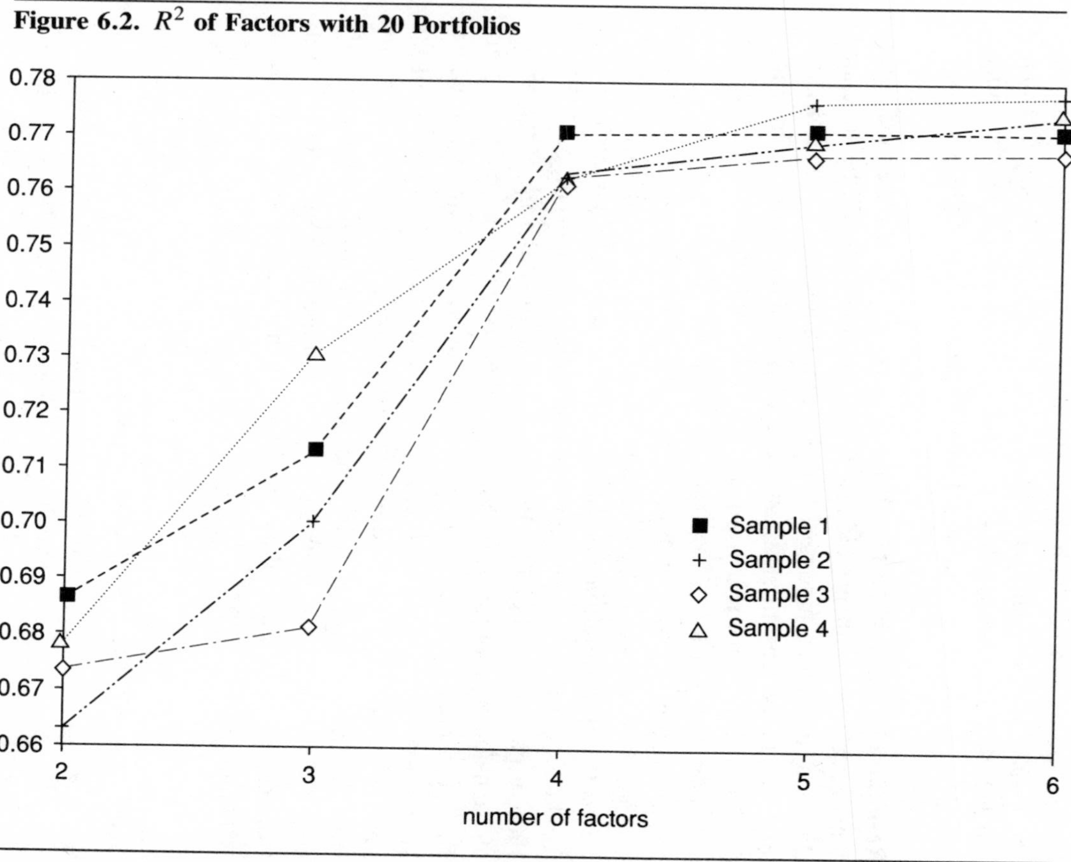

Correlation Tests. Table 6.4 presents for each of the four-factor solutions (one from each sample) both the correlation with a value-weighted index of the first section of the Tokyo Stock Exchange and the average correlation with the 20 portfolios formed from the NRI 400. The results are very similar across the four samples. It appears that it makes little difference which of the samples (factor solutions) we pursue, though those based on samples 1 and 3 appear to do slightly better.

Residual Correlation Test. If we have correctly identified the return-generating process then residuals from our model should be unrelated. One way to choose among the alternative candidates is to look at the model that produces the smallest average residual correlation. Once again the 20 portfolios formed from the NRI 400 were used to perform the test. For each portfolio, the residuals from the four-factor model were computed at each moment in time. The correlations between all pairwise combinations of residuals were computed. Since we had 20 portfolios, we had 190 correlation coefficients. Since we had four estimates of the factor structures, we had four different estimates of each of the 190 correlation coefficients. We can examine the ordering of the ability of each factor solution to produce residual correlations close to zero. Table 6.5 presents this ordering of factor solutions from best to worst. While few of the entries are statistically significant, the ordering of the sample factor solutions is similar to that found earlier, with the factor solution from sample 1 being the best and that from sample 3 only slightly inferior. Based on these tests we will use the four factor solutions from sample 1 as the model of the return-generating process through the remainder of this paper.

Table 6.4. R^2 with Four-Factor Solutions

	from Sample 1	**from Sample 2**	**from Sample 3**	**from Sample 4**
TSE First Section:	0.925	0.902	0.928	0.912
Average with 20 size portfolios from Nomura 400:	0.771	0.763	0.764	0.763

Table 6.5. Differences in the Absolute Value of the Correlation Coefficient

	Column Value minus Row Value			
	1	3	2	4
1		−0.0051 (0.0047)	−0.0081 (0.0050)	−0.0161 (0.0039)
3			−0.0029 (0.0056)	−0.0110 (0.0054)
2				−0.0081 (0.0042)

The numbers not in brackets represent the absolute value of the correlations from the sample shown in the left hand column, minus the absolute value of the residual correlation from the sample shown at the top of the table. Thus, a negative number indicates the sample on the left performed better (produced lower residual correlation). These are mean differences and the numbers shown in parentheses are the standard deviation of the mean.

Summary on the Choice of a Factor Structure

Up to this point we have investigated the estimation of the return-generating process. Based on single group tests and canonical correlation tests that look for common influences across groups, we have concluded that there are four factors present in the return-generating process for large Japanese stocks. We have shown that while these factors can be estimated from any of our samples, sample 1 is certainly no worse than the other samples and so will be used for future testing. We will now turn to an examination of both the explanatory power of the four-factor model and the stability of the sensitivity to factors over time.

II. Model Explanatory Power and Factor Sensitivity Sationarity

Having determined that returns are related to four factors and having produced a particular four-factor solution, the next step is to examine how much of the total return is explained by these four factors and to compare this to the amount explained by the more conventional single-index model.

To examine this, we utilized the 20 groups ranked by size and discussed in the previous section. Grouping will of course increase the amount explained by any model. At the same time it creates a manageable set of data that can allow not only an examination of average explanatory power but an examination of explanatory power across sets of stocks.

Table 6.6 shows the sensitivities and adjusted R^2 when the returns on each of the 20 portfolios are regressed against the four factors for the 15-year period April 1971 to March 1986. Across the 20 portfolios the average adjusted R^2 is 78%. Of the 80 different sensitivity estimates all but 18 are significant at the 5% level.

As a standard of comparison we utilized the single-index model. This

Table 6.6. Sensitivities and Explanatory Power for the Four-Factor Model

	Beta Coefficients				
	F1	**F2**	**F3**	**F4**	**Adj R^2**
1	0.0428	0.0092	−0.0088	−0.0199	0.8168
2	0.0442	0.0048	−0.0048	−0.0203	0.8201
3	0.0427	0.0034	−0.0067	−0.0158	0.8580
4	0.0417	−0.0003*	−0.0060	−0.0137	0.8239
5	0.0421	0.0041	−0.0001*	−0.0121	0.7516
6	0.0396	0.0022*	−0.0030*	−0.0066	0.7689
7	0.0388	0.0077	0.0034*	−0.0028*	0.7504
8	0.0380	0.0078	0.0013*	0.0013*	0.7767
9	0.0417	0.0059	0.0011*	0.0010*	0.8130
10	0.0356	0.0025*	0.0020*	0.0001*	0.7266
11	0.0375	0.0023*	0.0071	0.0051	0.7732
12	0.0384	−0.0007*	0.0101	0.0053	0.7642
13	0.0347	−0.0037	0.0104	0.0084	0.7479
14	0.0374	−0.0029*	0.0084	0.0134	0.8112
15	0.0368	−0.0037	0.0100	0.0138	0.7605
16	0.0384	−0.0059	0.0118	0.0168	0.8086
17	0.0330	−0.0087	0.0134	0.0179	0.7395
18	0.0385	−0.0004*	0.0152	0.0151	0.7371
19	0.0364	−0.0022*	0.0163	0.0194	0.6995
20	0.0364	−0.0065	0.0171	0.0230	0.6626
Average:					0.7755

*Insignificant at the 5% level.

involved regressing returns on the 20 portfolios against the NRI 400 index. The NRI 400 index is a value-weighted index. It is made up of the same 400 stocks we are analyzing. Thus, the relationship between the 20 portfolios and the index is likely to be higher than if we had chosen another market index. Table 6.7 shows the results.[9] As one might expect given the construction of the index: the R^2 declines with size. However, the extent of the decline is dramatic. The adjusted R^2 is less than 50% for the last eight portfolios and less than 15% for the portfolio of smallest stocks.

The explanatory power of the single index model is much less than that of the four-factor model. The average R^2 is 55% compared to 78% for the four-factor model. Thus, the four-factor model explains considerably more of the time series of security returns.

Table 6.7. Sensitivity and Explanatory Power for 1-Index Model

	Beta Coefficient	Adj R^2	Alpha	Avg. Return
1	1.1373	0.9065	−0.0018	0.0117
2	1.1289	0.8790	−0.0030	0.0104
3	1.0283	0.8700	0.0000	0.0122
4	0.9610	0.8180	−0.0002	0.0112
5	0.9570	0.7649	0.0030	0.0144
6	0.8697	0.7525	0.0007	0.0110
7	0.7877	0.6675	0.0022	0.0115
8	0.7942	0.6693	0.0038	0.0132
9	0.8130	0.6904	0.0000	0.0096
10	0.7067	0.5650	0.0069	0.0153
11	0.7037	0.5610	0.0037	0.0121
12	0.7097	0.5081	0.0036	0.0120
13	0.6232	0.4174	0.0098	0.0172
14	0.6203	0.4022	0.0058	0.0132
15	0.6307	0.3663	0.0073	0.0147
16	0.6137	0.3365	0.0106	0.0179
17	0.4815	0.2137	0.0124	0.0181
18	0.6001	0.2916	0.0109	0.0180
19	0.5349	0.2083	0.0135	0.0199
20	0.4841	0.1439	0.0203	0.0260
Average:		0.5516		

Table 6.8. Explanatory Power of Regression of Returns of 20 Portfolio on Return of NRI 400 and Factor 1

	Adjusted R^2	
	NRI 400	F1
1	0.9065	0.6447
2	0.8790	0.6839
3	0.8700	0.7502
4	0.8180	0.7429
5	0.7649	0.6995
6	0.7525	0.7488
7	0.6675	0.7190
8	0.6693	0.7488
9	0.6904	0.7996
10	0.5650	0.7256
11	0.5610	0.7376
12	0.5081	0.7098
13	0.4174	0.6564
14	0.4022	0.6998
15	0.3663	0.6363
16	0.3365	0.6358
17	0.2137	0.5033
18	0.2916	0.5796
19	0.2083	0.4900
20	0.1439	0.4220
Average:	0.5516	0.6667

Time Period: 7204–8603 (NRI 400), 7104–8603 (Factor 1)

Examining the composition of the first factor shows that it resembles an equally weighted market index. Thus it is interesting to examine the explanatory power of this factor relative to the NRI 400. Table 6.8 shows the comparison. The average R^2 is 67%, which is higher than the average R^2 for the single-index model using the NRI 400. The explanatory power declines slightly as the size of the firm declines. However, the decline is nowhere near as pronounced as the decline when using the NRI 400 as the market factor. Thus, the first factor has a much more uniform explanatory power than does using the NRI 400 as the index.

Comparing the explanatory power of the first factor in the four-factor model with all four factors shows that the added three factors explain a significant proportion of the variability of returns.

The sensitivity of portfolio returns to the NRI 400 index (beta) also declines with size. This is not at all expected. Beta is usually considered a measure of risk. For U.S. data the beta coefficient increases as size decreases. Thus, smaller firms are viewed as having greater risk. For Japanese data the reverse is true. The smaller firms have much lower betas than the large firms. Some caution is in order. The firms in the sample are all fairly large. There are 1100 firms in the first section of the Tokyo Stock Exchange. The NRI 400 includes 400 companies selected from among the largest firms on the Tokyo Stock Exchange. Thus the relationship between size and beta is found in the larger firms of the first section of the Tokyo Stock Exchange. The second result that is evident from Table 6.7 is that return is strongly related to size. Examining the last column of Table 6.7 shows a difference between the return on the small and large firms of over 1% per month. Furthermore, the relationship is almost monotonic.

The reduction in beta as size decreases as well as an increase in average return means that the smaller firms provide a higher return as well as lower beta. If beta is a risk measure, this evidence strongly favors the purchase of small stocks. Alternatively, this could be viewed as evidence that beta is not a sufficient metric for risk. The relationship between return and size is also evident in the four-factor model. For example, the sensitivities shown to factor four are ranked by size. A similar pattern, although less pronounced, is seen in factors 2 and 3. Thus, part of what the four-factor model is picking up relative to the one-factor model is a size effect. In summary, the four-factor model does a much better job of explaining the time series pattern of return than does the single-index model. Most of the advantage comes from explaining return on stocks of companies below the average size of companies included in the NRI 400.

Another interesting question is the stability of the sensitivity of return to the factors. We will examine the stability of the sensitivities for factor 4. We concentrate on factor 4 for it generally has the least stable sensitivity of our four factors. Table 6.9 shows the sensitivity coefficients for factor 4 for the 15-year period and three nonoverlapping 5-year periods. While not identical, clearly the sensitivities have the same pattern across the 20 groups. The correlation between the sensitivities

Table 6.9. Sensitivity to Factor 4

Portfolio	7104–8603	8104–8603	7604–8103	7104–7603
1	−0.0199	−0.0261	−0.0196	−0.0155
2	−0.0203	−0.0219	−0.0193	−0.0164
3	−0.0158	−0.0180	−0.0162	−0.0135
4	−0.0137	−0.0173	−0.0109	−0.0127
5	−0.0121	−0.0068*	−0.0107	−0.0162
6	−0.0066	−0.0018*	−0.0073	−0.0074
7	−0.0028*	0.0040*	−0.0048*	−0.0045*
8	0.0013*	0.0042*	−0.0009*	0.0031*
9	0.0010*	−0.0006*	0.0018*	0.0002*
10	0.0001*	0.0031*	0.0005*	−0.0008*
11	0.0051	0.0055*	0.0057*	0.0043*
12	0.0053	0.0073	0.0069	0.0037*
13	0.0084	0.0126	0.0049*	0.0060
14	0.0134	0.0084	0.0156	0.0140
15	0.0138	0.0180	0.0172	0.0083
16	0.0168	0.0125	0.0164	0.0177
17	0.0179	0.0187	0.0133	0.0155
18	0.0151	0.0133	0.0134	0.0132
19	0.0194	0.0230	0.0165	0.0153
20	0.0230	0.0238	0.0234	0.0216

*Insignificant at 5% level.

between the years 1971–1976 and 1976–1981 is 0.97. The correlation between the years 1976–1981 and 1981–1986 is 0.95. The average absolute difference in sensitivity between 1971–1976 and 1976–1981 was 0.0024 when the average absolute value of the sensitivity in 1971–1976 was 0.0105. Thus on average, the change was less than 23%. Likewise, the average absolute difference in sensitivity between 1976–1981 and 1981–1986 was 0.0039, with an average absolute value of the sensitivity in 1976–1981 of 0.0139. Thus, the average change was about 28%. The sensitivity measures between nonoverlapping periods are very stable for factor 4. The stability is even more pronounced for other factors.

In this section we have shown that a four-factor model explains returns better than a one-factor model. In addition, we have examined the stability of the sensitivities and have shown them to be very stable over time.

III. Index Tracking

In the prior section we showed that the four-factor model explained a significantly greater percentage of return variability than did the market (one-factor) model. Some increase in explanatory power in not surprising given the greater number of factors. However, the four-factor model consistently has a high explanatory power across all portfolios, where the explanatory power for the one-factor model deteriorates badly with size. A much more powerful test would be to make comparisons in a forecast mode. One method of doing this is analyzed in this section.

The test we will perform involves index matching. First, based on each model a portfolio of a small number of stocks that most clearly matches the return pattern of a preselected index is formed. In the case of the market model, we construct a portfolio with the same sensitivity (beta) as the index in question with minimum residual risk, and with (approximately) a fixed number of securities. In the case of the four-factor model, we construct a portfolio that has the same sensitivity as the index on each of the four factors, with minimum residual risk and with (approximately) a fixed number of securities. The second step in this test is to examine the ability of these portfolios to match the index over a period of time subsequent to when they are formed.

The index matching test is a joint test of a number of hypotheses. One aspect affecting performance is whether there are one or four factors in the market. Even if there are four factors, the one-factor model could still perform better if the historically estimated sensitivities for the four-factor model were poor forecasts of future sensitivities, while the historical sensitivity for the single index model was a good predictor of future sensitivities. Finally, we might not be able to distinguish differences in the performance of our two models even if the four-factor model was a superior description of reality, if the sensitivity of the market to these four factors was very stable over time. In this case, matching market betas is equivalent to matching factor sensitivities. Thus, our tests are joint tests of the model, stability of the sensitivities, and the stability of the relationship of the market to the factors.

The index we selected to match was the Nikkei 225. We attempted to match the index over the five years from January 1, 1981, to December 31, 1986. The first step was estimating sensitivities for each security. Sensitivities had to be estimated for both the market model and the four-factor model. Sensitivities were estimated on a quarterly basis for each model. For the market model we simply ran a regression of the return on each of the 393 stocks in our study versus the TSE Index at the beginning of each quarter using the previous 5 years of data. For the four-factor model a factor analysis was run at the beginning of each quarter using the prior 11 years of return data to determine the composition of the factors. Then, at the beginning of each quarter we ran a regression over the same period of returns on the 393 securities that comprise our samples versus return on the four factors. The regression coefficients were the sensitivities or betas used in the next step. In order to study the ability of our four-factor model or the market model to produce portfolios that matched a particular index (e.g., the Nikkei 225), the sensitivity of that index was measured by regressing it against both the TSE Index for the market model and the four indexes for the four factor model.

Once the sensitivities were determined, we calculated the composition of the portfolio intended to match the index. Matching portfolios were determined for portfolios of about 25, 50, and 100 securities.

For example, for the market model and 25 securities, the following quadratic programming problem was solved:

minimize:

$$\sum_i X_i^2 \sigma_{\epsilon i}^2$$

subject to:

1. $\sum X_i \beta_i = \beta_p$ (sensitivity matching)
2. $0 \leq X_i \leq 0.04$ (no short sales and upper bond)

where

1. X_i is the proportion in security i.
2. β_i is the sensitivity of a security to the market.
3. β_p is the sensitivity of the Nikkei 225 to the market.
4. $\sigma_{\epsilon i}^2$ is the residual risk from the market model.

The first constraint causes a matching of sensitivities. For the one-factor model this causes the beta on the matching portfolio to be the same as the beta on the Nikkei 225.

For the four-factor model the first constraint presented is replaced by a constraint that requires that the beta (sensitivity) be matched on each of the four factors. We wanted to have the same number of securities in the portfolio whether we matched using the one-factor model or the four-factor model. This guarantees that relative performance is unaffected by differences in the size of the portfolios. The constraint on the maximum invested in a security guarantees that there will be roughly the same number of securities in the two portfolios. In subsequent tables we will examine alternative values of the constraint on maximum investment. We shall use upper limits of 0.04, 0.02, and 0.01 and refer to the portfolios as having 25, 50, or 100 securities. In actual practice, a number of the portfolios had slightly more securities than the number shown. The same procedure was repeated every quarter, or 20 times over the five-year period.

Having determined the portfolio composition at the beginning of each quarter, we then calculated the return on the Nikkei 225 adjusted for dividends each month as well as the return on the matching portfolio using the market model and the matching portfolio using the four-factor model.[10] To examine which model matches the adjusted Nikkei 225 more closely, we calculated the monthly difference in return between the index and the matching portfolio and squared it. We then computed the average squared difference between the index and the two matching portfolios (Figure 6.3). Results for portfolios of size 25, 50, and 100 are presented. We also performed one further test. Since financial stocks are thinly traded, we excluded financial stocks from those that could be held in the matching portfolio. Since financial stocks are believed to move together, this tests the ability to match when a segment of the market is excluded. We tested this for a 50 stock portfolio.

In all four tests the matching portfolios formed using four factors outperformed the matching portfolios using one factor. Using the four-factor model cut the average squared forecasting error in some cases by more than 1/2. This test involves forecasting the model and parameters. Thus the difference in number of factors during the fit period does not bias the results. The ability of the four-factor model to allow the construction of a portfolio that better tracks a second portfolio is powerful evidence that the four-factor model better describes reality.[11]

IV. Relationship of Factors to Economic Variables

In earlier sections, we constructed and presented evidence on the existence of four factors in the return-generating process for Japanese securities. It would be convenient in predicting and understanding these

Figure 6.3. Comparison of Single and Four-Factor Model (Difference in Return)

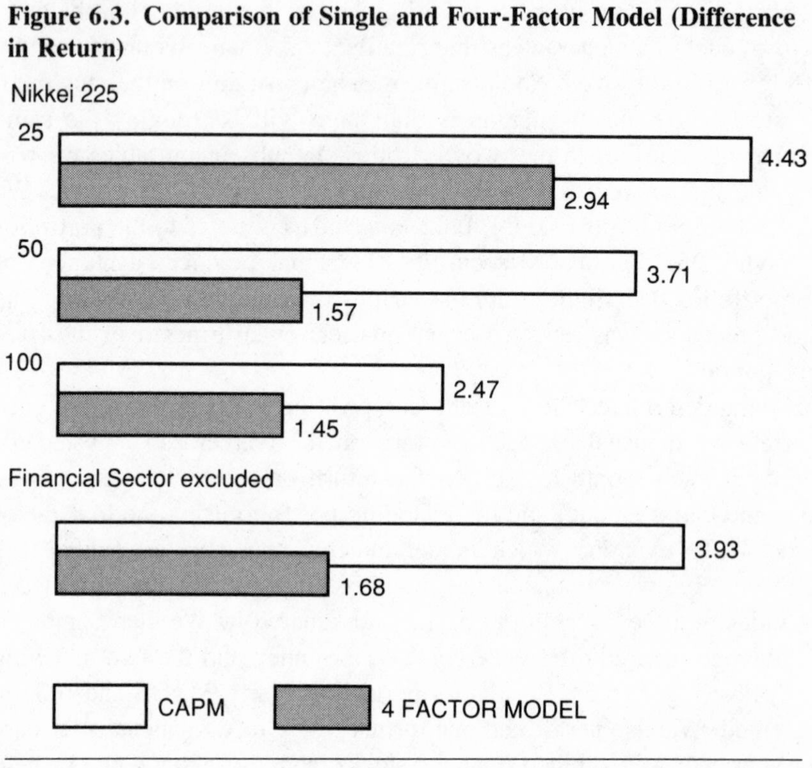

factors if they were associated with economic variables. There is a difficulty with this approach. Since the four factors are not unique to a linear transformation, there are, of course, an infinite number of four-factor models that would serve equally well. Thus, which factor is associated with which economic variable or set of economic variables is arbitrary.

Any information contained in the current level of economic variables should be incorporated in security prices. What should affect security returns is an unanticipated change in the level of the variables. We were unable to obtain expectational data on the variables we used. Thus we were forced to compromise. As our unanticipated change we used the continuously compounded change in the level of the variable. This definition of unanticipated change implicitly assumes that investors predicted zero change in the economic index. This is not dissimilar to the approach taken by others. A more complicated procedure would involve detailed research to determine a forecasting technique for each variable and would involve extensive research projects by themselves. Error in our determination of the forecast model should result in our finding less association than truly exists.

Table 6.10 lists the economic variables that we used. These variables can be classified as measures of inflation rates, interest rates, foreign trade, petroleum prices, economic conditions, and U.S. interest rates and inflation.

As discussed earlier, there are a large number of alternative four-factor models that are identical in their ability to explain returns. Thus it would be very arbitrary to simply relate any single factor to the economic variables. Rather, what we did was calculate the canonical correlation between the four factors and the economic variables. The cumulative correlation for the four canonical variables is 29.6% in the 15-year period from April 1971 to March 1986, and 63.9% in the 5-year period from April 1984 to March 1986. Thus, the statistically determined factors do have a strong relationship to the economic variables.

While the work in this brief section is preliminary in nature it does indicate that economic factors have an influence on the risk structure of security returns. These results suggest that continuing work in this area should prove promising.

V. Cross-Sectional Tests

In this section of the paper we examine the relationship of average returns to the factor sensitivities. This is considered a standard APT-type test. Factors are generally divided into two types of factors, so-called priced factors and unpriced factors. Priced factors are factors that not only explain the time series of returns but also have their sensitivities related to average returns. Unpriced factors are factors that affect the time series of returns but whose sensitivities are not related to average return.

Both types of factors are important in trying to explain the time series of returns. However, for explaining expected return, only price factors are important.

The examination of priced and unpriced factors was determined in a procedure similar to Roll and Ross (1980). At the beginning of each year a regression was run using data from the prior five years. The regression related return on our 20 portfolios to the return on the four factors. After estimating the sensitivities from the time series regression, a cross-sectional regression was run in each of the next 12 months. The

Table 6.10. Macrovariables

1. Inflation Rate:	
	Consumer Price Index
	Wholesale Price Index
	Yen/Dollar Rate (U.S. Dollar Central Rate)
	Export Price Index (Yen base)
	Import Price Index (Yen base)
	Nikkei Commodity Price Index
	Expected Inflation Rate
2. Interest Rate:	
	Call Rate
	10-yr Gov't Bond Yield
	Difference in Rates between Short– and Long-Term Interest
	Difference in Short-Term Interests between Japan and U.S.A.
3. Foreign Trade:	
	Exports Quantum Index
	Imports Quantum Index
	Crude Oil Import Quantity
4. Petroleum Prices:	
	Crude Oil Import Price
5. Economic Conditions	
	Workers' Households Disposable Income
	Production Index
	Inventory Index
	Value of Public Contracts
	Number of Corporate Bankruptcies
	Index of Business Outlook about Small Enterprises
	Retail Trade Index (seasonally adjusted)
	Forecast Industrial Production Rate
6. U.S. Interest Rate & Inflation:	
	Consumer Price Index of U.S.A.
	3-Month TB Rate
	Treasurites Securities Yields (20 years, avg.)

regression has the form:

$$\text{Return on Portfolio } i = \lambda_0 + \sum_{j=1}^{4} \lambda_i \beta_{ij}$$

where

1. β_{ij} are the sensitivities estimated from the five-year time series regression.
2. λ_j are estimated from the regression.

The λ_j were estimated for each of the 12 months. At the end of the year (beginning of the next), a new five-year time series regression was run to estimate sensitivities. These sensitivities were then used in the next year, and so forth. Since we had 15 years of data and need 5 years to estimate the time series regression, we had 10 years of monthly λ_j's, or a total of 120.

Table 6.11 shows the results. The average for each λ_j is the average value over the 120 months. The T values are calculated by using the 120 observations on λ_j to obtain a standard deviation of the mean and this is used to calculate T. The last two columns report one more measure of significance. For each of the 120 cross-sectional regressions we obtain a T value. The last two columns show how often the absolute value of this T is greater than 1 or 2.

By any normal measures of significance only factor 4 is priced. Thus, factors 1, 2, and 3 affect return but the investor does not earn excess return by having a portfolio whose returns are sensitive to these factors. Since these factors are important in affecting the risk of a large portfolio but not the return, the investor should make the sensitivity to these factors for the portfolio as close to zero as possible.

Table 6.11. Values of Lambda

	Average	S.D.	*T* Value	# $\lvert T\rvert > 1^*$	# $\lvert T\rvert > 2^*$
Lambda 1	0.098	1.214	0.884	51/120	17/120
Lambda 2	−0.063	0.934	−0.738	62/120	22/120
Lambda 3	0.005	0.873	0.062	54/120	21/120
Lambda 4	0.193	1.127	1.880	69/120	33/120

Conclusion

In this paper we have estimated the return-generating process for large stocks on the Tokyo Stock Exchange. We have found that four factors are sufficient to describe the return-generating process. In determining if four factors were sufficient, a new methodology for identifying the factors that make up the return-generating process was described and applied. In addition, we have found that the impact of these factors on returns is reasonably stable over time and that at least in one application (replicating the performance of stock indexes) the factors have meaningful forecasting ability. Next we showed that the factors are highly correlated with changes in a set of economic variables. Finally, we examined the ability of the factors to explain cross-sectional differences in return.

Notes

1. See Roll and Ross (1980), Brown and Weinstein (1983), and Dhrymes, et al. (1984).
2. See Roll and Ross (1980), Brown and Weinstein (1983), Dhrymes, et al. (1984), Gibbons, Elton, and Gruber (1987).
3. This problem is separable from but also associated with determining the number of factors that are priced.
4. Cho, et al. (1984) have demonstrated that maximum likelihood factor analysis is robust in identifying the correct number of factors under reasonable sets of assumptions.
5. Our sample was the NRI 400. Seven stocks were discarded because of data problems.
6. See, for example, Roll and Ross (1980), Gibbons and Hamao (1989).
7. See Roll and Ross (1980), and Dhrymes, et al. (1984) for a debate on this issue.
8. For evidence on the Japanese market, see Nakamura and Terada (1984).
9. That the four-factor model has a higher explanatory power than a single-factor market model in the fit period is to be expected. The size of the difference is, however, different than for U.S. studies as is the deterioration with size. In the next section, we will analyze explanatory power in forecasting.
10. Dividends average about 1% per annum. Dividend payments were implicitly reinvested in the portfolio at the proportions existing at the time the stock went ex-dividend.
11. As we discussed earlier, this is a joint test. However, it is not very plausible that the four-factor model is more stable than the one-factor model. Its

superior performance is likely to be because of the presence of multiple factors rather than greater stability of sensitivities.

References

Akaike, H., (1974). "A New Look at the Statistical Identification Model," *IEEE Transactions on Automatic Control*, pp. 716–723.

Brown, Steve, and Mark Weinstein, (1983). "A New Approach to Testing Asset Pricing Models: The Bilinear Paradigm," *Journal of Finance*, June.

Chen, Nai-Fu, (1983). "Some Empirical Tests of the Theory of Arbitrage Pricing," *Journal of Finance*, Vol. 38 No. 5, December, pp. 1393–1414.

Cho, D. Chinhyung, (1984). "On Testing the Arbitrage Pricing Theory: Inter-Battery Factor Analysis," *Journal of Finance*, Vol. 19 No. 1, March, pp. 1–10.

Cho, D. Chinhyung, Edwin Elton, and Martin Gruber, (1984). "On the Robustness of The Roll and Ross Arbitrage Pricing Theory," *Journal of Financial and Qualitative Analysis*, Vol. 19 No. 1, March, pp. 1–10.

Dhrymes, Phoebus, Irwin Friend, and N. Bulent Gultekin, (1984). "A Critical Re-Examination of the Empirical Evidence on the Arbitrage Pricing Theory," *Journal of Finance*, Vol. 39 No. 2, June, pp. 323–346.

Elton, Edwin, and Martin Gruber, (1987). *Modern Portfolio Theory and Investment Analysis*, 3rd Ed., John Wiley.

Gibbons, Mike. "Empirical Examination of the Return-Generating Process of the Arbitrage Pricing Theory," Working Paper, Stanford University.

Hamao, Yasushi. "An Empirical Examination of the Arbitrage Pricing Theory: Using Japanese Data," Unpublished Manuscript, Yale University (1989).

Lawley, D. N., and A. E. Maxwell, (1971). *Factor Analysis as a Statistical Method*, New York, Macmillan.

Nakamura, Takeo, and Noboru Terada, (1984). "The Size Effect and Seasonality in Japanese Stock Returns," paper presented at the Institute for Quantitative Research in Finance.

Roll, Richard, and Steve Ross, (1980). "An Empirical Investigation of the Arbitrage Pricing Theory," *Journal of Finance*, Vol. 35 No. 5, December, pp. 1073–1103.

Schwartz, G., (1978). "Estimating the Dimension of a Model," *Annals of Statistics*, Vol. 6, pp. 461–464.

7

An Empirical Examination of the Arbitrage Pricing Theory: Using Japanese Data*

Yasushi Hamao
University of California, San Diego

I. Introduction

Chen, Roll, and Ross (1986) examined the validity of the Arbitrage Pricing Theory (APT) in U.S. security markets. Their analysis used innovations in U.S. macroeconomic variables as proxies for the underlying risk factors driving stock returns. They found that significantly priced factors include industrial production, inflation, risk premia, and the slope of the yield curve. Futhermore, given these sources of risk, CAPM betas have no marginal power in explaining expected returns. The purpose of this paper is to perform a parallel analysis in Japanese markets (using Japanese macroeconomic variables) as a test of the robustness of the Chen, Roll, and Ross results. A secondary goal, described at length in Hamao (1986), is to develop a standard database for the study of Japanese financial markets.

The Japanese capital market is second in size only to that of the United States. Equities have a market value of $500 billion and an average

* This paper is a part of my dissertation written at Yale. I thank Stephen Brown, Philip Dybvig, William Goetzmann, Koichi Hamada, Roger Ibbotson, Jonathan Ingersoll, an anonymous referee, and especially Stephen Ross for useful comments and discussions. I am also grateful to Japan Securities Research Institute, J. P. Morgan Investment, and Nomura Research Institute for providing the data, and to the Dean Witter Foundation for partial financial support.

daily trading volume of 300 million shares (1982 data).[1] There are two sections in Tokyo Stock Exchange (TSE), similar to the dominance of the New York and American Stock Exchanges in the United States.

After World War II, Japan developed an active equity market but did not develop an active bond market. Government-imposed interest rate ceilings that were intended to stimulate investments in private sector firms kept investors away.[2] Corporations depended on bank loans instead of bond issues and the bond market remained undeveloped. Moreover, no long-term government bonds were issued, because a balanced budget was strictly sustained in order to prevent recurrence of the post-war hyperinflation. A long-term government bond was first issued in 1966 on the amendment of the law requiring a balanced budget, and massive offerings started in 1975. Not until 1977 were financial institutions, the main purchasers of the government bonds, permitted to sell bond holdings in a secondary market. Table 7.1 based on Ministry of Finance (1983), characterizes the rapid growth of Japanese government bond issues after 1975.

A particular difficulty in performing the study is the lack of availability of macroeconomic variables that exactly parallel the U.S. series. To know the slope of the yield curve and the "risk premium" (computed by Chen, Roll, and Ross as a premium on junk bonds), we must have data from an active bond market. As just described, the secondary market for bonds did not exist before 1975 and that is when our study starts, thus restricting us to using only 10 years of data.

The paper is organized as follows. In Section II we discuss two ways to test the APT. Section III describes the data and derives macroeconomic factors. Section IV reports the pricing results. Section V concludes the paper.

Table 7.1. Public Offering of Government Bonds* in Billion Yen

Year	1972	1973	1974	1975	1976	1977	1978	1979
Amount	1718	1498	1769	4513	6113	8867	10,499	10,966

*Source: Japanese Ministry of Finance (1983)

II. Tests of the Apt

There is rapidly growing literature on empirical tests of the Arbitrage Pricing Theory. One approach, which was pioneered by Roll and Ross (1980), is to conduct a factor analysis to extract systematic factors influencing stock returns. Brown and Weinstein (1983) and Chen (1983) also utilize factor analysis. Although this approach enables us to find an appropriate number of factors that are significant in pricing and to statistically characterize them, and although it is closer to the spirit of the theory of the APT in a sense that it attempts to identify the factors that span the return space, the extracted factors lack intuitive economic meaning.

Another approach is to prespecify the factors, derive time series of these factors, and examine their significance in pricing relationship. Chen, Roll, and Ross were the first to pursue this direction using the U.S. data. Shanken and Weinstein (1985) and McElroy and Burmeister (1986) report results of different statistical tests using the same factors as Chen, Roll, and Ross. Although this method offers clear economic interpretation, it is sometimes criticized for its arbitrary specifications of economic factors. The problem with this procedure is that since the macroeconomic data are noisy and often not contemporaneous with the stock data, the spanning of the return space by these factors may not be very accurate. In order to avoid this noisiness of the macroeconomic factors, an earlier version of Chen, Roll, and Ross employed stock portfolios that mimic the macroeconomic factors as factors in testing pricing relationship. This approach, which is an extension of Chen's (1983) procedure to obtain desirable factor scores, however, may be biased toward acceptance since it uses factors derived from stock data to test the pricing of stocks.

Factor analysis is not utilized in our study, nor are the mimicking portfolios in deriving factors. Our factors are macroeconomic state variables parallel to those used in Chen, Roll, and Ross. The choice of the variables is dictated by the basic economic theory of asset pricing, which would be applicable regardless of the location of the markets. By taking this approach, we are able to discuss different magnitudes of pricing influence of similar macrofactors in a parallel but different economy. Since Japan is heavily dependent in trade, we consider factors related to international trade in addition to the basic economic variables.

III. The Data

Stock Data

The data used are monthly returns from TSE Section I for the period January 1975 to December 1984, provided by the Nomura Research Institute. Out of a total of 1066 companies, some are exluded because of missing observations. The number of stocks excluded varies month by month, ranging from 53 to 188. In order to average out individual eccentricities in the data, stocks are groups into 20 equally weighted portfolios with an approximately equal number of securities sorted by size (price of stock multiplied by outstanding volume) of a company at the end of the previous month. Portfolios are reformed monthly. Chen, Roll, and Ross found sorting by size most successful in their pricing test compared to sorting by beta or residual variability in the market model. Size is adopted here as a sorting means because (1) size data suffers least from missing observations in our database, and (2) there is empirical evidence of a relation between size and returns, similar to that found in the U.S. data.[3] We expect, then, that returns will be spread cross-sectionally by grouping by size.

Economic State Variables

The simplest of theories in finance prices a financial asset by discounting future cash flows. Thus we are looking for exogenous macrovariables that affect the future cash flows or the risk-adjusted discount rate of a company. Since our purpose is to identify macroeconomic forces influencing the stock market, we must be careful not to include macrovariables derived from equity-related data.

Industrial Production. The monthly index of production, *IP*(*t*) was obtained from the *Ministry of International Trade and Industry Statistics*. The growth rate of industrial production is its first difference in logs,

$$MP(t) = \ln IP(t) - \ln IP(t-1)$$

We lag it forward by one month since *MP(t)* actually reflects production change in month $t - 1$ (at least in part).

In order to eliminate the annual seasonal variation, the average *MP* over the previous five years for the same month is subtracted from the *MP* series, yielding the variable *MPSA(t)*.

Inflation. There is no Japanese counterpart to U.S. Treasury Bills. However, the Japanese interbank short-term loan rate (the call money rate) and the interest rate that is applied to bond transactions with repurchase (or resale) agreements (*Gensaki* rate) provide proxies for short-term, risk-free interest rates. The major participants in the bond repurchase market are nonfinancial corporations and insurance companies, which are not allowed to participate in the call money market. The size of the Gensaki market is quite large. Its outstanding balance was $21.5 billion in 1982, compared to $22.5 billion in the call money market in the same period. The Gensaki rate used here is not for a one-month repurchase contract, but for a three-month repurchase contract. Unfortunately, the three-month rates obtained from Nomura Securities Company and the Japan Securities Dealers Association are the only available data for the Gensaki market over the 1975–1984 period. The three-month rates were then compounded back to yield a one-month rate. (The call money rate available is "unconditional," in most cases with a one-month maturity.)

We compare the expected inflation variables derived from the call money rate and the repurchase agreement rate by regressing $I(t)$ on these variables. (The procedure is described as follows.) Table 7.2 shows the

Table 7.2. Comparison of Expected Inflation: Using Call Money Rate vs. *Gensaki* rate. 1/75–12/84

1) Expected inflation using the call money rate, *EIC*

$$I_t = 0.0004179 + 0.785215(EIC_{t-1}) + e_t$$
$$(0.337834) \quad (2.118549)$$
$$R^2 = 0.03664 \quad s(e) = 0.007685$$

Residual autocorrelations;

ρ_1	ρ_2	ρ_3	ρ_4	ρ_5
−0.0336	−0.2988	−0.0561	0.0201	0.1260

2) Expected inflation using the Gensaki rate, *EIG*

$$I_t = -0.0006499 + 1.06815(EIG_{t-1}) + e_t$$
$$(-0.335194) \quad (2.598486)$$
$$R^2 = 0.064124 \quad s(e) = 0.0076153$$

Residual autocorrelations;

ρ_1	ρ_2	ρ_3	ρ_4	ρ_5
−0.0380	−0.3053	−0.0851	0.0315	0.1333

*T statistics in parenthesis

result. In terms of (a) conditional unbiasedness (i.e., an intercept close to zero and a regression coefficient close to 1.0), (b) serially uncorrelated residuals, and (c) low residual standard error, there is a slight bias in the regression coefficient of *EIC*, the expected inflation using the call money rate. It is known that the interest rate in the call money market has frequently been manipulated by the monetary authority, while in the Gensaki market such manipulation remains minimal. For this reason, the repurchase rate is used as the short-term, risk-free interest rate throughout the paper.

We use the Fama and Gibbons (1984) methodology as in Chen, Roll, and Ross to derive the expected inflation variable. Let $I(t)$ be the monthly first-order log relative of the realized CPI, and $E[\cdot \mid t]$ be the expectation operator, conditional on information at the end of month t. CPI data is obtained from *Bank of Japan Monthly Statistics*. Following Irving Fisher, the one-month interest rate (Gensaki rate in our case), $GR(t-1)$ observed at the end of month $t-1$ applicable to month t can be broken down into two components: an expected real return for month t, $E[\rho(t) \mid t-1]$ and an expected inflation rate, $E[I(t) \mid t-1]$,

$$GR(t-1) = E[\rho(t) \mid t-1] + E[I(t) \mid t-1] \tag{7.1}$$

The *ex post* real return for month t is

$$GR(t-1) - I(t) = E[\rho(t) \mid t-1] + \xi(t)$$

where $\xi(t) = E[I(t) \mid t-1] - I(t)$, and taking the difference of the real returns, we have

$$[GR(t-1) - I(t)] - [GR(t-2) - I(t-1)] =$$
$$E[\rho(t) \mid t-1] - E[\rho(t-1) \mid t-2] + \xi(t) - \xi(t-1)$$

Assuming that expected real returns follow a random walk, we can write this difference as a first-order, moving average process as follows:

$$[GR(t-1) - I(t)] - [GR(t-2) - I(t-1)] = u(t) - \theta \cdot u(t-1)$$

Using an estimation method described in Box and Jenkins (1976) we get the estimate of θ,

$$[GR(t-1) - I(t)] - [GR(t-2) - I(t-1)] =$$
$$\hat{u}(t) - 0.97645\hat{u}(t-1)(s(\theta) = 0.0126)$$

The estimate of expected real return is given by the fitted value

$$E[\rho(t) \mid t-1] = [GR(t-2) - I(t-1)] - 0.97645\hat{u}(t-1)$$

and the expected inflation is given by Equation 7.1.

The inflation variables are then contructed as

$$UI(t) = I(t) - E[I(t) \mid t-1]$$
$$DEI(t) = E[I(t+1) \mid t] - E[I(t) \mid t-1]$$

where *UI* is the unanticipated inflation and *DEI* is the change in expected inflation. If the inflation forecast is based on information other than the previous forecast errors, *DEI* would have different information from *UI*.

Risk Premia. Changes in risk premia in the financial market affect the value of an asset through changes in discount rates. One variable we might look at is the spread between government and corporate bonds since it is a function of risk aversion. The most readily available data for bonds is in "yield" form. We do not use it here since Japanese "yield" is not the same as yield to maturity and is computed without taking present values into consideration.[4] Instead, monthly returns are calculated for long-term government bonds with 10 years of maturity and long-term electricity company bonds with 10 years (12 years since March 1981) of maturity by using prices including accumulated interest. The raw data, which include quoted prices, dates, and amounts of coupon payments, and maturity dates, was obtained from *Monthly Report of Government and Corporate Bonds* of the Japan Underwriters Association. When there are quotations for many government or electricity company bonds, the bond with the longest maturity is used.

There are nine regional electricity companies and the data includes returns on the newest issues by any of the nine companies. Thus, the derived electricity company bond data is a series of returns of similar but not the same kind of bonds. While data on other corporate bonds are very difficult to obtain, returns on a managed fund of government and corporate bonds are available.

Optimally, in computing the "junk bond premia," we would like returns on a portfolio of low-grade corporate bonds with the same maturity as the long-term government bond. A well-diversified portfolio is desirable to obtain economy-wide figures. The same maturity is needed to separate risk premia from the term structure effect. However, neither electricity bond returns nor a managed fund's returns satisfy these conditions. The electricity bond is not a low-grade issue and its return series might contain fluctuations specific to this industry. The managed fund has an average maturity of only eight years and contains government bonds as well. We will use these simply because superior return series are not yet available.

Our candidates for risk premia variables are thus

$$UPREL(t) = EL(t) - LGB(t)$$
$$UPRMF(t) = MF(t) - LGB(t)$$

where *EL(t), LGB(t)*, and *MF(t)* are the returns on the electricity bond, the long-term government bond, and the managed fund, respectively.

The Term Structure. To capture effects of changes in interest rates, the return difference between long bonds and Gensaki is employed. The variable used is

$$UTS(t) = LGB(t) - GR(t-1)$$

If *UTS* is positive, then long bonds have risen implying that their yield has fallen, which lowers the slope of the yield curve.

Foreign Exchange. The Japanese economy is heavily oriented toward international trade, and one might suspect that volatility in foreign exchange rates would have a substantial systematic effect on Japanese equities.

Let ${}_{t-1}F_t$ be the forward exchange rate (yen/dollar) at the end of month $t - 1$ applicable to the end of month t, and S_t be the spot rate at the end of month t. Assuming risk-neutrality and presuming efficiency of the forward exchange market, we can use ${}_{t-1}F_t$ as a forecast of S_t. The innovation variable for the exchange rate change is then expressed as

$$UYEN(t) = \ln {}_{t-1}F_t - \ln S_t$$

Another variable that might capture more directly the effect of changes in foreign exchange on the economy is changes in the terms of trade. Terms of trade (*TT*) data, which is obtained from *Bank of Japan Monthly Statistics*, is defined as

$$TT = \frac{\text{(Price index of export goods)}}{\text{(Price index of import goods)}}$$

The change in *TT*, *DTT*(t) is constructed as

$$DTT(t) = \ln TT(t) - \ln TT(t-1)$$

Market Indices. Although we are constructing nonequity related macrovariables, the market indices are included since they may capture unexpected shocks to the economy more rapidly than smoothed, averaged, monthly series of macrovariables. They are also of interest in their own right as proxies whose efficiency is relevant to CAPM tests. The following two indices are used:

$VW(t)$ = Return on the value-weighted TSE-I index including dividends

$EW(t)$ = Return on the equally weighted TSE-I index including dividends

Oil Prices. Since the Japanese economy is heavily dependent on foreign oil, the price of oil is included as a systematic factor influencing the Japanese stock market. The oil price growth variable *OG* is constructed as the monthly log difference of the Arabian Light Spot price translated into Japanese yen using month-end spot exchange rates.

Statistical Characteristics of the Economic State Variables

Table 7.3 shows a correlation matrix of the macroeconomic variables computed over the 10-year period. The relatively low correlation (0.648) between *VW* and *EW* suggests the existence of more than two factors; that is, *VW* alone would not be sufficient to explain stock returns. Besides *VW* and *EW*, high correlations are seen between (1) *OG* and *UYEN*, (2) *UPRMF* (*UPREL*) and *UTS*, and (3) *UPRMF* and *UPREL*. This is not surprising since, with the exception of *EW* and *VW*, these pairs have common variables; the spot exchange rate is used in *OG* and *UYEN* and the long-term government bond return is used in *UPRMF* (*UPREL*) and *UTS*. Although *UYEN* is an innovation and *OG* is not, the high negative correlation between them is plausible. For example, unanticipated depreciation of the Japanese yen against the U.S. dollar would coincide with an oil price increase in terms of yen. These pairs, if used together, would result in multicolinearity and thus then to weaken

Table 7.3. Correlation Matrix of Economic Variables, 1/75–12/84

	MP	MPSA	DEI	UI	UPRMF	UTS	UPREL	DTT	UYEN	OG	VW	EW
MP	1.000											
MPSA	0.315	1.000										
DEI	0.035	0.106	1.000									
UI	−0.079	0.020	0.043	1.000								
UPRMF	0.052	−0.002	−0.112	0.044	1.000							
UTS	−0.101	−0.090	−0.196	−0.089	−0.630	1.000						
UPREL	0.134	−0.016	0.049	0.110	0.748	−0.776	1.000					
DTT	−0.137	−0.059	−0.187	−0.041	−0.150	0.217	−0.203	1.000				
UYEN	−0.093	−0.001	−0.153	−0.059	−0.130	0.408	−0.329	0.234	1.000			
OG	0.169	0.006	0.127	0.045	0.154	−0.318	0.276	−0.340	−0.535	1.000		
VW	−0.104	−0.048	−0.108	−0.015	0.109	0.147	−0.016	0.038	0.224	−0.156	1.000	
EW	0.053	0.004	−0.179	−0.015	0.058	0.193	−0.071	0.174	0.297	−0.193	0.648	1.000

Glossary:

MP	monthly growth rate of industrial production (raw data)
MPSA	monthly growth rate of industrial production (filtered)
DEI	change in expected inflation
UI	unanticipated inflation
UPRMF	unanticipated change in risk premium using managed bond fund return
UTS	unanticipated change in the term structure of interest rates
UPREL	unanticipated change in risk premium using electricity company bond return
DTT	change in terms of trade
UYEN	unanticipated change in foreign exchange rates
OG	growth rate of oil prices
VW	return on the value-weighted TSE-I index
EW	return on the equally weighted TSE-I index

the individual impact of these variables. Other correlations are not too strong and the variables are quite far from perfectly correlated.

Table 7.4 shows autocorrelations for the macrovariables computed over the same period. The *DTT* series is moderately autocorrelated. While a high autocorrelation of the *MP* series at the 12th lag indicates the presence of annual seasonality, the *MPSA* series does not exhibit any seasonality. The *UI* variable also has a peak in its lag at the 12th month, indicating that seasonality of the change in CPI is not captured by the expected inflation variable we constructed.

IV. The Pricing Result

We employ a variant of the classical Fama and MacBeth (1973) approach. First, the following type of time series regressions are run over a five-year (or 10-year) period for the 20 portfolios, sorted by the market value and reformed each month;

$$R_p = a_p + b_{1p}(MPSA) + b_{2p}(DEI) + b_{3p}(UI) + b_{4p}(UPR) + b_{5p}(UTS) + \epsilon_p$$

Then the following cross-section regressions are run using estimates of the b's obtained by the time series regressions as the independent variables;

$$R_{pt} = \lambda_{Ot} + \lambda_{1t}b_{1p} + \lambda_{2t}b_{2p} + \lambda_{3t}b_{3p} + \lambda_{4t}b_{4p} + \lambda_{5t}b_{5p} + \epsilon_p$$

This generates a time series of estimates of the risk premium (λ's) associated with each macrovariable. The time series mean of these estimates are tested by a t-test for significant difference from zero.

Table 7.5 shows results of the cross-section regressions. In this table the cross-section regressions are run simultaneously with the time series regressions. That is, the time period used to get estimates of b's by the time series regressions is the same 10-year time period as that used for the cross-section regressions.

Although running cross-section regressions over the same 10-year period as the time series regressions takes advantage of a longer observation period, it imposes an assumption of stronger stationarity on estimates of b's.[5] Nevertheless, the result is encouraging: except for the marginal significance of *UTS*, all coefficients are statistically significant. Using another risk premium variable (*UPRMF*), which employs the managed

Table 7.4. Autocorrelations of Economic Variables, 1/75–12/84

	ρ_1	ρ_2	ρ_3	ρ_4	ρ_5	ρ_6	ρ_7	ρ_8	ρ_9	ρ_{10}	ρ_{11}	ρ_{12}
MP	−0.333	−0.408	0.389	−0.123	−0.047	0.126	−0.074	−0.084	0.376	−0.432	−0.298	0.865
MPSA	−0.212	0.053	0.181	−0.151	0.132	−0.038	−0.109	0.045	0.203	−0.115	0.063	0.120
DEI	−0.144	0.070	0.132	0.043	0.052	0.086	−0.024	−0.105	0.198	−0.146	−0.077	0.144
UI	−0.038	−0.303	−0.083	0.030	0.127	0.081	0.043	0.034	−0.064	−0.297	0.019	0.613
UPRMF	−0.063	0.039	0.034	0.067	−0.013	−0.055	−0.040	0.100	0.029	0.063	0.141	0.078
UTS	0.076	0.013	−0.087	0.080	0.064	−0.150	−0.048	0.161	0.134	0.182	0.047	0.035
UPREL	−0.256	0.119	−0.107	0.060	−0.054	−0.058	−0.075	−0.001	0.128	0.129	−0.033	0.016
DTT	0.689	0.473	0.378	0.295	0.292	0.318	0.271	0.169	0.048	−0.076	−0.055	−0.066
UYEN	0.094	−0.016	0.160	0.099	0.036	−0.044	−0.031	0.066	−0.053	−0.042	0.021	0.115
OG	0.079	−0.023	0.500	0.035	−0.069	0.287	−0.194	−0.018	0.138	−0.115	−0.111	0.042
VW	−0.017	−0.050	−0.035	−0.066	−0.110	−0.040	0.018	0.058	0.053	−0.021	0.014	0.013
EW	0.209	0.062	0.032	0.026	0.112	−0.111	0.050	−0.008	−0.122	−0.064	0.048	0.168

Glossary:

MP	monthly growth rate of industrial production (raw data)
MPSA	monthly growth rate of industrial production (filtered)
DEI	change in expected inflation
UI	unanticipated inflation
UPRMF	unanticipated change in risk premium using managed bond fund return
UTS	unanticipated change in the term structure of interest rates
UPREL	unanticipated change in risk premium using electricity company bond return
DTT	change in terms of trade
UYEN	unanticipated change in foreign exchange rates
OG	growth rate of oil prices
VW	return on the value-weighted TSE-I index
EW	return on the equally weighted TSE-I index

Table 7.5. Economic Variables and Pricing, Cross-section regressions run over the same period as time series regressions (1/75–12/84).

Constant	*MPSA*	*DEI*	*UI*	*UPREL*	*UTS*	*DTT*
			Part 1			
0.02327	0.01690	0.00094	0.00597	0.011731	−0.01999	
(4.366)	(3.064)	(2.964)	(2.616)	(2.678)	(−1.936)	
			Part 2			
0.02239	0.01688	0.00103	0.00552	0.00744	−0.02002	
(3.249)	(2.174)	(2.540)	(1.760)	(1.637)	(−1.465)	
			Part 3			
0.02316	0.01730	0.00093	0.00606	0.01730	−0.01973	−0.01027
(4.533)	(3.439)	(3.158)	(2.276)	(2.686)	(−1.997)	(−1.340)

In each part, numbers in the top rows represent the time series means of λ's. Numbers in parentheses are T statistics.

Glossary:

MPSA	monthly growth rate of industrial production (filtered)
DEI	change in expected inflation
UI	unanticipated inflation
UPRMF	unanticipated change in risk premium using managed bond fund return
UPREL	unanticipated change in risk premium using electricity company bond return
UTS	unanticipated change in the term structure of interest rates
DTT	change in terms of trade

fund returns, is uniformly unfavorable to the result. The coefficients increased their significance when change in the terms of trade is introduced, but *DTT* itself failed to show significance. This may be caused by autocorrelation present in the *DTT* variable.

Table 7.6 reports results from the cross-section regressions following the time series regressions. In this table, time series regressions are run over a five-year period to obtain $\hat{b}$'s. Then a cross-section regression is run for a month *immediately* following the five-year period. This procedure is repeated every month for five years and a five-year time series of $\hat{\lambda}$'s is obtained. Note that estimates of b's obtained by a five-year period are used as independent variables for a cross-section regression over only one month next to the five years. Thus we use the

Table 7.6. Economic Variables and Pricing, Time series regressions followed by cross-section regressions (1/75–12/84, time series regressions over five years)

Constant	*MPSA*	*DEI*	*UI*	*UPREL*	*UPRMF*	*UTS*	*DTT*	*UYEN*	*OG*	*VW*	*EW*
						Part 1					
0.02013	0.00592	0.00039	0.00453	0.013690		−0.01500					
(4.440)	(1.263)	(1.966)	(1.651)	(1.747)		(−1.452)					
						Part 2					
0.01832	0.00619	0.00036	0.00419		0.00555	−0.01340					
(3.952)	(1.385)	(1.954)	(1.520)		(1.478)	(−1.247)					
						Part 3					
0.01947	0.00725	0.00039	0.00436	0.01440		−0.01345	−0.01072				
(4.500)	(1.532)	(1.985)	(1.504)	(1.892)		(−1.348)	(−1.425)				
						Part 4					
0.01790	0.00442	0.00033	0.00394	0.01280		−0.01492		−0.007550			
(4.417)	(0.965)	(1.717)	(1.543)	(1.830)		(−1.470)		(−0.712)			
						Part 5					
0.02001	0.00470	0.00035	0.00043	0.01096		−0.01140			0.01253		
(4.700)	(0.990)	(1.811)	(1.586)	(1.459)		(−1.149)			(0.477)		
						Part 6					
0.02174	0.00877	0.00041		0.01920		−0.02572					
(4.522)	(1.830)	(2.096)		(2.259)		(−2.286)					
						Part 7					
0.02478	0.00966	0.00039		0.01893		−0.02199	−0.11896				
(4.476)	(1.963)	(1.972)		(2.331)		(−2.071)	(−1.551)				

Part 8										
0.01445	0.00640	0.00042		0.01280		−0.01849			0.00478	
(2.167)	(1.581)	(2.233)		(1.806)		(−1.914)			(0.680)	
Part 9										
0.02357	0.00584	0.00032		0.01590		−0.01632				−0.01215
(3.365)	(1.641)	(1.6658)		(2.277)		(−1.721)				(−1.716)
Part 10										
−0.00266									0.02190	
(−0.408)									(2.817)	
Part 11										
0.01445	0.00642	0.00047		0.01309		−0.01954			0.01107	
(2.167)	(1.605)	(2.579)		(1.846)		(−2.018)			(1.757)	

In each part, numbers in the top rows represent the time series means of λ's. Numbers in parentheses are T statistics.

Glossary:

MPSA	monthly growth rate of industrial production (filtered)
DEI	change in expected inflation
UI	unanticipated inflation
UPRMF	unanticipated change in risk premium using electricity company bond return
UPREL	unanticipated change in risk premium using managed bond fund return
UTS	unanticipated change in the term structure of interest rates
DTT	change in terms of trade
UYEN	unanticipated change in foreign exchange rates
OG	growth rate of oil prices
VW	return on the value-weighted TSE-I index
EW	return on the equally weighted TSE-I index

most recent update of $\hat{b}$'s for cross-section regressions so that we expect more explanatory power, cross-sectionally.

The significance is weaker for Part 1 of Table 7.6 than the simultaneous case (Part 1 of Table 7.5). Using *UPRMF* again did not favor the result (Part 2 of Table 7.6), and so *UPRMF* is dropped from the analysis. The addition of *DTT* (Part 3) increased the significance for *MPSA*, *DEI*, and *UPREL* but showed slightly decreased significance for *UI* and *UTS*. Like the simultaneous case, *DTT* did not show its own significance. When *UYEN* is added (Part 4), it reduced significance for *MPSA* but did not change it for the rest of the variables. *UYEN* itself is not significant at all. A similar situation applies to the addition of *OG* (Part 5). The interpretation is that the pricing influence of *UYEN* and *OG* is already taken into account by other factors.

Noting that the expected inflation (*EIG*) has a low R^2 and that *UI* does not capture seasonal variability of the inflation rate very well, we next drop the *UI* variable. Part 6 of Table 7.6 reports the result. Although *MPSA* is still marginal, all other variables show significance. When *DTT* is added to this, it enhances the significance of *MPSA* and does not change others (Part 7).

To test whether a systematic risk exists that may have been missed by the macroeconomic variables but captured by the market indices, *VW* and *EW* are added to Part 6. Parts 8 and 9 report the result. Both *VW* and *EW* fail to show statistical significance and *EW* has a negative sign. The inclusion of market indices reduced the significance of other coefficients in both cases. This implies that the market indices do not contain missing priced factors. Part 10 displays the risk premium associated with *VW*. It is obtained by running regressions without macrovariables and is significant itself.

Part 11 is a somewhat different test from Part 8, and it shows results from regressions that use $\hat{b}$ for *VW* obtained by simple time series regressions of Part 10 and $\hat{b}$'s for macrovariables obtained by time series regressions of Part 6. Again, *VW* itself does not display significance. Other coefficients either improve or worsen slightly but the overall influence of *VW* is not substantial. This result can be viewed as supporting evidence of the APT as opposed to the CAPM.

Signs for risk premia are consistent throughout the analysis but opposite for *DEI* and *UI* compared to results from Chen, Roll, and Ross. The positive sign for inflation risk premia in our study implies that stocks that rise in price with more inflation are more valuable, other things being equal. As for *DTT*, whose risk premium is negative, the story is reversed; stock whose returns are inversely related to changes in terms of trade are more valuable. Other macrovariables bear a similar sign relationship in the risk premia of Chen, Roll, and Ross.

The evidence of the risk premia on multiple factors shows the robustness of the approach in a different but parallel economy; prespecified macroeconomic variables fare well in asset pricing even though they are marred by obvious noises.

V. Conclusion

This paper has developed macroeconomic state variables and investigated their pricing effects as systematic risks using Japanese data. The variables used are similar to those derived in Chen, Roll, and Ross (1986) for the U.S. market. We found that changes in expected inflation, unanticipated changes in risk premium and unanticipated changes in the slope of term structure appear to have a significant effect on the Japanese stock market. Weaker evidence of the presence of a risk premium exists in changes in monthly production and changes in terms of trade.

The macroeconomic data used here are not ideal; the unanticipated change in the risk premium is derived using a high-grade corporate bond hence is a weak measure of risk premium, and changes in terms of trade has an apparent autocorrelation. Improving these variables may lead to stronger evidence in the pricing result. The change in monthly production could also be improved by a forecasting method that used past returns on the market index.

On the other hand, it is clear even with the current state of the macrovariables that the oil price changes and unanticipated changes in foreign exchange are not priced in the stock market. This is surprising given the importance of international trade in the Japanese economy. Value and equally weighted market indices themselves neither have statistically significant risk premia not do they capture extra systematic risks missed by other macroeconomic state variables.

The study also suffers from a short observation period. However, the evidence presented here is encouraging and it is certainly worth exploring further as new data become available.

Notes

1. See Japanese Ministry of Finance (1983) for institutional descriptions of the Japanese securities market.
2. See Kuroda (1982, Chapter 1) and Suzuki (1980, Chapter 3) for a detailed historical survey.
3. See Hamao (1986), Kato and Schallheim (1985), and Nakamura and Terada (1984) for size and seasonal anomalies in Japanese stocks.
4. In the case of an annual coupon payment, Japanese "yield" $\hat{Y}$ is calculated as

$$P = \frac{nC + F}{1 + n\hat{Y}}$$

where P = price, n = number of remaining years, F = face value, and C = coupon payment.
5. Treating the years 1975–1984 as one period might mask the effect of the 1980 amendment of the Foreign Exchange Control Law that made Japanese markets literally open. Gultekin, Gultekin, and Penati (1987) examines the effect of this particular deregulation using the APT framework.

References

Box, George, and Gwilym Jenkins, (1976). *Time Series Analysis*, Oakland, CA, Holden-Day.

Brown, Stephen, and Mark Weinstein, (1983). "A New Approach to Testing Asset Pricing Models: The Bilinear Paradigm," *Journal of Finance*, vol. 38, pp. 711–743.

Chen, Nai-fu, (1983). "Some Empirical Tests of the Theory of Arbitrage Pricing." *Journal of Finance*, vol. 38, pp. 1393–1414.

Chen, Nai-fu, Richard Roll, and Stephen Ross, (1986). "Economic Forces and the Stock Market," *Journal of Business*, vol. 59, pp. 383–403.

Fama, Eugene, and James MacBeth, (1973). "Risk, Return, and Equilibrium: Empirical Tests," *Journal of Political Economy*, vol. 38, pp. 607–636.

Fama, Eugene, and Michael Gibbons, (1984). "A Comparison of Inflation Forecasts," *Journal of Monetary Economics*, vol. 13, pp. 327–348.

Gultekin, Bulent, Mustafa Gultekin, and Alessandro Penati, (1987). "Capital Controls and International Capital Markets Segmentation: The Evidence from the Japanese and American Stock Markets," Working Paper, Wharton School, University of Pennsylvania.

Hamao, Yasushi, (1986). "A Standard Database for the Analysis of Japanese Security Markets," Working Paper, Yale School of Management.

Japanese Ministry of Finance (ed.), (1983). *Securities Market in Japan*, Tokyo, Japan Securities Research Institute.

Kato, Kiyoshi, and James Schallheim, (1985). "Seasonal and Size Anomalies and the Japanese Stock Market," *Journal of Financial and Quantitative Analysis*, vol. 20, pp. 243-260.

Kuroda, Akio, (1982). *Nihon no Kinri Taikei* (The Term Structure of Japanese Government Bonds), Tokyo, Toyo Keizai Shimpo Sha.

McElroy, Marjorie, and Edwin Burmeister, (1986). "Joint Estimation of Factor Sensitivities and Risk Premia for the Arbitrage Pricing Theory," Working Paper, University of Virginia.

Nakamura, Takeo, and Noboru Terada, (1984). "The Size Effect and Seasonality in Japanese Stock Returns," Paper presented at the Institute for Quantitative Research in Finance (The Q Group).

Roll, Richard, and Stephen Ross, (1980). "An Empirical Investigation of the Arbitrage Pricing Theory," *Journal of Finance*, vol. 35, pp. 1073–1103.

Shanken, Jay, and Mark Weinstein, (1985). "Testing Multifactor Pricing Relations with Prespecified Factors," Working Paper, University of Southern California.

Suzuki, Yoshio, (1980). *Money and Banking in Contemporary Japan*, New Haven, CT, Yale University Press.

8

Macroeconomic Factors and the Japanese Equity Markets: The CAPMD Project[1]

Stephen J. Brown
Yamaichi Faculty Fellow, Leonard N. Stern School of Business, New York University

Toshiyuki Otsuki
Professor, Graduate School of International Management, International University of Japan

I. Introduction

Recent studies of the Japanese equity markets provide only limited evidence that macroeconomic variables are associated with positive risk premia in the Japanese equity markets.[2] In particular, it does not appear that oil price changes or exchange rate sensitivity explains the pricing of Japanese equities. This paper explores alternative definitions of the macrofactors and the effect of controlling for industrial composition in the context of a new paradigm for estimating asset pricing models introduced by McElroy and Burmeister (1988). We find evidence that from six to seven macrofactors are priced sources of risk in the Japanese equity markets. This paper briefly describes the McElroy and Burmeister model in Section II, the data used in Section III, and the basic results in Section IV. Section V contains some suggestions for future work.

II. The Model

Very little work has been done to empirically validate the CAPM, multi-beta, or APT models in the Japanese context.[3] We employ an approach due to McElroy and Burmeister that does not depend on which of these competing models of asset pricing is responsible for observed security returns. It is easily implemented using standard statistical technology. For these reasons it is a very attractive tool for an exploratory analysis of macrofactors and asset pricing in the Japanese context. In this section, we will briefly outline this approach showing how the CAPM and multibeta models are special cases of the empirical APT model they propose, and review the estimation procedure they advocate for such models.

McElroy and Burmeister suggest an empirical representation of the APT that allows the CAPM and multibeta models to be valid as very natural restrictions on the parameters of the more general model. Suppose the vector of security returns $\mathbf{r}_t$ can be represented as a linear factor model of the form:

$$\mathbf{r}_t = \mathbf{a} + \mathbf{BF}_t + \mathbf{e}_t \tag{8.1}$$

where $\mathbf{f}_t$ represents a set of $(k-1)$ macroeconomic factors. A (potentially unobserved) market index r_{mt} must also be represented as a linear function of the same macroeconomic variables:

$$r_{mt} = a_m + \mathbf{b}_m{}'\mathbf{f}_t + e_{mt} \tag{8.2}$$

The errors in the linear factor model e_t may potentially involve a residual market factor term e_{mt}

$$\mathbf{e}_t = \mathbf{b}_k e_{mt} + \boldsymbol{\xi}_t \tag{8.3}$$

which may be thought of as representing the pervasive macrofactors omitted from the specification of $\mathbf{f}_t$. If the APT model is correct, the intercept term $\mathbf{a}$ will be given by

$$\mathbf{a} \approx r_f \iota + \mathbf{B}\boldsymbol{\gamma} + \mathbf{b}_k \gamma_k \tag{8.4}$$

where r_f is a risk-free rate of interest, γ is a vector of factor prices and ι is a vector of ones. The quantity γ_k represents the factor price associated with the residual market factor. The intercept term in the market equation a_m is given by

$$a_m \approx r_f + \mathbf{b}_m{}'\boldsymbol{\gamma} + \gamma_k + \delta \tag{8.5}$$

where the exposure to the residual market factor is normalized to unity, and where the δ term captures the potential for the observed market index to be mispriced. A sufficient condition for the CAPM model and the APT model to be simultaneously true is for the matrix of factor loadings $\mathbf{B}$ to be given by

$$\mathbf{B} = \mathbf{b}_k \cdot \mathbf{b}_m{}' \tag{8.6}$$

This sufficient condition provides a simple test of the CAPM within a more general APT alternative.[4] Equations 8.1 and 8.2 correspond to the multibeta representation of the asset pricing model introduced by Sharpe (1977) and discussed in Shanken (1987), where the factor prices are constrained to be proportional to the covariance between the market return r_{mt} and the factors $\mathbf{f}_t$.

McElroy and Burmeister point out that the system of Equations 8.1, 8.2, 8.3, and 8.5 can be estimated using standard nonlinear systems estimation procedures implemented in SAS. They suggest the following two step procedure:

a) Estimate Equation 8.1 using ordinary least squares.

b) Use the estimated residuals $\hat{e}_{mt}$ to estimate the nonlinear system of equations

$$\mathbf{r}_t = r_f \boldsymbol{\iota} + \mathbf{B}\boldsymbol{\gamma} + \mathbf{b}_k \gamma_k + \mathbf{B}\mathbf{f}_t + \mathbf{b}_k \hat{e}_{mt} + \boldsymbol{\xi}_t \tag{8.7}$$

This procedure differs from traditional approaches to estimating asset pricing relations in at least two major respects. The traditional approach, based in the work of Black, Jensen, and Scholes (1972), suggests using time series data to estimate factor sensitivities (*betas* in CAPM applications or factor loadings **B** in APT applications[5]) and then estimating factor prices γ through a cross-section regression of returns against these estimated factor sensitivities. An alternative approach that avoids the error in variables problem associated with regressing returns on estimates in the second stage regression is to consider estimating factor sensitivities and factor prices *simultaneously* using nonlinear least squares procedures.[6] McElroy and Burmeister advocate the latter approach, and argue that by considering the model as a multivariate nonlinear regression model with cross equation restrictions, one can use the highly developed least squares statistical machinery for such nonlinear systems.

Access to this statistical technology implies the second major respect in which the McElroy and Burmeister approach differs from the traditional approach. Most of the time series-cross section approaches to estimating asset pricing models assume, at least implicitly, that the error covariances $\boldsymbol{\xi}_t$ are independent and identically distributed in the cross-section of securities.[7] Nonlinear, seemingly unrelated regression methods suggested in Gallant (1975) relax this assumption. In the APT context this allows for multiple nonpriced factors to influence security returns.

The macrofactor realizations $\mathbf{f}_t$ were estimated using the forecast errors derived from a multivariate state-space representation[8] of six macroeconomic time series. A similar procedure has shown some utility for estimation of expected inflation.[9] The procedure includes as a special case the approach taken by Fama and Gibbons (1984) and applied several times in this context.[10] Given the exploratory nature of this research it was considered appropriate to extend the analysis to consideration of the other potential candidates for identification as macroeconomic factors. Once the macrofactors are identified, it is reasonable to consider estimating the system of equations by substituting the state-space representation of the macrofactors into Equation 8.7 and estimating the factor prices, factor loadings, and state-space representations simultaneously. For simplicity, we only report results from the two-step procedure of estimating the forecast errors and in a second stage estimating the system of Equations 8.7, although the simultaneous estimation route is attractive and the subject of current research.[11]

III. Data

The basic data for this study consists of rates of return on all securities trading on the first section of the Tokyo Stock Exchange from May 1980 through August 1988. For a particular month return to be included in the study, the security in question had to be listed for that month and for the previous month. The security also had to pass two further tests. Market capitalization data had to be available for the previous month and, in addition, data on the industrial composition of the issuing firm had to be available. For all but a very small fraction of these companies, Yamaichi Securities has computed sales by line of business for 101 industrial classifications. For certain months, particularly in the early years of the sample, no company listed particular industrial classifications as their major line of business.[12] Such classifications were eliminated from consideration, leaving the 94 industries given in Table 8.1.

For the purpose of the analysis described in the previous section, we aggregated these securities into portfolios and computed the returns on such portfolios. The portfolios formed were of three types:

1. Industry portfolios, where the industries were defined according to the lines of business, as reported by Yamaichi.
2. Industry portfolios, where each industry is defined according to the major reported line of business.

Table 8.1. Industry Groups Used in Study

1 Fishery & Agricultural Products	33 Drugs	65 Precision Machinery
2 Coal	34 Medical Products	66 Printing and Publishing
3 Crude Oil	35 Paints and Inks	67 Music Instruments
4 Construction	36 Toiletries	68 Trading
5 Civil Engineering	37 Magnetic Products	69 Restaurants
6 Electrical, Telecom Engineering	38 Refined Oil	70 Department Stores
7 Road Construction	39 Tires	71 Supermarkets
8 Marine Construction	40 Rubber Goods	72 Long-term Credit Banks
9 Bridges and Steelframes	41 Glass	73 Money Center Banks
10 House Construction	42 Cement	74 Regional Banks
11 Engineering	43 Steel	75 Trust Banks
12 Building Materials	44 Stainless Steel	76 Personal Loans
13 Flour Milling	45 Nonferrous Metals	77 Sogo Banks
14 Processed Foods	46 Metal Fabrication	78 Consumer Credit
15 Foodstuffs	47 Cables and Wires	79 Leasing
16 Sugar Refining	48 Machinery	80 Securities
17 Confectionary	49 Machine Tools	81 Property and Casualty Insurance
18 Dairy Products	50 Agricultural Machinery	82 Land and Office Leasing
19 Soft Drinks	51 Construction Machinery	83 Real Estate
20 Liquor	52 Office Equipment	84 Railroad and Bus
21 Oil and Fats	53 Household Appliances	85 Trucking
22 Textiles	54 Machinery Parts	86 Shipping
23 Synthetic Fibers	55 Heavy Electrical Machinery	87 Airlines
24 Apparel	56 Consumer Electronics	88 Warehouses
25 Paper and Pulp	57 Computers and Semiconductors	89 Broadcast Media
26 Industrial Chemicals	58 Electronic Components	90 Communication Equipment
27 Chemical Products	59 Batteries	91 Electric Power
28 Petrochemicals	60 Ship Building	92 Gas Distributors*
29 Agricultural Chemicals	61 Automobile Manufacturing	93 Entertainment*
30 Industrial Gas	62 Truck Manufacturing	94 Leisure and Hotels*
31 Petrochemical Products	63 Auto Parts	
32 Oleochemicals	64 Measuring Instruments	

†The asterisks (*) denote industries for which data was available, and returns were used to construct the value weighted index. However, they were excluded from further analysis to permit the full error covariance to be (numerically) nonsingular.

3. Size portfolios, where each portfolio is defined according to the relative value outstanding of the securities contained in it.

In the first portfolio formation procedure, the percentage of sales according to line of business was collected as of the previous month and used to infer industry returns.[14] The second portfolio formation procedure simply defines each industry return as the return on a portfolio comprising those firms that report that industry as the major line of business, with weights proportional to the value of equity outstanding as of the previous month. The third portfolio formation strategy is to sort securities by value of equity outstanding as of the previous month, and then form 94 equally weighted portfolios ranked by value of equity outstanding, lowest to highest.

To the extent that others have considered industry composition in the context of asset pricing studies, it is the second approach that is generally employed.[15] The reason this method is favored is because line of business data are considered difficult to find in machine readable form. Tests of asset pricing relations generally use size-ranked portfolios.[16] The line of business data is to be preferred because it allows the investigator to control for changes in risk exposure that arise from changes in the industrial composition of firms with equity trading on the Tokyo Stock Exchange.

The macroeconomic variables used to perform the exploratory analysis were the first difference in logarithms of the monthly average money supply (M1), the (seasonally adjusted) industrial production index, the wholesale price index crude oil price in $U.S. per barrel and exchange rate (¥/$U.S.) defined as of month end, and one plus the month average of the overnight call rate.[17] Results from fitting these data using a multivariate, state-space procedure with a maximum allowance of four lags on the basis of data from January 1978 to August 1988 revealed the necessity of taking a 12th seasonal difference of the money supply variable.[18] With this correction the innovations specified by the forecast errors appeared to be white noise processes, uncorrelated[19] with zero mean within the period of study (June 1980–August 1988). These innovations were used to form the vector of six macrofactors $\mathbf{f}_t$. The seventh macrofactor, a residual market factor, was constructed from the residuals of Equation 8.2, estimated using a value weighted market index constructed from the set of security returns used for the study.[20] At this exploratory stage of the analysis, extensive experimentation with other suggested macrofactors, such as the change in forecast values from the state-space procedure, seemed to add very little explanatory power to the analysis once the residual market factor was included as a potential macrofactor.

IV. Results

The basic results from estimation of the general factor pricing model (Equation 8.7) can be found in Table 8.2. In that table are the estimates of the risk premium factors γ and t-values computed from the associated asymptotic standard errors. The three panels of that table correspond to the three portfolio formation rules described in the previous section.[21] The first line in each panel refers to the results estimating the equations using nonlinear, ordinary least squares, while the second refers to results obtained by nonlinear, seemingly unrelated regression procedures, using the error covariance matrix estimated using the ordinary least squares results. The results are quite similar for the different portfolio formation rules,[23] with the crude oil price being the most significant source of priced risk. The nonlinear, ordinary least squares results are the closest in methodology to those reported by Hamao (1988) and Elton and Gruber (1988). Consistent with those results, the Table 8.2 results indicate limited evidence of macrofactor pricing except for the line of business portfolios not considered by the other work. The fact that the seemingly unrelated regression results confirm evidence of significant pricing of the macrofactors suggests the importance of accounting for residual covariance (potentially unpriced factors) in studies of asset pricing in Japan.

The intercept term recorded in this table can be thought of either as a test of the model, or an index of the adequacy of the monthly average overnight call rate as an index of the prevailing risk-free interest rate, since the dependent variable is the return in excess of the average call rate (expressed in percentage terms). With a positively sloped yield curve, one might expect the intercept to be positive. However, for the size portfolio the intercept is significantly negative. Since the average value of the call rate for the period in question was 0.497 percent, this implies a *negative* implied risk-free rate (though with a statistically insignificant t-value of 1.43). For other reasons, the call rate data is difficult to interpret.[24]

Table 8.2. Estimation of Risk Premium Factors Using Japanese Data, June 1980–August 1988*

	Intercept	Money Supply	Production Index	Wholesale Price Index	Crude Oil Price ($/Bbl)	Exchange Rate (¥/$)	Call Rate	Residual Market Factor
Industry Portfolios Defined Using Line of Business Data								
Ordinary Least Squares	1.005 (4.10)	0.00038 (0.15)	0.00211 (0.80)	0.00332 (3.35)	−0.02294 (−2.75)	0.00021 (0.04)	0.01499 (2.02)	0.81683 (2.26)
Seemingly Unrelated Regression	1.284 (11.41)	−0.00002 (−0.02)	0.00119 (2.62)	0.00289 (10.49)	−0.02054 (−9.91)	0.00040 (0.20)	0.01557 (7.84)	0.50526 (3.74)
Industry Portfolios Defined Using Major Line of Business								
Ordinary Least Squares	−0.084 (−0.12)	0.00691 (0.91)	0.02508 (1.68)	0.00856 (1.84)	−0.05074 (−1.68)	0.00128 (0.12)	−0.00266 (−0.15)	1.86800 (1.86)
Seemingly Unrelated Regression	−0.544 (−1.86)	0.00874 (4.54)	0.03156 (5.58)	0.01006 (6.85)	−0.05538 (−5.37)	0.05560 (1.04)	−0.00261 (−0.24)	2.52225 (6.88)

Portfolios Defined Using Size Categories

Ordinary Least Squares	0.092 (0.05)	0.01724 (0.76)	0.06306 (1.06)	0.01976 (1.13)	−0.03601 (−0.63)	0.11272 (0.98)	0.02437 (0.48)	5.20973 (0.98)
Seemingly Unrelated Regression	−1.166 (−2.49)	0.01039 (3.67)	0.04648 (8.16)	0.01415 (8.10)	−0.03049 (−9.14)	0.09075 (7.84)	−0.01654 (1.91)	5.30990 (9.07)

*T values in parentheses.

Table 8.3. Factor Loadings Estimated for Industry Groups (Portfolios Defined Using Line of Business Data), June 1980–August 1988*

Seemingly Unrelated Regression Results

Macrofactor	Industry With Most Significant Negative Exposure to Macrofactor	Industry With Most Significant Positive Exposure to Macrofactor
Money Supply	Textiles (−1.47)	Securities (3.38)
Production Index	Real Estate (−2.34)	Refined Oil (1.87)
Wholesale Price Index	Crude Oil (−2.31)	Construction (1.66)
Crude Oil Price ($U.S./Bbl)	Trust Banks (−3.24)	Batteries (2.07)
Exchange Rate (¥/$U.S.)	Consumer Credit (−3.19)	Precision Machinery (3.10)
Call Rate	Processed Foods (−3.56)	Electric Power (2.09)
Residual Market Factor	N.A.	Securities (11.87)

**T* values in parentheses

It is interesting to study the factor loadings estimated for the model. The industries with the most significant negative and positive exposures to the macrofactors are listed in Table 8.3. A number of these results are intuitive. The securities industry has the heaviest loading on money supply and residual market factors. The electric power industry should be dependent on shocks to the call rate because of the nature of rate of return regulation.[25] These loadings represent the sum of all direct and indirect effects. The indirect effects arise through complex industry interactions. These interactions can be described by the kind of empirical analysis reported here, but can only be fully understood through sophisticated input-output or related analyses.[26]

McElroy and Burmeister advocate using iterated procedures to estimate the parameters where the residual covariance matrix is successively updated and used to reestimate the parameters. In the iterated, ordinary, least squares methods reported in Table 8.4, the error covariance matrix is assumed diagonal, whereas the iterated, seemingly unrelated methods assume the error covariance matrix is a full matrix. This iterated procedure did not converge for either the second or the third portfolio formation data. However, the point estimates for the industry line of business (as well as the nonconvergent estimates for the other data) did not differ greatly from the noniterated results. One important observation is the fact that the iterated, ordinary, least-squares maximized likelihood function is very close to the likelihood for the full error covariance methods. This suggests that a simple heteroskedasticity correction may capture most of the value of the computationally more difficult seemingly unrelated regression results. The one new result by consideration of the iterated methods is the fact that the production index risk premium changes sign.

The results reported in Table 8.5 suggest that the results for the line of business data are remarkably stable over time, both in terms of the coefficient values and in terms of the maximized likelihood function.[29] The production index premium factor represents an exception to this rule, being larger and more significant in the later period. This difference between the subperiod results might tend to explain the counterintuitive sign of the production index risk premium factor using the iterated methods reported on the previous table.

V. Conclusion

An exploratory analysis of the effect of macrofactors in pricing of Japanese equities suggests that from six to seven macrofactors are associated with significant risk premia. These results differ from other findings. We attribute the difference to the use of a new and more complete data base that accounts for line of business reporting, and the application of an estimation methodology that is not sensitive to which particular model of asset pricing is applicable in the Japanese context.[30] This methodology is easy to apply and allows for the error covariance matrix to be other than diagonal. There does appear to be significant added value associated with the use of a full covariance matrix, although the data available to estimate it is somewhat limited, as evidenced by the fact that several industry groups had to be excluded from analysis to estimate a nonsingular matrix. Current research is studying the extent to which it is possible to capture the benefits of a full covariance matrix assumption by structuring this matrix to account for additional risk factors at an industry and firm level.

Table 8.4. Effect of Iterated Estimation Procedures, Industry Portfolios Defined Using Line of Business Data, June 1980–August 1988*

	Intercept	Money Supply	Production Index	Wholesale Price Index	Crude Oil Price ($/Bbl)	Exchange Rate (¥/$)	Call Rate	Residual Market Factor
Results Assuming a Diagonal Error Covariance Matrix:								
Ordinary Least Squares	1.005 (4.10)	0.00038 (0.15)	0.00211 (0.80)	0.00332 (3.35)	−0.02294 (−2.75)	0.00021 (0.04)	0.01499 (2.02)	0.81683 (2.26)
Maximized Log Likelihood = −433,810.76								
Iterated Ordinary Least Squares	0.842 (3.91)	−0.00041 (−0.19)	0.00155 (0.67)	0.00243 (3.17)	−0.02067 (−2.90)	−0.00015 (−0.04)	0.00777 (1.23)	0.86062 (2.71)
Maximized Log Likelihood = −8269.48								

Results Assuming a Full Error Covariance Matrix:

Seemingly Unrelated Regression	1.284 (11.41)	−0.00002 (−0.02)	0.00119 (2.62)	0.00289 (10.49)	−0.02054 (−9.91)	0.00040 (0.20)	0.01557 (7.84)	0.50526 (3.74)
Maximized Log Likelihood = −8251.13								
Iterated Seemingly Unrelated Regression	1.776 (22.56)	0.00082 (1.27)	−0.00077 (−2.32)	0.00136 (8.28)	−0.01185 (−8.53)	0.00448 (2.87)	0.01543 (9.53)	−0.27947 (−3.40)
Maximized Log Likelihood = −8251.13								

*T values in parentheses.

Table 8.5. Effect of Estimation Period on Results

	Seemingly Unrelated Regression Results							
	Intercept	Money Supply	Production Index	Wholesale Price Index	Crude Oil Price ($/Bbl)	Exchange Rate (¥/$)	Call Rate	Residual Market Factor
Whole Period (June 1980–August 1988)	1.284 (11.41)	−0.00002 (−0.02)	0.00119 (2.62)	0.00289 (10.49)	−0.02054 (−9.91)	0.00040 (0.20)	0.01557 (7.84)	0.50526 (3.74)
Maximized Log Likelihood = −8251.13								
First Half (June 1980–June 1985)	1.286 (7.15)	0.00001 (0.04)	−0.00021 (−0.28)	0.00222 (6.60)	−0.01578 (−6.63)	−0.00287 (−0.87)	0.01426 (4.70)	0.43791 (2.07)
Maximized Log Likelihood = −3804.23								
Second Half (July 1985–August 1988)	1.297 (7.39)	−0.00101 (−1.13)	0.00205 (2.95)	0.00373 (8.43)	−0.02541 (−7.26)	0.00219 (0.85)	0.01790 (5.59)	0.68394 (3.51)
Maximized Log Likelihood = −3807.19								

Notes

1. This work is part of a research project entitled CAPMD, and is supported by generous funding from Yamaichi Securities Co. Ltd. We wish to acknowledge the support of Mr. Matsumoto of Yamaichi and Mr. Takano, the project team leader. Mr. Oshige and Dr. Om Sarda were very helpful in making available the relevant data and some of the computational procedures used in this study.
2. Hamao (1988) finds that macroeconomic variables defined using the growth rate of industrial production and inflation measures are associated with positive risk premia in the Japanese equity markets, while oil prices and exchange rates are not associated with such premia. Elton and Gruber (1988) find evidence of four pervasive factors in Japanese equity returns. These factors are associated with macroeconomic variables, but do not appear to imply positive risk premia.
3. Early work attempting to validate the Capital Asset Pricing Model (CAPM) in the Japanese context can be found in Lau, Quay, and Ramsey (1974). Empirical work studying the Arbitrage Pricing Theory (APT) of Ross (1976) using Japanese data can be found in Hamao (1987). The work of Elton and Gruber (1988) in this context can be interpreted either in an APT or multibeta (Sharpe, 1977) context.
4. This model is similar to that of Shanken (1987), who provides an even more restrictive set of conditions on the factor price vector γ and obtains a test of the efficiency of an observed index against an unspecified alternative.
5. As in the work of Chen, Roll, and Ross (1986) and Hamao (1988).
6. This is suggested by Gibbons (1982) in the context of CAPM and Brown and Weinstein (1983) in the context of APT.
7. The work of Litzenberger and Ramaswamy (1979) is a notable exception to this general statement. These authors assume the errors are independent in the cross-section but allow the error variances to differ from security to security.
8. This procedure and algorithms used to implement it are due to Akaike (1974).
9. See Burmeister, Wall, and Hamilton (1986).
10. In the work of Chen, Roll and Ross (1986), Hamao (1988), and Shanken and Weinstein (1987).
11. See Otsuki (1988).
12. Such examples being the Fishery Foods classification, and the Audio-Visual Software industry.
13. These data were computed in such a way that each industry return is in fact the return on a portfolio of securities and trading on the first section of the Tokyo Stock Exchange.
14. See, for example, Brown and Weinstein (1983).

15. Examples being the work of Chen, Roll, and Ross (1986) and Hamao (1988).
16. All data were obtained from TIS™ (a database of Yamaichi Securities). The original sources of data are the Bank of Japan (the money supply, wholesale price index, and call rate), the Ministry of International Trade and Industry (industrial production index), Jiji Tsushin (the exchange rate), the Ministry of Finance (crude oil price), and Yamaichi (security rates of return).
17. As with all such macroeconomic variables there is a serious question as to the extent to which they are actually synchronous in time. In particular, discussion has centered on the extent to which the production index should be lagged [Chen, Roll, and Ross (1986), Hamao (1988)]. After filtering the data with the multivariate state-space procedure discussed in the text, extensive experimentation showed that the use of the lagged production index did not add significantly to the explanatory power of the model.
18. The innovations were uncorrelated, with the important exception that the wholesale price index innovation appeared correlated with the exchange rate innovation ($\hat{\rho}$ = 0.4976) within the period of study (June 1980–August 1988). The only other significant pairwise correlation was that between the production index and call rate innovations ($\hat{\rho}$ = 0.2067).
19. This regression had a small but significant R^2 of 0.1289 ($F_{6,91}$ = 2.244), where the most significant variable was the oil price innovation ($t = -2.19$). This indicates either that the residual market factor captures significant macrofactors not otherwise explained by the model, or that the market risk exposures changed significantly over this period. Both hypotheses appear to be supported in the data.
20. In each case the number of portfolios had to be reduced from 94 to 91 due to numerical singularities in the estimated covariance matrices for the seemingly unrelated regression results.
21. This is true not only in terms of the estimated coefficient values but also the maximized likelihoods. For the first portfolio formation rule, the maximized log likelihood is −8251.13, for the second it is −8262.56, and for the third size portfolios it is −8255.64.
22. See Hamao (1987).
23. See Brown and Sibley (1987) for a discussion of these issues.
24. For an example of such an analysis, see Higgs (1988).
25. We should note that the covariance matrix assumed for the subperiod results was given by the error covariance matrix estimated for the entire period. In principle, to evaluate the stability of the relationship over time, one would wish to estimate the error covariance matrix using subperiod data, and then maximizing the likelihood function for the entire period using the subperiod estimated error covariance matrix. This was not possible, since the error covariance matrix has a higher dimension (91) than the number

of observations in each subperiod (48), implying the subperiod estimated covariance matrices would be singular.

26. Having written this, we note that it was of interest to study the extent to which the data supported the particular restrictions of the CAPM. On the basis of the nonlinear, seemingly unrelated regression results, the maximized likelihood function for the CAPM restricted model with 638 parameters was $-568,172.24$ as opposed to the maximized likelihood for the unrestricted model of 644 parameters of -8251.13 for the industry line of business data. The corresponding likelihoods were $-97,269.87$ as opposed to -8262.56 for the major line of business industry data, and $-82,099.18$ as opposed to -8255.64 for the size data. In each case this difference is significant at the 1% level. In addition, for all databases, the implied risk-free rate is significantly negative on imposition of the CAPM restrictions.

References

Akaike, H., (1974). "Markovian representation of stochastic processes and its application to the analysis of autoregressive moving average processes," *Annals of the Institute of Statistical Mathematics,* Vol. 26, pp. 363–387.

Black, Fischer, Michael Jensen, and Myron Scholes, (1972). "The capital asset pricing model: Some empirical tests," in *Studies in the Theory of Capital Markets,* Michael Jensen, ed., New York, Praeger.

Brown, Stephen, and Mark Weinstein, (1983). "A new approach to testing asset pricing models: The bilinear paradigm," *Journal of Finance,* Vol. 38, pp. 711–743.

Brown, Stephen, and David Sibley, (1987). *The Theory of Public Utility Pricing,* New York, Cambridge University Press.

Burmeister, Edwin, Kent Wall, and James Hamilton, (1986). "Estimation of unobserved expected monthly inflation using Kalman filtering," *Journal of Business and Economic Statistics,* Vol. 4, pp. 147–160.

Chen, Nai-fu, Richard Roll, and Stephen Ross, (1986). "Economic forces and the stock market," *Journal of Business,* Vol. 59, pp. 383–403.

Elton, Ned, and Martin Gruber, (1988). "A multi-index risk model of the Japanese stock market," *Japan and the World Economy,* Vol. 1, forthcoming.

Fama, Eugene, and Michael Gibbons, (1984). "A comparison of inflation forecasts," *Journal of Monetary Economics,* Vol. 13, pp. 327–348.

Gallant, Ronald, (1975). "Seemingly unrelated nonlinear regressions," *Journal of Econometrics,* Vol. 3, pp. 35–50.

Gibbons, Michael, (1982). "Multivariate tests of financial models: A new approach," *Journal of Financial Economics,* Vol. 10, pp. 3–27.

Higgs, Peter, (1988). "A forward-looking approach to portfolio analysis using a computable general equilibrium model," Unpublished Working Paper IP-37, Impact Research Centre, The University of Melbourne.

Hamao, Yasushi, (1988). "An empirical examination of the Arbitrage Pricing Theory using Japanese data," *Japan and the World Economy,* Vol. 1, forthcoming.

Hamao, Yasushi, (1987). Unpublished dissertation, School of Organization and Management, Yale University.

Lau, Sheila, Stuart Quay, and Carl Ramsey, (1974). "The Tokyo Stock Exchange and the Capital Asset Pricing Model," *Journal of Finance,* Vol. 9, pp. 507–514.

Litzenberger, Robert, and Krishna Ramaswamy, (1979). "The effect of personal taxes and dividends on capital asset prices: Theory and empirical evidence," *Journal of Financial Economics,* Vol. 7, pp. 163–195.

McElroy, Marjorie, and Edwin Burmeister, (1988). "Arbitrage pricing theory as a restricted nonlinear multivariate regression model," *Journal of Business and Economic Statistics,* Vol. 6, pp. 29–42.

Otsuki, Toshiyuki, (1988). "Modeling the APT and innovation generating process," Unpublished Working Paper, International Management Research Institute, International University of Japan, forthcoming.

Roll, Richard, and Stephen Ross, (1980). "An empirical investigation of the arbitrage pricing theory," *Journal of Finance,* Vol. 35, pp. 1073–1103.

Ross, Stephen, (1976). "The arbitrage theory of capital asset pricing," *Journal of Economic Theory,* Vol. 13, pp. 341–360.

Shanken, Jay, and Mark Weinstein, (1987). "Macroeconomic variables and asset pricing: Estimation and tests," Unpublished Working Paper, University of Rochester.

Shanken, Jay, (1987). "Multivariate proxies and asset pricing relations: Living with the Roll critique," *Journal of Financial Economics,* Vol. 18, pp. 91–110.

Sharpe, William, (1977). "The capital asset pricing model: A "Multi-Beta" interpretation," in *Financial decision making under uncertainty,* Haim Levy and Marshall Sarnat, eds., New York, Academic Press.

9

International Capital Markets Segmentation: The Japanese Experience*

Mustafa N. Gultekin
The University of North Carolina at Chapel Hill

N. Bulent Gultekin
The Wharton School, University of Pennsylvania, also Chief Advisor to the Prime Minister of the Republic of Turkey

Alessandro Penati
Director of Research, Akros S.P.A.

I. Introduction

The assumption of a unified and integrated world capital market is central to most theoretical developments in both international finance and macroeconomics; indeed, it also lies behind much of the recent international policy discussion.[1] Nevertheless, it remains one of the least tested propositions in the field. Segmentation may arise either because of government impediments to capital movements or because of individuals' inhibitions or irrationality. If the hypothesis that the international markets are integrated is rejected, there is still an important empirical question left unanswered that is related to the source of segmentation. Although there is a rich body of theoretical research on the international market

---

* The views expressed here are solely those of the authors and do not necessarily represent the views of the Prime Ministry or the Akros S.P.A.

We thank Bernard Dumas, Bob Litzenberger, Craig MacKinlay, Jennifer Conrad, Bob Harris, Naoki Kishimoto, and Rene Stulz for many useful suggestions. We are grateful to the University of Pennsylvania Research Fund for its generous financial suppport and especially to Nomura Research Institute for providing us with the Japanese stock returns.

integration, only a few studies have tried to investigate this important question empirically.

A first group of empirical studies on market integration have generally adopted an international single-index asset pricing model *à la* Sharpe-Lintner-Mossin to test whether a purely domestic factor—usually the part of the return on the domestic market portfolio that is orthogonal to the world portfolio—has explanatory power in a regression of stock returns on a world market index.[2] The finding that the domestic factor is often priced is then taken to support market segmentation.

Although appealing on theoretical grounds, the interpretation of this empirical evidence, however, is not so clear cut due to intractable problems. A single-index, international, capital asset pricing model can only be obtained under the restrictive assumptions of a universal logarithmic utility function (Adler and Dumas, 1983), or purchasing power parity (PPP) (Grauer, et al., 1976), or no correlation between exchange rate movements and stock returns as well as deterministic domestic consumption deflators (Solnik, 1974a). With deviations from purchasing power parity and more risk aversion than the logarithmic investor, for example, the equilibrium rate of return on an asset would also depend on its correlation with the inflation rates in various countries (Adler and Dumas, 1983; Stulz, 1985), so that the pricing of purely domestic factors would not necessarily indicate lack of integration.

Single-index models also do not address the question of whether segmentation arises from government policies or from market inefficiency. Theoretically, a powerful test could be devised by specifying two asset pricing models—one without and one with barriers to international investments—and then verify whether the additional restrictions implied by capital controls are supported by the data. Unfortunately, the pricing models will be different depending on the type of barrier imposed by governments (Stulz, 1981, 1981b; Eun and Janakiramanan, 1986) and, realistically, one cannot hope to capture the characteristics of the various countries' capital controls regimes with just one model specification. Furthermore, both the extent and form of the impediments to capital movements imposed by a country vary through time in response to balance of payments developments. During the oil crises of the seventies many of the industrialized countries adopted capital controls in order to face the ensuing balance of payment crises. Asset pricing models have to incorporate the anticipation of future governments' actions, which will render the testability of any model nearly impossible.[3]

A second group of studies has used an international version of the Arbitrage Pricing Theory (APT).[4] Because the pricing in this model is based on an arbitrage condition of nominal returns, APT has the advantage of eluding the problem of PPP deviations. However, if this framework is applied to a large set of countries, it may not provide information as to the sources of segmentation, namely government policies versus market failures.

Another approach is to test the equality of the marginal rate of substitution in consumption in different countries if agents have access to the same risk-free interest rate. This approach is adopted by Obstfeld (1986) who cannot reject the null hypothesis of integration. It would be difficult to extend this approach, however, to the pricing of risky assets. On empirical grounds, international consumption-beta models do not offer a solution to the problem because the knowledge of the state variables driving the system is needed in order to estimate them.[5]

Given the current status of the theory and the complexity of the problem, we believe that general tests of capital markets integration are either not viable or deemed to be uninformative. The difficulties associated with testing international capital asset pricing models have long been recognized in the literature. Solnik (1977) contains an early discussion of the issue. Therefore, in this paper, we try a different approach by focusing on the experience of just one country, Japan, at the time of the implementation of its new Foreign Exchange and Foreign Trade Control Law in December 1980. This law amounted to a true regime switch that virtually eliminated most capital controls in an economy where the financial markets had been highly regulated until then. If the controls were the only source of segmentation, we should be able to reject the hypothesis that the *price of risk* in any currency—defined in terms of various multifactor asset pricing models—was the same in the Tokyo and in the New York stock markets before the end of 1980, but not after that date. The approach that we follow is similar to an event study; as such, the results lack generality but they are more informative.

In the four years after the liberalization, we cannot find any sign of segmentation between the Japanese and U.S. security markets. Arbitrage has thus ensured that risk carries the same price in the two countries, when expressed in a common numéraire. By contrast, we often reject the equality of both the risk premia and the return on the risk-free asset before the liberalization of December 1980. The data support the view that government policies, rather than individual investors' behavior, create international capital markets segmentation.

In Section II we briefly review the Japanese experience with capital controls. In Section III we describe the model and the hypotheses being tested. In Section IV we explain the data and in Sections V and VI we present empirical tests utilizing prespecified risk factors for individual securities and portfolios. In Section VII we present tests utilizing risk factors estimated with factor analysis. Section VIII contains concluding remarks.

II. The Japanese Experience with Capital Controls: A Brief Account

Until 1974, no Japanese security firm could buy foreign financial assets and no foreign company could buy Japanese securities. Domestically, there was no free market for short-term assets. A steady liberalization process of domestic financial markets began after that date although interest rates in the money markets were completely deregulated only in 1978–1979.[6] Controls on international capital flows were instead effectively maintained, even in the second part of the seventies, as a policy tool to manage the exchange rate (Otani and Tiwari, 1981; Ito, 1986).

In an attempt to check the sharp appreciation of the yen from mid-1977 to the end of 1978, capital outflows were encouraged and inflows discouraged: nonresidents were prohibited from purchasing Japanese securities with maturities less than five years and one month; the marginal reserve requirement on yen accounts by nonresidents was also increased in steps to 100%; while Japanese institutions were for the first time allowed to purchase foreign securities. After a brief relaxation of the controls in 1979, Japanese authorities resorted to their use in 1980, this time to support a falling yen: the reserve requirements on nonresidents' deposits were rolled back to zero, Japanese banks were encouraged to raise funds in London and to transfer them to Tokyo and, at the same time, foreigners were allowed to trade in the domestic money market.

A sharp change in the capital control regime has occurred since December 1980 when the enactment of the new Foreign Exchange and Foreign Trade Control Law completely liberalized short-term capital movements. Since then, the Japanese government has also supported the "internationalization" of the yen and improved foreigners' access to all Japanese security markets.

The dramtic impact of Japanese controls between 1977 and 1980 and of the subsequent liberalization are clearly visualized in Figure 9.1, depicting the interest rate differential between three-month euroyen deposits traded in London and three-month repurchase agreements (*Gensaki*) in Tokyo—a market that has been least affected by administrative controls. Before 1981, the interest rate differential is substantial—it was negative until 1979 when capital was prevented from flowing into Japan and positive in 1980 when the opposite occurred—but has been practically zero after then, an indication that any government-induced segmentation of the market had ceased its effects on market prices. Even though the interest rate differential is a measure of money markets segmentation, data on stock-related capital movements in and out of Japan presented in Table 9.1 reveal a sharp increase in two-way flows after 1980.

Given the depth of the controls and the extent of the subsequent liberalization program, the Japanese experience constitutes a unique opportunity for a semicontrolled experiment to test international capital markets segmentation. If government policies, as opposed to investor attitudes, were the only source of segmentation, the price of risk in the U.S. and Japanese stock markets (expressed in the same currency) should

Table 9.1. Gross Equity-Related Capital Movements (in million dollars)

Fiscal Year[1]	Japanese Trade in Foreign Stocks[2]	Foreign Trade in Japanese Stocks[2]
1977	466	6131
1978	653	11,385
1979	1030	12,034
1980	1132	25,383
1981	1533	44,699
1982	2663	35,905
1983	3356	70,025
1984	4503	77,825

1. Fiscal years in Japan begin on April 1.

2. Sum of stock purchases and sales.

Source: Bank of Japan, Annual Report 1987.

Figure 9.1. Spread Between Three-month Euroyen in London and Three-Month Gensaki in Tokyo

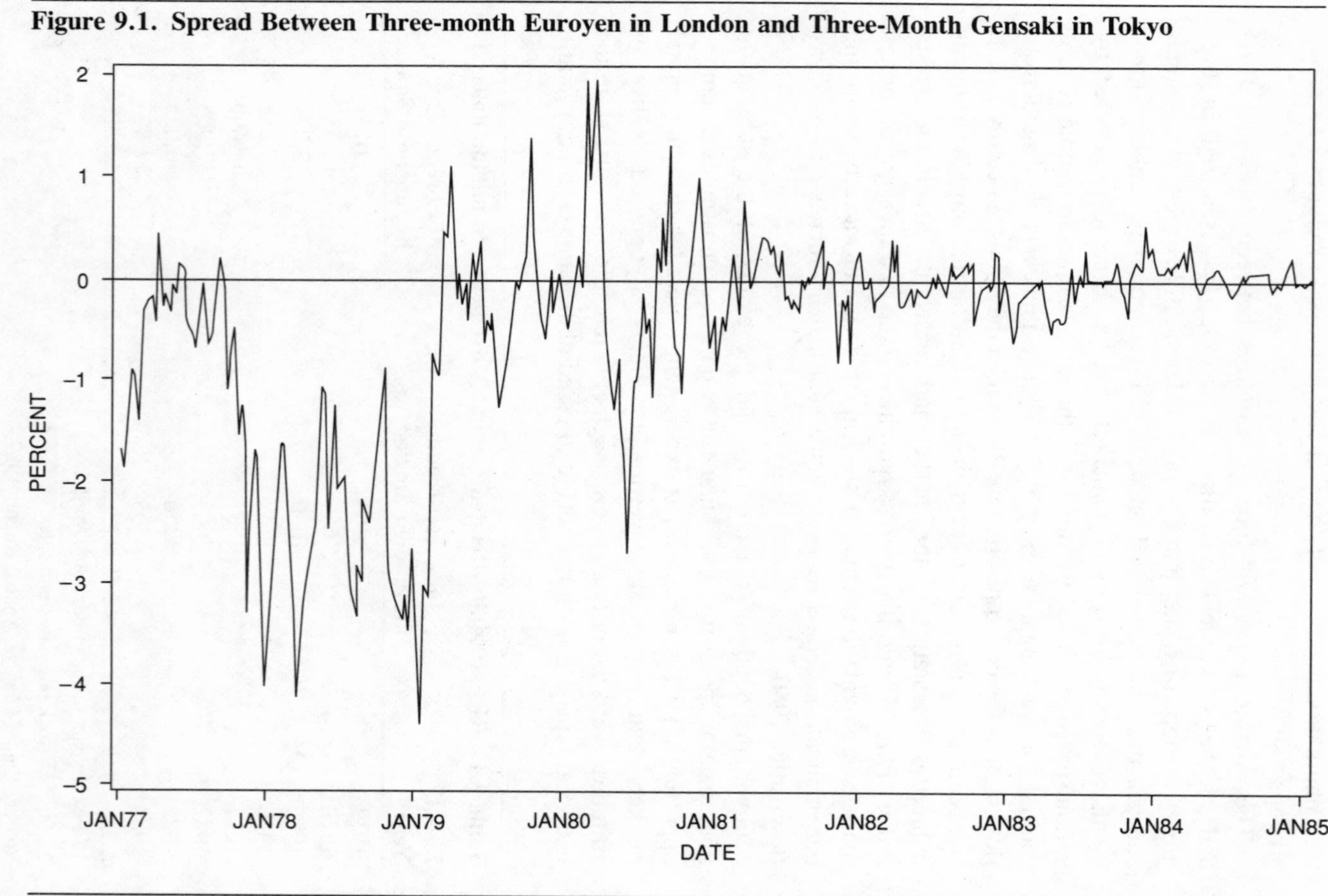

be different before 1981, but the difference should disappear afterwards. This is the hypothesis that we test in the following sections.

III. Testing Market Segmentation with APT

In order to test the equality between the price of risk in the two markets, and thus the proposition of market integration, we need a model that defines risk. We choose an international version of APT for two reasons. First, earlier empirical evidence indicates that more than one factor may affect security prices in an international setting, but it is difficult to derive the exact form of the pricing equation. Second, APT can be based on an arbitrage relation of nominal rates of returns so that one need not worry about deviations from purchasing power parity. It is worthwhile to note, however, that this paper is by no means a test of APT; rather, the APT framework is used to generate a benchmark that is used to compare pre– and postliberalization rates of return.

In our two-country case we have $N + 2$ securities traded in the United States and Japan, which are indexed by i. We assume that security 0 is the risk-free rate in U.S. dollars and security 1 is the Japanese risk-free asset, which, however, is risky in dollar terms. The remaining N assets are Japanese and American stocks. If the U.S. dollar is used as numéraire, APT postulates that the return-generating function for the $N + 1$ risky securities is linear:

$$r_t = E_t + BF_t + e_t \tag{9.1}$$

where r_t is the $(N + 1) \times 1$ vector of nominal rates of return (in dollars) at time t, **E** is the vector of expected return, **F** is the $k \times 1$ vector of risk factors with mean zero and covariance matrix of unity, **B** is the $(N + 1) \times k$ matrix of the sensitivity coefficients to the risk factors, and **e** is the vector of idiosyncratic terms with a diagonal covariance matrix **S**.

It is well known that in the absence of arbitrage, APT asserts that expected returns (in dollars) should be linear in **B**, that is,

$$E_t = \gamma_{0t} i + B\gamma_t \tag{9.2}$$

where γ is the vector of risk premia associated with risky factors, γ_0 is the risk-free rate, and **i** is an $(N + 1) \times 1$ vector of ones.

Solnik (1983) has shown that the same arbitrage portfolio will hold for the Japanese investor who calculates rates of returns in yen provided that the $/yen rate follows the linear return-generating function given in

Equation 9.1. The empirical counterpart of the equilibrium pricing equation is given at any point in time t by substituting Equation 9.2 into 9.1:

$$r_t^c = \gamma_{0t}^c i + B^c \gamma_t^c + v_t^c, \quad c = US, JA \tag{9.3}$$

where v_t is the vector of error terms ($v_t = BF_t + e_t$), and the superscript c indicates whether it is a Japanese or an American stock.

Because of the specification in Equation 9.3 our empirical tests of market segmentation are based on a well-known, two-stage estimation approach. In the first stage the elements of **B** are estimated for each security by using the time series of returns. In the second stage, estimated matrix **B** is used as independent variables to estimate γ_0 and vector γ for each country both for the sample period 1977–1980, during which the capital controls were in effect, and for the subsequent four years 1981–1984 that were characterized by free capital movements. Then, the composite null hypothesis that

$$\gamma^{US} \neq \gamma^{JA} \qquad \gamma_0^{US} \neq \gamma_0^{JA} \qquad \text{in } 1977 - 1980$$

and

$$\gamma^{US} = \gamma^{JA} \qquad \gamma_0^{US} = \gamma_0^{JA} \qquad \text{in } 1981 - 1984$$

is tested formally.

Because there is no agreement on the empirical implementation and testing of multifactor models, we used several approaches—prespecified factors and factor analysis with individual securities and portfolios of securities—as well as different multivariate testing techniques. If the impact of the capital market liberalization had a sufficiently strong impact on rates of return around the time of the regime switch, as we conjecture, then we should expect the results to be robust with respect to the alternative testing procedures and inevitable model specification errors. The approach that we follow is thus similar in the spirit to an event study; as such, the results lack generality but, we hope, they are more conclusive than previous empirical research in the field.[7]

IV. Data

We used weekly stock returns calculated from daily prices quoted at the close of the markets on Wednesdays from January 1, 1977, to December 31, 1984. As indicated before, we focus on the two sample periods, January 1977 to December 1980 and January 1981 to December

1984. We took two equal, four-year periods around the December 1980 liberalization measures because that was the longest for which we felt comfortable with the assumptions of risk factor stationarity.[8] In addition, the Bank of Japan did not officially admit a free money market until 1977, even though one started to develop as early as 1971.

We selected two sets of Japanese and U.S. securities, each consisting of 110 stocks, which reproduced the industry composition of the two countries' market portfolios as closely as data availability permitted us. The choice of an equal number of stocks and the attention paid to their industrial classification were dictated by the concern of introducing spurious risky factors in either of the securities sets. In Table 9.2 we show the proportion of the companies in the sample relative to the total number of companies in each industrial sector for two broad market indexes: the total of the publicly traded companies in Japan as reported by *Toyo Keizai Shinposha* (1985) and the largest 1000 corporations in the United States as ranked by *Business Week* (1986).[9]

We converted Japanese stock returns into dollars. We tried to match the timing of stock transactions with that of the exchange transactions as closely as possible. An investor who wants to get the Wednesday dollar rates of return at the closing prices of the Japanese stock market will buy the stock on Wednesday at 3 P.M. Tokyo time and sell it at the same time one week later. Given that it takes three business days to settle stock transactions in Tokyo, the investor needs yen on Monday, but will receive yen the next Monday. Two business days are needed for settlement in foreign exchange markets. Therefore, the foreign exchange transaction must occur on Friday in Tokyo. By taking the $/yen exchange rates quoted 1 P.M. New York time on Thursdays we lead the opening of the Tokyo foreign exchange market by four hours (1 P.M. in New York on Thursday is 4 A.M. in Tokyo on Friday). A far more serious problem, albeit unsolvable, is that of nonsynchronous trading given that trading hours in Tokyo and New York markets never overlap.[10]

V. Prespecified Factors with Individual Stock Returns

The first approach was to identify the sources of risk explicitly by "guessing" the economic variables that have a systematic effect on stock prices (Chan, et al., 1985; Chen, et al., 1986; Hamao, 1988). The approach can be criticized for its arbitrariness, but it was important to check the sensitivity of the results to all possible alternative implementations of the

Table 9.2. Industry Composition of Sample Portfolio and Market Portfolio

	Number of Companies in the Sample as Percentage of Market Portfolio	
Sectors	Japan[1]	U.S.A.[2]
Fishery	14.3	—
Construction	5.3	10.0
Foods	9.6	11.1
Textiles	6.5	13.3
Chemicals	16.1	11.4
Natural Resources	20.0	11.1
Rubber Goods	11.1	16.6
Iron and Steel	12.8	11.1
Nonferrous Metals	8.7	9.1
Machinery	4.9	10.0
Electronics and Computers	16.8	11.1
Transport Equipment	14.3	13.3
Precision Machinery	23.5	9.4
Miscellaneous Manufacturing	13.0	11.8
Commerce	8.6	11.0
Banking	6.1	11.3
Nonbanking Financial	28.0	11.1
Real Estate	15.8	20.0
Transportation	10.0	10.3
Utilities	14.3	10.8
Tobacco, Paper, and Forestry	—	10.0
Conglomerates	—	8.3

1. The industry composition of the market portfolio is obtained from *Toyo Keizai Shinposha* (1985).

2. The industry composition of the market portfolio is obtained from *Business Week* (1986).

multifactor model. In addition, this approach subsumes early empirical work in international finance. (Solnik, (1974b); Stehle, (1977)).

With weekly data, the choice of economic variables entering the stock return function is limited. We selected six variables. We take the change in the short-term interest rate in both Japan—three-month Gensaki rate (DIJ)—and the United States—three-month eurodollar deposit rates (DIU). These variables are used to capture movements in the term structure of interest rates in the spirit of recent single-state-variable theoretical model of the equilibrium structure. The third variable was the percentage change in the Dow Jones Commodity Futures Index (FUT)—an index of 12 commodities including foods, metals, and woods—as a proxy for world demand pressures and inflationary expectations.

In principle, stock market indexes should not enter the regressions if all relevant economic variables have been identified and properly measured; in practice, however, misspecifications are bound to occur, especially when the choice of variables is limited due to the weekly data frequency. Therefore, we added the percentage change in the world stock market index (WINDEX) which was calculated by weighing the stock markets of France, Germany, Switzerland, United Kingdom, Japan, Australia, Canada, and the United States—or 93.4% of total world stock markets shown in Table 9.3—with their capitalization at the end of 1980, the midpoint of our sample period.

Finally, we use two purely domestic market factors in the regressions, namely the part of the Japanese (JRES) and U.S. (USRES) stock indexes that were orthogonal to the world stock indexes. The last three variables typically have been used in many studies of international capital market integration. Changes in the exchange rate, by themselves, are not a source of systematic risk for stocks since the stockholder can hedge against it perfectly by borrowing the foreign currency. The changes, however, may be an indirect source of risk to the extent that they affect

Table 9.3. Equity Markets Capitalization[1] (U.S. dollars; end of 1980)

Countries Included in the World Index:	Billions $	% World Total	% World Index
France	53	2.2	2.3
Germany	71	2.9	3.1
Switzerland	46	1.9	2.0
United Kingdom	190	7.8	8.4
Japan	357	14.7	15.7
Australia	60	2.5	2.7
Canada	113	4.6	5.0
United States	1381	56.8	60.8
Total World Index	2271	93.4	100.0
Other Countries	159	6.6	—
Total World Equities	2430	100.0	—

1. Source: Ibbotson, Carr, and Robinson (1982).

the real exchange rate and, consequently the profitability of the export sector. The empirical evidence presented in Hamao (1988) shows that neither the exchange rate nor the terms of trade are priced factors in the Japanese stock market. In addition, any direct effect of foreign exchange movements should be already captured by the two domestic factors JRES and USRES.

The model specification imposes that the variables *F*, measures of risk, be mean zero and serially uncorrelated, although they may be contemporaneously correlated. Because all the variables are first differences of weekly data we do not find strong serial correlation—with the only exception of Japanese interest rates that moved in a stepwise fashion throughout most of the sample period—and the estimated means are comfortably close to zero, with the exception of the world stock index (Table 9.4).[11]

Table 9.4. Risk Measures: Descriptive Statistics (1977–1984)

	Mean (%)	t	ρ	$\sigma(\rho)$
WINDEX	0.19850	2.15	0.048	0.05
JRES	0.00000	0.00	0.032	0.05
USRES	0.00000	0.00	0.025	0.05
DIU	0.00017	0.31	0.076	0.05
DIJ	0.00001	0.00	−0.502	0.05
FUT	0.03195	0.31	0.127	0.05

Correlation Matrix (1977–1984)

	WINDEX	JRES	USRES	DIU	DIJ	FUT
WINDEX	1.00	0.00	0.00	−0.40	−0.15	0.37
JRES		1.00	−0.78	−0.08	−0.49	0.03
USRES			1.00	−0.17	0.46	−0.17
DIU				1.00	0.13	−0.18
DIJ					1.00	−0.10
FUT						1.00

WINDEX: Percentage change in world stock market index.
JRES : Domestic component of Japanese stock market index.
USRES : Domestic component of the U.S. stock market index.
DIV : Change in short-term interest rate in the U.S.
DIJ : Change in short-term interest rate in Japan.
FUT : Percentage change in the Dow Jones Commodity Futures Index.

The initial step is the estimation of the **B** matrix. In this section we use the time series of individual stock returns from the entire sample period 1977 to 1984. We assume thereby that the risk characteristics of the securities remained unchanged throughout the liberalization process even though the price of the risk factors changed between the two subperiods. There are two problems with this approach: the consistency of the risk premia estimates—because both **B** and γ are estimated from the same sample period—and the stationarity of **B**. Both problems will be dealt with in the next section by following the usual approach of forming portfolios and using out-of-sample betas; in this section, however, we do not want to lose the information that the grouping of securities would involve.

Some descriptive statistics for betas from individual stock returns are reported in Table 9.5. For the entire sample period all the risk factors had a strong impact on U.S. stock returns with the only exception of Japanese interest rates. For the Japanese stocks, instead, only Japanese variables seem to matter in addition to the world stock market. The table shows the differences in betas estimated for the two subperiods, 1977 to 1980 and 1981 to 1984. The U.S. stocks exhibit remarkable stability in the betas over this interval, even though the *t* statistics suggest rejection of the equality of the world index parameters.

As for the Japanese stocks, the betas are quite unstable—the Hotelling γ^2 rejects the null of equal **B**'s at any conventional level of significance. In particular, commodity futures and Japanese interest rates appear to have different effects in the two subperiods.[12]

The next step is to test the equality of the vector of risk premia for the U.S. and Japanese securities by using cross-sectional regressions of stock returns on the estimated betas. We use three testing procedures. First, we use mean rates of stock returns in each of the subperiods as the dependent variables in the cross-sections and estimate the vector of U.S. and Japanese premia jointly with seemingly nrelated regressions. Using our notations, we estimate the system of two equations;

$$\bar{r}_j^{US} = \bar{\gamma}_0^{US} i + \hat{B}_j^{US} \bar{\gamma}^{US} + v_j^{US} \qquad j = 1977\text{–}1980,$$

$$\bar{r}_j^{JA} = \bar{\gamma}_0^{JA} i + \hat{B}_j^{JA} \bar{\gamma}^{JA} + v_j^{JA} \qquad 1981\text{–}1984$$

with seemingly unrelated regression for each of the two subperiods, where r_j stands for the mean return over the period j. The equality of

Table 9.5. Security Betas: Descriptive Statistics

Estimation Period	WINDEX	JRES	USRES	DIU	DIJ	FUT	Hotelling[2] T^2
			Estimated Betas of Risky Factors[1]				
U.S. SECURITIES							
1977–1984							
Mean	1.079	0.097	1.179	−21.689	0.0003	−0.052	
Std. Dev.	0.396	0.195	0.678	37.833	0.112	0.108	
1977–1980							
Mean	1.185	0.102	1.195	−21.651	0.006	−0.052	
Std. Dev.	0.496	0.273	0.756	39.191	0.159	0.116	
1981–1984							
Mean	1.026	0.091	1.166	−21.291	−0.004	−0.052	
Std. Dev.	0.391	0.261	0.856	46.748	0.178	0.187	
JAPANESE SECURITIES							
1977–1984							
Mean	0.731	1.028	0.011	−0.368	−0.027	−0.015	
Std. Dev.	0.261	0.251	0.479	14.519	0.117	0.083	

1977–1980							
Mean	0.308	1.057	0.086	−0.658	0.021	−0.035	
Std. Dev.	0.237	0.313	0.745	21.464	0.147	0.102	
1981–1984							
Mean	0.922	1.006	0.014	0.437	−0.073	0.022	
Std. Dev.	0.326	0.322	0.645	28.488	0.177	0.139	
Equality of Betas between Subperiods (t values)							
U.S. SECURITIES	4.78	0.31	0.36	0.09	0.40	0.004	4.52 (0.0005)
JAPANESE SECURITIES	19.3	1.37	0.78	0.28	4.53	3.45	107.0 (0.000)

1. The definitions of the variables are given in Table 9.4.
2. *p* values in parentheses.

the premia is then tested with a standard F test of linear constraint (Theil (1971), p. 313).

Second, we follow the multivariate approach of Shkanken and Weinstein (1985) that takes into account the estimation errors of the betas in the first step of the procedure.[13] The test statistics, which we denote SW, are given by the ratio of two quadratic forms and are distributed γ^2.[14]

Third, we adopt the Fama and MacBeth (1973) procedure and we estimate the risk premia for both countries in each week of the two subperiods, or 208 weeks for each subperiod. In this way we obtain two time series of premia differentials which should have a zero mean if capital markets were perfectly integrated. The Hotelling γ^2 statistics are then used to test the vector of mean differentials.

The results are presented in Table 9.6. Cross-sectional estimates of risk premia are obtained by OLS shown in Panel A. More sources of risk seem to be priced before the liberalization of capital controls than after; this is particularly true for the Japanese securities. In Panel B we present the statistics and procedures testing the equality of premia with and without the intercept term. Without the intercept, the SW and γ^2 statistics indicate that capital market integration is supported by the data in both subperiods, even though the absolute value of the statistics declines substantially after 1980. The F statistics suggest instead that the hypothesis of segmentation cannot be rejected at the 0.05 significance level in the 1977–1980 period, but can be rejected in the subsequent years.

The results are substantially the same when the equality of the intercept term is tested together with the equality of the premia. This time, however, even the F statistics do not detect segmentation before 1981, which is somewhat surprising given that we have imposed an additional restriction. Based on the analysis of individual securities, we mostly find that the price of risk has been successfully arbitraged between the U.S. and Japanese stock markets, notwithstanding the capital controls existing before 1981. These controls appear to have segmented only the Japanese money market, as clearly illustrated in Figure 9.1. As we pointed out, lack of stationarity and consistency of the parameter estimates may mar the analysis of individual stock returns. In the next section we repeat the test by grouping securities into portfolios, which is the usual procedure to minimize these two sources of bias (Black, et al., 1972).

VI. Prespecified Factors with Portfolios of Securities

Given the small number of securities in each country sample, 110 in each, we can only form 22 portfolios of five securities. In each subperiod, 1977–1980 and 1981–1984, we took the first two years, 1977–1978 and 1981–1982, and estimated the securities beta with respect to their domestic market index. This beta was used to rank securities and form the portfolios. We then estimated the portfolios' betas with respect to all the six sources of risk specified in the previous section using again the returns from the first two years only. The portfolios' betas estimated in this way were used as independent variables to obtain estimates of the risk premia in the second half of the two subperiods, that is, 1979–1980 and 1983–1984.

There are no theoretical reasons for using the domestic market beta to rank securities; it simply turned out to be an effective way to spread securities returns out-of-sample.[15] We could not use firm size—a more popular choice in the literature—because both the U.S. and Japanese samples comprised the largest companies in the two countries, which lacked sufficient dispersion in the data.

Table 9.7 reports the estimated portfolio betas for the two subperiods. As for individual securities, U.S. betas seem more stable than Japanese betas. Surprisingly, changes in Japanese interest rates are correlated with U.S. portfolio returns but not with Japanese returns.

In Table 9.8 we show the same three test statistics that we introduced in the previous section and the risk premia estimates for portfolios. The results are clear cut. With or without the intercept term included, the hypothesis of integration is rejected at the 0.05 significance level by both *SW* and *F* statistics for the 1979–1980 period. By contrast, the same hypothesis cannot be rejected at any significance level for the years 1983–1984. Only the γ^2 statistics, with a significance level of 0.18, do not provide evidence of segmentation before the liberalization process. The significance of the results is somewhat reduced, however, by the lack of precision with which the risk premia are estimated in the second subperiod.

VII. Factor Analytic Approach

Factor analysis is an alternative methodology where one determines the number of factors k and estimates the elements of $\mathbf{B}$ jointly. We

Table 9.6. Risk Premia Based on Individual Stock Returns[2]

Estimation Period	Risk Premia[1] INTERCEPT	WINDEX	JRES	USRES	DIU	DIJ	FUT	R^2
A. 1977–1980								
U.S. Securities (*t* value)	0.078	0.315	0.174	0.084	0.003	0.421	−0.087	0.33
	(0.86)	(3.25)	(0.85)	(1.18)	(3.66)	(1.71)	(0.34)	
Japanese Securities (*t* value)	−0.010	0.097	0.328	−0.197	0.0008	−0.018	−0.300	0.24
	(0.09)	(0.82)	(2.52)	(3.68)	(0.67)	(0.11)	(1.38)	

Tests of Equality of Risk Premia[3]

Excluding Intercept		Including Intercept	
$F=$	2.17	$F=$	1.86
(p value)	(0.047)	(p value)	(0.076)
$SW=$	1.01	$SW=$	0.950
(p value)	(0.413)	(p value)	(0.467)
$T^2=$	0.802	$T^2=$	0.686
(p value)	(0.569)	(p value)	(0.683)

B. 1981–1984								
U.S. Securities								
(t value)	0.405	−0.176	−0.161	0.112	−0.001	−0.097	−0.207	0.24
	(6.40)	(2.60)	(1.12)	(2.24)	(2.46)	(0.56)	(1.15)	
Japanese Securities								
(t value)	0.020	0.015	0.213	−0.0032	−0.0017	0.014	−0.127	0.08
	(0.15)	(0.12)	(1.32)	(0.04)	(1.41)	(0.07)	(0.47)	

Tests of Equality of Risk Premia[3]

Excluding Intercept		**Including Intercept**	
$F=$	1.49	$F=$	1.83
(p value)	(0.183)	(p value)	(0.082)
$SW=$	1.32	$SW=$	1.10
(p value)	(0.243)	(p value)	(0.361)
$T^2 =$	0.390	$T^2 =$	0.470
(p value)	(0.855)	(p value)	(0.855)

1. The dependent variables are the mean returns of 110 U.S. securities and 110 Japanese securities.
2. The definition of the variables is given in Table 9.4.
3. The F statistics test the equality of the premia for Japanese and U.S. securities estimated by seemingly unrelated regression. The SW statistics are described in the text. The T^2 statistics test the equality of premia using Fama-MacBeth procedure.

Table 9.7. Portfolio Betas: Descriptive Statistics

Estimation Period	Estimated Betas of Risky Factors[1]					
	WINDEX	JRES	USRES	DIU	DIJ	FUT
U.S. PORTFOLIOS						
1977–1978						
Mean	1.484	0.072	1.198	−21.612	0.020	−0.014
Std. Dev.	0.623	0.198	0.724	38.000	0.067	0.066
1981–1982						
Mean	0.999	0.115	1.025	−18.868	0.050	−0.037
Std. Dev.	0.285	0.132	0.694	21.168	0.111	0.107
JAPANESE PORTFOLIOS						
1977–1978						
Mean	0.213	1.077	0.348	7.327	0.0003	−0.036
Std. Dev.	0.102	0.286	0.462	42.189	0.098	0.064
1981–1982						
Mean	0.979	1.107	−0.304	6.097	0.004	0.020
Std. Dev.	0.178	0.230	0.320	18.753	0.135	0.082

1. The definitions of the variables are given in Table 9.4.

extracted the factor loadings from the full covariance matrix of U.S. and Japanese stock returns, as well as the dollar return on the Japanese risk-free rate, which we assumed to be equal to the three-month interest rate on euroyen deposits. The matrix was calculated by using the time series of returns for the entire sample period, from 1977 to 1984, thereby assuming stationarity of the individual stocks' "riskiness." In this respect the analysis is similar to that of Section V.

A well-known issue in the estimation of APT models is the decision about the number of factors to be extracted. Because the number of factors required grows with the number of securities in the sample, the model soon loses its empirical content unless one arbitrarily fixes the number of priced factors (Roll and Ross, 1980; Dhrymes, et al., 1984). In our case the covariance matrix of returns contains 221 securities and the number of factors needed to explain the covariance structure of security returns would exceed 30. We limited the number of factors to 5, 10, and 20 as is done in most current empirical tests of the APT.

Once we had obtained the securities factor loadings, we estimated and tested the equality of the risk premia for the two countries in each of the two subperiods. We estimated weekly cross-sections of the premia with a generalized least square.[16] We then obtained a time series of premia differentials, $\gamma_t = \gamma_t^{US} - \gamma_t^{JA}$, with covariance matrix $\mathbf{D}$.[17] Under the null hypothesis that the mean differential is equal to zero, the statistic, $T\gamma' D^{-1}\gamma \sim \chi_k^2$, is a distributed chi square with k degrees of freedom.[18]

The results for the three models are shown in Table 9.9. The first statistic for each model is an overall chi-square test significance for the vector of estimated risk premia. This is an important piece of information because the null hypothesis of equal premia in the two countries could not be statistically rejected, even with perfectly segmented capital markets, if no factors were priced. For all three models we find that at least one factor is indeed priced.[19]

The chi-square tests of equality of risk premia are consistent with the findings of the previous section. There are significant differences in risk premia based on 5–, 10–, and 20-factor models during the regime of capital controls in Japan before 1981. We do not find any difference in risk premia for the U.S. and Japanese stocks after 1981.

Even though the results presented in this section support the notion that government policies are the source of segmentation, one might argue about the robustness due to asynchronous trading across markets. To avoid the problem of asynchronous trading, one must estimate the factors

Table 9.8. Risk Premia Based on Portfolio Returns[1]

	Risk Premia[2]							
Estimation Period	**INTERCEPT**	**WINDEX**	**JRES**	**USRES**	**DIU**	**DIJ**	**FUT**	R^2
A. 1979–1980								
U.S. Securities								
(*t* value)	0.104	0.362	0.198	−0.184	0.0007	−0.118	1.08	0.61
	(1.31)	(3.05)	(0.73)	(1.40)	(0.91)	(0.23)	(2.02)	
Japanese Securities								
(*t* value)	0.706	−0.529	−0.460	0.077	0.0004	1.44	−1.17	0.59
	(4.84)	(1.46)	(3.27)	(1.25)	(0.61)	(3.84)	(2.39)	

Tests of Equality of Risk Premia[3]

Excluding Intercept		**Including Intercept**	
$F =$	2.42	$F =$	3.52
(*p* value)	(0.049)	(*p* value)	(0.007)
$SW =$	2.58	$SW =$	2.90
(*p* value)	(0.023)	(*p* value)	(0.008)
$T^2 =$	1.52	$T^2 =$	1.41
(*p* value)	(0.18)	(*p* value)	(0.20)

B. 1983–1984								
U.S. Securities								
(t value)	0.569 (4.03)	−0.235 (1.27)	0.083 (0.32)	−0.017 (0.19)	0.0015 (0.93)	−0.75 (0.25)	−0.045 (0.20)	0.41
Japanese Securities								
(t value)	−0.212 (0.70)	0.567 (1.09)	−0.022 (0.06)	0.027 (0.17)	−0.005 (1.48)	−0.771 (2.14)	0.804 (1.39)	0.29

Tests of Equality of Risk Premia[3]

Excluding Intercept		**Including Intercept**	
$F=$	0.71	$F=$	1.02
(p value)	(0.642)	(p value)	(0.435)
$SW=$	1.08	$SW=$	0.74
(p value)	(0.380)	(p value)	(0.639)
$T^2 =$	0.76	$T^2 =$	0.676
(p value)	(0.60)	(p value)	(0.69)

1. The risk premia were obtained by regressing mean portfolio returns during the period indicated on the betas estimated from 1977–78 and 1981–82, respectively. The sample consisted of 22 portfolios of U.S. and Japanese stocks, respectively. Each portfolio contained five stocks.
2. The definitions of the variables are given in Table 9.4.
3. The F statistics test the equality of the premia for Japanese and U.S. securities estimated by seemingly unrelated regression. The SW statistics are described in the text. The T^2 statistics test the equality of premia with the Fama-MacBeth procedure.

Table 9.9. Risk Premia Based on Factor Analysis[1]

Factor Models	Period 1977–1980 US	JA	1981–1984 US	JA
A. FIVE-FACTOR MODEL[2]				
Overall χ^2	21.63	1.85	2.31	10.77
(p value)	(0.0006)	(0.869)	(0.805)	(0.056)
Test of Equality of Risk Premia[3]				
Excluding Intercept	χ^2 =	11.92	χ^2 =	3.93
	(p value)	(0.035)	(p value)	(0.559)
Including Intercept	χ^2 =	15.06	χ^2 =	5.32
	(p value)	(0.019)	(p value)	(0.503)
B. TEN-FACTOR MODEL[2]				
Overall χ^2	29.89	6.60	8.09	12.55
(p value)	(0.0008)	(0.762)	(0.620)	(0.249)
Test of Equality of Risk Premia[3]				
Excluding Intercept	χ^2 =	17.20	χ^2 =	12.97
	(p value)	(0.070)	(p value)	(0.225)
Including Intercept	χ^2 =	20.97	χ^2 =	15.08
	(p value)	(0.034)	(p value)	(0.178)
C. TWENTY-FACTOR MODEL[2]				
Overall χ^2	45.15	12.05	16.08	23.95
(p value)	(0.001)	(0.914)	(0.711)	(0.245)
Test of Equality of Risk Premia[3]				
Excluding Intercept	χ^2 =	36.83	χ^2 =	25.58
	(p value)	(0.012)	(p value)	(0.180)
Including Intercept	χ^2 =	39.02	χ^2 =	28.97
	(p value)	(0.009)	(p value)	(0.114)

1. Factor analysis based on returns of 221 securities: 110 U.S. Securities, 110 Japanese securities and the dollar return on the Japanese risk-free asset.

2. The overall χ^2 tests that the vector of risk premia estimated with generalized least square is significantly different from zero.

3. The χ^2 statistics tests that the vector of differences in the two countries' premia estimated weekly by generalized least squares is equal to zero.

separately across markets. However, the tests of equality of risk premia can only be carried on the intercepts (Dhrymes, et al., 1984).[20] We, therefore, factor-analyzed 111 Japanese security returns (100 stocks and risk-free assets) and 110 U.S. security returns separately in each of the two periods (1977–1980 and 1981–1984). Since the number of factors is not known, we estimated the model with increasing number of factors until the procedure degenerated. For the period covering 1977–1980, we estimated the model with 1 to 7 factors with the Japanese data and 1 to 13 factors with the U.S. data. For the period covering 1981–1984, we estimated the model with 1 to 12 and 1 to 15 factors for the Japanese and the U.S. data, respectively. Since the estimate of the intercept in the second stage is not independent of the number of factors extracted in the first stage and the true number of factors is not known, one must resort to testing all possible combinations—admittedly, a weak test. We thus conducted pairwise tests of equality of Japanese and the U.S. intercepts—assuming the distribution of the estimates of intercepts across different number of factors, k, is stationary—for all possible cases (7×13 and 12×15 cases in each subperiod). For the period 1977–1980 the null hypothesis that intercepts are equal was rejected in each of the 91 pairwise tests. For the period 1981–1984 the null hypothesis was rejected in 71 of the 180 pairwise tests (39%) at 0.01 significance level. These tests support the other results we presented in the paper as well.

Results in this section support the proposition that government controls are the source of segmentation more strongly than previous sections since risk premia are estimated using individual stock returns rather than portfolios.

VIII. Conclusions

General tests of international capital markets integration are likely to be inconclusive both because it is difficult to specify a testable, capital asset pricing model in an open economy and because it is difficult to distinguish between segmentation due to objective restrictions to trade in financial assets from that arising because of individuals' inhibitions and irrationality. In this paper, therefore, we decided to focus exclusively on perhaps the most important recent episode of capital market liberalization in an industrialized country, Japan at the end of 1980, and analyze the dollar price of risk in the Japanese stock market at the time of the liberalization.

If governments, rather than individuals, are the source of segmentation, we should observe a price differential for risk between the Japanese and the U.S. capital markets before the liberalization but not after. On the whole, the empirical evidence presented in the paper supports this view. The data were examined using different model specifications and testing procedures but in the vast majority of cases we were unable to reject the hypothesis of perfect integration after 1980. Before that date, integration is instead rejected most of the time.

Notes

1. Capital markets are integrated if assets with perfectly correlated rates of return have the same price regardless of the location in which they are traded. This seems to be the natural way of defining capital market integration. (See Stulz, 1981).
2. This approach is used by Stehle (1977) and Jorion and Schwartz (1986). A similar framework is used in the empirical studies of Solnik (1974) and Errunza and Losq (1985).
3. The recent experiences of France, Japan, and Italy, among the major industrialized countries, are very illuminating on this point. The important relationship between asset pricing and government policies in an international context has been stressed in Stockman and Hernandez (1985) and Stockman and Dallas (1986).
4. Cho, Eun, and Senbet (1986) and Korajczyk and Viallet (1986) use an APT framework to test international capital markets integration. However, it is difficult to interpret their results to support any statement about international capital markets integration. In particular, nothing can be said about the role of government policies in segmenting markets given that these studies lump together countries with drastically different capital control regimes, which themselves are changing over time. See also Cosset (1984) and Berges (1981) for an empirical study using an international APT.
5. Some of the problems with consumption-based asset pricing models are discussed in Cornell (1981).
6. See Pigott (1983) for a detailed account of the Japanese experience with financial deregulation.
7. An "event study" approach to capital market segmentation is also used by Gordon, Eun, and Janakiramanan (1988) by looking at the dual listing of companies in the Canadian and U.S. markets.
8. Nomura Research Institute very kindly computed the stock returns for us which had to be adjusted for frequent stock splits in Japan.

9. Because the original data on Japanese stocks were classified into 20 industry categories, we regrouped the U.S. companies according to that classification as close as our data allowed us.
10. Nonsynchronous trading may bias not only risk premia but also the returns covariance and, therefore, the estimation of risk factors. (See Shanken, 1986).
11. An alternative would have been to filter the data with univariate models or vector autoregressions, but we were afraid of the potential bias caused by a wrong specification of the processes for the time series.
12. We checked whether the liberalization of capital movements could account for the changes in the Japanese betas, in addition to the risk premia, by using the differential between domestic yen and euroyen deposits of the same maturity as proxy variable. This variable is plotted in Figure 9.1. Perhaps the proxy was inappropriate; when we reestimated the betas with the capital control proxy added at the right hand side, its coefficient was never significant.
13. The test draws on the work of Shanken (1985).
14. See Shanken (1985) and Gultekin, Gultekin, and Penati (1989) for the details of test statistics.
15. Multivariate tests reject the equality of portfolio mean returns in each of the subperiods. Thus, we can safely rule out the possibility of results being an artifact of the experimental design.
16. Formally, for each week of the sample period the risk premia were estimated by $\gamma_t = (\hat{B}^{*\prime} \hat{W}^{-1} \hat{B}^{*})^{-1} \hat{B}^{*\prime} \hat{W}^{-1} r_t$ and $\hat{W} = \hat{B}\hat{B}' + \hat{S}$ where $\hat{B}^{*}$ are now the estimated factor loadings augmented with a column of ones, $[i_{N+1}{:}B]$, and **S** is the specific variance or idiosyncratic risk associated with individual securities. See Roll and Ross (1980) and Dhrymes, Friend, and Gultekin (1984).
17. See Gultekin, Gultekin, and Penati (1989) for details.
18. See Dhrymes, Friend, and Gultekin (1984) and Gultekin, Gultekin, and Penati (1989).
19. The individual risk premia are not reported, however, since they are identified only up to an orthogonal transformation and no economic significance can be attributed to them (Dhrymes, et al., 1984).
20. Such a test will be robust if the overall mean returns—mean return of all Japanese stocks and mean return of the U.S. stocks—are statistically different. Indeed, the overall mean returns are statistically different and the tests—especially for the period of 1981–1984—are expected to be robust.

    A test of the intercept is equivalent to testing the equality of the risk-free rate (with the risk-free rate version of APT). The evidence provided in Figure 9.1 strongly supports the notion that money markets were segmented before 1980 but not afterwards.

References

Adler, Michael, and Bernard Dumas, (1983) "International Portfolio Choice and Corporation Finance: A Synthesis," *Journal of Finance,* Vol. 38, June, pp. 925–984.

Berges, Angel, (1981). "Test of Arbitrage Pricing Theory in International Capital Markets," unpublished manuscript, presented at the European Finance Association Meetings, Jerusalem, Israel, September.

Black, Fischer, Michael Jensen, and Myron Scholes, (1972). "The Capital Asset Pricing Model: Some Empirical Tests," in M. Jensen, ed., *Studies in the Theory of Capital Markets,* New York, Praeger.

Business Week, (1986). "The Top 1000," Special Issue, April 18.

Chan, K., Nai-Fu Chen, and David Hsieh, (1985). "An Exploratory Investigation of the Firm Size Effect," *Journal of Financial Economics,* Vol. 14, pp. 451–471.

Chen, Nai-Fu, Richard Roll, and Stephen Ross, (1986). "Economic Forces and the Stock Market," *Journal of Business,* Vol. 59, July, pp. 383–403.

Cho, Chinhyung, Eun Cheol, and Lemma Senbet, (1986). "International Arbitrage Pricing Theory: An Empirical Investigation," *Journal of Finance,* Vol. 41, June, pp. 313–329.

Cornell, Bradford, (1981). "The Consumption Based Asset Pricing Model: A Note on Potential Tests and Applications," *Journal of Financial Economics,* March, pp. 103–108.

Cosset, Jean-Claude, (1984). "On the Presence of Risk Premiums in Foreign Exchange Markets," *Journal of International Economics,* pp. 139–154.

Dhrymes, Phoebus, Irwin Friend, and Bulent Gultekin, (1984). "A Critical Reexamination of the Empirical Evidence on the Arbitrage Pricing Theory," *Journal of Finance,* Vol. 39, June, pp. 323–346.

Errunza, Vihang, and Etienne Losq, (1985). "International Asset Pricing Under Mild Segmentation: Theory and Test," *Journal of Finance,* Vol. 40, March, pp. 105–124.

Eun, Cheol, and S. Janakiramanan, (1986). "A Model of International Asset Pricing with a Constraint on the Foreign Equity Ownership," *Journal of Finance,* Vol. 41, September, pp. 897–914.

Fama, Eugene, and James MacBeth, (1973). "Risk, Return, and Equilibrium: Empirical Tests," *Journal of Political Economy,* Vol. 81, May–June, pp. 607–636.

Gordon, Alexander, Cheol Eun, and S. Janakiramanan, (1988). "International Listings, Stock Returns, and Capital Market Integration: Theory and Evidence," *Journal of Financial and Quantitative Analysis,* June.

Gultekin, Mustafa N., N. Bulent Gultekin, and Alessandro Penati, (1989). "Capital Controls and International Capital Markets Segmentation: The Evidence from the Japanese and American Stock Markets," forthcoming, *Journal of Finance*.

Grauer, Frederick, Robert Litzenberger, and Richard Stehle, (1976). "Sharing Rules and Equilibrium in an International Capital Market Under Uncertainty," *Journal of Financial Economics,* Vol. 3, June, pp. 233–256.

Hamao, Yasushi, (1988). "An Empirical Examination of the Arbitrage Pricing Theory: Using Japanese Data," forthcoming, *Japan and the World Economy: International Journal of Theory and Policy.*

Ibbotson, Roger, Richard Carr, and Anthony Robinson, (1982). "International Equity and Stock Returns," *Financial Analysts Journal,* Vol. 38, July-August, pp. 61–83.

Ito, Takatoshi, (1986). "Capital Controls and Covered Interest Parity between the Yen and the Dollar," *The Economic Studies Quarterly,* Vol. 3, September, pp. 223–241.

Jorion, Phillips, and Eduardo Schwartz, (1986). "Integration vs. Segmentation in the Canadian Stock Market," *Journal of Finance,* Vol. 41, May, pp. 603–613.

Korajczyk, Robert, and Claude Viallet, (1986). "An Empirical Investigation of International Asset Pricing," Unpublished Manuscript, Northwestern University, November.

Obstfeld, Maurice, (1986). "How Integrated Are World Capital Markets? Some New Tests," National Bureau of Economic Research, Working Paper #2075, November.

Otani, Ichiro, and Siddharth Tiwari, (1981). "Capital Controls and Interest Rate Parity: The Japanese Experience, 1978–81," IMF Staff Papers 28, December, pp. 793–815.

Pigott, Charles, (1983). "Financial Reform in Japan," *Economic Review,* Federal Reserve Bank of San Francisco, Vol. 1, Winter, pp. 25–45.

Roll, Richard, and Stephen Ross, (1980). "An Empirical Investigation of the Arbitrage Pricing Theory," *Journal of Finance,* Vol. 35, December, pp. 1073–1103.

Shanken, Jay, (1985). "Multivariate Tests of the Zero-Beta CAPM," *Journal of Financial Economics,* Vol. 14.

Shanken, Jay, (1986). "Nonsynchronous Data and the Covariance Factor Structure of Returns," *Journal of Finance,* Vol. 42, June, pp. 221–231.

Shanken, Jay, and Mark Weinstein, (1985). "Testing Multifactor Pricing Relations with Prespecified Factors," Unpublished Manuscript, University of Southern California, October.

Solnik, Bruno, (1974a). "An Equilibrium Model of the International Capital Market," *Journal of Economic Theory,* Vol. 8, August, pp. 400–424.

Solnik, Bruno, (1974b). "The International Pricing of Risk: An Empirical Investigation of the World Capital Market Structure," *Journal of Finance,* Vol. 29, May, pp. 48–54.

Solnik, Bruno, (1977). "Testing International Asset Pricing: Some Pessimistic Views," *Journal of Finance,* Vol. 32, May, pp. 503–511.

Solnik, Bruno, (1983). "International Arbitrage Pricing Theory," *Journal of Finance,* Vol. 38, May, pp. 449–457.

Stehle, Richard, (1977). "An Empirical Test of the Alternative Hypotheses of National and International Pricing of Risky Assets," *Journal of Finance,* Vol. 32, May, pp. 493–502.

Stockman, Alan, and Harris Dallas, (1986). "Asset Markets, Tariffs and Political Risk," *Journal of International Economics,* Vol. 21, November, pp. 199–213.

Stockman, Alan, and Hernandez Alejandro, (1985). "Exchange Controls, Capital Controls, and International Financial Markets," National Bureau of Economic Research, Working Paper No. 1755, October.

Stulz, Rene, (1981a). "A Model of International Asset Pricing," *Journal of Financial Economics,* Vol. 9, December, pp. 383–406.

Stulz, Rene, (1981b). "On the Effects of Barriers to International Investment," *Journal of Finance,* Vol. 36, September, pp. 923–934.

Stulz, Rene, (1985). "Pricing Capital Assets in an International Setting: An Introduction," in *International Financial Management,* D. Lessard, ed., New York, John Wiley and Sons.

Theil, Henri, (1971). *Principles of Econometrics,* Santa Barbara, John Wiley and Sons.

Toyo Keizai Shinposha, (1985). Japan Company Handbook.

PART III

Patterns in Stock Prices and Effects of Expectational Data

10

Seasonal and Size Anomalies in the Japanese Stock Market

Kiyoshi Kato
Nanzan University, Japan

James S. Schallheim*
University of Utah, Salt Lake City

I. Introduction

Little attention has been paid by the academic community in the United States to the Japanese stock market and its structure. Japan has the second largest economy in the Western world, and the Tokyo Stock Exchange (TSE) is second only to the New York Stock Exchange (NYSE) in terms of aggregate market values and sales volume. Analysis of the Japanese stock market is useful given its relative importance, but, in addition, examination of the Japanese market may offer insights into controversies surrounding U.S. markets. This study focuses on two such current controversies: the January and size anomalies.

The January effect refers to the phenomenon that January stock returns are, on average, higher than in other months. The size effect is the empirical regularity with which firms with small market value exhibit returns that, on average, significantly exceed those of large firms. The January effect was noted as early as 1942 by Wachtel (1942) for the U.S. stock market. Banz (1981) and Reinganum (1981a) provide substantial evidence for the existence of the small firm effect in the U.S. stock market.

* The authors wish to express their appreciation to Sanjai Bhagat, James Brickley, Jeffrey Coles, Frederick Dark, Yoshio Iihara, Ronald Lease, and Steven Manaster for their helpful comments, and especially to Michio Kunimura for the use of the facilities at Nagoya City University.

Recent studies have found a relationship between the January and size effects. Keim (1983) reports that small firm returns during January are significantly higher than large firm returns and that approximately 50% of the size effect appears in January. Other studies have documented the same effect noted by Keim.[1] Therefore, there appears to be a link between the January effect and the small firm effect. To date, however, no one has been able to explain this market behavior satisfactorily.

This study seeks to test whether the January-size effect exists in the Japanese stock market. Substantial differences between the Japanese and U.S. tax systems offer a unique opportunity to test one possible explanation, the "tax loss selling hypothesis," as a cause for the anomalies. Evidence is presented to suggest that the January-size effect does exist in Japan. In fact, the remarkable similarity between the January-size effects in the United States and those in Japan is an interesting result of this study. In addition, there also appears to be a June-size effect in the Japanese return data. Several possible explanations for this market behavior are suggested.

The organization of the paper is as follows. The next section reviews the literature on the January and size effects. Section III describes the data sources and the methodology. In Section IV, the tests for the January-size effects are presented. Section V offers several explanations for the evidence discovered. The last section summarizes the findings.

II. January And Size Anomalies: Previous Literature

The first study that combined the January and size anomalies was by Keim (1983). He reported that small firm returns during the month of January are significantly higher than large firm returns and that approximately 50% of the size effect appears in January. Furthermore, Keim discovered that over 50% of the January effect occurs during the first week of January. Keim briefly discussed two possible theoretical explanations for this effect: the tax-loss-selling hypothesis and the information hypothesis.

The tax-loss-selling hypothesis is derived from the consequences of the U.S. tax code and the tax year end of December 31. Properties of the U.S. tax code provide the motivation for individual investors to sell shares before the end of the year, particularly those shares for which losses have occurred. The difference between long-term and short-term capital gains/losses also influences this tax loss selling.[2] In addition, the group of small firms will contain a relatively larger number of the firms with capital losses. Reinganum (1983) examined U.S. stock returns to investigate whether the tax-loss-selling hypothesis can fully explain January-size effects. He found that small firms exhibit high returns after controlling for tax-loss-selling pressures. Reinganum concluded that the January abnormal returns for small firms were consistent with tax loss selling; however, tax-loss-selling cannot explain the entire seasonality effect.

The information hypothesis refers to the supposition that smaller firms have less publicly available information than do large firms. This lack of information leads to greater uncertainty and risk, resulting in higher returns. Brown and Barry (1984) attempted to test the information hypothesis as a possible explanation of the small firm effect. Using "time of listing on the exchange" as a proxy for the availability of information, they found that "time of listing" does explain some of the small firm effect. Brown and Barry concluded that information uncertainty does play at least a partial role in explaining the small firm effect.

Several studies provide some evidence on the international extent of the January-size effects. Gultekin and Gultekin (1983) examined the monthly value-weighted indices in 17 countries with different tax laws and tax year ends. They found a persistent January effect in most of the countries, including Japan. However, as they admitted, one of the weaknesses of their paper is that a single market index does not discriminate the size effect from the January effect.

Brown, Keim, Kleidon, and Marsh (1983) examined the tax-loss-selling hypothesis using Australian stock returns. Since Australia has a tax year that ends in June, analysis of Australian stock returns provides a good contrast to the U.S. stock returns to test this hypothesis. Brown et al. find that December, January, July, and August have significantly higher raw returns than do the other months. In addition, the small firm premium appears in all months. This is unlike the U.S. data in which the size effect is concentrated in January. They concluded that the tax-loss-selling hypothesis is not consistent with the Australian evidence.

Berges, McConnell, and Schlarbaum (1984) also test whether the tax-loss-selling hypothesis explains January-size effects, this time using Canadian stock return data. They focus on the fact that, until 1972,

Canada had no taxes on capital gains. So, for the period prior to 1972, there should not be January-size effects, according to the tax-loss-selling hypothesis. However, they find that January-size effects in Canada are similar to those in the United States both before and after 1972. This evidence is either inconsistent with the tax-loss-selling hypothesis or consistent with a well-integrated market between U.S. and Canadian investors. An integrated market means that U.S. investors are active participants in the Canadian market and vice-versa.

Japanese tax law offers an interesting opportunity to test the tax-loss-selling hypothesis. There is no tax on capital gains for individual investors in Japan nor is there a tax benefit for losses. Japanese corporations are taxed on capital gains; however, each firm can choose its fiscal year arbitrarily. There is no reason to believe there will be tax loss selling in December. In fact, approximately 50% of Japanese firms have tax years ending in March. However, the potential integration of the U.S. and Japanese stock market precludes the total rejection of the tax-loss-selling hypothesis.

III. Data Description and Methodologies

The rates of return for this study are drawn from the Nissho Monthly Stock Returns file. This data file contains all firms listed on the First Section of the TSE.[3] Because stock prices are required to construct size portfolios, the stock prices are obtained from the Nissho Monthly Stock Price file. The stock return and price files contain data for the 29-year period of 1952 to 1980. In order to obtain the number of shares and total assets for each firm, the Nikkei Needs Financial Data file for the 18-year period of 1964 to 1981 is used.

Due to the necessity of combining data from the three different sources, some companies are necessarily excluded from this study. The Nikkei Needs Financial Data does not contain firms in the banking and insurance industries. As a result, 102 of these firms are excluded from our sample (when the firm size is required). Furthermore, companies that delisted during the 1964 to 1981 period are not contained on the Nikkei Needs file. These firms number 87. Finally, 15 firms are lost due to missing data. Consequently, the number of firms in our sample ranges from a low of 529 in 1964 to a maximum of 844 in 1980.

Since a fairly large number of firms are excluded from the sample due to data availability, a careful examination of the missing firms is warranted. Excluding the group of firms that were delisted opens the door to survivorship bias. We analyze this group of firms separately, and find similar results to those reported as follows concerning the January effect.[4] Excluding the firms in the banking and insurance industries also may cause a systematic bias to the results. However, a modified examination of this group did not change the results significantly.[5]

In order to test January-size effects, 10 portfolios are created based on stock market capitalization.[6] The market capitalization of all firms in the sample is computed by multiplying the price per share by the number of shares of common stock. The 10 portfolios are rearranged every year based on market value of equity for each firm. Because of the limitation due to data availability, we use 17 years of data for portfolio analysis and 29 years of data for index analysis.[7]

The analysis of the data is performed using two alternative methodologies. We first examine the data for the January-size effects using raw returns. Secondly, we adjust the returns to account for systematic risk by use of the market model. Since few financial scholars believe the market model is stationary over long periods of time, we estimate the market model on the basis of a moving procedure of the prior 60 months of data for each security in the sample. The market model estimates a_i and b_i are obtained from the following regression equation

$$R_{it} = a_i + b_i R_{mt} + e_{it} \qquad (10.1)$$

$t = (t - 60), (t - 59), \ldots, (t - 1)$
$i = 1, 2, \ldots, n$ is the number of firms

R_{it} and R_{mt} represent returns on the security and market index, respectively, over the prior estimation period. The excess return for each security for each period is computed as

$$e_{it} = R_{it} - a_i - b_i R_{mt} \qquad (10.2)$$

This procedure is repeated for each month during the period 1964–1980 with the market model parameters being reestimated each month on the basis of data for the prior 60 months.[8]

IV. Results

Documentation of the January Effect

We begin the analysis of the Japanese stock market by examining two market indexes, a Value Weighted Index (VWI) and an Equally Weighted Index (EWI). To test for a January effect for these indices, we estimate the following regression coefficients

$$R_{it} = a_{i1} + \sum_{j=2}^{12} a_{ij} D_{jt} + e_{it} \qquad (10.3)$$

i = VWI or EWI (the market index)
R_{it} = return on idex i in month t
D_{jt} = seasonal dummy for calendar month j
j = February(2) to December(12)

The intercept a_{i1} indicates average returns for January, and the coefficients of the dummy variables ($a_{i2}, \ldots, a_{i12}$) represent the average differences in return between January and each individual month. As a supplemental test, the Kruskal-Wallis[9] nonparametric test is also used to examine the Japanese stock returns.

Table 10.1 reports the results of the analysis of the market indices. A January seasonal is indicated using either the VWI or the EWI. The F statistics, reported in column 13 of Table 10.1, are significant at traditional levels. This result is compatible with the results of Gultekin and Gultekin (1983). However, it is interesting to note that the January average return for the EWI is higher than that for the VWI. In fact, the monthly average return for the 29-year period (1952–1980) is 0.42% higher for the EWI than it is for the VWI. This evidence is indicative of a possible small firm effect because the EWI is influenced more by small firms than is the VWI.

To examine the small firm effect more directly, we need to know the size of the individual firms. As noted in Section III, however, we were able to calculate firm size only for the period 1964 to 1980, due to data limitations. In addition, 1964 marks a potentially fundamental change in the Japanese economy and markets. Prior to 1964, the Japanese economy, including the stock market, was very restrictive to foreign investors. Japan assumed the obligations of Article 8 of the International

Table 10.1. Tests for Seasonal Effects Using Market Indices

	Jan.	Feb.	Mar.	Apr.	May	Jun.	Jul.	Aug.	Sep.	Oct.	Nov.	Dec.	F ratio[a]	K-W[b]	Prob.
VWI(52-80)	4.48	−3.86	−2.52	−3.18	−3.84	−1.94	−4.25	−3.76	−2.74	−4.66	−2.73	−2.67			
		(−2.96)[c]	(−1.93)	(−2.44)	(−2.95)	(−1.49)	(−3.26)	(−2.88)	(−2.10)	(−3.57)	(−2.10)	(−2.05)	1.81*	22.03	0.024
EWI(52-80)	7.08	−6.01	−5.30	−5.67	−6.50	−4.25	−6.19	−5.89	−6.05	−6.55	−5.31	−4.55			
		(−4.18)	(−3.69)	(−3.95)	(−4.53)	(−2.96)	(−4.32)	(−4.10)	(−4.22)	(−4.56)	(−3.70)	(−3.17)	3.08**	35.43	0.000
VWI(52-63)	5.99	−6.02	−4.51	−3.25	−6.67	−1.81	−6.32	−3.57	−3.62	−5.70	−3.19	−5.07			
		(−2.51)	(−1.88)	(−1.36)	(−2.78)	(−0.75)	(−2.63)	(−1.49)	(−1.51)	(−2.38)	(−1.33)	(−2.11)	1.36	14.81	0.192
EWI(52-63)	8.27	−7.42	−7.08	−5.19	−9.08	−4.96	−7.89	−5.59	−6.68	−6.85	−4.12	−5.61			
		(−2.65)	(−2.53)	(−1.85)	(−3.24)	(−1.77)	(−2.82)	(−2.00)	(−2.38)	(−2.44)	(−1.47)	(−2.00)	1.36	12.00	0.363
VWI(64-80)	3.41	−2.34	−1.11	−3.13	−1.85	−2.04	−2.79	−3.89	−2.12	−3.92	−2.14	−0.98			
		(−1.62)	(−0.77)	(−2.17)	(−1.28)	(−1.41)	(−1.93)	(−2.69)	(−1.47)	(−2.72)	(−1.67)	(−0.68)	1.29	14.08	0.229
EWI(64-80)	6.24	−5.01	−4.04	−6.01	−4.67	−3.74	−4.99	−6.10	−5.61	−6.34	−6.15	−3.81			
		(−3.42)	(−2.77)	(−4.11)	(−3.12)	(−2.56)	(−3.42)	(−4.17)	(−3.84)	(−4.34)	(−4.21)	(−2.61)	2.87**	32.38	0.001

a. For the F statistics:
*0.05 significance level.
**0.01 significance level.

b. The statistic used for K-W test is a chi-square distribution.

c. t statistics in parentheses.

Monetary Fund in 1964 and the Japanese markets slowly opened to foreign investors thereafter.[10] Therefore, we decided to examine the market indices before and after 1964 to see if there any changes in the data.

In this experiment, only the EWI during the post-1964 period is significant, as shown in Table 10-1. This result may indicate that the January effect began in Japan at approximately the same time the Japanese economy began to open up to foreign investors, thus supporting the international integration of capital markets hypothesis.

The January effect may be industry related. In Section II, the information hypothesis was described as a possible explanation for the small firm effect. Also, it is possible that the January effect may be related to information due to the proliferation of annual reports and other information at year's end. If the firms within certain industries are more likely to report information at year's end, then industry classification may proxy for this information effect.

To test this hypothesis, we created 28 industry indexes. Each industry index is computed by taking the simple arithmetic average of the returns of each firm in the industry. Equation 10.3 is then calculated for each industry index. The results are reported in Table 10.2. Seven out of the 28 industries do not display significant seasonal effects. It is possible that these industries are related to the size phenomenon, however, a careful examination of the firms within these industries indicated no systematic size relationship. For example, in the oil and coal industry, about half of the companies could be labeled relatively large, and the remaining companies are small. It may also be possible that these industries are related to the information effect. There may be other important and systematic reasons why these 7 industries do not exhibit seasonalities. More research is needed to resolve this anomaly.

Examination of the Seasonal and Size Anomalies

The size effect is examined with the use of the 10 portfolios described in Section III. Table 10.3 reports the OLS betas and the autocorrelation functions for the 10 portfolios (again, this is monthly data for the period 1964 to 1980). Interestingly, the OLS betas are not related to firm size in a systematic way. This result is remarkably similar to the result found by Keim (1983) using U.S. data. Keim found that the two smallest portfolios also have the smallest OLS betas.[11] Table 10.3 reports the

Table 10.2. Tests of Seasonal Effects Using Industry Indices

	K-W[a]	Significance Level	N[b]
Fisheries Agriculture and Forestry	17.71	0.089	6
Mining	26.07	0.006	6
Construction	22.87	0.018	79
Foods	29.30	0.002	49
Textile	21.23	0.031	42
Pulp and Paper	13.52	0.261	17
Chemicals	34.95	0.000	106
Oil and Coal Products	12.56	0.323	10
Rubber Products	37.22	0.000	9
Glass and Ceramics Products	36.94	0.000	30
Iron and Steel	37.00	0.000	35
Nonferro Metals	28.04	0.003	72
Metal Products	26.99	0.005	17
Machinery	36.04	0.000	73
Electrical Machinery	21.90	0.025	92
Transportation Equipment	32.70	0.001	43
Precision Instrument	20.44	0.040	16
Other Products	25.84	0.007	21
Commerce	23.22	0.016	87
Banking and Insurance	38.47	0.000	102
Real Estate	19.42	0.054	13
Land Transportation	31.47	0.001	23
Marine Transportation	10.85	0.456	15
Air Transportation	28.92	0.002	3
Warehouse and Services Incidental to Transportation	14.63	0.200	10
Communication	19.15	0.059	3
Electric and Gas	29.56	0.002	14
Service	24.30	0.012	18
Total			961

a. The statistic used for K-W test is a chi-square distribution.

b. N stands for the number of firms within each industry in 1980.

Table 10.3. OLS Beta Estimates and Autocorrelations for the Ten Portfolios

Portfolio	OLS Beta (VWI) EWI	ρ_1	ρ_2	ρ_3	ρ_4	ρ_5	ρ_6	ρ_7	ρ_8	ρ_9	ρ_{10}	ρ_{11}	ρ_{12}	ρ_{13}	ρ_{14}
	1.07	0.042	0.083	−0.027	0.007	−0.195*	−0.042	−0.009	0.137*	0.004	0.048	0.063	−0.089	−0.076	0.011
Largest	(0.84)	(0.069)[a]	(0.068)	(0.068)	(0.068)	(0.068)	(0.068)	(0.068)	(0.067)	(0.067)	(0.067)	(0.067)	(0.067)	(0.067)	(0.067)
	0.98	0.024	0.070	−0.022	0.021	−0.109	−0.071	−0.009	0.056	−0.009	0.060	−0.005	−0.065	−0.033	0.056
2	(0.85)	(0.069)	(0.069)	(0.069)	(0.069)	(0.068)	(0.068)	(0.068)	(0.068)	(0.068)	(0.068)	(0.067)	(0.067)	(0.067)	(0.067)
	0.97	0.022	0.052	0.017	0.039	−0.107	−0.112	0.054	0.007	−0.068	0.030	0.010	−0.075	−0.065	0.040
3	(0.92)	(0.069)	(0.069)	(0.069)	(0.069)	(0.068)	(0.068)	(0.068)	(0.068)	(0.068)	(0.068)	(0.067)	(0.067)	(0.067)	(0.067)
	1.00	0.069	0.065	0.064	0.002	−0.117	−0.119	−0.076	−0.006	−0.098	−0.067	0.060	−0.051	−0.028	0.035
4	(1.03)	(0.069)	(0.069)	(0.069)	(0.069)	(0.068)	(0.068)	(0.068)	(0.068)	(0.068)	(0.068)	(0.067)	(0.067)	(0.067)	(0.067)
	1.02	0.075	−0.005	0.039	0.041	−0.096	−0.075	0.114	−0.020	−0.092	−0.074	0.074	−0.088	−0.056	0.023
5	(1.08)	(0.069)	(0.069)	(0.069)	(0.069)	(0.068)	(0.068)	(0.068)	(0.068)	(0.068)	(0.068)	(0.067)	(0.067)	(0.067)	(0.067)
	1.01	0.074	−0.011	0.013	0.034	−0.116	−0.112	0.095	−0.007	−0.172*	−0.075	0.090	−0.040	−0.099	−0.001

6	(1.13)	(0.069)	(0.069)	(0.069)	(0.069)	(0.068)	(0.068)	(0.068)	(0.068)	(0.068)	(0.068)	(0.067)	(0.067)	(0.067)	(0.067)
	0.96	0.127	0.019	−0.033	0.007	−0.009	−0.071	0.109	−0.015	−0.130	−0.110	0.021	0.031	−0.039	−0.010
7	(1.13)	(0.069)	(0.069)	(0.069)	(0.069)	(0.068)	(0.068)	(0.068)	(0.068)	(0.068)	(0.068)	(0.067)	(0.067)	(0.067)	(0.067)
	0.92	0.129	0.026	0.014	−0.023	−0.017	−0.025	−0.070	−0.043	−0.181*	−0.147*	0.016	0.047	0.001	−0.099
8	(1.13)	(0.069)	(0.069)	(0.069)	(0.069)	(0.068)	(0.068)	(0.068)	(0.068)	(0.068)	(0.068)	(0.067)	(0.067)	(0.067)	(0.067)
	0.86	0.180*	−0.024	0.019	0.048	0.034	−0.040	0.060	−0.044	−0.175*	−0.164*	−0.041	0.049	−0.061	−0.061
9	(1.12)	(0.069)	(0.069)	(0.069)	(0.069)	(0.068)	(0.068)	(0.068)	(0.068)	(0.068)	(0.068)	(0.067)	(0.067)	(0.067)	(0.067)
	0.79	0.219*	−0.050	0.034	−0.089	0.114	0.064	0.047	−0.077	−0.078	−0.160*	−0.062	0.086	−0.051	−0.155
Smallest	(1.13)	(0.069)	(0.069)	(0.069)	(0.069)	(0.068)	(0.068)	(0.068)	(0.068)	(0.068)	(0.068)	(0.067)	(0.067)	(0.067)	(0.067)

a. Standard error in parentheses.

*Sample autocorrelation is at least two standard errors to the left or to the right of its expected value under the hypothesis that the true autocorrelation equals zero.

autocorrelation function for each size portfolio up to 14 lags. Most of these estimates of the autocorrelations are not significantly different from zero. Two noticeable exceptions are the autocorrelations of lag 1 for the two smallest portfolios. A possible explanation for these significant lags is the infrequent trading of small firms.

Regression Equation 10.3 was run for each of the 10 size portfolios. The results are presented in Table 10.4. This table contains several important results. First, small firms, on average, earn higher returns than do large firms in January. Second, the *F* statistic (and the Kruskal-Wallis nonparametric test) reported in Table 10.4 indicates that the null hypothesis of no difference across months can be rejected at traditional significance levels for all but the three largest portfolios. This result supports the contention by several authors that the January effect is primarily a small firm effect. Finally, the coefficients on the monthly dummy variables for all non-January months are uniformly negative for all 10 portfolios, except for the month of December in the largest portfolio. This finding indicates that January returns are higher than those for all other months for this sample period.

In addition to the raw returns analysis reported in Table 10.4, we also adjusted the returns for systematic risk using the market model. Since both the Value Weighted Index and the Equal Weighted Index were used, Table 10.5 contains the 10 portfolio *excess* return regressions (again, employing Equation 10.3) using the VWI, and Table 10.6 contains results using the EWI. For both tables, the January excess returns are monotonically increasing as the size of the portfolios decreases. In addition, the January excess returns for the largest portfolios are negative.

Examination of the *F* statistic in Tables 10.5 and 10.6 indicates an interesting phenomenon. In Table 10.5, the two largest portfolios do not display seasonalities as indicated by the insignificant *F* statistic and K-W test. Since the VWI is used for the results reported in Table 10.5, it is interesting to note that large firms have a greater influence on the index than do small firms. In Table 10.6, the three medium-size portfolios (portfolios 5 through 7) do not indicate seasonalities. This result seems to indicate that the January-size effect may be very sensitive to the choice of the market index. Incidently, the results of Table 10.6 display a close resemblance to the results of Keim (1983), using U.S. data and an equally weighted portfolio.

Table 10.4. Month-to-Month Average Rate of Return for 10 Portfolios and Tests of Equality of Mean Returns for the Period January 1964 to December 1980

Portfolio	Jan.	Feb.	Mar.	Apr.	May	Jun.	Jul.	Aug.	Sep.	Oct.	Nov.	Dec.	F ratio[a]	K-W[b]	Prob.
	3.18	−1.83	−0.35	−2.75	−1.65	−2.41	−2.52	−3.46	−1.88	−3.51	−1.82	0.14	1.15	13.77	0.246
Largest		(−1.13)[c]	(−0.22)	(−1.70)	(−1.02)	(−1.49)	(−1.56)	(−2.14)	(−1.16)	(−2.17)	(−1.13)	(0.09)[c]			
	3.82	−2.18	−0.29	−3.69	−2.67	−2.89	−3.26	−4.15	−2.54	−3.97	−2.85	−1.18	1.66	19.49	0.053
2		(−1.47)	(−0.20)	(−2.48)	(−1.80)	(−1.95)	(−2.19)	(−2.79)	(−1.71)	(−2.67)	(−1.92)	(−0.79)			
	4.42	−2.56	−1.02	−4.41	−3.43	−3.13	−4.03	−4.20	−3.01	−4.40	−3.62	−2.86	1.59	19.47	0.053
3		(−1.68)	(−0.67)	(−2.91)	(−2.26)	(−2.06)	(−2.66)	(−2.77)	(−1.98)	(−2.90)	(−2.38)	(−1.88)			
	6.25	−4.24	−2.99	−5.72	−4.52	−4.62	−5.63	−6.07	−5.82	−6.42	−5.96	−4.01	2.55**	28.86	0.002
4		(−2.67)	(−1.88)	(−3.60)	(−2.84)	(−2.91)	(−3.55)	(−3.82)	(−3.66)	(−4.04)	(−3.75)	(−2.52)			
	6.12	−4.14	−3.39	−5.88	−4.92	−3.83	−5.33	−5.20	−5.58	−6.82	−6.19	−3.62	2.33*	27.07	0.004
5		(−2.49)	(−2.04)	(−3.54)	(−2.96)	(−2.31)	(−3.20)	(−3.13)	(−3.36)	(−4.10)	(−3.72)	(−2.18)			
	7.16	−5.44	−4.78	−7.21	−4.82	−4.27	−5.72	−6.72	−6.80	−7.44	−7.09	−4.85	2.82**	30.91	0.001
6		(−3.17)	(−2.79)	(−4.21)	(−2.81)	(−2.49)	(−3.34)	(−3.92)	(−3.97)	(−4.34)	(−4.14)	(−2.83)			
	8.15	−7.01	−5.63	−8.36	−6.74	−5.26	−6.74	−7.55	−7.27	−8.34	−9.02	−5.86	3.83**	38.27	0.000
7		(−4.15)	(−3.33)	(−4.95)	(−3.99)	(−3.11)	(−3.99)	(−4.47)	(−4.30)	(−4.93)	(−5.34)	(−3.47)			
	8.20	−6.94	−6.68	−8.22	−7.03	−4.53	−6.06	−8.34	−8.28	−8.10	−8.52	−5.20	4.02**	39.94	0.000
8		(−4.06)	(−3.91)	(−4.81)	(−4.11)	(−2.65)	(−3.54)	(−4.88)	(−4.84)	(−4.74)	(−4.98)	(−3.04)			
	8.55	−7.91	−7.55	−8.16	−6.80	−4.52	−6.28	−8.06	−8.13	−8.50	−9.21	−6.46	3.98**	35.76	0.000
9		(−4.50)	(−4.30)	(−4.64)	(−3.87)	(−2.57)	(−3.58)	(−4.59)	(−4.63)	(−4.84)	(−5.24)	(−3.68)			
	8.68	−9.23	−9.24	−7.34	−6.20	−4.07	−6.15	−7.96	−9.27	−7.56	−9.90	−4.97	4.10**	43.28	0.000
Smallest		(−4.68)	(−4.69)	(−3.72)	(−3.15)	(−2.06)	(−3.12)	(−4.04)	(−4.70)	(−3.84)	(−5.02)	(−2.52)			

a. For the F statistics:
  *0.05 significance level.
  **0.01 significance level.

b. The statistic used for K-W test is a chi-square distribution.

c. t statistics in parentheses.

Table 10.5. Month-to-Month Excess Rates of Return Relative to the Market Model for 10 Portfolios Using the Value Weighted Index

Portfolio	Jan.	Feb.	Mar.	Apr.	May	Jun.	Jul.	Aug.	Sep.	Oct.	Nov.	Dec.	F ratio[a]	K-W[b]	Prob.
	−0.98	0.38	0.86	0.62	0.59	−0.16	0.68	0.70	0.37	0.75	0.98	1.49	1.47	18.70	0.06
Largest		(0.74)[c]	(1.69)	(1.23)	(1.16)	(−0.32)	(1.34)	(1.38)	(0.74)	(1.48)	(1.92)	(2.94)			
	−0.19	0.22	0.53	−0.92	−0.084	−0.78	−0.31	−0.49	−0.35	−0.27	−0.34	−0.17	1.37	16.37	0.128
2		(0.43)	(1.02)	(−1.78)	(−1.63)	(−1.52)	(−0.60)	(−0.94)	(−0.67)	(−0.51)	(−0.67)	(−0.32)			
	0.61	−0.56	0.18	−1.78	−1.47	−1.19	−1.67	−0.29	−1.18	−0.50	−1.20	−1.71	2.36**	27.48	0.004
3		(−0.89)	(0.28)	(−2.81)	(−2.31)	(−1.89)	(−2.64)	(−0.46)	(−1.86)	(−0.78)	(−1.90)	(−2.70)			
	1.49	−1.47	−1.37	−1.82	−2.51	−1.58	−2.28	−1.46	−3.12	−1.37	−2.22	−2.34	2.44**	24.89	0.009
4		(−2.06)	(−1.91)	(−2.55)	(−3.52)	(−2.21)	(−3.19)	(−2.04)	(−4.37)	(−1.91)	(−3.11)	(−3.28)			
	2.18	−2.01	−2.28	−3.09	−3.17	−2.00	−2.47	−1.90	−4.02	−2.94	−3.89	−2.83	3.04**	33.17	0.000
5		(−2.33)	(−2.64)	(−3.58)	(−3.67)	(−2.32)	(−2.86)	(−2.20)	(−4.66)	(−3.41)	(−4.50)	(−3.28)			
	3.34	−3.19	−4.10	−4.37	−3.21	−2.22	−3.05	−2.72	−4.89	−3.65	−4.87	−4.14	3.70**	34.78	0.000
6		(−3.21)	(−4.13)	(−4.40)	(−3.24)	(−2.24)	(−3.07)	(−2.74)	(−4.93)	(−3.68)	(−4.91)	(−4.17)			
	4.05	−4.23	−4.51	−5.02	−4.77	−2.66	−3.87	−3.82	−5.69	−3.85	−6.17	−4.78	4.13**	38.77	0.000
7		(−3.82)	(−4.08)	(−4.53)	(−4.31)	(−2.41)	(−3.49)	(−3.46)	(−5.14)	(−3.48)	(−5.57)	(−4.32)			
	4.38	−4.50	−5.33	−5.36	−4.98	−2.11	−3.62	−4.72	−6.02	−3.78	−6.11	−3.89	4.11**	36.47	0.000
8		(−3.71)	(−4.40)	(−4.43)	(−4.11)	(−1.74)	(−2.99)	(−3.90)	(−4.97)	(−3.12)	(−5.05)	(−3.21)			
	4.87	−5.20	−6.16	−5.28	−4.89	−2.31	−3.50	−5.23	−6.16	−4.80	−6.88	−5.59	3.57**	31.63	0.001
9		(−3.65)	(−4.32)	(−3.70)	(−3.43)	(−1.62)	(−2.46)	(−3.66)	(−4.32)	(−3.37)	(−4.83)	(−3.92)			
	5.16	−6.81	−7.31	−4.41	−4.59	−1.78	−3.60	−4.74	−7.24	−3.63	−7.83	−3.43	3.74**	39.50	0.000
Smallest		(−3.92)	(−4.21)	(−2.54)	(−2.64)	(−1.02)	(−2.07)	(−2.73)	(−4.17)	(−2.09)	(−4.51)	(−1.98)			

a. For the F statistics:
*0.05 significance level.
**0.01 significance level.

b. The statistic used for K-W test is a chi-square distribution.

c. t statistics in parentheses.

Table 10.6. Month-to-Month Excess Rates of Return Relative to the Market Model for 10 Portfolios Using the Equally Weighted Index

Portfolio	Jan.	Feb.	Mar.	Apr.	May	Jun.	Jul.	Aug.	Sep.	Oct.	Nov.	Dec.	F ratio[a]	K-W[b]	Prob.
Largest	−2.48	1.94	2.90	2.19	2.51	0.74	1.85	1.88	2.87	1.83	3.49	3.62	2.14*	18.84	0.064
		(1.91)[c]	(2.86)	(2.16)	(2.47)	(0.73)	(1.83)	(1.86)	(2.83)	(1.80)	(3.44)	(3.57)			
2	−2.01	2.19	2.89	1.24	1.45	0.40	1.31	1.23	2.58	1.34	2.55	2.10	3.06**	28.27	0.003
		(3.07)	(4.05)	(1.74)	(2.03)	(0.56)	(1.83)	(1.73)	(3.61)	(1.87)	(3.57)	(2.95)			
3	−1.44	1.67	2.77	0.69	1.05	0.21	0.24	1.61	2.01	1.40	2.09	0.82	4.08**	42.41	0.000
		(2.77)	(4.61)	(1.15)	(1.75)	(0.34)	(0.40)	(2.67)	(3.35)	(2.33)	(3.48)	(1.36)			
4	−0.84	1.00	1.52	1.09	0.34	−0.01	−0.07	0.85	0.47	0.92	1.33	0.28	2.21*	25.68	0.007
		(1.93)	(2.92)	(2.09)	(0.66)	(−0.01)	(−0.14)	(1.63)	(0.90)	(1.77)	(2.57)	(0.53)			
5	−0.52	0.87	0.90	0.21	−0.00	−0.19	0.13	0.87	−0.05	−0.15	0.13	0.16	1.20	13.58	0.257
		(1.66)	(1.72)	(0.41)	(−0.00)	(−0.37)	(0.24)	(1.66)	(−0.09)	(−0.29)	(0.25)	(0.30)			
6	0.53	−0.11	−0.78	−0.83	0.08	−0.31	−0.33	0.16	−0.73	−0.68	−0.60	−0.97	1.02	11.97	0.366
		(−0.20)	(−1.42)	(−1.52)	(0.15)	(−0.56)	(−0.60)	(0.30)	(−1.34)	(−1.24)	(−1.09)	(−1.78)			
7	1.08	−1.00	−1.04	−1.28	−1.30	−0.58	−0.95	−0.68	−1.45	−0.62	−1.77	−1.56	1.58	14.69	0.197
		(−1.81)	(−1.87)	(−2.30)	(−2.33)	(−1.04)	(−1.71)	(−1.23)	(−2.60)	(−1.11)	(−3.18)	(−2.80)			
8	1.40	−1.26	−1.94	−1.53	−1.54	−0.02	−0.59	−1.48	−1.78	−0.48	−1.65	−0.65	2.21*	18.90	0.063
		(−1.92)	(−2.95)	(−2.33)	(−2.35)	(−0.03)	(−0.90)	(−2.25)	(−2.72)	(−0.74)	(−2.51)	(−0.99)			
9	1.82	−1.88	−2.75	−1.32	−1.44	−0.17	−0.42	−1.89	−1.88	−1.37	−2.28	−2.25	2.02*	19.27	0.056
		(−2.16)	(−3.16)	(−1.52)	(−1.66)	(−0.20)	(−0.48)	(−2.18)	(−2.16)	(−1.58)	(−2.62)	(−2.59)			
Smallest	2.02	−3.34	−3.82	−0.36	−1.16	0.44	−0.45	−1.26	−2.91	−0.02	−3.03	0.01	3.13**	34.56	0.000
		(−2.73)	(−3.12)	(−0.29)	(−0.95)	(0.36)	(−0.37)	(−1.03)	(−2.38)	(−0.02)	(−2.48)	(0.01)			

a. For the F statistics:
*0.05 significance level.
**0.01 significance level.

b. The statistic used for K-W test is a chi-square distribution.

c. t statistics in parentheses.

A June Effect?

Returning to the raw return data, we plotted the average monthly returns for the 10 portfolios. This plot is presented in Figure 10.1. The surprising results of Figure 10.1 are the "spikes" at certain months other than January. That is, the plot appears to indicate significant above-average returns for the months of January, June, and December. To test statistically this casual observation, the following regression was run

$$R_{pt} = a_p + b_p R_{Mt} + c_{p1} D_t^{\text{Jan}} + c_{p2} D_t^{\text{Jun}} + c_{p3} D_t^{\text{Dec}} \qquad (10.4)$$

R_{Mt} = VWI or EWI
D_t = Dummy for January, June, and December

The results are given in Table 10.7 (using VWI as a market index) and in Table 10.8 (using EWI as a market index). Both a January and

Figure 10.1. Mean Monthly Returns on the Ten Size Portfolios.

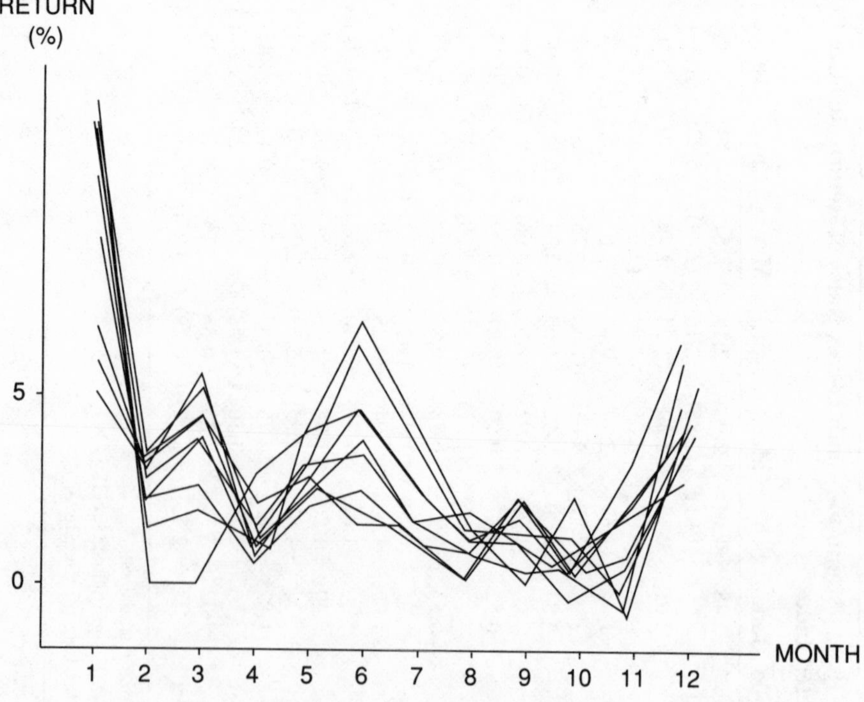

Table 10.7. Estimates of Average Excess Rate of Return for the Months of January, June, and December Relative to the Market Model Using the Value Weighted Index

	a_p	p_p(VWI)	cp_1	cp_2	cp_3	F ratio[a]
Largest	0.14	1.07 (48.75**)[b]	−0.61 (−1.81)	−0.84 (−2.51*)	0.58 (1.73)	615.97**
2	0.20	0.97 (38.33**)	0.29 (0.75)	−0.62 (−1.60)	0.07 (0.19)	384.53**
3	0.24	0.97 (33.07**)	0.87 (1.91)	−0.29 (−0.65)	1.04 (−2.31*)	288.05**
4	0.22	0.97 (26.41**)	2.72 (4.79**)	0.07 (0.13)	−0.34 (−0.60)	196.98**
5	0.07	0.99 (23.88**)	2.68 (4.20**)	0.86 (1.37)	0.03 (0.05)	161.30**
6	0.17	0.98 (20.48**)	3.67 (5.01**)	1.39 (1.92)	−0.22 (−0.30)	124.44**
7	0.03	0.91 (17.55**)	5.02 (6.28**)	1.61 (2.05*)	0.06 (0.07)	100.06**
8	−0.05	0.85 (14.86**)	5.34 (6.04**)	2.54 (2.92**)	0.98 (1.12)	76.48**
9	0.08	0.79 (12.41**)	5.76 (5.84**)	2.85 (2.93**)	0.04 (0.06)	74.45**
Smallest	0.03	0.71 (8.61**)	6.23 (4.88**)	3.61 (2.87**)	1.96 (1.55)	31.24**

a. For the F statistics and t statistics:
*0.05 significance level.
**0.01 significance level.

b. t statistics in parentheses.

June seasonal are statistically significant for the small firms. However, the interesting observation is that the significance of the coefficients is dependent on which index is used. For example, when the VWI is used as a market index, either a January or June seasonal is not observed for large firms (with one exception). Alternatively, when we use the EWI as a market index, either January or June effects are not shown for medium-size firms. Again, these anomalies appear to be highly dependent on the market index used. Some conjectures about these observations are presented in the next section.

Table 10.8. Estimates of Average Excess Rate of Return for the Months of January, June, and December Relative to the Market Model Using the Equally Weighted Index

	a_p	b_p(EWI)	cp_1	cp_2	cp_3	F ratio[a]
	0.26	0.90	−2.68	−1.73	0.88	98.67**
Largest		(19.37**)[b]	(−3.57**)	(−2.43*)	(1.23)	
	0.24	0.90	−2.04	−1.57	0.20	166.63**
2		(25.14**)	(−3.52**)	(−2.86**)	(0.37)	
	0.22	0.97	−1.87	−1.36	−1.03	310.74**
3		(34.36**)	(−4.07**)	(−3.14**)	(−2.37*)	
	0.15	1.04	−0.40	−1.12	−0.44	514.41**
4		(43.02**)	(−1.01)	(−3.01**)	(−1.18)	
	−0.03	1.09	−0.64	−0.40	−0.12	534.57**
5		(43.94**)	(−1.60)	(−1.05)	(−0.31)	
	0.03	1.12	0.12	0.06	−0.45	593.35**
6		(45.65**)	(0.29)	(0.15)	(−1.20)	
	−0.15	1.11	1.40	0.28	−0.25	581.38**
7		(44.00**)	(3.43**)	(0.71)	(−0.65)	
	−0.25	1.09	1.66	1.20	0.61	392.86**
8		(35.68**)	(3.37**)	(2.57*)	(1.29)	
	−0.17	1.08	1.99	1.50	−0.37	258.98**
9		(28.77**)	(3.27**)	(2.61**)	(−0.64)	
	−0.27	1.07	2.29	2.22	1.39	104.24**
Smallest		(17.90**)	(2.37*)	(2.42*)	(1.51)	

a. For the F statistics and t statistics:
*0.05 significance level.
**0.01 significance level.

b. t statistics in parentheses.

V. Further Comments on the Results

As with any empirical study, some of the results of this study may be subject to criticism concerning methodology and measurement error. We would like to elaborate on several potential problems.

First, there are problems concerning the return-generating process. We have chosen the market model as our benchmark for calculating excess returns. Although the market model is not equivalent to the Capital Asset Pricing Model (CAPM), some of the criticism concerning the CAPM applies. Roll's (1977) critique of the CAPM concerning the choice of the proxy for the market index is very appropriate. The evidence presented in Section IV indicates that the January-size anomalies are sensitive to the choice of the market index. Therefore, it is possible that the entire January-size anomalies are products of an incorrect proxy for the true market portfolio.

The true return-generating process may be more complex than the one-factor market model. Arbitrage Pricing Theory (APT) suggests a multi-factor model as the true return-generating process. Although we have no evidence concerning the APT applied to the Japanese stock market, there are two studies of the U.S. market concerning the size effect and the APT. Unfortunately, the two studies reach opposite conclusions. Reinganum (1981b) finds the size effect still remains after adjusting for three-, four-, and five- factor models, whereas Chen (1983) finds no size effect after adjusting the returns with a five-factor model.

Other possible explanations of the January-size effects have been explored thoroughly by other authors. These include the problems of infrequently traded small firms, transaction costs, and other statistical artifacts.[12]

Two possible explanations of the January-June anomalies documented in this study deserve further attention. First, there is a correlation between the January and June effects and "bonuses" peculiar to Japanese society. Most Japanese companies pay large bonuses twice a year to their employees, most frequently in June and December. These bonuses can amount to two or three months' salary. After the employees purchase traditional gifts—called *Ochugen* in the summer and *Oseibo* in the winter—we assume that a portion of the remaining bonus money is available for investment in the capital markets. How this bonus money translates into the observed seasonal effects and size effects is not known. Whether the correlation of the January and June effects with the Japanese bonus represents causality or mere coincidence is subject to future research.

A second explanation for the January-size effects that appears to be the more fruitful for future research is the information hypothesis. It is possible that the release of financial reports during specific months is contributing to this phenomenon. For example, year-end (preliminary) financial reports may be contributing to the January effect. In Japan, earnings forecasts by corporate officers often occur in May, and earnings forecasts by financial analysts occur every March, June, September, and December (see Kunimura, p. 4). If these May-June forecasts offer new information to the financial market, they could potentially explain the June effect found in this study.[13]

VI. Conclusions

This study has examined stock returns on the TSE for the presence of January and size effects. Both of these anomalous effects appear to be present in the Japanese data. However, the January and size effects are sensitive to the type of market index used in the analysis. One of the most interesting findings is the remarkable similarity between the U.S. and Japanese stock markets in terms of these anomalies. This similarity between the capital markets may be indicative of well-integrated markets on an international scale. A further result of this study casts more doubt on the tax-loss-selling hypothesis as an explanation of the January-size effects. This is due in part to the differences between the Japanese and U.S. tax regimes. Further evidence is presented that indicates a possible June seasonal in the Japanese stock market.

Notes

1. For examples, see Brown, Kleidon, and Marsh (1983), Givoly and Avadia (1983), Reinganum (1983), and Roll (1983).
2. Constantinidies (1984) provides a detailed discussion of the so-called "tax timing option" that arises from this asymmetry in the tax code.
3. The TSE has two sections. The First Section dominates the Second Section since the size of the Second Section is less than 10% of the First in terms of market values and total sales. Although there are seven other stock exchanges in Japan, they are very small relative to the TSE. Analysis of the First Section of the TSE should be analogous to the study of the NYSE and the AMEX in the United States.
4. The group of delisted firms was examined for seasonalities in the same manner as the main sample. This subsample also exhibited a significantly higher January return relative to the other months. Therefore, there is no reason to believe that survivorship bias is driving the results.
5. Financial data are not available for the firms in the Banking and Insurance industries on the Nikkei Needs file. However, we were able to collect the number of shares outstanding for these firms for the year 1980. Assuming that the size rankings of the firms did not change over the period 1964–1980, we were able to include these firms in the total sample. The January-size effects remained.

6. Ten portfolios also were created based on total assets. The results are not significantly different from the portfolios based on market value of equity.
7. Fortunately, the Nissho Monthly Stock file contained a Value Weighted Index for the 29-year period. We were able to compute an Equally Weighted Index from the return data.
8. In the case of a missing monthly return for a particular firm, that month and the subsequent monthly return are excluded from the analysis.
9. The Kruskal-Wallis (K-W) nonparametric test is used as a supplemental test to the regression analysis due to the uncertainty concerning the exact nature of the return distribution. The K-W test does not require normality for the return distributions and also is not sensitive to extreme outliers. This test is most widely used for testing the null hypothesis that several samples have been drawn from the same population. Our basic model for returns is

$$R_t = u + d_m + e_t$$

where u is the (unknown) overall mean, d_m is the unknown month (m) effect, and e_t is the purely random disturbance term. The null hypothesis is

$$H_0 : d_1 = d_2 = \ldots = d_{12} = 0$$

The alternative hypothesis is that at least one "d" differs from zero.
10. Article 8 of the International Monetary Fund agreement prohibits direct restrictions on payments based on current transactions. Current regulation of the Japanese security markets allows a single foreign investor to hold up to 10% of a Japanese firm without special permission from the Japanese government.
11. Keim also estimates Scholes/Williams and Dimson betas. However, Keim uses daily data where the asynchronous trading problem is more pronounced. This study uses only monthly data.
12. Roll (1981) and Reinganum (1982) examine the asynchronous trading bias on small firm excess returns created by the infrequent trading problem. However, this bias is not sufficient to explain the small firm effect. Stoll and Whaley (1983) claim that transaction costs (including the bid-ask spread) explain at least part of the small firm effect. Schultz (1983) counters the Stoll and Whaley argument with additional data and concludes that transaction costs do not explain the small firm effect nor the January effect (unless transaction costs are also seasonal). Roll 1983 discusses several possibilities related to other statistical artifacts.
13. Kalay and Loewenstein (1985) provide evidence that the risk increases around the information release for anticipated events (e.g., dividend announcements). Thus, the returns to stockholders also will increase

given the positive relationship between risk and return. This argument could explain the seasonal effects reported in this study if the months with abnormal returns are truly new "information" months.

References

Banz, R. W., (1981). "The Relationship between Return and Market Value of Common Stocks," *Journal of Financial Economics,* Vol. 9, March, pp. 3–18.

Barry, C. B., and S. J. Brown, (1984). "Differential Information and the Small Firm Effect," *Journal of Financial Economics,* Vol. 13, June, pp. 283–294.

Berges, A., J. J. McConnell, and G. G. Schlarbaum, (1984). "An Investigation of the Turn-of-the-Year Effect, the Small Firm Effect and the Tax-Loss-Selling Pressure Hypothesis in Canadian Stock Returns," *Journal of Finance,* Vol. 39, March, pp. 185–192.

Brown, P., A. W. Kleidon, and T. A. Marsh, (1983). "New Evidence on the Nature of Size-Related Anomalies in Stock Prices," *Journal of Financial Economics,* Vol. 12, June, pp. 33–56.

Brown, P., D. B. Keim, A. W. Kleidon, and T. A. Marsh, (1983). "Stock Return Seasonalities and the Tax-Loss-Selling Hypothesis: Analysis of the Arguments and Australian Evidence," *Journal of Financial Economics,* Vol. 12, June, pp. 105–127.

Chen, N., (1983). "Some Empirical Tests of the Theory of Arbitrage Pricing," *Journal of Finance,* Vol. 38, December, pp. 1393–1414.

Constantinides, G. M, (1984). "Optimal Stock Trading with Personal Taxes: Implications for Prices and the Abnormal January Returns," *Journal of Financial Economics,* Vol. 13, March, pp. 65–89.

Givoly, D., and A. Ovadia, (1983). "Year-End Tax-Induced Sales and Stock Market Seasonality," *Journal of Finance,* Vol. 38, March, pp. 171–185.

Gultekin, M. N., and N. B. Gultekin, (1983). "Stock Market Seasonality: International Evidence," *Journal of Financial Economics,* Vol. 12, December, pp. 469–481.

Kalay, A., and U. Lowenstein, (1985). "Predictable Events and Excess Returns: The Case of Dividend Announcements," *Journal of Financial Economics,* Vol. 14, September, pp. 423–450.

Keim, D. B., (1983). "Size-Related Anomalies and Stock Return Seasonality: Further Empirical Evidence," *Journal of Financial Economics,* Vol. 12, June, pp. 13–32.

Kunimura, M. "The Information Content of Forecast by Corporate Officials and by Financial Analysts in the Japanese Capital Market," Working Paper, No. 84-3, University of Pennsylvania.

Reinganum, M. R., (1981a). "Misspecification of Capital Asset Pricing: Empirical Anomalies Based on Earnings Yields and Market Values," *Journal of Financial Economics,* Vol. 9, March, pp. 19–46.

Reinganum, M. R., (1981b). "Empirical Test of Multi-Factor Pricing Model, the Arbitrage Pricing Theory: Some Empirical Results," *Journal of Finance,* Vol. 36, May, pp. 313–321.

Reinganum, M. R., (1982). "A Direct Test of Roll's Conjecture on the Firm Size Effect," *Journal of Finance,* Vol. 37, March, pp. 27–36.

Reinganum, M. R., (1983). "The Anomalous Stock Market Behavior of Small Firms in January: Empirical Tests for Year-End Tax Effect," *Journal of Financial Economics,* Vol. 12, June, pp. 89–104.

Roll, R., (1977). "A Critique of the Asset Pricing Theory's Tests," *Journal of Financial Economics,* Vol. 4, May, pp. 129–176.

Roll, R., (1981). "A Possible Explanation of the Small Firm Effect," *Journal of Finance,* Vol. 36, September, pp. 879–888.

Roll, R., (1983). "Vas ist Das? The Turn-of-the-Year Effect and the Return Premia of Small Firms," *Journal of Portfolio Management,* Vol. 9, Winter, pp. 18–28.

Schultz, P., (1983). "Transaction Costs and the Small Firm Effect: A Comment," *Journal of Financial Economics,* Vol. 12, June, pp. 81–88.

Stoll, H. R., and R. E. Whaley, (1983). "Transaction Costs and the Small Firm Effect," *Journal of Financial Economics,* Vol. 12, June, pp. 57–79.

Wachtel, S. B. (1942). "Certain Observation on Seasonal Movement in Stock Prices," *Journal of Business,* Vol. 15, pp. 184–193.

11

Day of the Week Effects in Japanese Stocks

Kiyoshi Kato
Nanzan University

Sandra L. Schwartz
University of Tsukuba

William T. Ziemba*
Yamaichi Research Institute,
Tokyo University of Tsukuba
and University of British Columbia

Many of the anomalies in the U.S. markets also occur in Japan. Although literature on Japanese stock market anomalies is just starting to be written, we do have some good independent studies of interday and day of the week, small firm, and January effects, as well as the development of data bases and arbitrage pricing equations. In this paper, we survey several studies on the day of the week effect.[1] Other anomalies are discussed in Ziemba (1989ab). For other aspects of the Japanese stock market see Ziemba (1989c) and Ziemba and Schwartz (1990).

Jaffe and Westerfield (1985ab) investigated the day of the week effect in the Nikkei Dow, a price-weighted index of 225 large capitalization securities traded on the first section of the TSE and the TSE 1000 (at that time), a value-weighted index of all stocks on the first section, called TOPIX.

* Without implicating them William T. Ziemba would like to thank his colleagues, particularly A. Komatsu and H. Shintani at the Yamaichi Research Institute for their help and useful discussions on anomalous behavior in Japanese security markets. This research was supported by the Yamaichi Research Institute and by a grant from the Centre for International Business Studies, University of British Columbia. William T. Ziemba's research on this topic was conducted at the Yamaichi Research Institute and he thanks the institute for permission to publish the new results. This paper is a modified version of a chapter in Ziemba and Schwartz (1990).

The Nikkei Dow index is computed in a fashion similar to the Dow Jones Industrial Average. It is a price-weighted index computed by adding the prices of the 225 component stocks in the index and dividing by a divisor that changes over time due to stock splits, rights issues, et cetera. At the end of December 1988, the divisor that had originally been 225 was 10.287. The index is calculated and announced at one-minute intervals during trading hours. At the end of December, 1988, the Nikkei Dow closed at its high of the year which was 30,159.

The Nikkei Dow is a theoretical number and should be distinguished from the real average price in the marketplace. The meaning of the level ¥30,159 is as follows. Supposing one had bought one share of each of the 225 component stocks listed on the Tokyo Stock Exchange at the time of the post-war inauguration of the exchange (May 16, 1949), then held them until December 17, 1988, without putting additional funds into new shares issued through rights offerings to shareholders. Instead one had reinvested the value of every right evenly in all of the component stocks. The average price would then have increased from ¥176.21 on the date of the original investment on May 16, 1949, to ¥30,159 or about 171 times, not counting dividends and taxes. In U.S. dollars the increase is about 495 times since the yen/dollar exchange rate was 360 in 1949, closed at 124.58. The average is compiled by summing the value of the 225 stocks and dividing by the current divisor. The divisor is adjusted by the formula:

$$\frac{\text{Price Totals Before Ex-Rights Date}}{\text{Old Divisor}} = \frac{\text{Price Totals Before Ex-Rights Date} - \text{Value of Rights}}{\text{New Divisor}}$$

Every time a component stock goes ex-rights, the divisor is reduced.

The ND suffers from the same criticisms as the DJIA. It is not a true representation of the real market since it only has a small percentage of all the stocks on the TSE and in addition the price-weighting scheme is not as accurate a measure as a value-weighting scheme. In the words of the Tokyo Stock Exchange (1988):

> The Tokyo Stock Exchange stopped computing its Dow formula based average and replaced it with TOPIX on July 1, 1969, as the Exchange found the average inappropriate for measuring the market for the following reasons: Firstly, investors are apt to confuse the

> average with the real price, despite the fact that the average is a theoretical arithmetic mean enlarged by applying a multiplier. Secondly, as the average is not weighted, it tends to be affected by price changes in a handful of smaller companies' stocks trading on high prices. Thirdly, as component stocks of the average have virtually been fixed since 1949, except for occasional substitutions caused by delistings and company mergers, the average does not reflect the change in industrial structure and therefore does not serve as an appropriate measure of the market as a whole. In order to eliminate all of these problems, the Exchange developed and began computing and publishing TOPIX on July 1, 1969.

TOPIX value-weights all 1135 stocks (at the end of December 1988) on the First Section of the TSE. The index is simply the value-weighted average of all the stocks on the TSE. Adjustments are made to any corporate activities that affect the current market value, other than price changes, via an adjustment to the base value, such as new listings, assignment of stocks from the Second Section to First Section and vice versa, delisting, rights offerings, public offerings, private placements, mergers, exercises of stock, subscription warrants, or conversion of convertible bonds or preferred stock into common stock. In contrast to the actions above, a corporate decision that entails no change in the market value of shares of the company has nothing to do with the basic market value adjustment. Stock splits, capitalization issues, bonus issues, and stock dividends are thus eliminated from the adjustment, as the new stock price multiplied by the increased (or decreased) number of shares is theoretically the same as the old stock price multiplied by the old number of shares.

The formula for the adjustment is

$$\text{New Base Market Value} = \text{Old Base Market Value} \times \frac{\text{New Market Value}}{\text{Old Market Value}}$$

By doing so it is a better measure of overall market movements than the S&P 500 in the United States. The corresponding index measures in the United States are the NYFE index of all stocks on the New York Stock Exchange or the broader-based Wilshire 5000 index.

TOPIX is computed and published via the TSE's Market Information System every 60 seconds. It is reported to securities companies across Japan and is available worldwide through computerized information networks. TOPIX's initial value was set at 100 on July 4, 1968 and its value at the end of December was 2357.03. For dates before 1968 TOPIX traded below 100—in fact it was around 10 near the start of the new phase of the TSE in 1949. Currently, the Nikkei Dow has a beta of 0.84 relative to the TOPIX's market index of 1.00. Large capitalized stocks (over 200 million shares outstanding) have a beta of 1.16 and small capitalized stocks (less than 60 million shares outstanding) have a beta of only 0.37. The latter is an underestimate because of the thin trading of many of these stocks and the fact that the TSE's beta estimates do not use the Dimson or Scholes-Williams procedures for estimation in such circumstances.

Using data from January 5, 1970, to April 30, 1983, on the Nikkei Dow (ND), TOPIX and the S&P 500, Jaffe and Westerfield (1985b) found that there was a substantial day of the week effect. This is detailed in Table 11.1.

The United States results indicate typically sharp average losses on Mondays, with large gains on Wednesdays and Fridays, and modest gains on Tuesdays and Thursdays. In Japan, there are small losses on Mondays and more substantial losses on Tuesdays. In sum, Japan's Tuesday losses are more or less in the ballpark of Monday's United

Table 11.1. Percent of Returns on Country Common Stock Indexes by Day of Week

	Mon	Tues	Wed	Thurs	Fri	Sat	All Days
			U.S. S&P500 1970–83				
mean	−0.129	0.020	0.097	0.032	0.078		0.021
std. dev.	1.015	0.883	0.924	0.823	0.827		0.889
			Japan ND 1970–83				
mean	−0.020	−0.090	0.150	0.026	0.063	0.115	0.038
std. dev.	0.876	0.788	0.815	0.875	0.788	0.668	0.817
			Japan TOPIX 1970–83				
mean	−0.014	−0.064	0.124	0.026	0.057	0.099	0.035
std. dev.	0.701	0.684	0.671	0.741	0.626	0.530	0.672

Returns are computed as $r_t = [(V_t/V_{t-1}) - 1] \times 100$, where V_t is the value of the country index at the end of day t.

Source: Jaffe and Westerfield (1985b).

States losses. One would suspect that these losses would be highly correlated, especially since Japan's trading day starts 14 hours before New York's. But, this was not the case during 1970–83; the correlation between Monday's return in New York and Tuesday's return in Japan is only 0.076 for the ND and 0.004 for the TOPIX.

Corresponding to the Wednesday and Friday high mean returns in the United States are large average gains in Japan on Wednesdays and Saturdays. These gains are about three times the average daily gain of 0.038% and 0.035% on the ND and TOPIX, respectively. Jaffe and Westerfield looked at leads and lags of up to five days throughout the week. The lead and lag effects are minuscule with the lead +1 correlation being 0.072 and 0.086, respectively, for the ND and TOPIX. The same day correlations are larger being 0.163 and 0.154, respectively. Still it is a minor relationship during this time period.

More recent studies of the day of the week effect in Japan were done by Ikeda (1985, 1988), in Japanese, Kato and Schallheim (1985), and by Kato (1988ab). The results of Ikeda (1988) and Kato (1988a) are summarized in Table 11.2. These studies are based on the TOPIX

Table 11.2. Percent of Returns on the TOPIX Stock Index by Day of Week

	Mon	Tues	Wed	Thurs	Fri	Sat	All Days
			Jan. 1, 1977–Dec. 31, 1986: Ikeda (1988)				
mean	0.039	−0.110	0.153	0.028	0.082	0.138	0.052
t-value*	1.61	−4.21	6.11	0.95	3.36	6.08	4.88
			April 4, 1978–June 18, 1987: Kato (1988a)				
mean	0.0039	−0.0902	0.1449	0.0648	0.1049	0.1397	0.0581
t-value	0.13	−3.08	4.95	2.22	3.60	4.11	4.72
			April 4, 1978–Dec. 31, 1981: Kato (1988a)				
mean	0.0007	−0.0852	0.1283	−0.0273	0.0834	0.0957	0.0302
t-value	0.02	−2.58	3.89	−0.83	2.54	2.54	2.17
			Jan. 1, 1982–June 18, 1987: Kato (1988a)				
mean	0.0061	−0.0935	0.1561	0.1279	0.1195	0.1707	0.0771
t-value	0.14	−2.15	3.58	2.92	2.74	3.33	4.19

*All returns are significantly different from zero at the 5% level, except all Monday results and Thursdays during 1978 to 1981.

index which now has 1,135 securities (end of December 1988 count) on the entire first section of the TSE, for the periods January 1, 1977, to December 31, 1986, and April 4, 1978, to June 18, 1987, respectively. Kato also split his data into subperiods from April 4, 1978, to December 31, 1981, and from January 1, 1982, to June 18, 1987. In general, these results are consistent with and reinforce those of Jaffe and Westerfield.

Kato (1988a) tested but did not report results from the Nikkei Dow since they were similar to his TOPIX findings. Monday is more or less even, Tuesday is quite negative, Wednesday and Saturday are strongly positive, and Thursday and Friday are moderately positive. One change in Kato's study is that Thursdays became very positive during 1982–1987, and in this later period they nearly rival Wednesday and Saturday.

The distribution of returns is weighted a bit more to the right on Mondays and on Wednesdays to Saturday, and to the left on Tuesdays than a normal distribution would be. Kato's (1988a) data yield the visual display of this in Figure 11.1.

Kato (1988a) also investigated the intraday and close-to-open effects. Data on the TOPIX for each 15 minute period of trading are publicly available in Japan in the Japanese Securities newspaper, *Nihon Shoken Shimbun*. Trading occurs during 9–11 A.M. and 1–3 P.M. on weekdays and 9–11 A.M. on Saturdays. During the period of this study there was trading on Saturdays on the first and fourth weeks of the month and fifth if there is one. Historically, there was trading on all Saturdays until the end of 1972. Then until July 1983 it was closed on the third Saturday, and later the second Saturday closed from August 1983–July 1986. Saturday trading stopped at the end of January 1989. The trading time lost will be made up with additional trading on December 29 and 30 and with an additional half hour of trading in the afternoon session which now begins at 12:30.

A visual display of the interday effects appears in Figure 11.2 for the period January 1, 1982, to June 19, 1987. We see that all days have an initial surge, except for Tuesdays which start out flat. Wednesdays to Fridays are—remember this is all averages; if only the market could be this straightforward—roughly flat until they have a kick at the end of the day, similar to what Harris (1986) found on the NYSE. Mondays lose their initial gains and drift negatively except for the final kick which puts them about even. Tuesdays have a pattern similar to Monday but without the early gains. They close down about −0.15% despite the final kick. Saturdays are very positive throughout the day. They open up

Figure 11.1. Histograms of Returns of the TOPIX, in %, 1978–1987

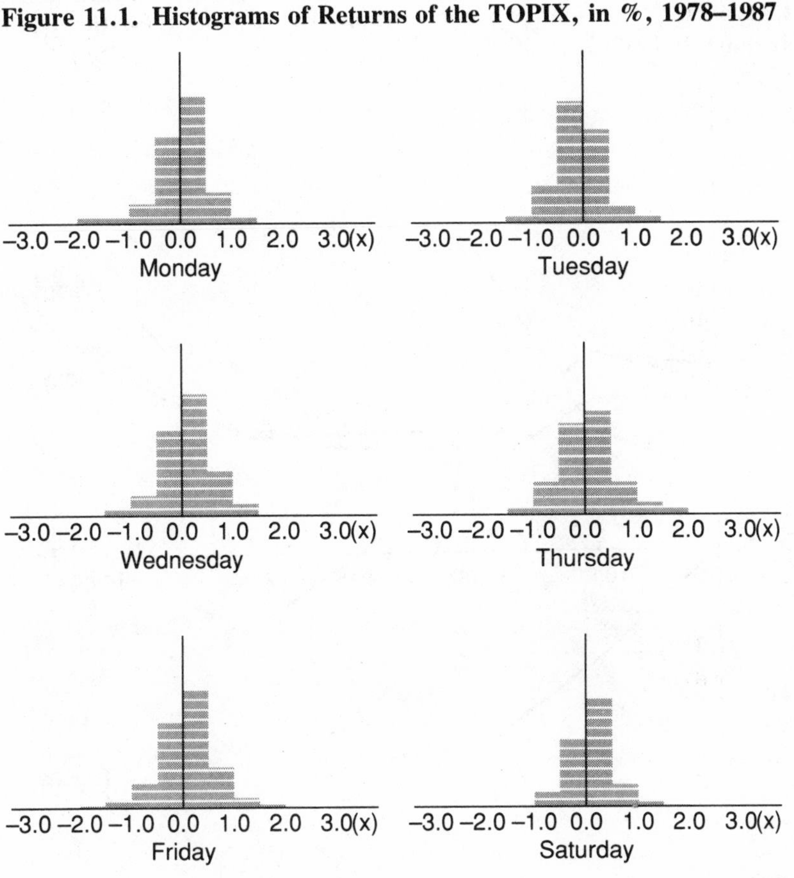

and continue increasing until the final bell. Interestingly, the nontrading periods are all positive; gains occur during the night and the market opens up, even on Tuesdays. Table 11.3 shows Kato's results including the intraday returns using the previous close to the open as the starting point. Except for Mondays, which are strongly negative, not much happens during the lunch break, although Kato's data for this period has 15 minutes of trading in it so this conclusion is a little muddled.

The effects of Saturday trading are very interesting. First, Saturdays are extremely positive. Second, Saturdays are even more positive if the previous week had Saturday trading—at present during the first week of the month (See Table 11.4). Third, Mondays are negative if the previous Saturday is closed (the third and fourth weeks) and more so if this week

Figure 11.2. Cumulative Mean Intraday Returns in % for the TOPIX, January 1, 1982–June 1989.

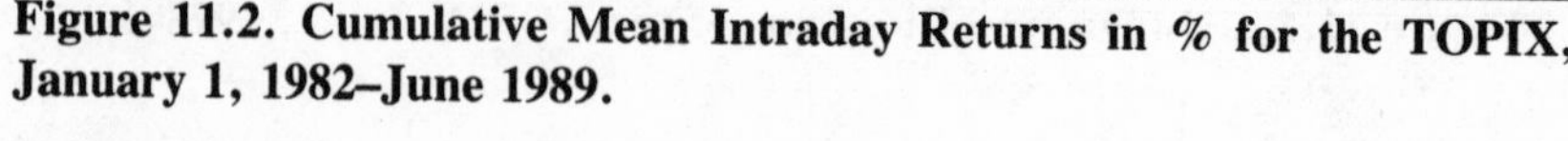

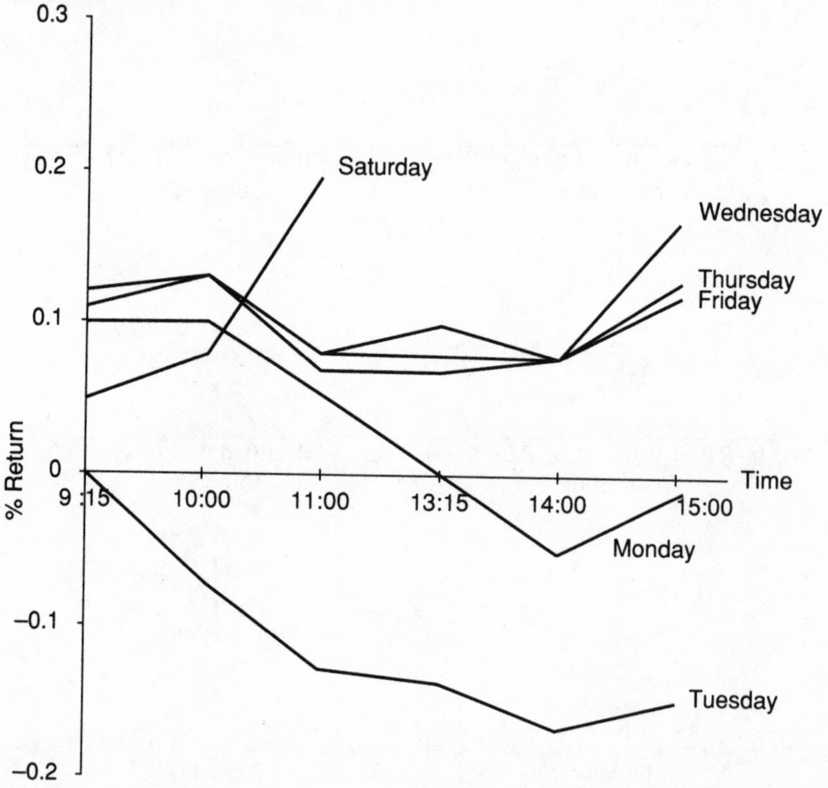

has no Saturday Trading, that is, the third week. However, Mondays are positive if Saturday had trading and especially so if this week has no Saturday trading, that is, the second week of the month.

Before we continue snooping into this data, let us pause to see if this makes any sense. We know from U.S. data that there is strong one-day serial correlation of returns, so if Saturday is positive (and we need it to be open to be so), then Monday likely will be positive and we will have the usual negative Tuesday. Suppose Saturday is closed, then the Friday is stronger than usual and somehow the long weekend gives traders more time to think about selling. Then with Monday so negative, Tuesday can be positive but only in weeks that end with Friday trading.

For weeks ending with Saturday trading the loss is more or less split over the Monday and Tuesday.

When the anomalous effect does not show up as expected, plan for it to be pushed around a little. The Friday-Friday weeks have the most negative Monday following the first Friday, and then the rest of the week is very strong. Is it the sight of a positive Tuesday giving the market life? We do not know, but the effect seems to be there. Kato's data covers a period of more than nine years with differing rules on Saturday trading so that may affect the results as well.

Table 11.4 lists the weeks of the month corresponding to the current trading data rules so that you can data snoop some more. Kato (1988a) also plots the intraday patterns by day of the week using the 1982–1987 data; they have similar interpretations. (See Figure 11.3). Kato has a little more information on this, namely the effect of the New York Dow on the Tokyo TOPIX. He researched this with and without Saturday to explain, in particular, the switching of the negative Tuesdays to Mondays when there is no Saturday trading. This is discussed in what follows.

Ikeda (1985, 1988) and Kato (1988a) discuss the settlement hypothesis as a possible explanation of the day of the week effect. The idea is that on certain days the time that one has to pay for stock or receive money for sales is different, and thus there should be a premium for the additional interest foregone or earned from this process. The delivery of securities and receipt of payment takes place on the third business day after the transaction. See Figure 11.4 for rules on this settlement. The results found by Kato and Ikeda, like those in North America, are mixed. This is a partial explanation of the day of the week phenomenon. However, the returns on Tuesdays are negative except they are strongly positive in the third week, which has no Saturday trading, following a week without Saturday trading days is inconsistent with this theory. If we let R be the rate of return on the stock in question and i be the cost of capital, then the differences in return across days of the week, with and without Saturday trading, should be as follows, see Ikeda (1985, 1988)—assuming that there are no holidays in this period:

	Mon	Tues	Wed	Thurs	Fri	Sat
Saturday Trading	$2R + i$	$R + i$	$R + 3i$	R	$R + i$	$R + i$
No Saturday Trading	$3R + i$	$R + i$	$R + 3i$	$R + i$	$R + i$	—

Table 11.3. Trading, Nontrading, and Intraday Returns in % for the TOPIX January 1, 1982–June 18, 1987

Period	Statistic	Monday	Tuesday	Wednesday	Thursday	Friday	Saturday	All Days	*F*
Close	Mean	−0.0213	−0.1331	0.1792	0.1201	0.1212	0.1983	0.0723	6.88**
to Close	*T*-Value	(−0.41)	(−2.60)	(3.52)	(2.35)	(2.38)	(3.28)	(3.35)	
Close	Mean	0.1002	0.0013	0.1177	0.1211	0.1134	0.0487	0.0855	23.58**
to Open*	*T*-Value	(5.08)	(0.07)	(6.11)	(6.26)	(5.88)	(2.13)	(10.47)	
Open	Mean	−0.1217	−0.1344	0.0611	−0.0017	0.0069	0.1490	−0.0135	4.54**
to Close	*T*-Value	(−2.73)	(−3.07)	(1.41)	(−0.04)	(0.16)	(2.89)	(−0.74)	
9:15–	Mean	−0.0040	−0.0671	0.0114	0.0065	0.0237	0.0278	−0.0016	3.67**
10 A.M.	*T*-Value	(−0.24)	(−4.13)	(0.70)	(0.40)	(1.47)	(1.45)	(−0.23)	
10:00–	Mean	−0.0543	−0.0589	−0.0457	−0.0546	−0.0627	0.1210	−0.0330	10.46**
11 A.M.	*T*-Value	(−0.26)	(−2.90)	(−2.26)	(−2.69)	(−3.11)	(5.05)	(−3.84)	

11:00– 1:15 P.M.	Mean	−0.0514	−0.0097	0.0232	0.0029	0.0019	−0.0070	4.47**
	T-Value	(−4.22)	(−0.81)	(1.95)	(0.24)	(−0.16)	(−1.295)	
1:15– 2:00 P.M.	Mean	−0.0516	−0.0251	−0.0160	−0.0035	0.0070	−0.0175	3.24**
	T-Value	(−3.44)	(−1.71)	(−1.09)	(−0.24)	(0.48)	(−2.65)	
2:00– 3:00 P.M.	Mean	0.0387	0.0215	0.0885	0.0466	0.0407	0.0473	8.55**
	T-Value	(2.12)	(1.20)	(4.97)	(2.62)	(2.29)	(5.90)	

*The market opens at 9 A.M.. Kato's close to open is from the previous day's close to 9:15, a period when most stocks have opened.

**These F statistics all indicate that the regression model used to fit these returns, namely

$$R_t = \sum_{k=1}^{6} B_k D_{kt} + E_t$$

where $D_{1t} = 1$ for Mondays, $D_{2t} = 1$ for Tuesdays, . . . , $D_{6t} = 1$ for Saturdays, and zero otherwise, is significant at the 1% level.

Source: Kato (1988a)

Table 11.4. Effects of Saturday Trading on the TOPIX April 4, 1978–June18, 1987

Week of Month	Category Trading Ends This Week	Last Week	Monday	Tuesday	Wednesday	Thursday	Friday	Saturday	*F*	Sample Size
1st, 5th A1	Sat	Sat	0.0198	−0.1072	0.1790	0.0581	0.0605	0.1678	8.67**	1406
4th A2	Sat	Fri	−0.1008	−0.1102	0.1074	0.0306	0.1582	0.0793	2.53*	649
2nd B1	Fri	Sat	0.1135	−0.0649	0.0980	0.0933	0.1341		4.05**	539
3rd B2	Fri	Fri	−0.3489	0.1931	0.2479	0.2609	0.2193		0.46	58
	All	Weeks	0.0039	−0.0902	0.1449	0.0648	0.1049	0.1397		
Sample Size			449	464	464	465	467	343		2652

**indicates significance at the 1% level and * at the 5% level and similarly in succeeding tables.

Source: Kato 1988a

Figure 11.3. Cumulative Mean Intraday Returns by Four Group Classified by Saturday Trading, TOPIX, 1983–1987

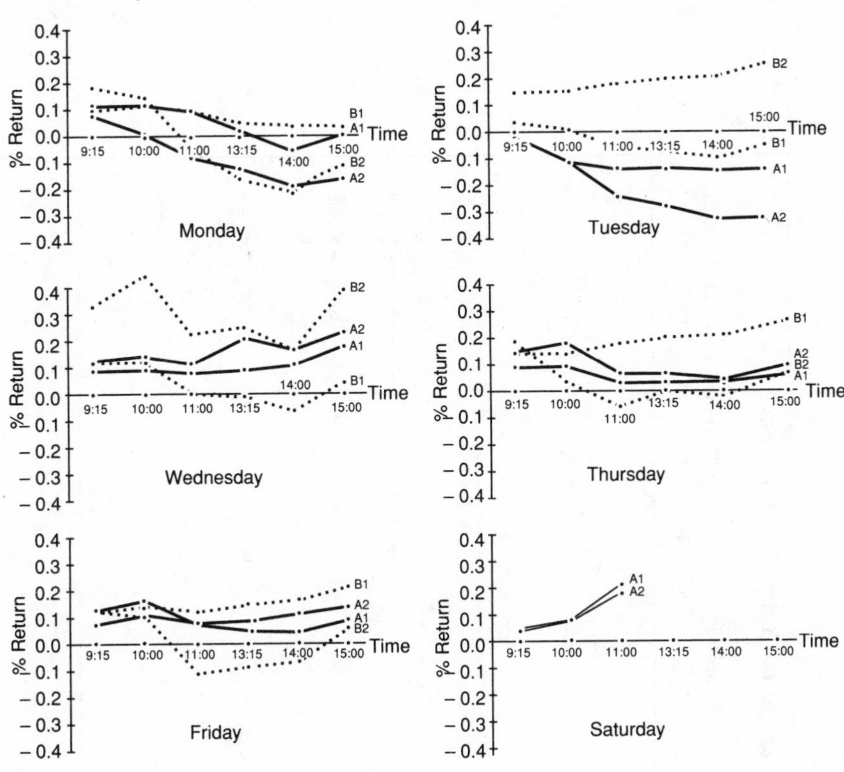

Hence the returns should be highest on Mondays and Wednesdays, with or without Saturday trading. The returns should be the same on Tuesdays, Thursdays in weeks without Saturday trading, Fridays and Saturdays. One very important implication of the settlement rates is that stocks can be purchased on Wednesdays, sold on Thursdays and have settlement on the same day, Monday.[2] This is widely believed to have a positive effect on Wednesdays something that is consistent with the data. As we can see from the previous results, some of this is consistent with the facts but it is far from a proper explanation of the day of the week phenomenon. See Ikeda (1988) for some calculations adjusting the returns for this theory. He concludes that once adjustment for these settlement differences are made, the day of the week differences are less anomalous than before in a statistical sense.

Figure 11.4. Settlement Procedure in the Tokyo Stock Exchange

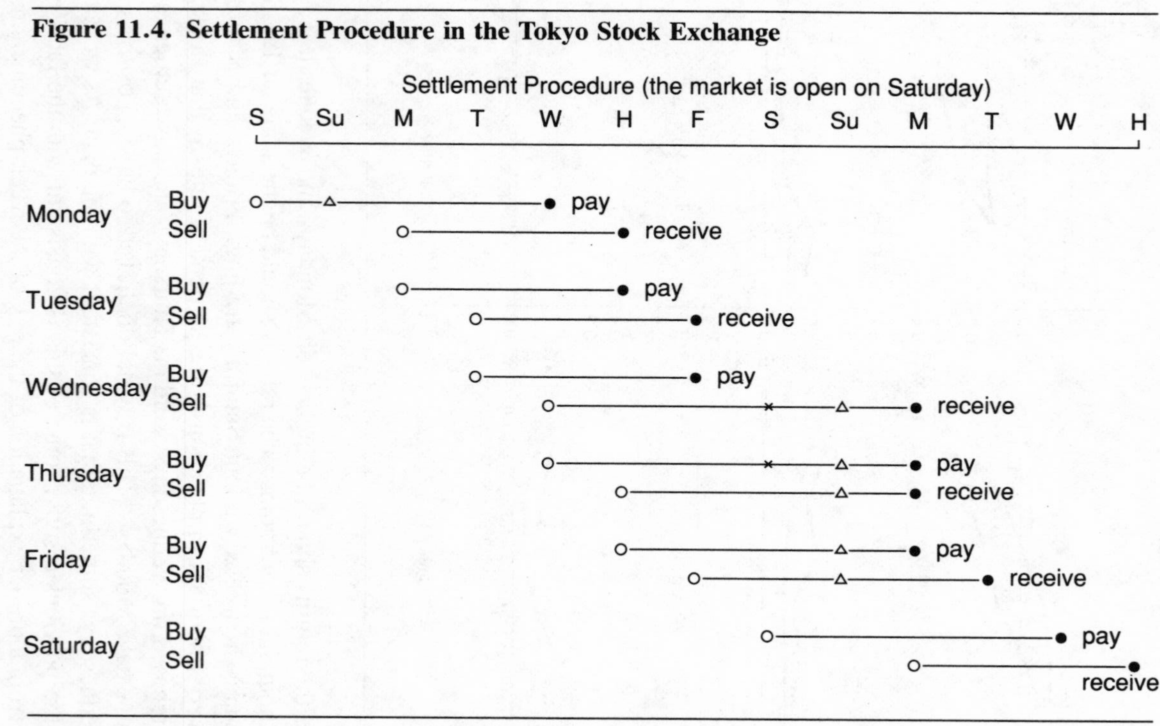

Figure 11.4. (Continued)

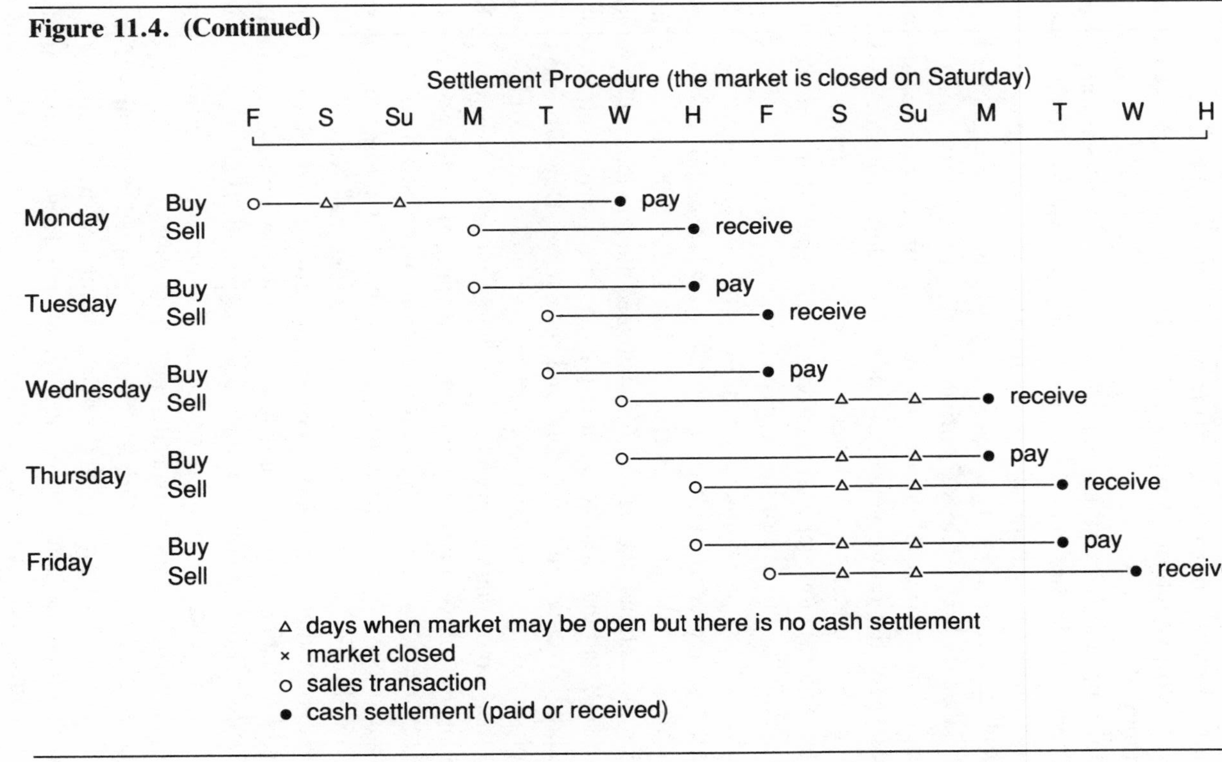

Since the day of the week effect casts doubt on the homogeneity of the return-generating process across the week, not only the mean but higher moments of the return distribution should be taken into consideration for each day of the week. Ikeda (1988) examined the skewness and kurtosis, and also presented a test regarding "the stability under addition property" to reject a stable Paretian distribution hypothesis. He found that when the interval used for calculating returns is extended from a day to a week, a week to two weeks, two weeks to a month, et cetera, the kurtosis and skewness become less significant to reject normality, and that leads to use of the mixture of normal distributions (or subordinated stochastic process) for the return generating process of Japanese stocks. He also presented a model which relates the mixture of normals hypothesis to the "information generating process" and applied that model to the explanation of the day of the week effect.

Kato (1988a) re-examined the earlier study by Jaffe and Westerfield (1985b) on the correlation between the New York and Tokyo markets with his more recent data. For the period 1980–1987, he found much higher correlations, namely 53.6%, between the previous day's return in New York and the close-to-open returns in Tokyo, using the Dow Jones Industrial Average in New York and the Nikkei Dow in Tokyo. This is not surprising since the two markets have grown over time to watch the other's movements very closely. The previous day's return in New York is the most relevant information leading into Tokyo's opening. The reverse effect, namely the correlation between Tokyo's close-to-close and New York's close-to-open on the next trading day is only 10.96%. So Tokyo's effect on New York is less than New York's effect on Tokyo. Other correlations are smaller for each directional effect, but still statistically significant. Kato's results are summarized in Table 11.5. Since this data covers a relatively long period, 1980–87, one would expect many changes in these correlations over time. Additional results on this appear in Hamao, Masulis and Ng (1989).

The trading or nontrading on Saturday coupled with the effects of New York trading on Tokyo, provides a method to investigate more fully why there are such different Monday and Tuesday effects in these two circumstances. To investigate this Kato (1988a) ran the following regression.

$$R_{T_0t} - R_{NY,t-1} = \sum_{K=1}^{6} \beta_k D_{kt} + \epsilon_t$$

Table 11.5. Correlation Coefficients Between the Dow Jones Industrial Average and the Nikkei Dow, 1980–87

	New York			Tokyo ($t=0$)		
New York's Effects on Tokyo	(t=-1)	Close-to-Open	r	0.3306	0.2817	0.3721
		Open-to-Close	r	0.3823	0.1091	0.2453
		Close-to-Close	r	0.5363	0.2551	0.4313
Tokyo's Effects on New York	(t=0)	Close-to-Open	r	0.1556	0.0565 (0.0138)	0.1096
		Open-to-Close	r	−0.0057 (0.8031)	0.0591	0.0484 (0.0348)
		Close-to-Close	r	0.0887	0.0929	0.1145

All coefficients are significant at 1% or lower level except those with p values in ()'s. So the only effect that is statistically zero is Open-to-Close in New York on $t=0$ versus Close-to-Open in Tokyo on $t=0$ which had a small negative correlation.

Source: Kato, 1988a.

where $R_{T,t}$ is the return in Tokyo on day t and $R_{NY,t-1}$ is the return in New York on the previous day, the β's are the coefficients, and the D_{kt}'s are "dummy" variables to pick up the day of the week effects. That is, if t is a Tuesday then $D_{1t} = 0, D_{2t} = 1, D_{3t} = \ldots D_{6t} = 0$, et cetera, and ϵ_t is the error in this equation. He found that when there is Saturday trading, the F statistic for the fit is 0.32, which is not significant even at the 10% level. However, when there is no Saturday trading the F statistic is 3.48, which is significant at the 1% level. This fit is caused mainly because of the low Monday return on the Nikkei Dow relative to the high return on Friday's New York Dow. When there is Saturday trading and Monday is excluded from Tokyo's data, that is, New York is MTWThF and Tokyo is TWThFS, then the hypothesis that the weekly patterns of both markets are identical cannot be rejected. In particular, the low Monday in New York lines up with the low Tuesday in Tokyo, and the high Friday in New York matches with the high Saturday in Tokyo. The other days are correspondingly similar. Hence, whatever reasons are the true causes for the day of the week effect in New York, they are probably similar to those in Tokyo. Perhaps in weeks with Saturday trading, investors do not have enough time to vacation and contemplate their portfolios leading to Monday sales, so the fall is on Tuesday. See Miller (1988) on this.

The studies discussed above utilize data from the 1970s and 1980s to study the day of the week effects, and they aggregate the results over large subsets of these periods. Hence, the results are smoothed out and do not show yearly differences. Figure 11.5, *abcd* show the effects year by year for both the TOPIX and the Nikkei Dow indices for the 40 years from 1949 to 1988. There is considerable variation over time but in general the previous results of low or negative Monday and Tuesday returns and high Wednesday to Saturday returns are supported by this data. Tuesday was consistently negative from 1973 to 1987. Tuesdays have been slightly positive so far in 1988. Mondays are negative or slightly positive throughout the whole 40 years. Wednesdays became positive in 1970 and have remained positive during each of the past 19 years at levels of about 0.2% per day. Thursdays show great variation over the entire sample period with wide swings in average returns from year to year, switching from highly positive to negative returns and back to positive returns in short periods. Recently they have been more positive. On the TOPIX each year, since 1983 shows positive average returns reaching levels of 0.2% to 0.3% per day in 1986 and 1987. For

Figure 11.5. Mean Return by the Day of the Week

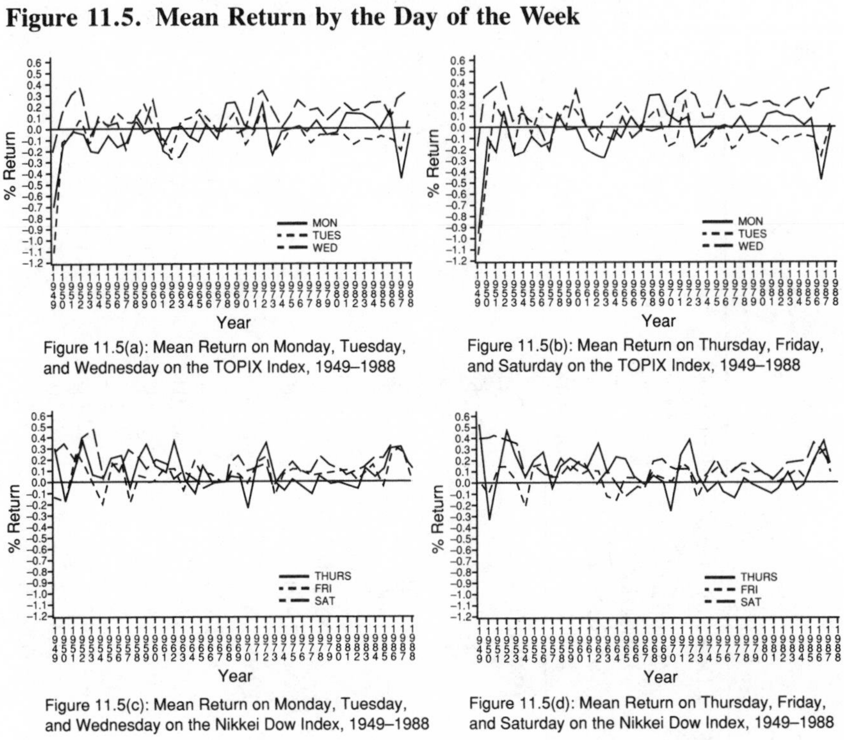

Figure 11.5(a): Mean Return on Monday, Tuesday, and Wednesday on the TOPIX Index, 1949–1988

Figure 11.5(b): Mean Return on Thursday, Friday, and Saturday on the TOPIX Index, 1949–1988

Figure 11.5(c): Mean Return on Monday, Tuesday, and Wednesday on the Nikkei Dow Index, 1949–1988

Figure 11.5(d): Mean Return on Thursday, Friday, and Saturday on the Nikkei Dow Index, 1949–1988

the Nikkei Dow the returns on Thursday are not positive until 1985. Since then they have been very positive and they have provided average gains in every year on both indices since 1974. Saturdays are even more positive with gains throughout the 40-year sample period except for a brief period in the mid-1960s on the Nikkei Dow.

Table 11.6 investigates the returns during the past four decades in the Nikkei Dow by day of the week. We see that: (a) Mondays and Tuesdays were negative in the 1950s, with Wednesday, Thursday, and Saturday having progressively higher returns. Saturdays returned over four times the average daily returns and provided gains nearly two-thirds of the time; (b) in the 1960s, Mondays were still negative but Tuesdays were slightly positive. Thursdays were again strong but Wednesdays were essentially even. Saturdays had gains but only 50% higher than all days compared to 350 + % higher in the 1950s; (c) Mondays and Tuesdays were negative in the 1970s with Tuesdays now switching to be the more negative day by a 7 to 1 ratio. Only 44% of Tuesdays had positive returns

Table 11.6. Returns by Day of the Week by the Nikkei Dow, by Decade, 1949–1988

	Day	Sample Size	Mean Return %	Standard Deviation of Return %	*t*-Statistic	*p*-Statistic	Percent of Positive Returns
				1949–1959			
1	All	3193	0.0565	1.1189	2.85	0.0044	53.6
2	Mon	531	−0.1545	1.1544	−3.08	0.0022	43.3
3	Tue	531	−0.0284	1.1120	−0.59	0.5571	50.3
4	Wed	534	0.0957	1.1860	1.87	0.0627	53.0
5	Thu	531	0.1488	1.277	2.68	0.0075	56.9
6	Fri	535	0.0467	1.0986	0.98	0.3258	53.3
7	Sat	531	0.2302	0.7849	6.76	0.0001	65.5
				1960–1969			
1	All	3000	0.0368	0.8675	2.32	0.0201	52.8
2	Mon	501	−0.0396	0.8767	−1.01	0.3119	50.5
3	Tue	499	0.0643	0.8500	1.69	0.0915	50.5
4	Wed	501	0.0004	0.9075	0.01	0.9919	50.7
5	Thu	501	0.1221	0.9705	2.82	0.0050	56.7
6	Fri	495	0.0160	0.8973	0.40	0.6911	51.9
7	Sat	503	0.0575	0.6686	1.93	0.0543	56.7

				1970–1979			
1	All	2892	0.0391	0.8560	2.46	0.0140	52.3
2	Mon	488	−0.0135	0.9182	−0.33	0.7453	54.1
3	Tue	502	−0.0968	0.8129	−2.67	0.0079	44.4
4	Wed	494	0.1702	0.8454	4.47	0.0001	61.7
5	Thu	499	0.0091	0.9497	0.21	0.8307	54.5
6	Fri	496	0.0660	0.8412	1.75	0.0810	55.6
7	Sat	413	0.1136	0.7018	3.29	0.0011	62.5
				1980–1988			
1	All	2444	0.0625	0.8242	3.75	0.0002	56.0
2	Mon	417	−0.0135	0.7585	−0.36	0.7169	57.3
3	Tue	427	−0.1183	1.0205	−2.40	0.0170	43.8
4	Wed	431	0.2151	0.8696	5.14	0.0001	63.3
5	Thu	428	0.0606	0.7797	1.61	0.1088	52.3
6	Fri	433	0.0944	0.7669	2.56	0.0108	58.0
7	Sat	308	0.1601	0.5933	4.74	0.0001	63.6

Source: Yamaichi Research Institute.

versus 55% on all days. Wednesdays replaced Thursdays as the strong midweek day and Saturdays were again very strong. Both Wednesdays and Saturdays had positive returns on more than 60% of the time; (d) the 1980s are quite similar to the 1970s with very negative Tuesdays, mildly negative Mondays, stronger Thursdays (than the 1970s), as well as stronger Fridays. Wednesdays again were the strongest days, returning 0.215% on average and providing positive returns 63.3% of the time. Saturdays were again very positive as well, returning 0.16% per day and being positive 63.6% of the time. The Nikkei Dow results are, not surprisingly, quite similar to the TOPIX results for the 1970s and 1980s discussed earlier.

Obviously many of the anomalies affect one another and interact. Kato (1988a) has investigated the interaction of the January and small firm effects by days of the week to attempt to isolate the separate influences of these anomalies using TOPIX data from January 4, 1974, to June 8, 1987. His results are detailed in Tables 11.7 and 11.8 and Figure 11.6. Among his findings: The strong days—Wednesday, Friday, and Saturday—have positive gains during the day which essentially nullify the losses on the weekdays—Monday, Tuesday, and Thursday. Only on the very strongest days—Wednesday and Saturday—are there positive returns during the day for all levels of capitalized stocks outside of January.

All the gains are at night and there are positive returns on every trading day. Moreover, the small cap stocks make their major gains then. Then in total we have the advantage of the small stocks over the big stocks day by day in the close-to-close returns on every day of the week regardless if the day is positive like Wednesday or Saturday or negative as on Tuesdays.

There is little discussion here or anywhere else of convincing reasons why this anomalous day of the week as well as other security market regularities occur. Indeed, even in the books on anomalies such as Coulson (1987), Dimson (1988), Hirsch (1986), and Ziemba (1990), the authors are fairly silent on this point. Connolly (1988a,b) argues with much data and strong statistical tools that the day of the week effect in the United States is not as clear cut as previously believed and may not have even existed recently in United States security markets.

The main reason anomalies are anomalies is that we cannot explain them. Indeed, the various anomalies have pestered hardline financial economists to such an extent that they are now quite fashionable and such results can now be published and indeed are encouraged in the most prestigious journals in the field. The anomalies, of course, do seem to violate traditional equilibrium models of asset behavior over time. They do have causes which we do not understand. Some thoughts along these lines regarding day of the week effects appear as follows. Obviously the rigorous testing of the validity and percent explained by the various hypotheses will entail considerable effort and statistical ingenuity. Initial research on this appears in Hiraki, Aggarwal, and Rao (1988) and Komatsu and Ziemba (1989).

Some Possible Reasons for Day of the Week Anomalies:

1. Negative Tuesdays with Saturday trading
   - Investors are more likely to sell if they have a weekend to think it over
   - Sales representatives have a more difficult time getting buy orders after Saturday, especially with a rise on Saturday
   - You must sell on Tuesday if you need money on Friday because of the three day business settlement rules since there are no Saturday settlements
   - There is a lag from New York's Monday fall via the correlation effect
   - It takes time to get into the market again in the new week
2. Negative Mondays after Saturdays Closed
   - It takes time to get into the market again in the new week
   - Sales on Monday provide receipts before the end of the week
   - Investors are more likely to sell if they have a weekend to think it over
   - Dealers have a harder time to round up buy orders
   - Individuals are net sellers especially of small capitalized stocks. Their sell orders accumulate over the weekend and outweigh the buy orders of brokers recommendations since brokers are not soliciting orders on the weekend. Hence, contrary to the other days of the week, there is net selling on Monday; see Miller (1988).
3. Positive Wednesdays
   - According to the settlement hypothesis, Wednesdays should be very strong

Table 11.7. Mean Portfolio Close-to-Close, Close-to-Open, and Open-to-Close Returns by Day of the Week and Firm Size on the TOPIX, January 4, 1974–June 18, 1987

	Firm Size	Monday	Tuesday	Wednesday	Thursday	Friday	Saturday	*F*
Close	All Firms	0.0544	−0.0406	0.2188	0.0604	0.1119	0.1489	30.67**
to	Smallest	0.1249	0.0240	0.2803	0.1157	0.1583	0.2059	51.73**
Close	2	0.0855	−0.0277	0.2325	0.574	0.1348	0.1674	34.15**
	3	0.0519	−0.0472	0.2114	0.0287	0.1297	0.1590	27.80**
	4	0.0500	−0.0491	0.1899	0.0321	0.1067	0.1459	24.10**
	Largest	0.0340	−0.0672	0.1591	0.0357	0.1053	0.1447	17.41**
	F's	10.20**	4.00**	83.32**	7.20**	31.23**	61.86**	
	N	3225	3350	3350	3340	3360	2460	
Close	All Firms	0.1776	0.0483	0.1176	0.1510	0.1252	0.0532	116.95**
to	Smallest	0.2616	0.1030	0.1844	0.2084	0.1673	0.1381	191.77**
Open	2	0.2324	0.0805	0.1537	0.1942	0.1577	0.0961	174.54**
	3	0.2039	0.0679	0.1325	0.1639	0.1509	0.0813	144.77**
	4	0.1661	0.0393	0.0952	0.1207	0.1106	0.0409	87.02**
	Largest	0.0959	−0.0113	0.0425	0.0793	0.0707	0.0022	23.25**
	F's	234.77**	33.92**	127.10**	197.06**	102.22**	43.91**	
	N	3225	3350	3350	3340	3360	2460	

Open	All Firms	−0.1234	−0.0889	0.1008	−0.0908	−0.0134	0.0952	30.25**
to	Smallest	−0.1367	−0.0792	0.0952	−0.0929	−0.0093	0.0676	28.98**
Close	2	−0.1469	−0.1082	0.0783	−0.1368	−0.0230	0.0711	35.23**
	3	−0.1519	−0.1151	0.0785	−0.1352	−0.0214	0.0775	33.57**
	4	−0.1160	−0.0884	0.0944	−0.0888	−0.0040	0.1048	25.27**
	Largest	−0.0621	−0.0559	0.1164	−0.0440	0.0346	0.1422	18.13**
	F's	50.21**	23.84**	25.11**	34.00**	1.50	46.07**	
	N	3225	3350	3350	3340	3360	2460	

Source: Kato (1988a).

Table 11.8. Mean Returns in Percent for Trading and Nontrading Periods on the TOPIX, January 4, 1974–June 8, 1987

Firm Size	Monday	Tuesday	Wednesday	Thursday	Friday	Saturday	All Days	*F*'s
				January Returns				
Open to Close Returns:								
Smallest	0.4450	0.2976	0.4416	0.3970	0.4198	0.1402	0.3801	25.88**
2	0.3118	0.2056	0.3664	0.2870	0.3500	0.2138	0.2932	15.66**
3	0.1972	0.1559	0.3066	0.2270	0.3252	0.1596	0.2326	9.85**
4	0.1293	0.1113	0.2759	0.1518	0.2455	0.1392	0.1779	6.42**
Largest	0.0592	−0.0225	0.2499	0.0415	0.2791	0.1321	0.1242	4.56**
Close to Open Returns:								
Smallest	0.4003	0.2353	0.2929	0.2713	0.2827	0.1522	0.2781	48.58**
2	0.3523	0.1687	0.2220	0.2365	0.2162	0.1396	0.2263	39.82**
3	0.2829	0.1568	0.1685	0.1987	0.2097	0.1101	0.1914	26.98**
4	0.2085	0.1284	0.1381	0.1565	0.1587	0.3417	0.1432	16.88**
Largest	0.1281	0.0358	0.0879	0.0793	0.1529	0.0361	0.0893	5.96**
Open to Close Returns:								
Smallest	0.0440	0.0618	0.1481	0.1250	0.1364	0.0875	0.1015	4.33*
2	−0.0408	0.0367	0.1439	0.0500	0.1335	0.0738	0.0665	2.51*
3	−0.0858	−0.0010	0.1377	0.0280	0.1152	0.0493	0.0410	1.99
4	−0.0794	−0.0172	0.1374	−0.0050	0.0867	0.0973	0.0345	2.08
Largest	−0.0691	−0.0572	0.1617	−0.0380	0.1259	0.0957	0.0348	2.65*

All Months But January

Close to Close Total Returns:								
Smallest	0.0962	0.0005	0.2661	0.0914	0.1350	0.2030	0.1290	39.72**
2	0.0652	−0.0477	0.2208	0.0377	0.1156	0.1634	0.0894	26.98**
3	0.0389	−0.0646	0.2030	0.0116	0.1122	0.1589	0.0731	23.19**
4	0.0429	−0.0629	0.1824	0.0218	0.0943	0.1465	0.0675	10.46**
Largest	0.0317	−0.0711	0.1512	0.0352	0.0898	0.1457	0.0602	14.47**
Close to Open Returns:								
Smallest	0.2492	0.0916	0.1749	0.2030	0.1570	0.1369	0.1697	158.46**
2	0.2217	0.0729	0.1477	0.1906	0.1524	0.0924	0.1482	145.83**
3	0.1968	0.0603	0.1293	0.1609	0.1457	0.0788	0.1304	123.10**
4	0.1623	0.0316	0.0915	0.1176	0.1063	0.0408	0.0936	73.87**
Largest	0.0930	−0.0153	0.0385	0.0793	0.0633	0.0007	0.0447	19.36**
Open to Close Returns:								
Smallest	−0.1529	−0.0913	0.0906	−0.1117	−0.0223	0.0659	−0.0409	32.17**
2	−0.1564	−0.1207	0.0725	−0.1529	−0.0370	0.0708	−0.0590	37.66**
3	−0.1578	−0.1249	0.0733	−0.1493	−0.0335	0.0799	−0.0574	34.60**
4	−0.1194	−0.0946	0.0906	−0.0960	−0.0120	0.1055	−0.0262	24.33**
Largest	−0.0615	−0.0558	0.1124	−0.0445	0.0265	0.1462	0.0153	16.17**

Source: Kato (1988a)

Figure 11.6. Mean Returns by the Day of the Week, Close-to-Close, Close-to-Open, and Open-to-Close, TOPIX, 1974–1987

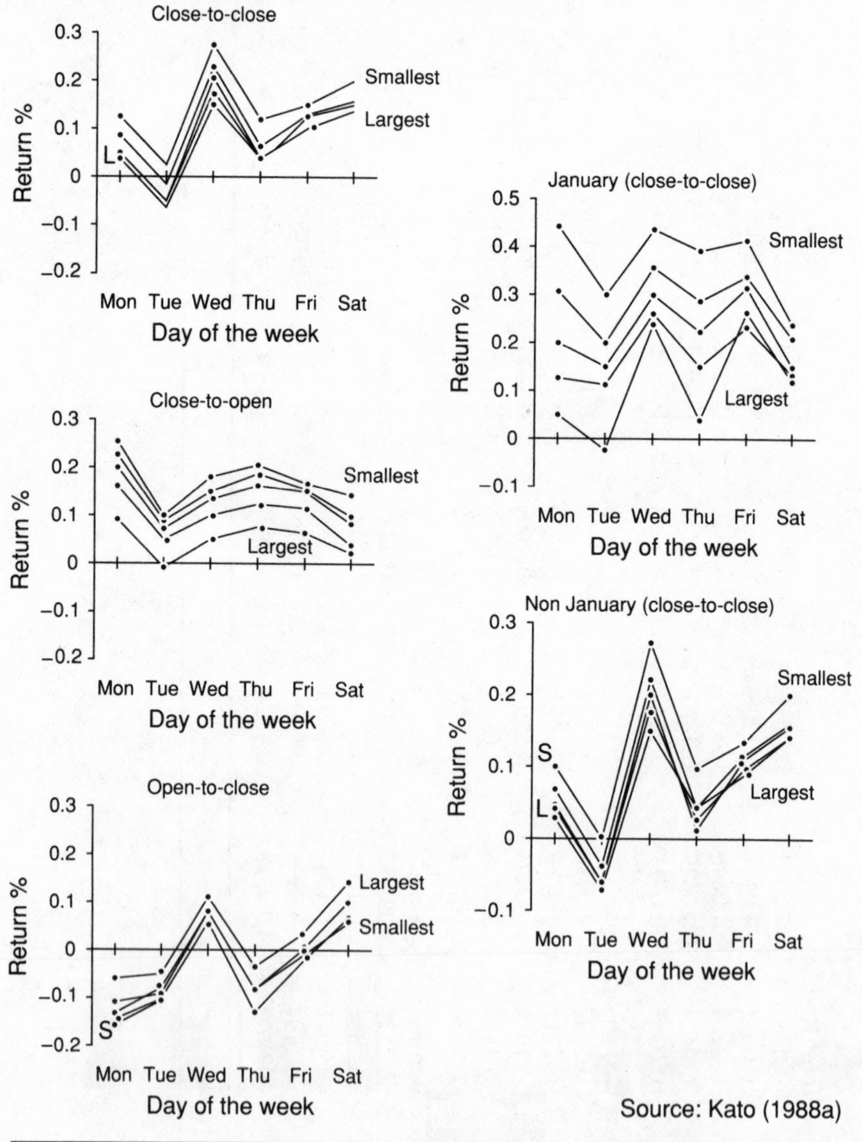

Source: Kato (1988a)

Figure 11.7. Days of the Week Effects in the ND Spot Market and the Osaka 50 Spot Market in Tokyo and the Kabusaki 50 Futures in Osaka, June 6, 1987 to Sept. 20, 1988

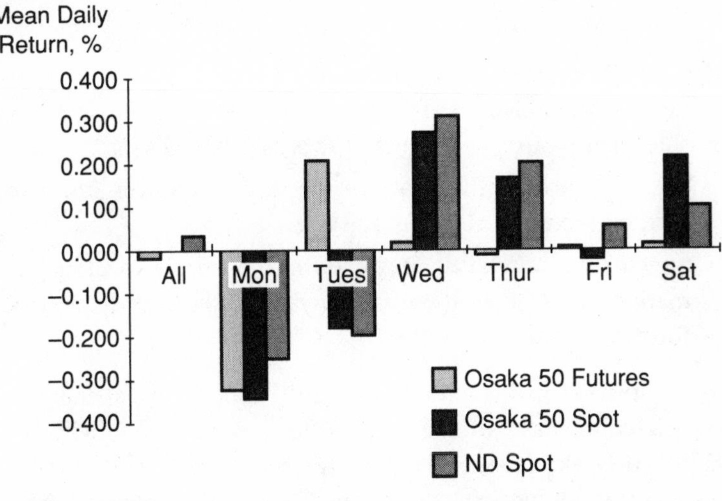

Figure 11.8. Days of the Week Effects in the ND Spot Market in Tokyo and the SIMEX Futures Markets in Singapore, Sept. 3, 1986 to Sept. 19, 1988

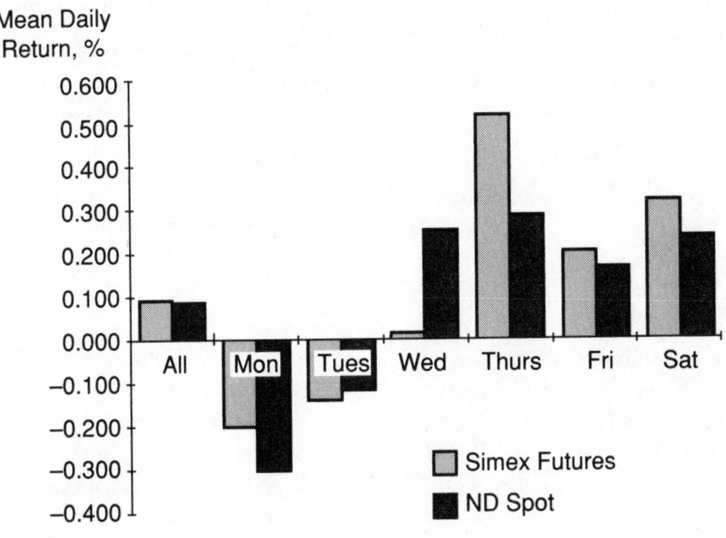

- Some brokerage dealers buy on Wednesday then sell on Thursday. The settlement for both is on Monday. Since transaction costs are almost zero and Wednesdays are typically strong this can be a profitable strategy. This is the only day that brokers can use this strategy.

4. All Gains Overnight
   - Orders are collected after the close of trading for open by salesmen's push with a bias towards buy orders
   - There is cross selling late in the day to recover funds to match purchases made on the open
   - Speculative purchases are made at the open expecting the market to rise then there is covering at the end of the day for these trades

Ziemba (1989b) investigates seasonality effects in Japanese futures markets including days of the week effects using the SIMEX Nikkei Dow 225 and Osaka Kubusaki 50 contracts for the period 1986–1988.

The spot effect of weak Mondays and Tuesdays and strong Wednesday to Saturday is continuing. Wednesdays are the strongest days followed by Thursdays and Saturdays in the spot market. The Simex futures in Singapore look just like the spot market in Tokyo except in the Wednesday–Thursday period. Possibly this market is following rather than leading, although other evidence suggests the leading hypothesis. The futures seem to rise and fall with the spot. The Osaka 50 seems to anticipate the days of the week effect. Saturdays hardly rise at all in the futures markets despite the spot gains, thus anticipating Monday's fall. Then these futures fall on Monday to anticipate a further fall on Tuesday. They then rise on Tuesday to anticipate the gains on Wednesday, Thursday, Friday, and Saturday. They are then flat until the fall the next Monday. Figures 11.7 and 11.8 on page 277 visually show the results.

Notes

1. For a sampling of the U.S. literature on the day of the week effect, the reader may consult Connolly (1988ab), Dimson (1988), Flannery and Protopapadakis (1988), French (1980), Gibbons and Hess (1981), Harris (1986), Hirsch (1986), Jacobs and Levy (1988), Keim and Stambaugh (1984), Lakonishok and Levi (1982), Lakonishok and Smidt (1989), McInish and

Wood (1985), Miller (1988), Rogalski (1984), Smirlock and Starks (1980), and Ziemba (1990).

2. The law governing this was enacted in 1978 and is titled "*maigetsu no daini doyoubi igai no doyoubi ni kansuru gyoumukitei, shinyoutorihiki oyobi taishaku torihiki kitei narabini jutakukeiyaku junsoku no tokurei.*" As Ikeda had pointed out to us in a private communication, the discussion in Jaffe and Westerfield (1985a), p. 267 on this point is incorrect.

References

Connolly, Robert A., (1988a). "An Examination of the Robustness of the Weekend Effect," Working Paper, University of California, Irvine.

Connolly, Robert A., (1988b). "A Posterior Odds Analysis of the Weekend Effect," Working Paper, University of California, Irvine.

Coulson, D. Robert, (1987). *The Intelligent Investor's Guide to Profiting from Stock Market Inefficiencies,* Chicago, Probus.

Dimson, E., ed., (1988). *Stock Market Regularities,* Cambridge, Cambridge University Press.

Flannery, Mark, and Aris Protopapadakis, (1988). "From T-Bills to Common Stocks: Investigating the Generality of Intra-Week Return Seasonality." *Journal of Finance,* Vol. 43, pp. 431–450.

French, Kenneth, (1980). "Stock Returns and the Weekend Effect." *Journal of Financial Economics,* Vol. 8, pp. 55–69.

Gibbons, Michael R., and Patrick Hess, (1981). "Day of the Week Effects and Asset Returns." *Journal of Business,* Vol. 54, pp. 579–596.

Hamao, Yasushi, Ronald W. Masulis, and Victor Ng, (1989). "Correlations in Price Changes and Volatility Across International Stock Markets," Working Paper, University of California, San Diego.

Harris, Lawrence, (1986). "A Transaction Data Study of Weekly and Intradaily Patterns in Stock Returns," *Journal of Financial Economics,* Vol. 16, pp. 99–117.

Hiraki, Takato, Raj Aggaarwal, and Ramesh P. Rao, (1988). "Stock Market Anomalies and Investors Behavior in Japan," Working Paper, International University of Japan.

Hirsch, Yale, (1986). "Don't Sell Stocks on Monday," *Facts on File Publications.*

Ikeda, M. (1985). "The Day of the Week Effects and Monthly Effects in the Tokyo Stock Exchange," Working Paper, University of Tokyo, October.

Ikeda, M., (1988). "The Day of the Week Effect and the Mixture of Normal Distributions Hypothesis," *Japan Financial Review,* Vol. 8, pp. 27–53.

Jaffe, J., and R. Westerfield, (1985a). "The Weekend Effect in Common Stock Returns: The International Evidence," *Journal of Finance,* Vol. 40, pp. 433–454.

Jaffe, J., and R. Westerfield, (1985b). "Patterns in Japanese Common Stock Returns: Day of the Week and Turn of the Year Effects," *Journal of Financial and Quantitative Analysis,* Vol. 20, pp. 243–260.

Jacobs, Bruce I., and Kenneth N. Levy (1988). "Calendar Anomalies: Abnormal Returns at Calendar Turning Points," *Financial Analysts Journal,* November–December, 28–39.

Kato, Kiyoshi, (1988a). "Weekly Patterns in Japanese Stock Returns," Working Paper, Nanzan University, Nagoya, Japan, April.

Kato, Kiyoshi, (1988b). "A Further Investigation of Anomalies on the Tokyo Stock Exchange," Working Paper, Nanzan University, Nagoya, Japan, August.

Kato, Kiyoshi, and James S. Schallheim, (1985). "Seasonal and Size Anomalies in the Japanese Stock Market," *Journal of Financial and Quantitative Analysis,* Vol. 20, No. 2, pp. 243–272.

Keim, Donald B., and Robert F. Stambaugh, (1984). "A Further Investigation of the Weekend Effect in Stock Returns," *Journal of Finance,* Vol. 39, pp. 819–840.

Komatsu, Asaji, and William T. Ziemba, (1989). "Some Tests of Plausible Causes for Anomalous Behavior in Japanese Security Markets," Working Paper, Yamaichi Research Institute.

Lakonishok, Josef, and Maurice Levi, (1982). "Weekend Effects on Stock Returns: A Note," *Journal of Finance,* Vol. 37, pp. 883–889.

Lakonishok, Josef, and Seymour Smidt, (1989). "Are Seasonal Anomalies Real? A Ninety-Year Perspective," *Review of Financial Studies,* forthcoming.

McInish, Thomas H., and Robert A. Wood, (1985). "Intraday and Overnight Returns and Day-of-the-Week Effects," *Journal of Financial Research,* Vol. 8, pp. 119–126.

Miller, Edward M., (1988). "Why a Weekend Effect?" *Journal of Portfolio Management*, Fall, pp. 42–48.

Rogalski, Richard J., (1984). "New Findings Regarding Day-of-the-Week Returns over Trading and Non-Trading Periods: A Note," *Journal of Finance,* Vol. 39, pp. 1603–1614.

Smirlock, Michael, and Laura Starks, (1986). "Day of the Week Effects in Stock Returns: Some Intraday Evidence," *Journal of Financial Economics,* Vol. 17, pp. 197–210.

Tokyo Stock Exchange, (1988). *Fact Book,* forthcoming.

Ziemba, William T., (1990a). *Strategies for Making and Keeping Excess Profits in the Stock Market*, William Morrow, New York.

Ziemba, William T., (1989a). "Japanese Security Market Regularities: Monthly, Turn of the Month and Year, Holiday and Golden Week Effects," mimeo, Yamaichi Research Institute, Tokyo.

Ziemba, William T., and Sandra L. Schwartz, (1989). *Investing in Japan,* forthcoming.

Ziemba, William T., (1989b). "Seasonality Effects in Japanese Futures Markets," Yamaichi Research Institute, Tokyo, forthcoming in *Research on Pacific Basin Capital Markets,* S. Ghon Rhee and Rosita P. Chang, eds, American Elsevier, forthcoming.

Ziemba, William T., (1989c). *The Chicken or the Egg: Land and Stock Prices in Japan,* mimeo, Yamaichi Research Institute, Tokyo.

12

Analysts' Expectations and Japanese Stock Prices*

Edwin J. Elton
Nomura Professor of Finance, The Graduate School of Business Administration, New York University

Martin J. Gruber
Nomura Professor of Finance, The Graduate School of Business Administration, New York University

A number of articles that analyze the impact of (earnings and) earnings estimates on security returns have appeared.[1] The majority of this literature has been concerned with the relationship between consensus estimates of earnings and security returns. While the results of this literature are occasionally ambiguous the major conclusions are that

1. Actual earnings impact stock returns.
2. The consensus forecast of growth in earnings is already incorporated in stock price and hence does not impact returns.
3. Knowing the change in consensus forecast of growth in earnings ahead of time leads to excess returns.
4. Changes in consensus ranking of stocks may have an impact on returns after they are made public. The evidence here is more ambiguous than the evidence supporting the first three conditions.

While the results for consensus earnings forecasts and general performance forecasts are reasonably clear, the results for individual forecasters are much more ambiguous. For example, Elton, Gruber, and Grossman (1986) found that past forecast accuracy could not be used to select individual forecasters who would subsequently perform well. In

* This paper owes much to our collaboration with the quantitative analysis team of Nomura Securities and in particular to two individuals Mr. Y. Akeda and Mr. Y. Kato of the Nomura Research Institute.

contrast, studies of the investment advice of Value Line show superior forecasting ability.[2]

The bulk of the research on analysts' predictions and performance has been done on U.S. markets. The purpose of this paper is to examine the impact of forecasts of earnings and sales in the Japanese economy. The study is interesting because of the similarity and differences between the Japanese and U.S. markets. The aggregate value of shares listed on the Tokyo Stock Exchange is larger than the value of shares listed on the New York Stock Exchange. Given the volume of shares traded it should be as competitive as the New York Stock Exchange. On the other hand, the number of suppliers (brokerage firms and institutions) of information and, in particular, forecast data to the market is much smaller in Japan than in the United States. The average number of analysts supplying forecasts of earnings per share for the 400 largest NYSE stocks according to IBESS is 22, while for the 400 largest firms on the Tokyo Stock Exchange IBESS reports 6 estimates. Given the difference in number and the fact that for many Japanese stocks only one forecast exists, the impact of any forecaster can potentially be much more important in Japan than in the United States. The Japanese market may be more informationally inefficient than the U.S. markets.

In this article we examine the forecasts of earnings and sales prepared by Nomura Research Institute for Japanese stocks. We selected a single forecasting source rather than the consensus forecast since there is only a short history for consensus forecasts and for many stocks Nomura is the only forecaster in the consensus. Nomura was selected because it is the largest financial institution in Japan and because it prepares forecasts for more stocks than any other Japanese or non-Japanese participant in the market.

This paper has three sections. In the first section we examine the impact of four types of variables on returns: actual growth, forecasted growth, errors in forecasted growth, and changes in forecasted growth. The results broadly indicate that earnings and sales impact share price and that estimates of these variables contain information. To study the impact of forecasts, returns had to be examined as excess returns. The problem of measuring expected returns in order to determine excess returns is at least as complex for the Japanese market as it is for the U.S. market. The first section starts with a discussion of the method for estimating expected returns and hence excess returns.

The second section examines whether changes in estimates of earnings are incorporated in stock prices sufficiently slowly that information about changes can be used to earn a high rate of return. While the evidence of high return is strong, the risk associated with buying on analysts' change in opinion is high. Hence, the third section examines the utilization of changes in analysts' estimates to construct a portfolio, highly correlated with an index, that capitalized on analysts' forecasts while controlling risk. Using information that is clearly available to a decisionmaker, a portfolio is constructed that closely resembles the market and yet earns a consistently higher rate of return. Tests of the performance of this portfolio involve the incorporation of realistic transaction costs.

I. The Importance of Growth in Sales and Earnings

The purpose of this section is to analyze the impact of estimates of growth in sales and earnings on share prices. In order to do so we need to employ a model of return expectations.

Estimating Expected Returns

In most studies of earnings surprises in the U.S. market, excess returns from following any strategy are measured relative to expectations formed from a single-index (market) model. Though a single-index model may do an adequate job of describing risk in the U.S. market (debate continues as to whether it does or does not), empirical evidence strongly suggests that one index is not a sufficient description of the risk structure of the Tokyo Stock Exchange. For example, the empirical work of Elton and Gruber (1988) and Hamao (1988) indicate that four indexes are necessary to describe risk. Some of the problems involved with the single-index model are shown in Elton and Gruber (1988) who find that by using the single-index model:

1. Return is inversely related to beta in the Japanese market.
2. One index accounts for less than 25% of the return of the four portfolios representing the smallest 20% of the stocks included in the NRI 400. The four-index model accounts for better than 70% of the return on these same four portfolios.

The poor explanatory power of the one-index model combined with the inverse relationship between return and risk when risk is taken as the beta from a one-index model have motivated us to use the four-index model to adjust for risk in all the research that follows.

The description of the methodology behind the four-index model is beyond the scope of this paper. The interested reader is referred to Elton and Gruber (1988) for a detailed description and performance evaluation of the four-index model we employed. In the last section of this paper, however, the validity of the four-index model will be demonstrated by its usefulness in constructing an index fund.

Tests

Having constructed a model of return expectations we now turn to the impact of earnings and sales and earnings estimates on price.

The tests in this section are based on all companies listed on the Tokyo Stock Exchange which had a March fiscal year and for which Nomura Research Institute prepared earnings and sales forecasts for the fiscal years 1985 and 1986. We chose March since more firms had a March fiscal year than any other. Thus, the choice of March gave us the largest number of firms in our sample. We chose a common fiscal year because for some of our tests we wanted all firms to be subject to the same economic influences. Our sample consisted of 941 firms for fiscal year 1984 and 864 firms for fiscal year 1985.

To examine the importance of sales and earnings growth as variables affecting price we ranked all stocks from highest to lowest value on the variable being examined. The stocks were then divided into three groups equal in number of stocks. The return on each portfolio was calculated by taking an equally weighted average of the return on each stock in a group.

We then calculated an excess return for each group relative to the excess return for the whole sample. As discussed earlier, expected return was calculated using the four-factor model. In each case the four-factor model was fit by regressing the actual return of the three ranked portfolios on the return on the four factors for the five-year period prior to the period being analyzed. Expected return was calculated using actual return on the factors during the sample period and the coefficients estimated in the prior five-year period. Excess return is the difference between actual return of the three ranked groups and the expected return estimated from the four-factor model. The excess return was adjusted by subtracting out the average percentage excess return for the whole sample. This last adjustment has the effect of making the excess return net to zero across the three subsamples and adjusts for abnormal performance for the stocks for which earnings and sales are forecasted.

We will now discuss the definition of each of our variables in more detail. The first variable we analyzed was actual growth. If actual growth does not impact share prices, then estimated growth, even if the estimate is correct, should not impact share prices. If growth in earnings and sales impact share price, then knowledge about the future value of these variables should lead to excess returns. Actual growth in earnings and sales was calculated as follows:[3]

$$\text{Actual Earnings Growth} = \frac{\text{Actual Earnings } T + 1}{\text{Actual Earnings } T} - 1$$

$$\text{Actual Sales Growth} = \frac{\text{Actual Sales } T + 1}{\text{Actual Sales } T} - 1$$

For example, for the 1984 sample period, actual sales for the fiscal year ending March 1985 were divided by actual sales for the fiscal year ending March 1984.

Table 12.1 shows the results for actual earnings growth and sales growth. The results are the cumulative excess return for 13 months, starting 2 months after the end of the earlier fiscal year (T). For example, for the year titled 1984 the results are the cumulative returns for the 13 months beginning June 1984 and ending June 1985. An investor would not know actual growth over this period, so that if growth in earnings or sales affect security prices knowledge about the future value of these variables, it should lead to excess return. The period during which we cumulated excess returns was selected for the following reason. First, we start cumulating returns in June because the fiscal year ends in March, and by June data on prior year earnings and sales are public. We present results ending in June of the subsequent year because analyzing monthly returns for 24 months after the start of the sample period showed that in all cases any impact was fully captured by the end of June.

Table 12.1 shows that knowledge concerning actual earnings leads to excess returns being earned. The one-third of the stocks with the highest actual growth in earnings had excess returns that exceeded those of the lowest one-third by over 8% in 1984 and over 18% in 1985. This is evidence that earnings growth is an important factor in determining

Table 12.1. Cumulative Excess Return

	1985			1984		
	Top	**Middle**	**Low**	**Top**	**Middle**	**Low**
			Earnings			
1. Actual Growth	8.96	0.63	−9.59	2.49	3.47	−5.96
2. Forecasted Growth	−3.62	3.74	−0.12	−3.74	−1.85	5.59
3. Error in Forecast	11.54	−0.10	−11.44	9.65	−1.20	−8.45
4. Change in Forecast	12.41	−0.04	−12.37	5.26	−0.58	−4.68
5. Forecast Revision	4.00	−0.34	−3.65	1.88	−0.38	−1.50
			Sales			
1. Actual Growth	4.06	−0.42	−3.64	1.89	2.99	−4.89
2. Forecasted Growth	−7.52	4.35	3.18	−7.48	5.69	1.79
3. Error in Forecast	8.27	−0.30	−7.95	3.90	1.87	−5.77
4. Change in Forecast	4.67	4.91	−9.59	−0.54	1.63	−1.09

share price. If we had performed the same analysis with a variable that did not affect share price, excess returns would not have been earned. While the results are consistent for both years, they are much weaker in the 1984 sample period.

We also earn excess returns with knowledge concerning sales growth. What is surprising, and the same result consistently shows up in our other tests, is that the importance of sales growth is less than earnings growth. This is consistent with U.S. results but is inconsistent with popular beliefs about the Japanese markets. The popular belief is that Japanese share prices are driven by sales, while U.S. prices are driven by earnings. Here we find evidence that in Japan earnings is the more important variable affecting share prices. This is consistent with results using U.S. data.

The second variable we examined is expectations about earnings growth. The variables we examined were

$$\text{Forecasted Earnings Growth} = \frac{\text{June Forecasts of Earnings at } T + 1}{\text{Actual Earnings at } T} - 1$$

$$\text{Forecasted Sales Growth} = \frac{\text{June Forecasts of Sales at } T + 1}{\text{Actual Sales at } T} - 1$$

We used the June forecast since we believe that by June the prior year's actual figures are known. To clarify the dates, the 1984 figures are calculated by taking the June 1984 forecast of earnings for the fiscal year ending March 1985 and dividing by actual earnings for the fiscal year 1984. We would expect that forecasts were fully incorporated into share price so that no excess return could be earned. When consensus data are used for an analysis of U.S. security markets we find no excess return. However, here we are examining the forecasts prepared by a single firm in the Japanese market. The results could be different.

Examining Table 12.1 shows that although excess returns are earned, it is the low-forecasted growth firms that have positive excess returns. This is evidence that investors have overreacted to the forecast. However, not much importance should be placed on these results since the month-by-month pattern is very unstable. For all other variables that we analyze the month-by-month pattern is very consistent. The results for sales are even more ambiguous than the result for earnings.

The third variable we examined was errors in the forecast. If expectations are important, then knowledge that forecasts are in error should lead to excess return. We computed percentage error. The measures were (ERROR IN EARNINGS FORECAST) = [(Actual Earnings at $T + 1$) − (June Forecast of Earnings in $T + 1$)] ÷ (Actual Earnings in $T + 1$) and (ERROR IN SALES FORECAST) = [(Actual Earnings at $T + 1$) − (June Forecast of Earnings in $T + 1$)] ÷ (Actual Earnings in $T + 1$). For example, the number shown for 1984 uses the forecast of earnings prepared in June of 1984 for earnings reported in March 1985 and compares this forecast with the actual earnings reported for March 1985.

Knowledge that forecasts were in error produced larger positive excess returns than knowledge of the actual values of the variables themselves.

The excess return differential between the top and bottom portfolio was over 18% in 1984 and 22% in 1985. This is evidence of the importance of the variables and that expectations drive security prices. Note that the use of sales forecasts rather than earnings forecasts once again produces positive but smaller differentials between portfolios.

The fourth variable we analyzed is change in the forecast. If we are analyzing variables that affect share price, and if expectations are important in determining share price, then knowledge concerning changes in expectations should be more important than knowledge about the actual value of the variable itself. The variables we examined were (CHANGE IN EARNINGS FORECAST) = [(December Forecast of Earnings in $T + 1$) − (June Forecast of Earnings in $T + 1$) ÷ (June Forecast of Earnings in $T + 1$) and (CHANGE IN SALES FORECAST) = [(December Forecast of Sales in $T + 1$) − (June Forecast of Sales in $T + 1$)] ÷ (June Forecast of Sales in $T + 1$). For example, the number shown under 1984 utilizes the difference between the December 1984 forecasts and the June 1984 forecasts. Both forecasts are of earnings reported March 1985. In this case excess returns are examined from June 1984 to June 1985.

Table 12.1 shows the results. Knowing how earnings forecasts will change results in greater excess returns than knowledge of actual growth. This is strong evidence that expectations affect share price and that in particular Nomura's forecasts impact share price. Once again, knowledge concerning earnings is more important than knowledge concerning sales.

The results for these four variables are remarkably similar to U.S. results. In both markets the pattern across variables is the same. Thus, in both markets knowledge about expectations is more important than knowledge about the variables themselves. This is evidence that expectations drive security prices. The results analyzed here are for one firm rather than consensus forecasts used in the U.S., but these results show that this firm has an important influence on share price. The surprising result given general beliefs is that earnings growth is more important than sales growth. This is the U.S. result, but popular belief is that it differs in Japan. Here we see it does not.

Before leaving this section we will reexamine the change in forecasted earnings to see if some of the change is captured in market price after it becomes public. This is a topic that will be examined in great detail in later sections of the paper where we examine month-by-month changes.

To get a rough idea of the phenomenon let us return to the change in forecast variables, and look at the excess returns that would accrue for an investor who bought after the change in estimates was realized (in 8501 or 8601) and held for three months.

Examining the row labeled Forecast Revision in Table 12.1 indicates that a considerable amount of the excess returns associated with a revision of analysts' estimates is realized after the date of the revision. In fact, approximately one-third of the excess returns accrue after the revision is made. We now turn to a further exploration of this phenomenon.

II. Change in Analysts' Estimates

In this section we will examine the results of purchasing stocks for which analysts have increased their estimate of earnings. In the previous section of the paper we showed that earnings was a more important variable than sales. For American stocks a number of studies have shown that changes in analysts' estimates are not immediately incorporated in share prices.[4] If changes in analysts' estimates of earnings are not immediately incorporated in share price for the Japanese stocks, then excess returns might be earned by buying stocks for which analysts have increased their earnings estimates. We will examine the question in this section.

Since short sales are not permissible in Japan and we wanted to formulate a strategy that could be followed by a Japanese institution, we did not report strategies involving short sales.[5] Earnings estimates are collected from the analysts during the course of each month. Although we do not know exactly on which day they become available, we do know for certain that they have been collected and are available by the end of the month. Hence, the more conservative method is to make all purchases and sales at month's end. More explicitly, we will test the following strategy for the period June 1985 through May 1987:

1. At the end of each month, using forecasts prepared during the month, buy all stocks with increased earnings estimates.[6]
2. Sell any stock that has had a decrease in its earnings estimate.
3. Sell any stock not added to the portfolio in the previous six months.

The portfolio was updated at the end of each month over the sample period. Two weighting schemes were used, the first with equal amounts in each stock. Each time a stock has an increase in earnings estimates it is treated as a new stock. Thus, under the equal-weighting scheme the same stock may be included more than once and in this sense have more invested in it. At the extreme, a stock could be included six times. If changes in estimates contain information, then larger percentage changes might contain more information than small changes. Thus, a second weighting method was examined where each stock, rather than being weighted equally, was weighted proportionally to the size of its percentage change in earnings.

Before we examine the results of these trading rules let us look at the performance if analysts' estimates are available at the beginning of the month in which they are prepared. This represents the maximum gain that possibly could be achieved by access to analysts' estimates, and is interesting as such. Furthermore, it may not be an unrealistic return since analysts' estimates tend to be available during the first week or two of the month, and hence it is very conservative to assume they are not available until the end of the month.

The results of holding an equally weighted portfolio formed from stocks that have had an increase in earnings estimates as previously described are presented in Table 12.2. In constructing this table we have defined differential (above market return) as the return on the portfolio we construct minus the return on the NIKKEI 225 Index. Note first that the differential return is positive and statistically different from zero at better than the 1% level.[7] The differential return of 1.07% per month is not only statistically different from zero but also large enough to suggest economic importance. To judge economic importance, returns should be examined after transaction costs. Transaction costs are fixed rather than negotiated in the Japanese market. Adjusting for transactions costs on the turnover of 11.2% only reduced the differential return from 1.07% to 0.93% per month. Although this indicates a sizeable return, other statistics in Table 12.2 indicate that the portfolio that results is not highly correlated with the market. In the next section of this paper we will examine excess returns from employing analysts' estimates in a portfolio strategy that more closely replicates the market.

The second row in Table 12.2 shows the results of following an equally weighted portfolio strategy based on changes in forecasts where implementation takes place at the end of the month in which estimates are prepared. Notice that the monthly differential return is still economically significant and persists over time. It has dropped to 0.84% per month,

Table 12.2. Statistics on Performance of Portfolio Strategies

Basis of Portfolio Formation	Monthly Return	Beta	R^2	Differential Monthly Return	T Value	Turnover
Begin Month Equal Weights	2.41	0.79	0.74	1.07	4.25	11.29
End Month Equal Weights	2.19	0.78	0.73	0.84	3.31	11.44
End Month Proportional Weights	2.75	0.69	0.37	1.41	3.04	17.05

a decrease of only 21%. Thus, 79% of the information in changes in analysts' estimates is still present even if action is taken only at the end of the month in which estimates become available. If we make the adjustment for transaction costs, excess return is reduced to 0.70% per month. This is still a large enough differential over market returns to be of interest.

Finally, when we make portfolio holdings proportional to the size of the earnings surprise, we see a marked increase in returns. The excess return goes from 0.84% per month in the equally weighted case to 1.41% per month, an increase of 68%. Turnover and transaction costs also increase. However, after deducting transaction costs the excess return is still 1.20% per month.

In this section we have shown that constructing a portfolio based on earnings surprises provides a return that is both economically and statistically significantly better than that which can be earned by holding a market portfolio. Even when analysts' estimates are assumed to be available only at the end of the month in which they are made the results are robust. Constructing the portfolio by using weights proportional to the size of changes in analysts' estimates leads to much greater excess returns than assuming that stocks with favorable changes are held in equal proportions.

Although the strategies using end-of-the-month forecasts are all feasible investment strategies, they lead to construction of portfolios that are significantly different from market portfolios. Consistent differential return is interesting, but the investor might also be interested in controlling risk. This leads us to the next section of this article on employing analysts' estimates in a portfolio with risks similar to those of an index fund.

III. An Indexed Earnings Estimate Change Model

We have shown that the selection of stocks for which analysts have changed their estimates of earnings growth can result in an extra return even after transaction costs. Though the results are quite encouraging it seems reasonable to perform a second type of analysis. In the previous section we allowed the inclusion of small stocks. We wished to test whether these results still held when we restricted ourselves to a portfolio that was appropriate for institutional ownership. In addition, in the last section there was no attempt to match market risk. Since the beta was less than one and the market increased, this should not account for our results. However, over a small number of years positive returns might be due to a fortuitous choice of industries. In addition, while an investor might desire to benefit from the forecast change model, he or she might also want to limit risk by holding a portfolio that more closely resembles a market index.

For all of these reasons an experiment was conducted that involved designing a portfolio that (a) was composed of highly liquid stocks; (b) closely matched the performance of the first tier of the Tokyo Stock Exchange index; and (c) capitalized on the informational content of changes in analysts' earnings estimates.

The procedure used involved the following steps: Design an initial sample of highly liquid stocks from the first tier of the Tokyo Stock Exchange. Select from the approximately 1100 stocks on the Tokyo Stock Exchange 600 stocks with high liquidity. The 600 stocks selected were divided into 13 industry sectors. In each month for each stock the rate of change in analysts' estimates of earnings was computed. For each industry sector the one-third of the stocks for which analysts had the largest percentage increase in estimates was considered a candidate for the index fund. Using these 200 stocks, a quadratic programming problem was solved that formed a portfolio that minimized residual risk from the four-factor model (described in Section I) while matching the Tokyo Stock Exchange index in its sensitivities to each of the four factors, and involved holding no more than 100 securities. The portfolio was held for one month, the sample reformed, and the quadratic programming problem resolved to develop a new portfolio. The output was the monthly composition and return on a series of portfolios formed from January 1983 through December 1987. Each portfolio was formed using only data that was available at the time of its construction and returns recorded for the month subsequent to its formation.

In Table 12.3 we summarize the results of performance. First note that the beta is 1.05 and the coefficient of determination is 0.93. The beta is considerably closer to 1 and the R^2 much higher than the results of Section II, where no attempt was made to match a market index. However, the indexing is not without cost. The turnover is higher and the return (after transaction costs) falls to 0.41% per month. This excess return of better than 40 basis points per month on a portfolio that closely resembles the Tokyo Stock Exchange is surely of economic significance.

Table 12.3. Earnings Surprise Index Fund

	Percent per Month				
Year	Portfolio Return	Excess* Return	Excess Return After Transaction Cost	Periods Better than Index	Percent Turnover
1983	2.685	0.689	0.356	10/12	31.6
1984	2.791	0.551	0.263	8/12	28.3
1985	1.920	0.512	0.272	8/12	25.7
1986	4.350	0.606	0.343	8/12	33.8
1987	2.069	0.949	0.775	9/12	24.6
AVG.	2.763	0.661	0.405	43/60	28.9

Beta = 1.0495
R^2 = 0.927

*Excess Return is defined as the return on the portfolio minus the return on the TOPIX.

Note also that in each of the five years tested the earnings surprise index fund outperformed the market portfolio. The minimum average monthly differential over a year holding period is 26 basis points, and the maximum is 78 basis points.[8]

In summary, using only data that are available to an investor we have constructed a portfolio that contains 100 stocks, closely resembles an index fund on the Tokyo Stock Exchange, and outperforms such an index fund by over 40 basis points per month.

Conclusion

In this paper we have examined the interaction of one firm's estimates of earnings and sales and stock prices in the Japanese market. We have shown that contrary to popular belief, earnings, not sales, drive stock prices in Japan. Analysts' estimates are incorporated in stock prices but changes in analysts' estimates are incorporated with a lag. Because of this lag extra returns can be earned by buying stocks immediately after an upward revision in analysts' earning estimates. Furthermore, by using changes in forecasts a fund that mirrors the first tier of the Tokyo Stock Exchange but that offers a greater return can be created.

Notes

1. See Brown, Foster, and Noreen (1985), Dimson and Marsh (1984), and Elton, Gruber, and Gultekin (1981) and (1984) for an extensive bibliography.
2. See, for example, Black (1973). The Value Line studies as well as many others in this area are suspect because of selection bias. After the fact a forecaster or firm such as Value Line is identified as doing well and then back testing shows that the forecaster did in fact do well.
3. In all cases we deleted firms with negative earnings or such small earnings that growth in excess of 100% was found. This is consistent throughout.
4. See, for example, Givoly and Lakonishok (1979) and Hawkins, Chamberlin, and Daniel (1990).
5. Allowing short sales would have increased returns beyond those reported in the text.
6. If a stock is already included in the portfolio and it has an increase in earnings estimate, then it is treated as a new stock and enters a second time.
7. To test statistical significance, we computed the means and standard deviation of the difference between the portfolio return and the market return.

From the central limit theorem the mean return should be normally distributed, and hence the *t*-test is appropriate.

8. Subsequent to examining this simple rule for selection, more complex rules were examined with different revision intervals and different populations of stocks. While turnover changed, the results of superior returns (positive alpha) with high R^2 was robust across a wide range of model parameters and samples.

References

Black, Fisher, (1973). "Yes Virginia there is Hope: Tests of the Value Line Ranking System," *Financial Analysts Journal,* Vol. 29, No. 5.

Brown, Philip, George Foster, Eric Noreen, (1985). "Security Analysts Multi-year Earnings Forecasts and the Capital Market," *Studies in Accounting Research,* No. 21, American Accounting Association.

Dimson, Elroy, and Paul Marsh, (1984). "An Analysis of Brokers' and Analysts' Unpublished Forecasts of U.K. Stock Returns," *Journal of Finance,* December, pp. 1257–1292.

Elton, Edwin J., and Martin J. Gruber, (1988). "A Multi-Index Model of the Japanese Stock Market," *Japan and the World Economy,* Vol. 1.

Elton, Edwin J., Martin J. Gruber, and Seth Grossman, (1986). "Discrete Expectational Data and Portfolio Performance," *Journal of Finance,* July, pp. 699–712.

Elton, Edwin J., Martin J. Gruber, and Mustafa Gultekin, (1981). "Expectations and Share Prices," *Management Science,* September, pp. 975–987.

Elton, Edwin J., Martin J. Gruber, and Mustafa Gultekin, (1984). "Professional Expectations: Accuracy and Diagnosis of Errors," *Journal of Financial and Quantitative Analysis* December, pp. 351–363.

Givoly, D., and J. Lakonishok, (1979). "The Informational Content of Financial Analysts' Forecasts," *Journal of Accounting and Economics,* Winter, pp. 165–185.

Hamao, Yasushi, (1988). "An Empirical Examination of the Arbitrage Pricing Theory: Using Japanese Data," *Japan and the World Economy,* Vol. 1.

Hawkins, E. H., S. C. Chamberlin, and W. E. Daniel, (1990). "Earnings Expectations and Security Prices," *Financial Analysts Journal,* forthcoming.

PART IV

Futures

13

The Japanese Stock Index Futures Markets: The Early Experience*

Menachem Brenner
Hebrew University and New York University

Marti G. Subrahmanyam
New York University

Jun Uno
Nihon Keizai Shimbun Inc.

I. Introduction

The first futures contract based on an index of Japanese stocks to be traded was one based on the Nikkei Stock Average (NSA). This contract first started trading on September 3, 1986, on the Singapore International Monetary Exchange (SIMEX). Since then, other contracts on Japanese stock indices have been introduced in Japanese markets. The earliest of these is the Osaka Stock Futures 50 (OSF50), which opened for trading on the Osaka Securities Exchange (OSE) on June 9, 1987.[1]

In this study, we examine the behavior of the NSA contract on SIMEX and the OSF50 contract on the OSE in the early years of trading. In particular, we analyze the relationship between the "fair value" of the contracts in relation to the respective cash markets and their actual pricing, taking transactions costs into account.

In Section II, we describe the basic pricing models for stock index futures contracts. The next section, Section III, deals with the main

* We acknowledge with thanks helpful comments on this research provided by S. Park and W. Silber. We are grateful to Nihon Keizai Shimbun Inc. for providing us with the data. Some of the tables and graphs used in this Chapter have previously appeared in another paper we have published [Brenner, Subrahmanyam, and Uno (1986)], and are reproduced by permission.

features of the SIMEX and OSF50 contracts. In Section IV, we present the empirical evidence on the pricing of the two contracts for the first few expiration months. In the last section, Section V, we present a summary and our conclusions.

II. Pricing Of Stock Index Futures

The payoffs from stock index futures contracts can be replicated by positions in the underlying index (i.e., the basket of stocks making up the index) and the riskless asset. Hence, the "fair" price of an index futures contract can be computed form the price of the "replicating" portfolio that mimics the payoffs from the futures contract. In particular, the "fair" price of the futures contract can be shown to be equal to the price of the underlying spot index plus the "cost of carry" for the spot index between the current date and the expiration date of the futures contract.[2] In general, carrying costs for the underlying asset consist of interest costs and storage costs, less the amount of cash payments such as dividends that are made to owners of the spot asset. In the case of an underlying asset such as the stock index, storage costs are zero. Hence, the carrying costs represent the difference between the interest costs paid and the dividends received. We shall now explore this general proposition in some detail for specific cases relating to taxes, transactions costs, and restrictions on trading. In what follows, the possible differences in the pricing of forward and futures contracts, which are mainly due to the risk of being marked-to-market, are ignored.

Case 1: No transactions costs, short sales permitted

Suppose that there are no transactions costs and that short sales are permitted in the stocks that make up the spot index. Consider the strategy of buying the stocks making up the spot index on day t, receiving the dividends (which are assumed to be known ahead of time) between time t and the expiration date of the futures contract, T, and reinvesting them at the risk-free interest rate, and liquidating the portfolio at time T. This strategy replicates the payoffs from buying the futures contract, making investments equal to the dividend payments in the riskless asset, and liquidating the futures position at the expiration date, T. The reason is that the price of the futures contract equals the index value on the expiration date.

Alternatively, buying the stocks in the spot index (using borrowed funds) and selling the futures contract at time t, collecting the dividends from the stocks and reinvesting them at the risk-free interest rate, and liquidating the stocks at the expiration of the futures contract yields the following cash flow, C, net of interest costs at time T:

$$C = [S_T - S_t \exp(r\,\tau) + DIV_t] - [F_T - F_t] \tag{13.1}$$

where

t is the current date

T is the expiration date of the futures contract

S is the price of the spot asset

F is the price of the futures contract

r is the riskless annual interest rate at time t

$\tau = (T - t)/365$ is the fraction of the year represented by the time interval between t and T

D_{t+j} is dividend paid on the spot asset on date $t + J$

$DIV_t = \sum_j D_{t+j} \exp[r(T - (t + j))/365]$ is the future value at T of the dividends between t and T on the spot asset.

The first term in Equation (13.1) indicates the profit from the spot position after considering interest costs and dividends, while the second is the profit from the futures position. In an arbitrage-free market, this cash flow cannot be positive. Further, since $F_T = S_T$, by definition, we can write:

$$-S_t \exp(r\,\tau) + DIV_t + F_t \leq 0$$

or

$$F_t < S_t \exp(r\,\tau) - DIV_t \tag{13.2}$$

Thus, the futures price can be no larger than the compounded value of the current spot index less the compounded value of the dividend flow.

Now, consider the opposite strategy of buying the futures contract and selling short the stocks making up the spot index. The cash flow from this strategy is the negative of that given in Equation (13.1). Again, to avoid arbitrage, this cash flow cannot be positive. This implies that

$$S_t \exp(r\,\tau) - DIV_t - F_t \leq 0$$

or

$$F_t \geq S_t \exp(r\,\tau) - DI\,V_t \tag{13.3}$$

In other words, the futures price can be no less than the compounded value of the current spot index reduced by the compounded value of the dividend flow.

For the case of no transactions costs or restrictions on short sales, we can conclude, by combining (13.2) and (13.3), that the relationship holds as an equality:

$$F\,P_t = S_t \exp(r\,\tau) - DI\,V_t \tag{13.4}$$

where $F\,P_t$ is the "fair" futures price at time t.

Case 2: No transactions costs, short sales of stocks prohibited

In this case, the arbitrage transaction underlying Equation (13.3) is not permitted. Hence, only (13.2) holds, which means that there is an upper bound, but no lower bound, on the "fair" futures price:

$$F\,P_t \leq S_t \exp(r\,\tau) - DI\,V_t \tag{13.2$'$}$$

This analysis assumes that there is a segmentation in the financial markets, where those investors who hold the stocks in the index are not allowed to substitute them for futures contracts. The arbitrageur, on the other hand, does not possess the stocks to sell. Hence, the transactions underlying Equation (13.3) are not feasible.

Case 3: No transactions costs, short sales permitted, but proceeds of the short sales are not received

There is no difference between this case and the preceding cases for the arbitrage implied by buying the spot and selling the futures contract. Hence, Equation (13.2) holds in this case also. The difference arises when it comes to buying the futures contract and selling the spot asset.[3] Here, not receiving the proceeds of the short sales implies that the interest that could have been earned on this amount is foregone. In other words, the arbitrage restriction (13.3) is modified to:

$$F_t \geq S_t - DI\,V_t \tag{13.3$'$}$$

Combining (13.2) and (13.3′) yields:

$$S_t \exp(r\,\tau) - DI\,V_t \geq F\,P_t \geq S_t - DI\,V_t \qquad (13.4')$$

where $F\,P_t$ is the "fair" futures price.

Thus, there is a band within which arbitrage is not possible, because of the asymmetry of the cash flow stream. This asymmetry is due to not receiving the proceeds of the short sales, while payment is made for the long position in the stocks.

A minor variant of the above case is one where a fraction of the proceeds of the short sales, say K, are made available to the seller. Here (13.4′) can be modified as follows:

$$S_t \exp(r\,\tau) - DI\,V_t \geq F\,P_t \geq [K\,S_t \exp(r\,\tau) + (1-K)S_t] - DI\,V_t \qquad (13.4'')$$

Case 4: Transactions costs are incurred in both spot and futures markets

Transactions costs have an impact on each one of the above cases by creating a band within which arbitrage is not profitable. We shall illustrate the impact of transactions costs in the first case where there are no restrictions on short sales, that is, as a departure from Equation (13.4). The effect of transactions costs in the other cases is similar. There are six elements of transactions costs in carrying out the stock index arbitrage:

a) The brokerage commissions charged for buying and selling the underlying stocks.
b) The brokerage commissions charged for selling and buying back the futures.
c) The securities transfer tax paid when the stocks are sold.
d) The "market impact" cost in buying and selling the stocks.
e) The "market impact" cost in selling and buying back the futures contract.
f) The cost of "borrowing" the stocks when the stocks in the spot index are to be sold short.

Items a) and b) are the direct transactions costs and require no further explanation. Item c) is a tax charged in many countries, including Japan, when stocks change hands. Items d) and e) take into account the fact that a sizeable transaction cannot be put through in the spot and futures markets without changing the market price. At the very least, this would involve the current bid-ask spread for the average-sized transaction in the respective markets. However, this spread may widen for a larger transaction size. The last item refers to the institutional restriction that, for selling short, the stock should be in the "possession" of the seller. This is usually accomplished by "borrowing" it from another investor, such as a pension fund, that may charge the short seller a fee for "lending" the stock.

Define

s = Transactions costs in the stock market as a percentage of the stock price.

f = Transactions costs (round trip) per contract in the futures market in money terms.

i_s = "Market Impact" in one direction for the underlying stocks as a percentage of the stock price.

i_f = "Market Impact" in one direction for the futures contract in "ticks" per contract translated into money terms.

x = Securities transfer tax as a percentage of the stock price.

b = Cost of "borrowing" the stock as a percentage of the stock price.

The band within which the futures price should lie vis-a-vis Equation (13.4) can be written as:[4]

$$FP_t^+ = [S_t(l + c_t^+)]\exp(r\tau) - DIV_t \tag{13.5a}$$

$$FP_t^- = [S_t(l - c_t^-)]\exp(r\tau) - DIV_t \tag{13.5b}$$

where

$$c_t^+ = \frac{(2sS_t + f + 2i_sS_t + 2i_f + xS_t)}{S_t}$$

$$c_t^- = \frac{(2sS_t + f + 2i_sS_t + 2i_f + xS_t + bS_t)}{S_t}$$

FP_t^+ is the upper bound and FP_t^- is lower bound of the band, and c_t^+ and c_t^- are the deviations caused by transactions costs expressed as a percentage of the current spot price. We assume that the position is "unwound" at the expiration of the contract in the above computation. The band would be narrower if instead of unwinding the position at the expiration, it is "rolled over" into next contract date. To this extent, the band is conservatively defined in Equations (13.5a) and (13.5b).

In the above computation, we ignore the taxation of the profits from the arbitrage transactions. Of course, there are differences in the tax treatment of different types of arbitrageurs in many countries, ranging from tax-exempt entities to entities that are taxed at the same tax rates on all transactions.[5] In this analysis, we ignore the taxation of the arbitrage profits, that is, the analysis here refers to a tax-exempt arbitrageur who pays the same marginal tax rate on all sources of income.

A violation of the arbitrage conditions derived above for the various cases can be measured in different ways. The first is to compute the difference between the "fair" (i.e., arbitrage-free) price and the actual price, divided by the "fair" futures price. The second is to calculate an implied interest rate on the arbitrage transaction, that is, the interest rate at which the "fair" futures price equals the actual futures price.

The two measures are best illustrated by considering Case 4 when there is a total transactions cost per "contract-equivalent" trade, that is, buying the spot and selling one futures contract or the opposite transaction.[6] The violation of the arbitrage conditions in this case can be defined by the following alternative measures:

$$M_t = \begin{cases} \dfrac{(F_t - FP_t^+)}{FP_t^+}, \text{ if } F_t > FP_t^+ \\ 0, \text{ if } FP_t^+ > F_t > FP_t^- \\ \dfrac{(F_t - FP_t^-)}{FP_t^-}, \text{ if } F_t < FP_t^- \end{cases} \tag{13.6a}$$

$$R_t = \begin{cases} (1/\tau)[\ln\{\dfrac{F_t}{S_t(1 + c_t^+) - PV(DIV_t))}\}], \text{ if } F_t > FP_t^+ \\ r, \text{ if } FP_t^+ > F_t > FP_t^- \\ (1/\tau)[\ln\{\dfrac{F_t}{S_t(1 - c_t^+) - PV(DIV_t))}\}], \text{ if } F_t < FP_t^- \end{cases} \tag{13.6b}$$

where $PV(DIV_t)$ = Present Value of DIV_t.

In the above equation, M_t represents the mispricing, expressed in proportional terms, in relation to the theoretical futures price. R_t is the implied annual interest rate in the arbitrage. If it is greater than the opportunity cost, r, it pays to buy the spot and sell the futures contract and lock in a higher lending rate. If it is less than the opportunity cost, it pays to buy the futures and sell the spot and lock in a lower borrowing rate. Due to the size of the transactions cost band, it may happen that it does not pay to engage in either of the two possible arbitrage transactions. In other words, the best opportunity available is to invest at the riskless interest rate r. In the absence of transactions costs, Equations (13.6a) and (13.6b) are modified to include only a single "fair" price $F\,P_t$ which is equal to $F\,P_t^+$ and $F\,P_t^-$, since the band collapses to a single value.

III. Description of the Data

This study uses data on the NSA and OSF50 indices and the futures contracts on these indices. The NSA consists of 225 stocks traded on the First Section of the Tokyo Stock Exchange (TSE). The market value of the Nikkei stocks amounts to about 50% of the market value of all stocks on the First Section. These stocks accounted for about 75% of the trading volume on the First Section of the TSE during the period under study. The NSA is an arithmetic price average, like the Dow-Jones Industrial Average. The NSA is computed by adding the prices of all 225 stocks and dividing by a divisor that changes over time due to stock splits, rights issues, et cetera. Currently, the index is announced at one minute intervals during trading hours.

The futures contract on the NSA started trading on September 3, 1986, on the Singapore International Monetary Exchange (SIMEX). Each trading day, the futures contract starts trading with the opening of trading on the TSE and closes 15 minutes after the close of trading on the TSE. While the TSE trades between 9 A.M. and 11 A.M. and again between 1 P.M. and 3 P.M., Tokyo time, the futures contract trades *continuously* between 8 A.M. and 2.15 P.M., Singapore time. (Tokyo time is one hour after Singapore time.) The futures contract trades on weekdays and some Saturdays.[7] The contract has four maturities (March, June, September, December). The last trading day is the third Wednesday of the contract month. The settlement of the contract is in cash, based on the closing value of the NSA.

The OSF50 is also an arithmetic price average, but of 50 leading stocks. This index is highly correlated with the NSA but contains a smaller number of stocks. Adjustments to this index are made in a manner similar to those for the NSA index. The OSF50 futures contract was introduced on June 9, 1987, for trading on the OSE. The main characteristics that distinguish this contract from the NSA contract on SIMEX are settlement procedures and trading hours. Unlike most stock index futures contracts, in general, and the NSA contract, in particular, the OSF50 contract is settled by physical delivery of the underlying securities, for all contracts open on the last trading day of the delivery month. Additionally, in contrast to the NSA contract traded on SIMEX, the trading hours for the OSF50 contract coincide with those of the Japanese exchanges trading the underlying stocks (9 A.M. to 11 A.M. and 1 P.M. to 3 P.M., Monday to Friday, and 9 A.M. to 11 A.M. on trading Saturdays). The main features of the NSA and OSF50 futures contracts are listed in Table 13.1.

The trading volume of NSA futures on SIMEX averaged 30,000 contracts per month until the October 1987 crash and declined somewhat afterwards. The OSF50 futures was trading over 50,000 contracts per month in the study period.[8] Figures 13.1 and 13.2 provide charts of the trading volume in the OSF50 and NSA contracts since the inception of the OSF50 contract in June 1987.

An important distinction between the Japanese stock market and U.S. stock market is with regard to the dividend stream on the underlying stocks. Unlike American corporations, Japanese companies generally pay dividends twice a year (occasionally once). These payments are concentrated at the end of two months each year, March and September. For example, 77 companies went "ex-dividend" on September 26, 1987, and 121 companies, out of 225 in the NSA, went "ex-dividend" on March 27, 1988 (See Figure 13.3). After the dividends are announced, usually days before the payment, the actual dividend payments are known in most cases. However, even before their announcement, dividend forecast figures are provided by the financial newspapers and by the publications of the brokerage firms. The dividend stream is, for the most part, rather predictable. The pattern of dividends on the stocks in the two indices, the NSA and OSF50, are very similar, as illustrated by Figures 13.3 and 13.4.

The interest rate used in our analysis is the three-month Gensaki rate (a "repo" rate), that is commonly used as the analog of the short-term Treasury bill rate in the U.S.[9] The Gensaki rate declined from about 4.7% at the beginning of the analysis period (September 1986) to about

Table 13.1. Features of the NSA (SIMEX) and OSF50 (OSE) Stock Index Futures Contracts

	NSA	OSF50
1. Underlying Asset	Nikkei Stock Average of 225 stocks	Package portfolio of 50 stocks
2. Contract Size	Nikkei Stock Average multiplied by 500	One trading unit of package portfolio multiplied by 1000
3. Contract Months	March, June, September, December (Five Contract Months open at a time)	March, June September, December (Five Contract Months open at a time)
4. Expiration Day	Third Wednesday of contract month	15th day of contract month
5. Last Trading Day	Third Wednesday of contract month	Sixth business day prior to the 15th of contract month
6. Trading Hours	8 A.M., 2:15 P.M. Singapore Time (9 A.M., 3:15 P.M. Tokyo Time) on trading days	9 A.M., 11 A.M., 1 P.M., 3 P.M. Tokyo Time on trading days
	8 A.M., 10:15 A.M. Singapore Time (9 A.M., 11:15 A.M. Tokyo time) on half trading days	9 A.M., 11 A.M. Tokyo Time on half trading days
7. Method of Trading	Open outcry (Individual auctions)	Computerized—competitive bids and offers
8. Tick Size	¥ 5 × 500 = ¥ 2500	¥ 0.5 × 50,000 = ¥ 25,000
9. Settlement on Last Trading Day	Cash Settlement	Physical Delivery
10. Price Limits	No*	Yes

*After October 1987, price limits were introduced for the NSA contract by the SIMEX authorities.

Figure 13.1. Trading Volume, OSF50 Futures Contract

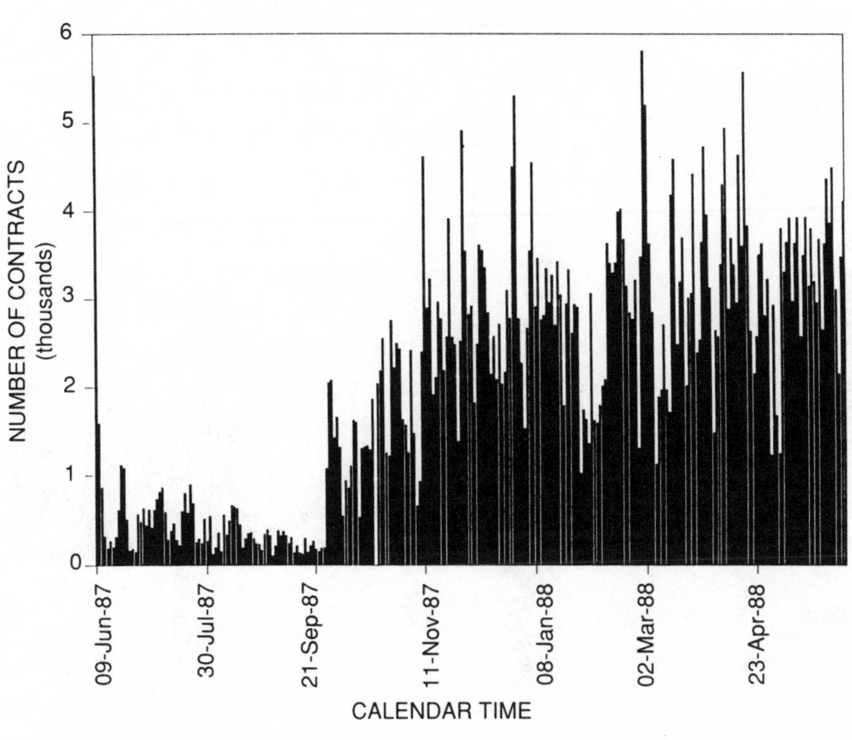

3.8% at the end of the period (June 1988). There is no interest rate for a maturity exactly matching the maturity of the futures contract each trading day. Although this rate could be estimated by interpolation between the one-month and three-month rates, the differences between the three-month rate and the interpolated rate are trivial. For example, the average three-month and one-month Gensaki rates over our sample period were 3.985% and 3.956% respectively, a difference of about three basis points.

Finally, we obtained estimates of the transactions costs involved in carrying out the spot-futures arbitrage from both published data as well as discussions with several traders. As discussed in Section II, there are six items that make up the transactions costs. We shall discuss an example of the transactions costs for the NSA arbitrage. The first item, commissions on the stocks, is given by the Table of General Commission Rates.[10] Brokerage commissions depend on the size of the transaction,

Figure 13.2. Trading Volume, SIMEX NSA Futures Contract

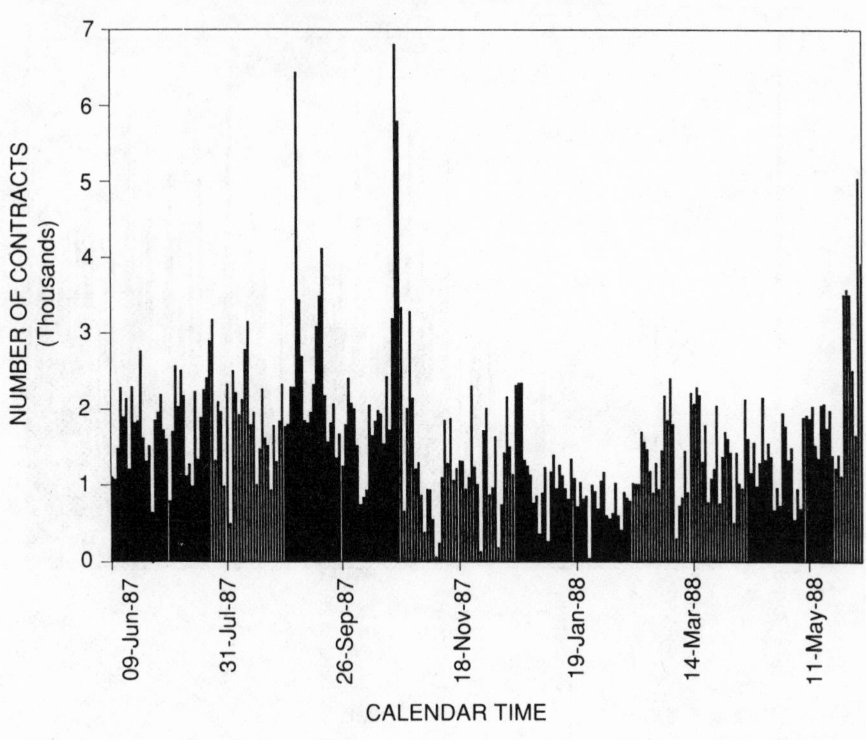

and on whether the trader is an investor or a broker. For example, on a transaction of value 10 million yen, the commission was 0.7% before October 1987. If the transaction was undertaken by a broker, only a small stock exchange fee of about 0.01% was payable.

Items b), the commissions on futures contracts, are fixed yen amounts per contract, round-trip (7500 yen per contract up to 10 contracts and 5000 yen per contract, thereafter). Item c), the securities transfer tax payable when stocks are sold, amounted to 0.55% for investors and 0.18% for brokers. Items d), the "market impact" costs for stocks, are estimated to be about 0.3% to 0.6% for a trade in range of 10–30 million yen per stock. In the futures market, the "market impact" (item e)) varies greatly depending on the level of activity in the market. In the first six months of trading, the bid-ask spread was as much as 10–12 ticks (1 tick is 2500 yen), or about 0.25% to 0.35% (round trip) of the average value of the contract during the period. Later on, this spread narrowed

Figure 13.3. Daily Dividend Yield, OSF50 Index

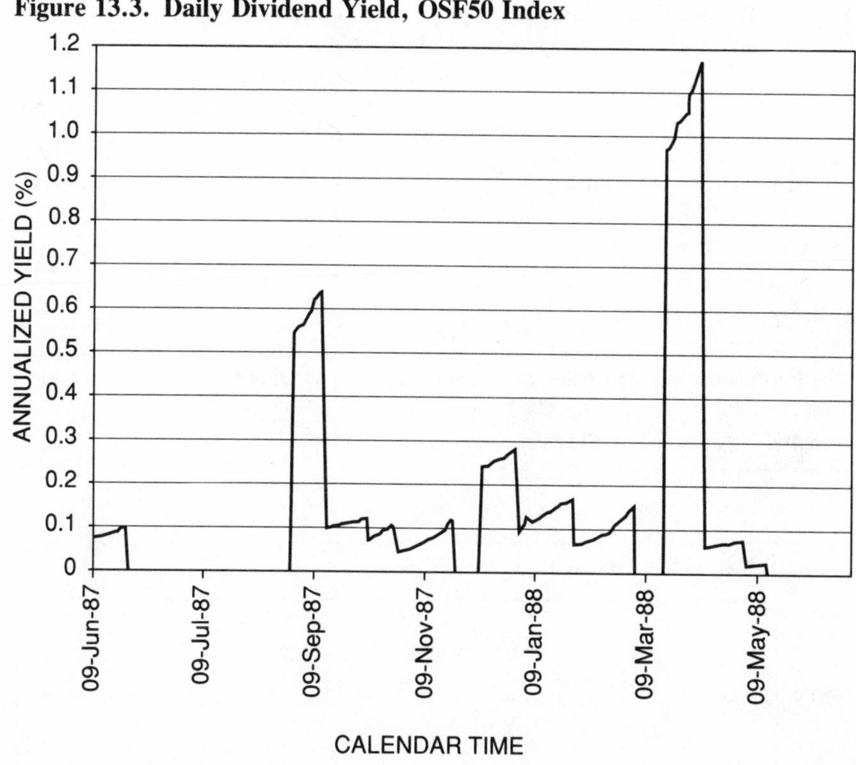

to about 2–4 ticks, or about 0.05% to 0.1% (round trip) of the value of the contract. Item f), the cost of "borrowing" stocks for short sales, is estimated to be about 0.10%.

Following are illustrative examples of transactions costs estimates for different traders:

Typical Transactions Costs for Spot-Futures Index Arbitrage on a One Billion Yen Trade* before October 5, 1987

	For Institutional Investors (%)	For Brokers (%)
a) Stock Commissions	1.40	0.01
b) Securities Transfer Tax	0.55	0.18
c) Market Impact (Stocks)	0.40	0.40

Typical Transactions Costs for Spot-Futures Index Arbitrage on a One Billion Yen Trade* before October 5, 1987 (Continued)

	For Institutional Investors (%)	For Brokers (%)
d) Market Impact (Futures)	0.30	0.30
e) Futures Commissions	0.04	0.04
f) Cost of "borrowing" the stocks for short sales**	0.10	0.10
Total	2.79	1.03

*Using a "basket" of 100 stocks with 10 million yen invested in each stock and a futures trade involving about 80 contracts.

**Applies only for selling short the stocks in the spot index.

Figure 13.4. Daily Dividend Yield, NSA Index

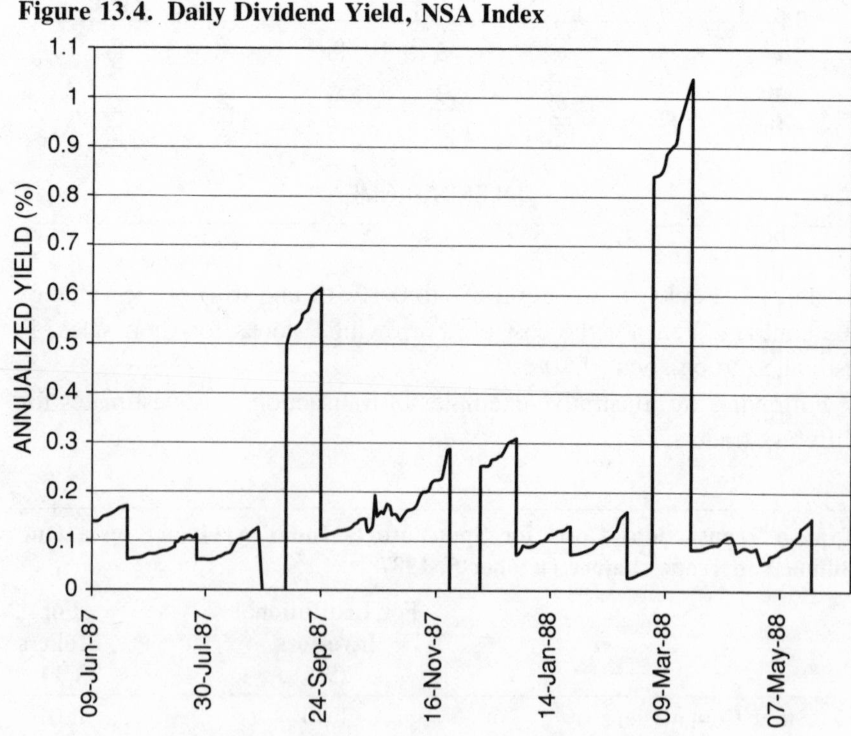

It is obvious that brokers' costs are significantly less than those of other investors. In summary, the total transactions costs can be estimated to be in the range 1%–1.25% for brokers and 2.5%–3% for institutional investors. The analysis in the following section is conducted from the view point of brokers, the arbitrageurs with lower transactions costs.[11]

IV. Methodology And Results

In the second section of this paper, we derived the relationship that should exist between the value of a stock index and the futures contract on the index in an arbitrage-free market. In the absence of transactions costs and without restrictions on short sales, the relationship is given by Equation (13.4). Any deviation from this relationship could be attributed to mispricing, but could also arise from measurement errors, due mainly to nonsimultaneity of transactions in the spot and futures markets. This source of error was examined by using time-stamped futures prices that closely match the closing value of the Nikkei index. In the case of time-stamped data, these short-term aberrations due to measurement errors are small, and cannot be systematic. Since both positive and negative deviations could be construed as mispricing, the mean deviation is not a meaningful statistic.[12] However, a transformation of the negative and positive deviations, such as the squared deviation (or the absolute value), may be a good indicator of mispricing.

In this study, we use the two statistics discussed in Equations (13.6a) and (13.6b) to measure the extent of mispricing. The first statistic is the percentage premium or discount as measured by M in Equation (13.6a). The second one is the implied rate of interest, R, that would be earned by constructing a portfolio consisting of the index and the futures contract as in Equation (13.6b). This implied rate is contrasted with the Gensaki rate.

As in the case of the U.S. markets, there is a 15–minute delay between the time the spot market closes and the time the futures market closes and the settlement price is determined, in the case of the NSA contract. There is no time delay between the closing spot index and the settlement price of the futures contract for the OSF50. In the case of the NSA index, we also examined an alternative set of data based on matched (i.e., synchronous) prices in both markets at the close of trading in Tokyo (on a weekday, 2 P.M., Singapore time or 3 P.M., Tokyo time and on trading

Saturdays, 10 A.M., Singapore time or 11 A.M., Tokyo time).[13] This data was available on the NSA futures contract for a limited period of time (the first three contracts are included).

The deviations based on the two sets of data for the SIMEX NSA contract are presented in Tables 13.2 and 13.3 and in Figures 13.5 and 13.6. Several interesting observations can be made based on these figures. First, there are many deviations and some are rather large. Second, the negative deviations are more common and larger than the positive ones. Third, deviations in either direction tend to persist for many days. This rules out the possibility that the mispricing detected is due to nonsimultaneity of the price data. In Tables 13.2 and 13.3, we provide some statistics on the extent of these deviations, for the whole sample and for each contract expiration respectively.

We now examine each of the tables in detail. In Table 13.2, out of 163 observations for the first three contracts, negative deviations are observed on 102 days with the largest deviations arising during the first three months of the first contract (September 1986 to December 1986). The average absolute deviation for the first contract was 1.54%, which includes mean positive deviations that are only less than one-third of the mean negative deviations. The magnitude of the deviations, both positive and negative, declined substantially during the second contract. The means were about 0.42% for the positive as well as the negative deviations. In the third contract, the deviations increased in size—the mean absolute deviation rose to 1.12%. There was a dominance of negative deviations throughout the period, however. The average negative deviation for the first three contracts is about 1.4% with some deviations being larger than 4.0%, which is larger than our estimate of transactions costs.[14] One explanation may be related to the issue of short selling. As discussed in Section II (in Cases 2 and 3), constraints on short selling place a smaller lower bound on the futures-spot relationship, that is, the futures may have to decline relative to its theoretical value by a substantial amount before an arbitrage opportunity arises. Indeed, if short sales are prohibited, there is no lower bound as stated in the discussion of Case 2 in Section II.[15] As the market matures and more participants realize that long positions in the market, like index funds, could be substituted by "cheaper" futures positions, we should find that most of the large discounts disappear as in the case of the U.S. markets.

Another possible explanation for the discounts observed in 86–87 is

Table 13.2. Summary Statistics of Premiums and Discounts SIMEX NSA Contract (Closing Cash vs. Settlement Futures Prices)

Contract	Number Positive	Number Negative	Mean Positive (%)	Mean Negative (%)	Mean Absolute (%)	Mean M^2 (%)	Number Obs.
DEC. 86	15	48	0.577	−1.845	1.543	4.082	63
MAR. 87	32	15	0.416	−0.423	0.418	0.267	47
JUN. 87	14	39	0.935	−1.185	1.119	1.711	53

Table 13.3. Summary Statistics of Premiums and Discounts SIMEX NSA Contract (Closing Cash vs. 3 P.M. Futures Prices)

Contract	Number Positive	Number Negative	Mean Positive (%)	Mean Negative (%)	Mean Absolute (%)	Mean M^2 (%)	Number Obs.
DEC. 86	17	46	0.509	−1.954	1.564	4.168	63
MAR. 87	31	16	0.470	−0.427	0.455	0.307	47
JUN. 87	14	39	0.838	−1.208	1.110	1.753	53

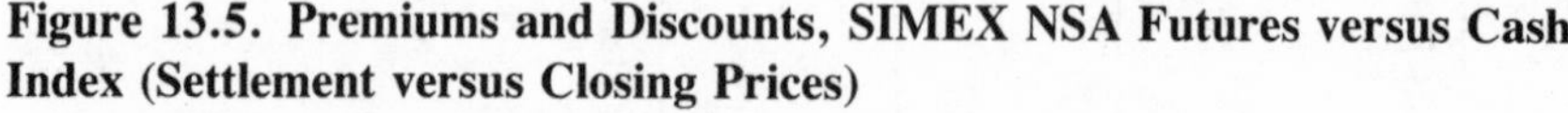

Figure 13.5. Premiums and Discounts, SIMEX NSA Futures versus Cash Index (Settlement versus Closing Prices)

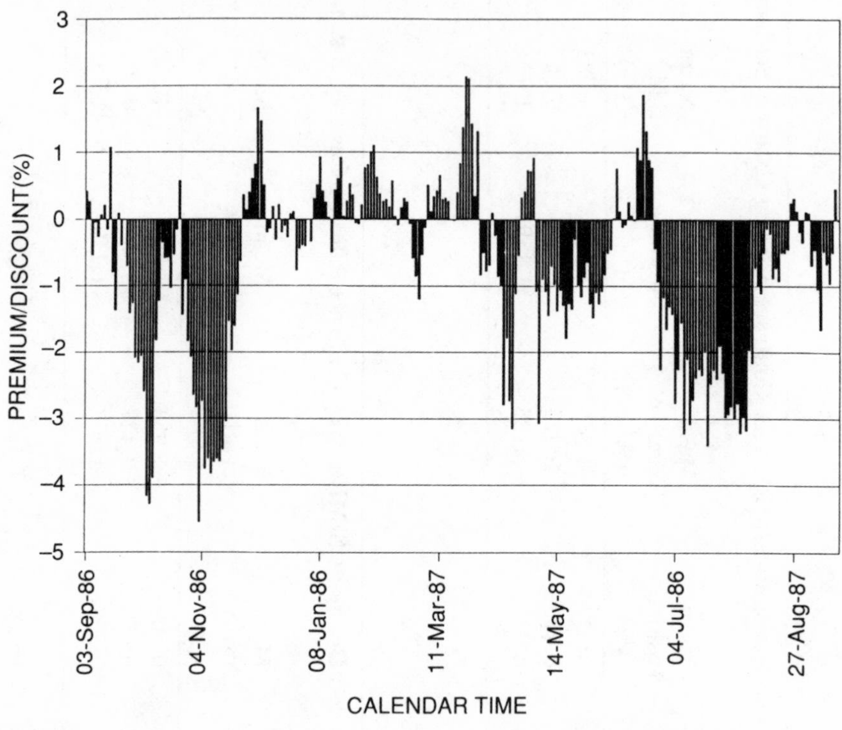

the prevalence of regulatory constraints on the participation of some financial institutions in the NSA futures market. Until December 1986, U.S. financial institutions were not permitted by the CFTC to trade the NSA futures contract. Further, U.S. financial institutions were allowed to become members of the TSE only in early 1986. It was as recently as May 1987 that the Japanese Ministry of Finance permitted Japanese financial institutions to trade financial futures contracts abroad. In some cases, the specific permissions were delayed until three months later.[16] This meant that entities like index funds could not easily engage in the arbitrage transaction when the futures were at a discount. The arbitrage operations may also have been hindered by the difficulty in "borrowing" stocks from institutions such as mutual funds and pension funds, since some of these investors are prohibited from "lending" their stocks.

Table 13.3 and Figure 13.6 show the percentage premium and dis-

Figure 13.6. Premiums and Discounts, SIMEX NSA Futures versus Cash Index (3 P.M. Index Value)

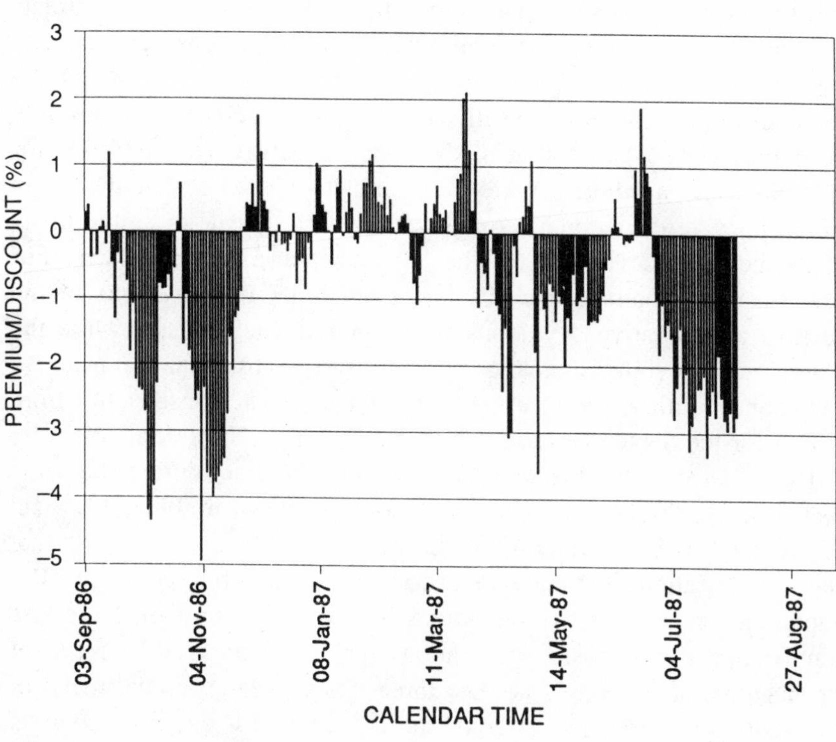

counts using the 3 P.M. futures prices. The results are essentially the same as in Table 13.2 and Figure 13.5, respectively, except that the discounts are slightly larger. Since the differences between settlement prices and 3 P.M. prices are so small, we believe that an analysis based on settlement prices is not affected by the difference in the close of trading for the NSA contract. Our analysis for the subsequent period is, therefore, based on settlement prices of the futures contracts.

We analyzed next the more recent period from June 1987 to June 1988.[17] This second year of futures trading on SIMEX happens also to be the first year of futures trading on the OSE in Osaka. We, therefore, analyze and compare the results in the two markets. In this analysis, we also take into account the transactions costs in both markets.

The prices used for the indices are the Tokyo Stock Exchange (TSE) prices, the largest and deepest cash market in Japan.[18] The evidence on the mispricing in the OSF50 contract in the absence of transactions costs is presented in Table 13.4 and graphically represented in Figure 13.7. Out of 272 observations, there are about 30% more positive than negative deviations—154 versus 118. The September and June contracts have more positive deviations while the December and March contracts have somewhat more negative deviations.[19] Turning to the size of the deviations, the mean of the positive deviations is much larger in absolute magnitude (1.03%) than that of the negative deviations (–0.77%), for the sample as a whole. A closer examination reveals that the mean of the positive deviations is roughly three times as large as the mean of the negative deviations for the September and June contracts. For the December contract, the absolute magnitudes of the means of the positive and negative deviations were approximately equal, while the March contract shows a smaller mean for the positive than the negative deviations. Further, the mean absolute deviation declines steadily from 1.31% for the September contract to 0.58% for the June contract.[20]

The pattern of the deviations for the NSA contract during the same period in the absence of transactions costs is shown in Table 13.5 and Figure 13.8. Unlike the OSF50 contract, the NSA contract shows that negative deviations dominate the observations for all four contracts. The importance of the negative deviations is accentuated by their large size compared with the positive deviations for all contracts. The mean of the negative deviations is at least three times as large as the mean of the positive deviations.[21] Overall, the deviations for the NSA contract are larger than for the OSF50 contract. For the sample as a whole, the mean absolute deviation is 1.22% for the NSA contract versus 0.92% for the OSF50 contract. Qualitatively, the results for the NSA contract are similar to those in the first nine months of the SIMEX (September 1986 to June 1987) discussed earlier, when large and negative deviations dominated the NSA market. It should be noted that, similar to the OSF50 market, the deviations in the NSA market declined in magnitude in the NSA marketover time. The mean absolute deviation fell from 1.48% to 0.47%, during the period under study. However, this is in contrast to the first year of the NSA contract, when no such trend is noticeable.

Tables 13.6 and 13.7 present the data on mispricing after adjusting for realistic transactions costs for brokers—0.75% before September 25 and 0.5% after September 25 for the OSF50 contract, and 1% for the NSA contract.[22] The deviations after taking transactions costs into account are plotted in Figures 13.9 and 13.10. The results indicate that a majority of

Table 13.4. Summary Statistics of Premiums and Discounts* OSF50 Futures Contract (Closing Cash vs. Settlement Futures Prices)

Contract	Number Positive	Number Negative	Mean Positive (%)	Mean Negative (%)	Mean Absolute (%)	Mean M^2 (%)	Number of Obs.
SEP. 87	40	32	1.83	−0.66	1.31	2.63	71
DEC. 87	30	37	0.94	−0.92	0.93	1.20	67
MAR. 88	30	35	0.68	−0.96	0.83	0.86	65
JUN. 88	54	14	0.67	−0.19	0.58	0.50	68
TOTAL	154	118	1.03	−0.77	0.92	1.32	272

*Cash Index calculated based on closing prices on the Tokyo Stock Exchange

Figure 13.7. Premiums and Discounts, OSF 50 Futures versus Cash Index

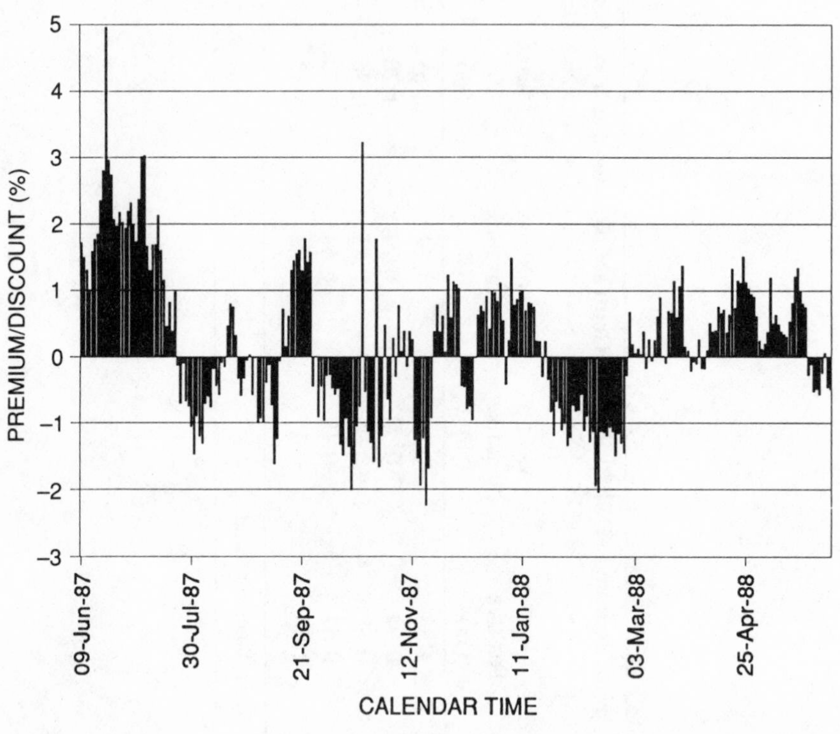

the deviations documented in Tables 13.4 and 13.5 are large enough to compensate for transactions costs. In the case of the OSF50 contract, 106 out of 154 positive deviations and 70 out of 118 negative deviations are outside the transactions costs bounds. In the case of the NSA contract, only 6 out of the 51 positive observations fall outside the transactions costs bounds against 110 out of the 211 negative deviations.

An interesting feature of the mispricing series, observed also in the U.S., is the persistence of the deviations, both positive and negative.[23] This path dependence shows up in the autocorrelation coefficients. The first-order coefficients are very high, between 0.64 and 0.89, and decline slowly.[24] One possible explanation for this persistence is the price discovery role of the stock index futures market in spite of the lack of arbitrage activity. In other words, even though the price of the futures

Table 13.5. Summary Statistics of Premiums and Discounts SIMEX NSA Futures Contract (Closing Cash vs. Settlement Futures Prices)

Contract	Number Positive	Number Negative	Mean Positive (%)	Mean Negative (%)	Mean Absolute (%)	Mean M^2 (%)	Number of Obs.
SEP. 87	18	52	0.76	−1.73	1.48	3.16	70
DEC. 87	8	58	0.41	−2.16	1.94	7.84	66
MAR. 88	4	58	0.20	−0.99	0.94	1.22	62
JUN. 88	21	43	0.17	−0.61	0.47	0.40	64
TOTAL	51	211	0.42	−1.41	1.22	3.21	262

Figure 13.8. Premiums and Discounts, SIMEX NSA Futures versus Cash Index

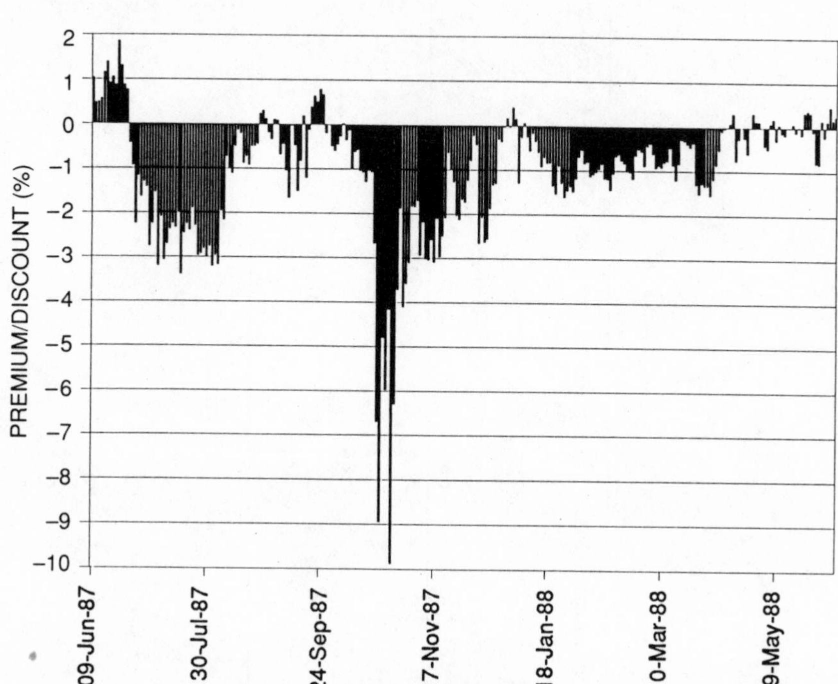

contract may deviate from its "fair" price, information affecting the spot market is speedily incorporated in the futures price, largely preserving the deviation on a day-to-day basis.

The data on mispricing can be looked at in a different manner as mentioned in Section II. Rather than measuring the mispricing as a deviation from the "fair" price, the interest rate implied by the market prices of the spot and futures contract can be computed and compared with the market interest rate. Taking into account the effect of transactions costs, the implied interest rate is given in Equation (13.6b). The implied interest rate on the stock index arbitrage in the two markets, when transactions costs are ignored, is plotted in Figures 13.11 and 13.12 respectively. These figures show clearly the large negative implied interest rates in the case of the NSA contract and the pattern of both large positive and negative implied interest rates for the OSF50 contract.

Table 13.6. Summary Statistics of Premiums and Discounts* with Transaction Cost OSF50 Futures Contract (Closing Cash vs. Settlement Futures Prices)**

Contract	Number Positive	Number Negative	Mean Positive (%)	Mean Negative (%)	Mean Absolute (%)	Mean M^2 (%)	Number of Obs.
SEP. 87	34	14	1.33	−0.29	0.69	1.16	48
DEC. 87	19	26	0.68	−0.68	0.46	0.45	45
MAR. 88	19	30	0.43	−0.55	0.38	0.27	49
JUN. 88	34	0	0.43	—	0.21	0.12	34
TOTAL	106	70	0.76	−0.55	0.44	0.51	176

*Cash Index calculated based on closing prices on the Tokyo Stock Exchange

**Transactions costs before and after September 25, 1987, are 0.75% and 0.5%, respectively.

Table 13.7. Summary Statistics of Premiums and Discounts with Transaction Cost* SIMEX NSA Futures Contract (Closing Cash vs. Settlement Futures Prices)

Contract	Number Positive	Number Negative	Mean Positive (%)	Mean Negative (%)	Mean Absolute (%)	Mean M^2 (%)	Number of Obs.
SEP. 87	6	35	0.30	−1.30	0.68	1.07	41
DEC. 87	0	41	—	−1.87	1.16	4.80	41
MAR. 88	0	26	—	−0.47	0.20	0.19	26
JUN. 88	0	8	—	−0.34	0.04	0.02	8
TOTAL	6	110	0.30	−1.25	0.53	1.55	116

*Transactions costs are 1%.

Figure 13.9. Premiums and Discounts with Transactions Costs, OSF 50 Futures versus Cash Index

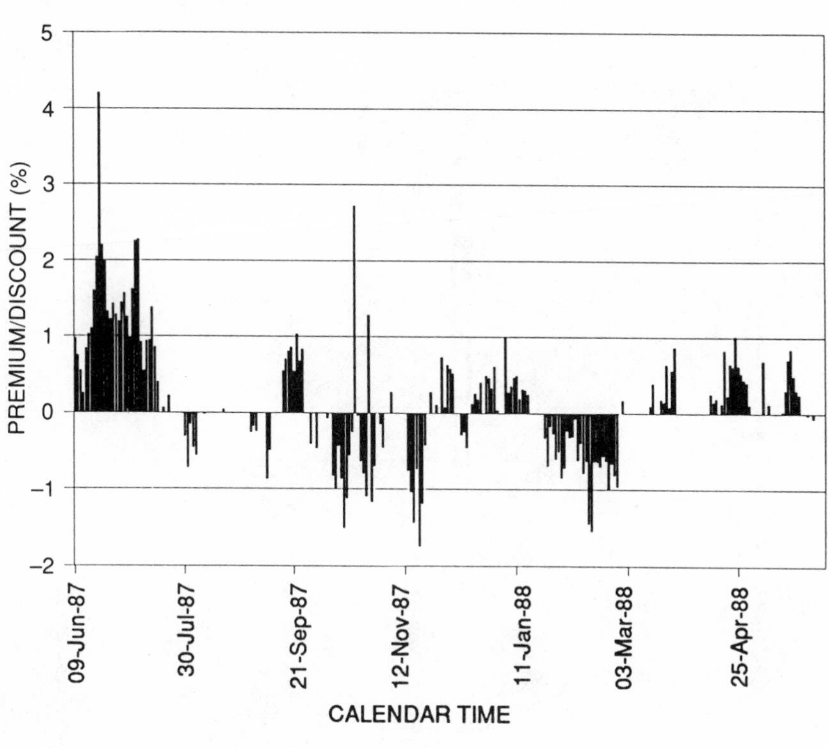

V. Summary and Conclusions

The persistent underpricing of stock index futures contracts in relation to their "fair" price in the early years of trading has been documented in many markets, in particular in the United States. The first year of trading in the NSA contract on SIMEX exhibited a similar pattern. However, the size of these negative deviations shows a downward trend in the second year.

Several general conclusions can be drawn from the analysis of the data for the two contracts in 1987–1988. First, there are large deviations from the "fair price" in the case of both the OSF50 and NSA stock index futures markets. Many of these deviations are large enough to compensate for realistic estimates of costs for traders with the lowest transactions costs. Second, in terms of magnitude, there are more large

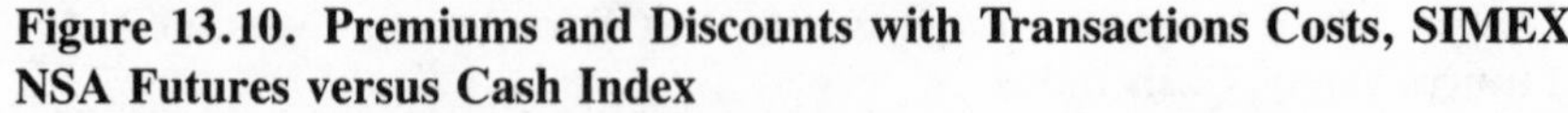

Figure 13.10. Premiums and Discounts with Transactions Costs, SIMEX NSA Futures versus Cash Index

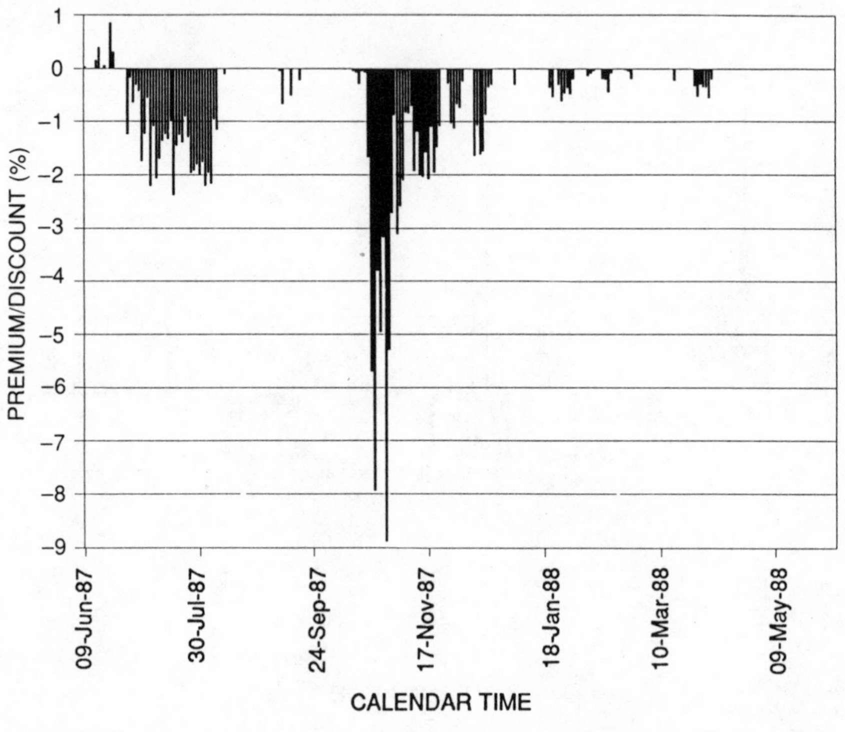

positive deviations than negative ones, in the case of the OSF50 contract. Positive deviations were somewhat more frequent also. In contrast, negative deviations are much more frequent, accounting for virtually all the mispricing, for the NSA market.

There are two major reasons for the deviations from "fair price" in these two index futures markets—transactions costs and restrictions on trading. Although these two sources of deviations are common to many markets, they are particularly important in the Japanese markets. Restrictions on trading, particularly relating to selling stocks short, are important impediments to the arbitrage process in the Japanese market. Trading restrictions are compounded by the cost and difficulty involved in borrowing stock for short sales. Other restrictions include restrictions placed on U.S. and Japanese financial institutions on participating in the Japanese stock index futures markets in the early period of trading.

Figure 13.11. Implied Interest Rate, OSF 50 Futures versus Cash Index

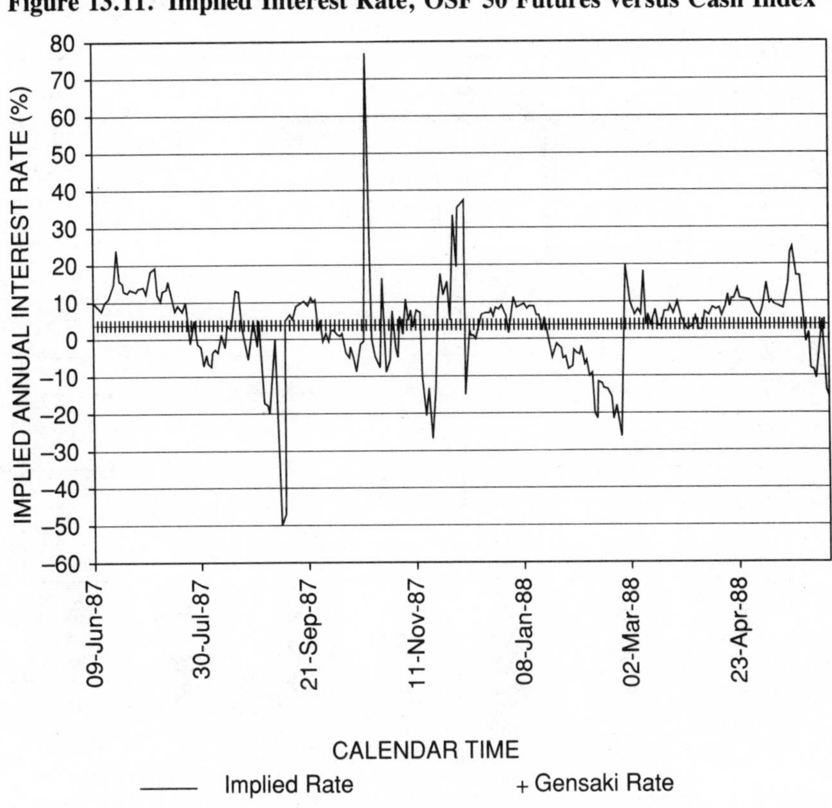

The decrease in the size of the absolute deviations over time, is indirect evidence that the transaction costs, and restrictions are less inhibiting than they were in the early months of trading in the NSA contract.

It is instructive to compare our results with those from research on U.S. markets. Stock index futures contracts in the United States have been trading now for over seven years. In general, mispricing has not disappeared in the U.S. markets, but the magnitudes have diminished substantially from the early days. Mispricing is less persistent and negative mispricing is not as common as it used to be. In contrast, the "younger" Japanese futures contracts exhibit behavior similar to that of the U.S. markets in the first few years. While it is tempting to argue that some of the mispricing is common to any new market, it is instructive to note some differences in trading practices between the two markets.

Figure 13.12. Implied Interest Rate, SIMEX NSA Futures versus Cash Index

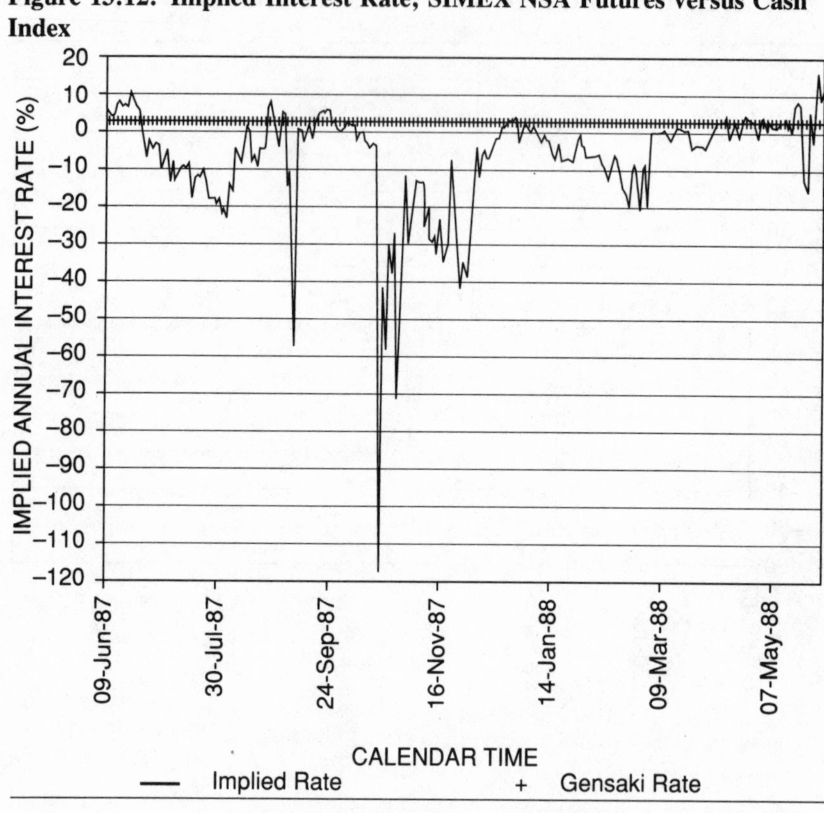

Restrictions on trading and execution risk are more important in the Tokyo Stock Exchange than in the New York Stock Exchange (NYSE). This may add to the "cushion" required to engage in the arbitrage. It is possible that the observed mispricing is reduced, if not eliminated, when this "cushion" is factored into the calculations.

An important aspect of execution risk is the speed with which transactions can be carried out. The speed of execution on the NYSE is greater than on the TSE due, among other reasons, to the "DOT" system (a 200 stock basket will take about five minutes to execute, and less if it qualifies for "Super DOT" execution). These capabilities do not yet exist on the TSE. Another important feature affecting execution risk and transactions costs has to do with the costs of closing a position on expiration. While there are no costs in closing a position, at expiration, on the NYSE, the costs on the TSE are the same as in opening a position. The difference is a result of a different trading system on both exchanges. A Market-on-Close (MOC) order on the NYSE eliminates the market impact cost at the expiration of the futures contract. Also, the arrangement between large institutional traders and the specialist not to be charged on MOC orders eliminates the commissions. On the TSE, where there is no specialist, there is no guarantee that a MOC order will actually be filled. Further, commissions are not waived on MOC orders. Analysis of transactions data may shed additional light on the effect of these institutional differences on stock index arbitrage.

The results of this study and others in U.S. markets may be interpreted in the context of the market efficiency hypothesis. Unlike many other tests of efficiency in financial markets, arbitrage-based tests do not require assumptions about the preferences of investors. In that sense, tests based, for example, on covered interest rate parity, put-call option, parity and futures-spot arbitrage are based on weaker assumptions. Hence, the evidence of profit opportunities in an arbitrage context raises stronger doubts about market efficiency.

Notes

1. Two major stock index futures contracts were introduced in 1988, another contract based on the NSA on the OSE and one based on the Tokyo Stock Price Index (TOPIX) on the Tokyo Stock Exchange (TSE).
2. The price of a futures contract is, in general, different from that of a forward contract on the same asset for the same maturity. However, in a world of nonstochastic short-term interest rates, there is no difference between the two prices. [See, for example, Cox, Ingersoll, and Ross (1981)]. There is some empirical support for the proposition that the difference between the two prices, which is due to the risk of being marked-to-market, is negligible. [See, for example, Cornell and Reinganum (1981), and Elton, Gruber, and Rentzler (1984)]. This may be due to the fact that uncertainty in the overnight interest rate over, say, a three-month horizon is negligible compared to uncertainty in the spot price, for most risky assets, over the same horizon.
3. In this case, too, we assume that holders of stocks cannot substitute them for futures contracts.
4. We ignore the time value effects in the computation of the total transactions costs, that is, we assume that all transactions costs are paid at the time the first trade is put on. We also neglect the small differences between proportions of S_t and S_T as a second-order effect.

5. See Cornell and French (1983) and Figlewski (1984) for a discussion on tax-induced effects in the pricing of stock index futures. In Japan, capital gains are exempt from taxes but for professional arbitrageurs (e.g., financial institutions), all profits are taxed at the same rate, and hence, there are no relative pricing effects caused due to differential taxation of income versus capital gains.
6. There is a difference between the transactions costs incurred in the two transactions, due to the cost of "borrowing" the stocks when they are to be sold short.
7. Since May 23, 1987, SIMEX also traded on the first, fourth, and the fifth (if there is one) Saturdays of each month, from 8 A.M. to 10:15 A.M., Singapore time. In general, both markets observe the same holidays although there are some exceptions. In the analysis that follows, we drop days when one or other of the two markets is closed.
8. In late 1988, with the introduction of cash settled futures contracts in Japan, the volume of the OSF50 declined dramatically.
9. The Gensaki rate used in the analysis is the average bid for the day, calculated at 10 A.M. (Tokyo time). There is no Gensaki rate available on Saturdays. In the case of trading on Saturdays, the Gensaki rate for Friday is used as the risk-free rate.
10. These rates were lowered on October 5, 1987.
11. This analysis does not take into account "tracking error," which arises due to the fact that the basket of stocks chosen may not perfectly match the cash index.
12. The mean deviation will, by definition, provide a statistic that is smaller than the actual mispricing, either positive or negative, that has occurred.
13. Our hypothesis, based on a somewhat casual examination of the data, suggests that this lack of synchronization is likely to be less serious for the Japanese data, since the NSA index is often being revised even after eight minutes beyond the close of trading in Tokyo. These revisions may be attributed to heavy order flow around the time of closing and the inability of the data processing system to reflect trades immediately in the quotations, and hence, in the index.
14. Such large discounts were also observed in the early days of the U.S. markets. See, for example, Figlewski (1984) and Modest and Sundaresan (1983).
15. Again, this assumes that the arbitrageurs in these markets do not start out with long positions in the spot, so that the short sales constraint becomes binding.
16. International subsidiaries of these financial institutions, especially those based in tax havens, had fewer constraints on their futures transactions.
17. Some of the tables and graphs used in the following few pages appeared

previously in Brenner, Subrahmanyam, and Uno (1989b). These are reproduced by permission of the publishers.

18. We also performed the analysis using the cash prices based on OSE for the OSF50 index and found that the results are virtually identical.
19. When the data for the June contract are broken into two subperiods, before and after stock exchange fees for futures trading were reduced on September 25, 1987, the first subperiod of the second contract had a preponderance of positive deviations similar to the first contract.
20. For the December contract, we excluded the data for October 20, since the stock market and OSF50 futures market stopped trading due to the triggering of price limits. The large positive deviation observed on that day in closing prices is due to the fact that the futures market stopped at a 3% limit down while the stock market stopped at roughly 15% down on the index. (Price limits on the TSE differ from stock to stock based on the price of the stock). Since the NSA futures on SIMEX had no price limits at that time, the futures declined to a much lower level, and therefore, show a large negative deviation.
21. Since the week after October 19 was very volatile and many stocks in Japan stopped trading on several occasions due to price limits, arbitrage activity became very risky. This may explain the large deviations during this period. When the seven trading days after October 19 are excluded from the sample, the mean negative deviation for the December 1987 contract declined substantially from –2.16% to –1.54% and the mean absolute deviations declined from 1.94% to 1.38%. Our general conclusions remain unaffected, however. The mean negative deviation, for the sample as a whole, is still about three times as large as the mean positive deviation—−1.23% versus 0.42%.
22. The stock exchange fee on futures trading on the OSE was reduced on September 25, 1987. The stock brokerage commissions were reduced on October 5, 1987, but this did not affect the transactions costs for brokers.
23. See, for example, MacKinlay and Ramaswamy (1988).
24. For details, see Brenner, Subrahmanyam, and Uno [(1989a) and (1989b)].

References

Brenner, M., M. G. Subrahmanyam, and J. Uno, (1989). "The Behavior of Prices in the Nikkei Spot and Futures Markets," *Journal of Financial Economics*, forthcoming.

Brenner, M., M. G. Subrahmanyam, and J. Uno, (1989). "Stock Index-Futures Arbitrage in the Japanese Markets," *Japan and the World Economy*, forthcoming.

Cornell, B., and K. R. French, (1983). "Taxes and the Pricing of Stock Index Futures," *Journal of Finance*, Vol. 38, June, pp. 675–694.

Cornell B., and M. Reinganum, (1981). "Forward and Futures Prices: Evidence from the Foreign Exchange Markets," *Journal of Finance*, Vol. 36, December, pp. 1035–1045.

Cox, J. C., J. E. Ingersoll, and S. A. Ross, (1981). "The Relation between Forward Prices and Futures Prices," *Journal of Finance Economics*, Vol. 9, December, pp. 321–346.

Elton, E. J., M. J. Gruber, and J. Rentzler, (1984). "Intra-day Tests of the Efficiency of the Treasury Bill Futures Market," *The Review of Economics and Statistics*, Vol. 46, February, pp. 129–137.

Figlewski, S., (1984). "Explaining the Early Discounts on Stock Index Futures: The Case for Disequilibrium," *Financial Analysts Journal*, Vol. 40, July–August, pp. 43–47.

MacKinlay, A., and K. Ramaswamy, (1988). "Index Futures Arbitrage and the Behavior of Stock Index Futures Prices," *Review of Financial Studies*, Vol. 1, Summer, pp. 137–158.

Modest, D. M., and M. Sundaresan, (1983). "The Relationship Between Spot and Futures Prices in Stock Index Futures Markets: Some Preliminary Evidence," *Journal of Futures Markets*, Vol. 3, Spring, pp. 15–41.

PART V

Mergers

14

The Market for Corporate Control, the Level of Agency Costs, and Corporate Collectivism in Japanese Mergers

Richard H. Pettway
University of Missouri-Columbia

Neil W. Sicherman
University of South Carolina

Takeshi Yamada
Hosei University, Tokyo

I. Introduction

There are major differences in the cultural and managerial environments between Japanese and American firms. Japanese business operates with lifetime employment, restricted labor mobility, seniority promotions, company unions, and corporate collectivism, whereby extensive mutual holdings of equity among affiliated firms reduces the ability of outside and independent shareholders to influence the decisions of managers. It is often said that Japanese firms are operated more for the benefit of managers and employees than for stockholders. Studies of Japanese managers find that they do not give high priority to maximization of shareholders' wealth. Under such conditions, there may be larger agency costs in Japanese mergers.

There is a potential for higher agency cost, or what Jensen and Meckling (1976) call "residual loss," in Japan than in the United States. With job security resulting from lifetime employment, seniority-based promotions, and little change of an employer during a career, Japanese managers face less *ex post* "settling up" constraints. Since stock option plans for managers are extremely rare in Japan, there are fewer bonding activities using this technique. Finally, because of large mutual holdings of stock among affiliated businesses and few independent stockholders, there are fewer monitoring activities in Japan. This reciprocal business ownership of shares is often called "corporate collectivism" in Japan. Most firms choose to operate with others in groups. Large reciprocal business ownership significantly reduces the role and influence of independent, outside investors on managerial decisions. This reduced role of independent outsiders may impact the competitiveness of the Japanese merger market. Thus, with fewer monitoring and bonding activities and fewer possibilities for *ex post* settling up constraints, there is a higher potential for agency cost in Japan than in the United States. Perhaps these differences explain the dissimilarities between the markets for corporate control in the United States versus Japan. The U.S. merger market is vast and very competitive, with many friendly as well as hostile takeovers.[1] The Japanese market is much smaller with almost exclusively friendly mergers, and most mergers take place as an exchange of shares.

Clearly, there are many cultural and business differences that may cause Japanese combinations to have different effects on shareholder's wealth than American mergers.[2] The objective of this paper is to determine the impact of Japanese mergers on shareholder's wealth, compare them with U.S. corporate combinations that take place in a competitive market, and deduce if there are larger agency costs in Japanese mergers than in U.S. mergers.

II. The Market for Corporate Control in Japan

In order to compare the financial effects of Japanese mergers with American mergers, it is necessary to understand the nature of Japanese business practices and mergers in particular. First, it is important to realize that many business firms in Japan operate within groups of affiliated firms. There are many interrelated activities among companies, very commonly including mutual stock ownership. Many companies persuade banks and other companies to buy and hold their shares to form and solidify a business relationship. This use of interrelated groups is called "corporate collectivism." Shimizu (1980) reports that of 894 firms he surveyed, 90% owned shares of other firms in the same affiliated group. As evidence of this "corporate collectivism," the Tokyo Stock Exchange reports that individual investor ownership had declined from 61.3% in 1950 to 20.1% in 1987 while shares owned by business corporations, securities companies, and financial institutions rose to 74% of all listed shares.[3] Nishiyama (1984) states that of the 78 largest nonbank Japanese firms in 1978, 61 firms had over three-quarters of their total shares held by financial institutions, primarily life insurance companies and to a lesser degree commercial banks. He argues that "management workers" control firms as shareholders do not provide any element of control due to the lack of stockholder leadership. This lack of leadership, for example, is because of the mutual form of the large life insurance companies that own a majority of the stock of large Japanese firms. He said, "Stockholders obviously are neither controllers nor owners. . . They are creditors who own claims on corporate dividends and thus resemble bond holders or loan creditors."

Interrelated groups of firms with mutual stock ownership is one of the most prevalent forms of business in post-war Japan. These combinations of affiliated companies within a group is what Franko (1983) and others call a *keiretsu*. Within a keiretsu there are wholly owned subsidiaries as well as various degrees of mutual stock ownership. Four types of ownership relationships among nonsubsidiary group members exist. First is what Ballon, Tomita, and Usami (1976), BTU, call *oya-ko*, or parent-child relationship of related companies. The definition of an affiliated company is where more than 50% of the shares of the child are owned by the parent company. Next is the *kanren gaisha*, or related companies, whose shares are owned from 20% to 50% by another company. Third are companies owned as an investment by another company, but not affiliated. Finally, firms could be customers and/or subcontractors, but not affiliated through stock ownership.

Japanese mergers present difficult organizational and human capital problems and perhaps for these reasons there are fewer mergers in Japan than in the United States. When expanding into a new or related field, Japanese businessmen prefer to form semiautonomous interrelated companies rather than purchase existing companies. A third party intermediary is often required for acquisitions to be effective. In fact, business marriages or *gappei* are often arranged by third parties. Usually the principal bank is the intermediary, although other important parties have been government and business leaders. BTU state that the acquiring firm rarely takes the initiative in mergers. Often the acquired firm will seek business or financial assistance from the acquiring company. Thus, a third party often is required to approach the acquiring firm.

The Japanese market for corporate control has not had many hostile or unfriendly takeovers. Perhaps because of the necessity of an intermediary, takeover mergers are rare in Japan. It is possible for a company to quietly accumulate some shares of the target firm without its approval, but it is far less popular and generally abhorrent to the public.[4] None of the mergers in this study were of the takeover type. Japanese mergers tend to be friendly, using an exchange of shares rather than a cash purchase, which is often used in U.S. mergers.

In any comparison of the financial performance of Japanese firms with American firms, it is important to realize that there are major differences in the managerial objectives between the two countries. Sato and Hoshino (1984) state that the reason for company unions being rather cooperative toward management in Japanese firms is "fundamentally because both management and labor believe that the company belongs to them, not to shareholders." Kagono, Nonaka, Sakakibara, and Okumura (1984) report from a questionnaire survey of 291 Japanese industrial firms listed on the Tokyo Stock Exchange and of 227 U.S. firms listed in *Fortune's* top 1000 industrial firms that the management objectives were very different between Japanese and American firms. In Japan, increasing the market share and return on investment were the top two of nine goals. Increasing the firm's share price was the lowest or last objective listed by Japanese managers. U.S. managers listed return on investment and increasing the share price as the top objectives. Suto (1981) classified managerial goals into two broad categories: stockholder's objectives and manager's objectives. She describes that not all goals of Japanese mergers satisfy the stockholder's objective of wealth maximization.

Shimizu (1980) examined the managers of 894 Japanese firms and found that no company stated that increasing its share price was most important, and only 0.2% said that it was the second most important objective of a firm's management. He reports that the financial factors influencing top management are: the rate of sales growth, profits, the profit/sales ratio, and the profit/equity ratio. Other factors such as the debt/equity ratio, the current ratio, stock prices, and dividend rates were not considered as important. It is interesting that not much importance is given by Japanese managers to stock prices and dividend rates, since this is contrary to the hypothesis common in the United States that managers should maximize the share price. Shimizu states, "In the United States, firms are managed from the standpoint of maximizing the interests of the stockholders, while in Japan the viewpoint is that of survival and growth of the firms themselves."

In Japanese firms, protecting their access to future loanable funds is often said to be more important than stockholder's wealth maximization. Aoki (1984b) reported that the primary group to be satisfied by Japanese firms is not always shareholders, but is often the bank. He found many activities of Japanese firms were inconsistent with the singular objective of shareholder wealth maximization. Japanese firms tend to have very high, by American standards, ratios of book-value financial leverage before adjustments.[5] Because of these large debt ratios, Japanese managers find it essential to maintain their ability to borrow to avoid economic disaster. Often bankruptcies of large firms are directly affiliated to the withdrawal of lending support by the firm's major bank.[6]

In a study of Japanese business groupings, Nakatani (1984) found that corporate groups maximized the joint utility of its corporate constituents: management, employees, financial institutions, and stock holders. He reported that as groups of affiliated companies grew in size they had higher financial leverage, lower profit, lower dividend payouts, lower risks, but much higher salaries for management and employees. The establishment of groups of affiliated companies with reciprocal shareholding reduces the "employment risk" of managers, isolates the management from takeover bids, and insulates the groups of firms from the threat of competition in capital markets. He confirms that Japanese reciprocal stock ownership groups operate more in management's interests rather than in maximizing the independent shareholder's wealth.

Itami, Kagono, Yoshihara, and Sakuma (1984) found in a study of 112 Japanese diversifying companies that there were declining benefits, to diversification in terms of profitability, after the size of the group of affiliated companies became medium sized. Any increase in diversification of large groups led to a reduction in profitability, which is also similar to the findings of Nakatani. There has been much discussion about Japanese companies being operated primarily for the management, employees, and the lead bank rather than for the firm's stockholders, therefore, implying the possibility of higher agency cost or residual loss in Japanese mergers.

There have been a few other studies of Japanese mergers. Suto (1981) analyzed the effects of Japanese mergers around the effective date using monthly data over a long test period and found that mergers had little impact on shareholders' wealth. Hoshino (1982, 1983, 1984) studied the accounting performance and other financial characteristics of Japanese firms that merged compared to unmerged firms. Generally, he found an adverse effect in accounting and financial ratios from merger as the group of companies that merged have poorer financial ratio performance than nonmerging firms. Pettway and Yamada (1986) studied the impacts of Japanese mergers on stockholders' wealth from 1977 through 1984 and found that the market for Japanese mergers was efficient and competitive, and that the acquiring firms' shareholders had positive but insignificant gains from the mergers. On the other hand, the acquired firms' shareholders had significantly positive returns, but they were smaller than returns for U.S. selling firms.

In sum, there are differences in the market for corporate control in Japan versus in the United States. These differences include the limited role of outside independent investors in monitoring managerial actions and stated managerial objectives that do not place shareholder's wealth maximization very high. This, coupled with a propensity to merge under friendly conditions, suggests an obvious potential for Japanese management to benefit at the expense of their shareholders. Further, in Japan potential selling firms tend to initiate the merger transaction through intermediary third parties, suggesting that the merger market may be less competitive in Japan than in the United States.

The purpose of this paper is to measure the impact of Japanese mergers on shareholder's wealth with emphasis on determining the effects of those characteristics that appear to be different in Japan versus the United States. Specifically, the impacts of corporate collectivism and shareholder-manager conflicts on market competitiveness and agency costs will be examined.

III. Research Design

Data

The decade from January 1, 1977, through December 31, 1986, was selected to study Japanese mergers. During this 10-year period, as the data in Table 14.1 indicate, there were 201 mergers involving nonfinancial firms in Japan, but only 88 acquiring firms were listed on the Tokyo Stock Exchange and had exchange ratios between the two firms at the date of the merger.[7]

For these 88 mergers, exchange ratios, places of listing, relative size ratios, the announcement dates (AD), and the effective dates (ED) of each merger were obtained. For the 88 mergers that had exchange

Table 14.1. Nonfinancial Mergers of Listed Companies

Categories	1977	1978	1979	1980	1981	1982	1983	1984	1985	1986	Total	Final Test Sample
Total Number of Acquiring Firms	17	20	15	15	20	22	30	18	21	23	201	
Mergers with Exchange Ratios and Listed on Major Exchange	8	11	7	3	8	9	12	7	13	10	88	72
Affiliated Listed Companies Mergers	1	4	3	1	5	5	5	4	5	5	38	28
Unaffiliated or Independent Listed Companies	7	7	4	2	3	4	7	3	8	5	50	44

Source: *Corporate Mergers*, Tokyo, Tokyo Stock Exchange, Various dates.

ratios, the financial statements for the period just prior to the merger announcement were analyzed to determine what was the nature of the relationship between the two firms.

Of these 88 mergers of listed companies, 38 were between companies that were affiliated[8] and 50 of these mergers were between firms where the acquiring firm owned less than 20% of the outstanding shares of the acquired firms before the merger. Thus, as is indicated in Table 14.1, 50 mergers were identified as the set of independent firms and are the most similar to U.S. mergers.[9]

To avoid bias due to reduced or limited trading, all acquiring firms that had trades on fewer than 90 business dates during the 180 day base period were omitted, as were firms without at least 70 days between the AD and ED. These omissions, mostly for inadequate trading, eliminated 16 mergers (6 independent acquisitions and 10 affiliated acquisitions) from the overall group of 88 total acquiring firms; therefore, the final test sample of 72 acquiring firms was selected as noted in Table 14.1. Thus, the final sample of 44 independent acquisitions and 28 affiliated acquisitions was analyzed.

Methodology

Daily holding period returns of all listed acquiring firms were gathered form 210 business days before the AD through 30 business days after the ED.[10] Since the period between the AD and ED was not constant across firms, the length of the data in each company array of returns is firm and merger specific. These return data were analyzed during the 180 day base period that began 210 days before and ended 30 days before the AD. The popular market model Equation (14.1) developed by Sharpe (1963) and later refined and expanded by Sharpe (1964), Lintner (1965), and others asserts that

$$R_{i,t} = \alpha_i + \beta_i R_{m,t} + e_{i,t} \tag{14.1}$$

where $R_{i,t}$ is the daily return of the acquiring firm i at time t; $R_{m,t}$ is the daily return at time t of the market index, the Tokyo Stock Exchange Price Index;[11] α_i and β_i are the estimated parameters of the market model; and $e_{i,t}$ is the error term of the model.

During the test period, which began 30 days before the AD and continued until 30 days after the ED, the residuals for each firm, $u_{i,t}$, were obtained using Equation (14.2).

$$u_{i,t} = R_{i,t} - [\alpha_i + \beta_i R_{m,t}] \tag{14.2}$$

These daily residuals were averaged across firms around two centering dates, the AD and ED, using Equation (14.3). AR_t is the average abnormal return of N firms on a common date, t, relative to centering dates, AD and/or ED. These average abnormal returns were accumulated to day T using Equation (14.4) for various beginning and ending dates.

$$AR_t = \frac{\sum_{i=1}^{N} u_{i,t}}{N} \tag{14.3}$$

$$CAR_T = \sum_{t=1}^{T} AR_t \tag{14.4}$$

To interpret the movements in the cumulative abnormal returns (CARs), the period from 30 days before the AD to 30 days after the ED was divided into subperiods. The first subperiod was from 30 days prior to AD to AD. The second interval, the interim period, was from AD +1 to –1 ED. The next measurement period was form ED to ED +30. The CARs from these periods were summed for a total effect. Additionally, 7 day periods centering on AD and ED were used to determine announcement and consummation effects.

Hypotheses

Because of the lower levels of monitoring and bonding activities and a less developed secondary labor market, the potential agency cost in the market for corporate control appears to be higher in Japan than in the United States. If this is true, buying-firm shareholders will gain less in Japan than in the United States. First, the full sample of Japanese mergers will be examined for comparison with U.S. results. Next, Japanese mergers that are most similar to U.S. mergers, independent acquisitions, will be examined and compared to American combinations. Japanese corporate collectivism infers that acquisition markets may be less competitive in Japan than in the United States. Thus, the comparison of the changes in stockholders' wealth from U.S. mergers and Japanese mergers will offer insight into the competitiveness of the Japanese market for corporate control.

The role of corporate collectivism will be further examined by comparing Japanese mergers on the basis of the acquired firm's previous affiliation with the buyer. More competition would be expected for unaffiliated, independent selling firms. However, the existing relationship between buying-firm management and affiliated sellers suggests less than arms-length agreements in this type of merger, and buying-firm shareholders may perceive little benefit of acquiring the remaining shares of an existing keiretsu member. Further, Mikkelson and Ruback (1985) report, for United States mergers, that the announcement of the purchase of a firm in which the buyer already has an investment position yields significantly negative abnormal returns. If these results are applied to Japanese mergers, then it would imply that acquiring-firm shareholders will gain less, at announcement (i.e., a lower announcement effect), from the purchase of affiliated firms than from the purchase of independent firms. However, in a completely competitive market there should be no total overall difference in wealth impact between the two types of acquisitions measured from before the announcement past the consummation date.

In summary, this paper will measure the impact of Japanese mergers on acquiring-firm shareholders' wealth. The analysis will focus on the role of independence versus affiliated mergers to attempt to measure the impact of higher potential agency costs due to reduced monitoring and bonding activities in Japanese corporations.

IV. Results

Full Sample Analysis of Acquiring Firms

The abnormal returns (ARs), found in Table 14.2, column 2 indicate that there are only a few significant values around the AD for the entire sample of firms.[12] The CAR value for the 31 day period prior to and including the announcement is a significant 2.346%. The 7 day announcement effect CAR, from AD –3 to AD +3, is a highly significant 2.102%. This positive announcement effect indicates that investors initially perceived the merger as favorable.

The interim period is the time period between the announcement (AD) and the consummation of the merger (ED). Since this period is unique to each transaction, the average residual accumulation (among the 72 firms) between AD and ED was used as the CAR value for the interim period. More specifically, each firm's residuals were accumulated from AD +1

Table 14.2. Cumulative Abnormal Returns, Total Effect from 30 days before the Announcement Date to 30 days after the Effective Date (in percent)

(1) Day	(2) ARs for All 72 Firms	(3) CARs for All 72 Firms	(4) CARs for 44 Independent Mergers
−30	−0.293	−0.293	−0.044
−20	0.251	0.216	0.440
−10	−0.408*	−0.038	0.657
−5	0.250	0.666	1.562
−4	0.237	0.903	1.642
−3	0.629***	1.532	2.464*
−2	0.227	1.759	2.794*
−1	0.542**	2.301*	3.279**
AD	0.045	2.346*	3.672**
Announcement Effect		2.102***	2.860***
Interim Period		−1.220	−2.398
Consummation Effect		−0.171	1.752**
ED	−0.304	−0.304	0.050
+1	0.154	−0.150	0.456
+2	0.000	−0.150	0.889*
+3	−0.016	−0.165	1.086*
+4	−0.480	−0.646	0.491
+5	0.101	−0.545	0.151
+10	−0.258	−1.084	−0.575
+20	0.206	−1.913*	−1.326
+30	0.272	−1.444	−1.365
Total Effect		−0.318	−0.091

*Significant at the 0.10 level.

**Significant at the 0.05 level.

***Significant at the 0.01 level.

to –1 ED, summed, and then averaged across the 72 firms.[13] It is clear that the interim period reaction, with significant abnormal returns of –1.220%, is not as positive as the period prior to and including the AD. The 7 day consummation effect, from –3 ED to ED +3, is negative but insignificant. After the ED the cumulative abnormal returns of these 72 firms are negative and becomes significantly negative at ED +20.

To place all of these separate effects into perspective, an overall or total effect for all 72 mergers measured the movements in abnormal return from 30 days before the AD through 30 days after the ED. The total effect from before the AD until after the ED is a CAR of –0.318%[14] These results indicate that, overall, information about the merger has an insignificant effect on shareholders' wealth.[15] These findings are similar to the studies of American mergers, which show that acquiring firms have insignificant returns from merger activity.

Analysis of Independent Acquisitions

To concentrate on mergers of firms which are similar to U.S. mergers, we tested a subsample of 44 unaffiliated or independent mergers. Column 4 of Table 14.2 includes the CAR values for the four different effects. The 31 day period prior to and including announcement yields a significant CAR of 3.672%. The 7 day announcement effect CAR is a significant 2.860%. The interim period CAR is negative but insignificant. The 7 day consummation effect is significantly positive but CARs after ED are generally insignificant. Over the entire period from –30 until ED +30, the total effect is –0.091% and insignificant. Since there is no significant overall wealth impact, Japanese acquisitions of independent firms yield similar results as U.S. mergers.

The Japanese literature on management and mergers presented in the second section of this paper clearly indicates that there is a higher potential for agency costs and residual losses to stockholders in Japanese firms than in U.S. firms. Notice, however, that the results of Japanese merger activity are similar to the results of U.S. mergers. Thus, it must be concluded that the Japanese market for mergers is just as competitive as the U.S. market and that the potential for higher agency costs in Japan does not impact stockholders' wealth differently around mergers than in the United States. Thus, it appears that agency costs in Japanese mergers are not higher than in U.S. mergers.

Comparison of Full Sample, Independent, and Affiliated Acquisitions

Japanese acquiring firms clearly have less information about independent sellers than already affiliated selling firms. This asymmetry of information may yield differential results between these types of mergers. Further, outside shareholders have less information than acquiring firm management. Thus, shareholders may view the acquisition of an affiliated firm as something less than an arm's-length transaction. They may see less value to this type of acquisition than an independent merger since the affiliated acquisition is already controlled by the acquiring firm. In such cases, abnormal returns to buying firms should be higher for independent acquisitions than for affiliated mergers.

CAR values were tested for significant differences between the overall sample, 44 independent mergers, and 28 affiliated mergers. These results are shown in Table 14.3. The first line for each effect shows the comparison CAR values and their individual level of significance from zero. The second line shows the difference in CAR values between the groups and whether the difference in CAR values is significant. The third line shows the number of mergers in each comparison.

The comparisons in Table 14.3 indicate that there is a significant difference in announcement effect of independent mergers versus affiliated mergers, with greater abnormal gains for independent acquisitions than for affiliated acquisitions. The consummation effects are also significantly different and again they indicate that the gains to the acquiring firm's stockholders are larger from the purchase of independent firms compared to the purchase of affiliated firms. Note that none of the total effects are significant from zero and none are significantly different from each other. Thus, it appears that there are no significant overall differences between the results for all the firms in the sample, independent acquisitions, and affiliated acquisitions.

The results reported in column 4 of Table 14.3 are somewhat consistent with the hypothesis that buying-firm shareholders see little benefit in acquiring an existing keiretsu member. Cumulative abnormal returns from affiliated acquisitions tend to be negative, whereas the CARs for independent mergers tend to be zero or positive. The announcement effect from the purchase of an independent firm is significantly higher than the announcement effect from the purchase of an affiliated firm. This result is consistent with findings of Mikkelson and Ruback (1985) for U.S. mergers.

Table 14.3. CAR Values and Differences: The Comparison Between Affiliated Versus Independent Firm Mergers (in percent)

(1) Different Effects or Periods	(2) All Firms vs. Independent (# of Firms)	(3) All Firms vs. Affiliated (# of Firms)	(4) Independent vs. Affiliated (# of Firms)
Announcement Effect −3AD to AD+3	2.10^{+++} vs. 2.86^{+++} dif = 0.76 (72 vs. 44)	2.10^{+++} vs. 0.91 dif = 1.19 (72 vs. 28)	2.86^{+++} vs. 0.91 dif = 1.95^{*} (44 vs. 28)
Interim Effect AD+1 to −1ED	−1.22 vs. −2.40 dif = −1.18 (72 vs. 44)	−1.22 vs. 0.63 dif = −1.85 (72 vs. 28)	−2.40 vs. 0.63 dif = 3.03 (44 vs. 28)
Consummation Effect −3ED to ED+3	−0.17 vs. 1.75^{++} dif = -1.92^{**} (72 vs. 44)	−0.17 vs. -3.19^{+++} dif = 3.02^{**} (72 vs. 28)	1.75^{++} vs. -3.19^{+++} dif = 4.95^{***} (44 vs. 28)
Total Effect −30AD to ED+30	−0.32 vs. −0.09 dif = −0.23 (72 vs. 44)	−0.32 vs. −1.54 dif = 1.22 (72 vs. 28)	−0.09 vs. −1.54 dif = 1.45 (44 vs. 28)

$^{+}$Different from zero at 0.10 level. *Different values at 0.10 level.

$^{++}$Different from zero at 0.05 level. **Different values at 0.05 level.

$^{+++}$Different from zero at 0.01 level. ***Different values at 0.01 level.

Conclusions

Compared to the very competitive market for corporate control in the United States, the Japanese market appears to operate in an environment that suggests a higher potential for agency cost or residual loss and at a level of reduced competition for acquisitions. Corporate collectivism governs most managerial decisions because of extensive mutual stock ownership among affiliated firms; thus, the role of independent shareholders is much less in Japanese firms than in their U.S. counterparts. Mergers tend to be friendly transactions that sellers typically initiate. Japanese managers do no face the same levels of monitoring activities as American managers. With lifetime employment and seniority based wages and promotions, Japanese managers also have lower employment risk and, therefore, are not as disciplined by a managerial labor market.

Even though there is a higher potential for agency costs in Japan because of the many major cultural and institutional differences between the Japanese and American business environments, the impacts of Japanese mergers on shareholder's wealth of acquiring firms are similar to results from U.S. mergers. Residual losses from mergers do not appear to be higher in Japan than in the United States. This study of 10 years of merger activity finds that, generally, the market for corporate control in Japan is similarly competitive.

It has been argued that Japanese managers and employees feel as if the company that they work for is theirs, not the stockholders'. However, this study of the impact of Japanese mergers on stockholders' wealth finds that the results are consistent with shareholder wealth maximization. Since Japanese managers have job security, perhaps they do not make decisions on the basis of reducing their employment risk at the expense of shareholders. Thus, it appears that the requirements of a high level of monitoring activities as well as a competitive managerial labor market with *ex post* settling up, are not necessary to assure that Japanese managers operate in a way that is consistent with the interest of stockholders. These results indicate that these requirements may not be necessary in the United States to limit residual losses from mergers as long as there is a competitive acquisitions market. This suggests that to avoid agency costs in mergers, managers, stockholders, analysts, and lawmakers should focus on maintaining the competitive acquisitions market and avoid all actions that reduce the competitiveness of the market for corporate control.

Notes

1. For studies of the U.S. merger market see: Asquith (1983), Dodd (1980), Ellert (1976), Halpern (1973), Jensen and Ruback (1983), Lantieg (1978), and Mandelker (1974).
2. See Hoshino (1982, 1983, 1984) for a good discussion of the differences between Japanese and American mergers. There is also a good discussion in Ballon, Tomita, and Usami (1976) as well.
3. In 1987, the following are the percentage of ownership based on market value of all listed companies on the TSE: financial institutions 41.5%, business corporations 30.1%, securities companies 2.1%, governments 0.9%, individuals and others 20.1%, and foreigners 5.3%. Thus, business concerns comprised of both financial and nonfinancial firms own the vast majority of the shares of Japanese firms. See *The TSE Fact Book* (1988), p. 51.
4. In fact, takeovers in Japanese are called either *nottori* (hijacking) or *baishu* (bribery). Thus, the unfriendly takeovers have a very negative, even immoral connotation in Japan.
5. See Aoki (1984a) for a discussion of the necessary balance sheet adjustments to reflect the true values of the debt ratios of Japanese firms and a comparison between adjusted ratios for Japanese and American firms. Even after adjustments, Aoki finds that debt ratios in Japan tend to be larger than U.S. firms. When the market value of equity is used, Kester (1986) finds that Japanese manufacturing firms are similar to U.S. manufacturing firms in terms of their book-value debt to market-value equity ratios.
6. When Sanko Steamship Company filed for bankruptcy August 13, 1985, the largest failure in Japanese history, it was reported that the critical factor was the lead banks stopping their line of credit to the firm. See: *The Wall Street Journal* (August 14, 1985), p. 26. This was also the case in the Nippon Netsugaku bankruptcy in 1974.
7. The source of these mergers is *Corporate Mergers*. These were verified against another source, *The TSE Shohou (Report)*. If there was no exchange ratio listed at the date of the merger, the acquired firm became a wholly owned subsidiary of the acquiring firm prior to the merger. These mergers were omitted from this study so as to concentrate on mergers between more independent companies.
8. An example of a merger between affiliated firms is the merger of Toyota Motor Company with Toyota Motor Sales announced on March 15, 1982. Both of these companies with separate security numbers were listed on the first section of the Tokyo Stock Exchange. There was a stated exchange ratio for the merger, but Toyota Motors owned 44.36% of the shares of Toyota Motor Sales. This merger is between affiliated companies rather than a true arm's-length merger between unaffiliated firms. Thus, this

merger was included in the sample study of 88 mergers with exchange ratios, as a merger between affiliated firms; therefore, it is included in the study of the 38 affiliated mergers.

9. It could be argued that many U.S. acquiring firms merge firms after some ownership position is first taken in selling firm. In the U.S. case these ownership positions prior to merger are most often less than 20% of the outstanding shares of the selling firm; therefore, the comparison of unaffiliated mergers in Japan which have less than 20% ownership is most similar to U.S. mergers.
10. The daily price data were obtained from either the Tokyo Stock Exchange or Daiwa Securities Research Institute in Tokyo.
11. The Tokyo Stock Exchange's Price Index is one of the most popular market indexes used in Japan and is defined as the total market value of all stocks listed on the TSE on a specific day compared to a base date of January 4, 1968. See *Securities Market In Japan* (1988), pp. 44–48, for details on its calculation.
12. The t values shown on Table 14.2 were calculated using the variance of raw residual returns during the 180 day base period for each company as suggested by Brown and Warner (1985), BW. These variances were averaged across all companies to determine the estimated variance of the residuals. This variance was used to test the significance of CAR from the expected value of zero at time T. See BW, p. 29.
13. The average length of this interim period was 115.625 days with a standard deviation of 36.861 days and a range of values from 71 to 254 days for the 72 mergers.
14. The total effect is calculated by taking the CAR at the AD, plus the CAR value for the interim period, plus the CAR at ED +30. Specifically, in column 2 of Table 14.2 the total effect is shown as −0.381, which was obtained by adding the independent accumulations of +2.346, –1.220, and –1.444. This format has been used previously in event studies by Asquith and Mullins (1986) and Pettway and Yamada (1986).
15. The percent positive values for average residual (AR) across all mergers for each time period that underlies the CAR values in Table 14.2, were determined and tested with the binomial test. Few significant P values were found, thus the lack of significant values indicates that the results were not affected significantly by outliers.

References

Aoki, M., (1984a). "Aspects of the Japanese Firm," in M. Aoki, ed., *The Economic Analysis of the Japanese Firm*, Amsterdam, North-Holland, pp. 3–43.

Aoki, M., (1984b). "Shareholders' Non-unanimity on Investment Financing: Banks vs. Individual Investors," in M. Aoki, ed., *The Economic Analysis of the Japanese Firm*, Amsterdam, North-Holland, pp. 193–224.

Asquith, P., and D. W. Mullins, Jr., (1986). "Equity Issues and Offering Dilution," *Journal of Financial Economics*, Vol. 15, January, pp. 61–89.

Asquith, P., R. F. Bruner, and D. W. Mullins, Jr., (1983). "The Gains to Bidding Firms from Merger," *Journal of Financial Economics*, Vol. 11, pp. 121–139.

Ballon, R. J., I. Tomita, and H. Usami, (1976). *Financial Reporting in Japan*, Tokyo, Kodansha International Ltd.

Brown, S. J., and J. B. Warner, (1985). "Using Daily Stock Returns, The Case of Event Studies," *Journal of Financial Economics*, Vol. 14, pp. 3–31.

Corporate Mergers, various dates. Tokyo, Tokyo Stock Exchange. In Japanese.

Dodd, P., (1980). "Merger Proposals, Management Discretion, and Stockholder Wealth," *Journal of Financial Economics*, Vol. 8, pp. 105–137.

Ellert, J. C., (1976). "Merger, Antitrust Law Enforcement and Stockholder Returns," *Journal of Finance*, Vol. 31, pp. 715–732.

Franko, L. G., (1983). *The Threat of Japanese Multinationals*, New York, John Wiley & Sons.

Halpern, P., (1973). "Empirical Estimates of the Amount and Distribution of Gains to Companies in Mergers," *Journal of Business*, Vol. 46, pp. 554–575.

Hoshino, Y., (1982), "The Performance of Corporate Mergers in Japan," *Journal of Business Finance and Accounting*, Vol. 9, pp. 153–165.

Hoshino, Y., (1983). *Corporate Mergers in Japan*, Research Paper No. 1, Tokyo University, Tokyo.

Hoshino, Y., (1984). *General Comparison of Financial Characteristics Between Merging and Nonmerging Firms in Japan*, Nagoya Economic Study Paper #61, Nagoya, Japan.

Itami, H., T. Kagono, H. Yoshihara, and A. Sakuma, (1984). "Diversification Strategies and Economic Performance," in K. Sato, and Y. Hoshino, eds., *The Anatomy of Japanese Business*, Armonk, NY, M. E. Sharpe, Inc., pp. 319–351.

Jensen, M. C., and W. H. Meckling, (1976). "Theory of the Firm: Managerial Behavior, Agency Costs and Ownership Structure," *Journal of Financial Economics*, Vol. 3, pp. 305–360.

Jensen, M. C., and R. S. Ruback, (1983). "The Market for Corporate Control: The Scientific Evidence," *Journal of Financial Economics*, Vol. 11, pp. 5–50.

Kagono, T., I. Nonaka, K. Sakakibara, and A. Okumura, (1984). "Mechanistic vs. Organic Management Systems: A Comparative Study of Adaptive Patterns of American and Japanese Firms," in K. Sato, and Y. Hoshino, eds., *The Anatomy of Japanese Business*, Armonk, NY, M. E. Sharpe, Inc., pp. 27–69.

Kester, W. C., (1986). "Capital and Ownership Structure: A Comparison of United States and Japanese Manufacturing Corporations," *Financial Management*, Vol. 15, pp. 5–16.

Langetieg, T. C., (1978). "An Application of a Three-factor Performance Index to Measure Stockholder Gains from Mergers." *Journal of Financial Economics*, Vol. 6, pp. 365–383.

Lintner, J., (1965). "The Valuation of Risk Assets and the Selection of Risky Investments in Stock Portfolios and Capital Budgets," *Review of Economics and Statistics*, pp. 13–37.

Mandelker, G., (1974). "Risk and Return: The Case of Merging Firms," *Journal of Financial Economics*, Vol. 1, pp. 303–335.

Mikkelson, W. H., and R. S. Ruback, (1985). "An Empirical Analysis of the Interfirm Equity Investment Process," *Journal of Financial Economics*, Vol. 14, pp. 523–553.

Nakatani, I., (1984). "The Economic Role of Financial Corporate Groupings" in M. Aoki, ed., *The Economic Analysis of the Japanese Firm*, Amsterdam, North-Holland, pp. 227–258.

Nishiyama, T., (1984). "The Structure of Managerial Control: Who Owns and Controls Japanese Business?" in K. Sato, and Y. Hoshino, eds., *The Anatomy of Japanese Business*, Armonk, NY, M. E. Sharpe, Inc., pp. 123–163.

Pettway, R. H., and T. Yamada, (1986). "Mergers in Japan and Their Impacts Upon Stockholders' Wealth," *Financial Management*, Vol. 15, pp. 43–52.

Sato, K., and Y. Hoshino, (1984). *The Anatomy of Japanese Business*, Armonk, NY, M. E. Sharpe, Inc.

Securities Market In Japan, (1988). Tokyo, Japan Securities Research Institute.

Sharpe, W., (1963). "A Simplified Model for Portfolio Analysis," *Management Science*, pp. 29–40.

Sharpe, W., (1964). "Capital Asset Prices: A Theory of Market Equilibrium Under Conditions of Risk," *Journal of Finance*, Vol. 19, pp. 425–492.

Shimizu, R., (1980). *The Growth of Firms in Japan*, Tokyo, Keio Tsushin.

Suto, M., (1981). "The Effect of Mergers on Stockholders," *Keisoku-shitsu Technical Paper*, No. 53, pp. 1–53. In Japanese.

The TSE Fact Book. (1988). Tokyo, International Department, Tokyo Stock Exchange.

The TSE Shohou (Reports), various dates. Tokyo, Tokyo Stock Exchange. In Japanese.

The Wall Street Journal, August 14, 1985, p. 26.

Author Index

R

S

T

U

V

W

Y

Z

Subject Index

A

B

C

P

R

S

ABOUT THE AUTHORS

Edwin J. Elton

Edwin J. Elton is Nomura Professor of Finance at the Stern School of Business of New York University. He has authored or coauthored five books and over 60 articles. These articles have appeared in such journals as *The Journal of Finance, Review of Economics and Statistics, Management Science, Journal of Financial Economics, Journal of Business, Oxford Economic Papers,* and *The Journal of Financial and Quantitative Analysis*. He was coeditor of *The Journal of Finance*. He has been a member of the Board of Directors of the American Finance Association and an Associate Editor of *Management Science*. Professor Elton has served as a consultant for many major financial institutions.

Martin J. Gruber

Martin J. Gruber is Nomura Professor of Finance and Chairman of the Finance Department at the Stern School of Business of New York University. He has published seven books and over 60 journal articles in such journals as *The Journal of Finance, Review of Economics and Statistics, Journal of Financial Economics, Journal of Business, Management Science, Journal of Financial and Quantitative Analysis, Operations Research, Oxford Economic Papers,* and *The Journal of Portfolio Management*. He was coeditor of *The Journal of Finance*. He has been a Director of the American Finance Association, the Computer Applications Committee, and the Investment Technology Symposium, both of the New York Society of Security Analysts. He was formerly Department Editor for *Finance of Management Science*. Professor Gruber has consulted in the areas of Investment Analysis and Portfolio Management with many major financial institutions.

The Institutional Investor Series in Finance

The Institutional Investor Series in Finance has been developed specifically to bring you—the finance professional—the latest thinking and developments in investments and corporate finance. As new challenges arise in this fast-paced arena, you can count on this series to provide you with the information you need to gain the competitive edge.

Institutional Investor is the leading communications company serving the global financial community and publisher of the magazine of the same name. Institutional Investor has won 36 major awards for distinguished financial journalism—including the prestigious National Magazine Award for the best reporting of any magazine in the United States. More than 560,000 financial executives in 170 countries read Institutional Investor publications each month. Thousands more attend Institutional Investor's worldwide conferences and seminars each year.